Trafficking in Women
Forced Labour and
Slavery-like Practices

in Marriage

Domestic Labour and

Prostitution

Marjan Wijers . Lin Lap-Chew

Published by
Foundation Against Trafficking in Women (STV)
Postbus 1455 / 3500 BL Utrecht
The Netherlands
Tel 31(0)30 - 271 60 44
Fax 31(0)30 - 271 60 84
e-mail STV @ inter . nl . net

Global Alliance Against Traffic in Women (GAATW)
191 Sivalai Condominium / Itsaraphal Road
SOI 33 / Bangkok 10600
Thailand
Tel 662 - 864 - 1427-28
Fax 662 - 864 - 1637

English editing
Olga Zoomer / Nani Lei Stam
Design & Lay-out
JT ONTWERPEN, Juul Tomasowa
Printing
Anraad

Printed in The Netherlands
ISBN 90-803620-1-8

PREFACE

This report presents the results of an international investigation on trafficking in women, forced labour & slavery-like practices in the contexts of marriage, domestic labour and prostitution. The investigation was carried out by the Dutch Foundation Against Trafficking in Women (STV) and the Global Alliance Against Trafficking in Women (GAATW). A preliminary version of the report was presented to the United Nations Special Rapporteur on Violence against Women, Mrs. Radhika Coomaraswamy, in November 1996, in order to inform her of the current situation and the discussions on the various issues pertaining to this phenomenon.

Many people co-operated in compiling the report. We would like to express our gratitude to the members of the Advisory Committee - Lesley Roberts, Gail Pheterson, Roelof Haveman, Siriporn Skrobanek and Welmoed Koekebakker - for their unfailing, critical and warm support and for sharing with us their knowledge and experience in their respective fields of expertise. Roelof Haveman and Gail Pheterson also assisted in writing the final report. Roelof Haveman assisted in writing chapter 2 and 5 and Gail Pheterson prepared the Summary. Special thanks are due to the regional consultants: Yamila Azize-Vargas, Florence Butegwa, Lisa Kois, Johanna Bond, Jyoti Sanghera, Sarah Johnston and Siriporn Skrobanek. Without their expertise, enthusiasm and above all hard work this report would not have been possible. We also thank Trees Mom, our research consultant. Marjolein Sol processed the data of the questionnaire and kept the office going; she was replaced by Corine van Reeuwijk. Without their support we would have been lost in chaos.

Last but not least, we thank all the organizations and persons who are actively addressing the issue in their local situations and who were willing to share with us their information and experiences by sending us their materials and by making the effort to complete the questionnaires. This certainly was not an easy job given the complexity and extent of the questionnaire.

The whole project, including the work of the regional consultants, was made possible through the generous financial support of the Dutch Ministry of Foreign Affairs, Directorate General Development Co-operation (DGIS), the Dutch development organizations NOVIB, ICCO, HIVOS and BILANCE, the Dutch feminist fund Mama Cash, and the Danish development organization KULU.

Finally, we thank the Special Rapporteur, who provided the unique and valuable opportunity to compile such a global report on a form of violence against women, which many people consider inconceivable in the twentieth century.

This report is written in the hope that it will contribute to the development of new conceptual frameworks and strategies to combat trafficking in women, forced labour & slavery-like practices which are based on the legal and social recognition of women as autonomous individuals in all spheres of life and work.

Marjan Wijers, Lin Lap-Chew
International Report Project Research Team
February 1997

TABLE OF CONTENTS

1 INTRODUCTION TO THE REPORT

1 Violence against women on the UN Agenda

At the end of the UN Decade for Women, the Forward Looking Strategies (FLS) adopted by the 1985 World Conference on Women in Nairobi, identified violence as a major obstacle to the achievement of the objectives of the UN decade for Women: Equality, Development and Peace.

The Commission on the Status of Women(CSW) and the Committee on the Elimination of All Forms of Discrimination against Women(CEDAW) put gender violence on their agenda.
The CSW completed a draft of a Declaration on the Elimination of Violence Against Women in 1992. Women's organizations globally lobbied for new and better instruments to address violence against women.

In June 1993, the World Conference on Human Rights in Vienna, acknowledged that violence against women in all its multiplicity of forms constitutes a serious violation of the human rights of women. In December 1993 the Declaration on the Elimination of Violence against Women was adopted by the UN General Assembly. One of the forms of violence against women included in the Declaration is "forced prostitution and trafficking in women".
In april 1994 a Special Rapporteur on Violence against Women, Ms Radhika Coomaraswamy, was appointed by the Commission on Human Rights for a period of three years. She received a broad mandate, within the framework of international human rights agreements, to investigate the "causes and consequences" of violence against women and to recommend ways to eliminate its causes and to remedy its consequences.
In 1995 Ms Coomaraswamy presented her first (preliminary) report to the Commission on Human Rights touching on the issues which are included in her mandate. In 1996 she presented the second report, which focussed on violence against women in the private (family) sphere. In 1997 she will present her third report, which will address the different forms of violence against women in the public sphere, including trafficking in women.

2 The International Report Project: double objectives

The International Report Project (IRP) was initiated in response to the invitation of the UN Special Rapporteur on Violence Against Women, its Causes and Consequences, to submit a global report on trafficking in women and forced prostitution. This is one of the issues which she will include in her report to the 53rd session of the UN Commission on Human Rights in 1997.

The Project had a double objective. Next to providing the Special Rapporteur with the relevant information for her report to the Commission on Human Rights, the project aimed at furthering the work of NGOs by strengthening and mobilising contacts in the field and bringing together information and networks. This second objective made it imperative to organise the investigation in a manner that involved as many people as possible, and set in motion a process of regional and international consultations which would contribute to network-building on the local, regional and international level.

This report presents the results of the investigation carried out between October 1995 and February 1997 by the Foundation Against Trafficking in Women (STV), based in The Netherlands, in collaboration with the Global Alliance Against Trafficking in Women (GAATW), based in Thailand. A preliminary version of the report has been submitted to the Special Rapporteur in October 1996.

3 Organization of the research

During the first phase of the project information sources were identified, as well as the agents of action and change at all levels. Around the world persons and organizations who could serve as information sources, were already involved in action to address the issue, or were interested to initiate action, were contacted. At the same time, regional consultants were identified and secured in Asia/Pacific, Africa, North America and Latin America & the Caribbean, in order to coordinate research and networking in their respective regions.

An important aim in this first phase was to clarify the analytical framework of the report through a process of consultations and discussions with the members of the Advisory Committee, international women's human rights experts and NGO workers. This was necessary as one of the fundamental problems in addressing the issue is the lack of a clear and unambiguous definition based on women's interests and perspectives. This consultative process resulted in the formulation of the working definitions as described in Chapter II, in correspondence with our own working experiences in the field and the current developments in the international debate on the issue. For analytical reasons two working definitions were developed which would address abusive brokerage practices, defined as "trafficking in women", as well as abusive working and living conditions, defined as "forced labour & slavery-like practices", in both public and domestic spheres. The basic principle underlying both definitions is the (human) right of women to have control over their own body and life.

In the second phase, a questionnaire (see annex 1) was designed, using the working definitions developed in the first phase. The questionnaire concentrated on trafficking and forced labour & slavery-like practices in the contexts of prostitution, domestic labour and marriage as defined in the working definitions. It was distributed by the research team and the regional consultants among the various organizations who are working on the issue and whom we expected to have actual and specific information on their own local, national or regional situation. In addition separate questionnaires were sent to international organizations and to embassies (see annex 2).

During this period of data-gathering, the regional consultants conducted visits to organizations in their respective regions and/or organised regional meetings in order to collect information, do in-depth studies, strengthen networks and stimulate new initiatives. This resulted in the production of regional reports on the situation in Asia, Latin America & the Caribbean and Africa, addressing the specific issues and concrete steps which need to be taken in the respective regions. The research team in The Netherlands attended various national and international conferences and meetings on trafficking and migrant workers in Europe with the same objective. At the same time secondary sources, including NGO and GO reports, documents and publications, were researched.

The third phase consisted of processing and analysing the responses to the questionnaire along with the other information collected: documents respondents sent along with the questionnaire, the reports compiled by the regional consultants, the various NGO and GO documents collected by the research team and the regional consultants, and the information resulting from the literature research. In order to analyse the findings, discuss the drafts for the report and formulate recommendations, a two-day meeting of the research team, the regional consultants and the Advisory Committee was organised.

In the fourth phase, starting from December 1996, regional conferences were organised by the regional consultants in collaboration with the research team to present both the regional reports (which are to be publicised separately) and the results of the international report. The objectives of the regional consultations are to share and discuss the findings of the research emphasizing on the specific issues of the respective regions, to strengthen the regional networks, to plan follow-up action and to build up an international campaign for adoption of Standard Minimum Rules for the Treatment of Victims of Trafficking in Women, Forced Labour & Slavery-like Practices by the United Nations.

4 The questionnaire

The objective of the questionnaires was to obtain an overview of the following issues:

- the nature and extent of contemporary manifestations of trafficking in women, forced labour & slavery-like practices in prostitution, domestic labour and marriage, as defined in the working definitions
- the existing national legislative and political instruments to combat trafficking in women and forced labour & slavery-like practices
- the strategies of governmental and non-governmental organizations addressing the issue in their countries.

In a separate introduction to the questionnaire the framework of the report, the working definitions and their underlying principles were presented (See annex 1, Introduction to the questionnaire). Respondents were asked to use these definitions in completing the questionnaire.

The questionnaire for NGOs consisted of four sections:

a Organizational information

b General questions on trafficking in women and forced labour & slavery-like practices in prostitution, domestic labour and marriage

c Specific questions on trafficking in women and forced labour & slavery-like practices in prostitution

d Specific questions on trafficking in women and forced labour & slavery-like practices in domestic labour.

All respondents received sections A and B. Sections C and D were sent to selected respondents, as these sections contained questions requiring more specialised knowledge of the respective situations. Due to the general lack of research on trafficking and forced labour & slavery-like practices within the context of marriage it was not possible to draw up a separate questionnaire pertaining to marriage.

Since the aim was to obtain as reliable information as possible on a country basis, respondents were selected according to the following criteria:

- being actually employed in activities aimed specifically at some aspect of the issues of trafficking in women and forced labour & slavery-like practices in the areas of our concern, e.g. running shelters, giving counselling, advocacy work etc.
- being involved in research on the issue
- being involved in policy making and/or networking levels in national and/or international forums.

The selection of respondents in Asia/Australia, Africa, North America and Latin America & the Caribbean was done in consultation with the respective regional consultants. Being well connected in various regional networks, they were in the best position to know where material would be available and whom to ask for information. The selection of respondents for Europe was done by the research team.

About 200 questionnaires were sent to NGOs in as many countries as feasible. The purpose was to get at least one questionnaire returned per country. Sixty-five organizations filled in and returned the general sections (section A and B), of which 61 were valid (4 questionnaires were completed in such a way that it was not possible to process the answers). In addition, 46 organizations filled in the specialised section on prostitution (section C), and 17 the section on domestic labour (section D) (See annex 3 for a list of NGOs which returned the questionnaire).

The highest response was received from NGOs in Europe (20) and Asia (19). From North America and Canada 5 organizations responded, from Africa 8, from Latin America & the Caribbean 7 and from Australia 2. In total, respondents came from 41 countries. Many NGOs sent various documents pertaining to their work and the situation in their country along with the questionnaire. Some organizations did not fill in the questionnnaire but sent us their annual reports or other documents pertaining to the issue.

In general, responses came mainly from those who have been working on a grass-root level on the issue for a number of years. In most cases they stated that their information was based on their own observations or research obtained in the course of their work.

In addition to the NGO questionnaires, separate questionnaires were send to 77 international organizations, pertaining to their programmes and activities on the issue. Of these, 13 returned a completed questionnaire.
Furthermore, 111 questionnaires were sent to embassies, asking for figures, laws and government activities on the issue. Only 8 embassies returned a completed questionnaire or sent documents. (See annex 4 for a list of international organizations and embassies which returned completed questionnaires.)

5 Limitations of the report and methodological problems

Finding reliable statistics on the extent of trafficking in women and forced labour & slavery-like practices in the three areas of our concern - marriage, domestic labour and prostitution - appeared to be virtually impossible. Similarly, it is practically impossible to indicate accurate numbers of women who pressed charges or the number of court cases or convictions.

There are several reasons for this dearth of statistics. Firstly, there is a significant lack of systematic research and where research exists, the issues investigated may differ widely due to the lack of a precise, consistent and unambiguous definition of the phenomena at hand. Secondly, many of the practices described in this report are - in theory - illegal, clandestine or criminal and thus more or less hidden. Thirdly, the issue has been widely neglected by many governments and international organizations, while in many countries prostitution is considered an illegal or criminal activity. Lastly, very little statistics, research or documentation on informal sector activities, including domestic work and prostitution exists.

If any figures are available, they pertain more generally to the number of national or migrant domestics, the number of national or migrant prostitutes or the number of bi-national marriages, without any indication as to the occurrence and/or extent of trafficking and/or forced labour & slavery-like practices as defined for this report.

The problem is even more immense with regard to figures relating to the number of cases filed and the number of suspects prosecuted or convicted. Cases are hardly registered and if they are, it is not clear to which offence they refer. As will be seen in chapter 4, national laws differ widely, which means that in one country a case may be registered as procuring or "living off the avails of prostitution", whereas in another country similar cases may be registered as "trafficking".

Most of the forthcoming information concerned trafficking in women in the context of prostitution, due to the fact that most of the organizations addressing the issue of trafficking have tended to do so exclusively in relation to prostitution. Prostitution appears to be the most accessible, visible and therefore most researched field. Details, statistics and documentation on the other domains are much more sparse and fragmentary. Contacts and information on the situation of domestic workers are difficult to obtain since they work in private homes. The same applies to trafficking for marriage and the issue of servile marriages.

It is significant to note that the information available varies greatly from country to country and region to region. In some regions, like Asia, Latin America and Europe, relatively much information is available because of the range of NGOs working directly with the women who have been addressing the issue for a considerable length of time. In other regions, such as Africa, North America and Canada, the issue has received little public attention until now, organizations working directly with the women are much more difficult to identify and factual information on the situation of the women involved is accordingly more difficult to gather. A great part of the documentation with regard to the situation in North America became only available in a late phase of the project, due to problems in finding relevant organizations and information sources. As a result, it has only been possible to process this information to a very limited extent. Chapter III and IV especially reflect this shortcoming. Other countries, like the ones in the Middle East, are so "closed" that it was not possible to collect any information within the scope of this report, which should be seen as a major deficit.

The results of the questionnaire are processed throughout the report. However, it must be kept in mind that they reflect the perception and assessments of the respondents, thus showing trends and not "facts" in the strict sense of the word. It should also be stressed that discourse and terminology are relative and that for example "frequently" used by a Thai respondent in the context of Thailand may mean something completely different from how a Canadian respondent might use the term in the Canadian context and experience.

It must also be noted that respondents were requested to complete the questionnaire according to the working definitions. Given the varying interpretations of the concept of "trafficking" in each national context, this sometimes required respondents to "translate" their information into a different framework, which inevitably presents certain difficulties.

However, notwithstanding the limitations described above, the results of the questionnaire, in combination with the other sources utilized, such as texts of legislation, governmental and non-governmental reports, research reports and other publications, yielded important and valuable information.
Finally, due to the limitation of time is has not been possible to include a more extensive analysis of the relevant international legal instruments on (forced) labour, slavery-like practices, the protection of migrant workers, human rights and women's rights and their usefulness from the perspective of the working definitions as developed for this report.

6 Choices and deliberate omissions

In line with the context of this report, the choice was made to focus exclusively on women. This does not mean that trafficking and forced labour & slavery-like practices do not occur in relation to men. Although there certainly are indications that men may also fall victim to the practices described, albeit to a much less extent, it is clear that the overwhelming majority of victims are women.

Secondly, although we are aware that trafficking in children - girls and boys - occurs extensively and with devastating effects on those affected, this report does not address trafficking and forced labour & slavery-like practices with regard to children, since these practices take place in a different legal context and need different approaches and strategies. It is difficult, however, to make a very strict distinction since the legal age may differ in particular countries. Moreover, many women are trafficked at the age of 15 or 16, when by international standards they are still children, and may stay for many years, long into their adulthood, in a situation of forced labour or slavery-like conditions. Nevertheless, where ever possible, we have tried to confine our focus to women of eighteen years and over.

Thirdly, although the working definitions as developed in chapter II pertain to all "work or services", we have concentrated for this report on trafficking, forced labour & slavery practices in the contexts of marriage, domestic labour and prostitution. The knowledge and experience of those presently engaged in addressing the issue indicate that trafficking and slavery-like practices occur predominantly in these fields. Some respondents indicated the occurrence of slavery-like practices and forced labour in other fields, such as sweatshops and the garment industry. Closer investigation into these areas is needed.

Fourthly, the term migration is generally used in the broad sense, referring to migration within a country, for example from rural to urban areas, as well as to intra-regional and international migration.

7 Contents

Chapter 1 gives an introduction to the survey and examines some methodological problems.

Chapter 2 contains a historical overview of the different definitions of "trafficking in women" and their development throughout the successive international conventions and within the various international organizations and political arenas. Based on an analysis of the trends and themes that emerge from this historical overview, the working definitions as formulated in this report are developed and the choices and principles underlying them are clarified.

Chapter 3 places the issue within the broader context of traditional female roles, a gendered labour market and the increase of female labour migration. The contributing factors are discussed, along with a description of the contemporary manifestations and trends of the exploitation of women's work within marriage, domestic work and prostitution under conditions of force or deceit ("forced labour and slavery-like practices" as defined for this report), as well as the recruitment for work or services under conditions of force or deceit ("trafficking in women" as defined for this report).

Chapter 4 looks into the different laws and state policies on prostitution, assessing the extent to which they prevent, address, sanction or legitimise trafficking and forced labour & slavery-like practices in prostitution as defined in the working definitions. The different legal systems are analysed in terms of prohibitions and regulations aimed at the distinctive activities and parties involved, including their impact on the living and working conditions of women working in prostitution. This chapter focuses solely on prostitution, since it appeared impossible to make a similar analysis in relation to domestic work and marriage, given both the limited time for the report and the limitations in available information.

Chapter 5 reviews the current strategies employed by both NGOs and GOs to address the issue in the light of the working definitions as developed in chapter 2. Strategies are analysed from the perspective of the distinctive dominant conceptualizations of the problem to be solved: morality, criminality, (illegal) migration, public order, labour conditions and human rights.

In ***Chapter 6*** conclusions and recommendations are formulated.

Chapter 7 contains a summary of the report.

2 TOWARDS NEW DEFINITIONS

I Introduction

A fundamental problem in addressing the issue of "trafficking in women"[1] is the lack of a clear and unambiguous definition. Although the term "traffic in women" was mentioned as early as the end of the last century, there is a persistent confusion as to what it means precisely.
This confusion is reflected today in the various, sometimes contradictory, definitions and concepts used in national legislation[2] and international conventions, as well as in the ongoing international debate.

From a theoretical point of view, this lack of a clear and internationally accepted definition is not surprising. "Trafficking in women" is a complex phenomenon which touches various, and often extremely sensitive issues, like sex and money. In practice however, the need for a clear understanding and definition of what constitutes "traffic in women", i.e. what practices exactly should be combated, is not just an academic or ideological issue. The strategies or policies that should be pursued, depend to a high extent on the definition of the problem. Logically, solutions vary, according to what is perceived as the problem to be solved: organised crime, illegal migration, prostitution, forced labour, violence and abuse of women, unequal economic relationships or poverty?

Without a good definition, attempts to deal with the problem will remain wishful thinking at best. At worst they can cause repercussions that have repressive instead of emancipatory effects on the already precarious situation of the women concerned. The fact that, today, we still need to grapple with the definition of "trafficking in women" is in itself indicative of at least part of the failure of past policies, based as they were on unclear or conflicting concepts.

The first part of this chapter will give a historical overview of the different definitions and how they developed throughout the successive international conventions and within the various international organizations and fora. It will become clear that there are multiple interpretations and common understandings of the term "trafficking" and that these have shifted and changed over time.
The second part will analyze the trends and themes that emerge from this overview, showing how each definition carries a different identification of the problem and, consequently, of the

[1] For clarity, the term "trafficking in women" is in quotation marks until it is well defined. Where in the remainder of the report "trafficking" is used in the sense of our working definitions as formulated at the end of this chapter, no quotation marks are used. Where it has a different meaning or where its meaning is unclear, as is e.g. the case in many laws or policy documents, it will appear in quotation marks.

[2] As will come across in Chapter 4 regarding the national legal context.

solutions. This analysis forms the basis for the last part of the chapter. Concluding that effective strategies on women's behalf require new definitions that clearly pinpoint violence against women within the scope or intent of what has been referred to as "trafficking", new working definitions are proposed in order to distinctly cover abusive brokerage practices (defined as "trafficking"), on the one hand, and abusive working and living conditions (defined as "forced labour & slavery-like practices"), on the other, in both public and private spheres.

2 Historical developments

2.1 Pre-war treaties

The first international conference on the prevention of "trafficking in women" was held in 1895 in Paris, followed by another in 1899 in London and one in Budapest. In 1904, sixteen states were represented at an international meeting in Paris, from which resulted the first international agreement against "White Slavery"[3]. "Being desirous of securing to women of full age who have suffered abuse or compulsion, as also to women and girls under age, effective protection against the criminal traffic known as the White Slave Trade", the 1904 International Agreement for the Suppression of the White Slave Trade aims to combat the procuring of women or girls for immoral purposes abroad according to the preamble, the convention is limited to the compulsive forms of procurement (inasfar it concerns adult women) and does not address those situations where there is no apparant compulsion or abuse. Six years later this Agreement is followed by a new convention, broadening its scope to include the "traffic in women" within national boundaries. The 1910 Convention[4] obliges States to punish:

Any person who, to gratify the passions of others, has by fraud or by the use of violence, threats, abuse of authority, or any other means of constraint, hired, abducted or enticed a woman of full age for immoral purposes.

Again, in case of minors the requirement of constraint does not apply.

Both conventions are limited explicitly to the process of recruitment, i.e. the process up to the moment the woman is actually handed over. Coercive conditions inside the brothels are not addressed, as is made clear in the closing statement of the 1910 Convention:

The case of the retention, against her will, of a woman or girl in a house of prostitution could not, in spite of its gravity, be included in the present Convention, because it is exclusively a question of internal legislation.

"Being anxious to secure more completely the Suppression of the Traffic in Women and Children", an additional convention is drafted in 1921[5]. The most important addition is the extension to the traffic in boys ("traffic in children of both sexes").

3 International Agreement for the Suppression of the White Slave Trade, signed in Paris, May 18 1904.

4 International Convention for the Suppression of the White Slave Trade, signed in Paris, May 4 1910.

5 International Convention for the Suppression of the Traffic in Women and Children, Geneva, Switzerland, September 30 1921.

In 1933 a new international agreement is signed in Geneva[6], removing the condition of constraint, but only with regard to the international "traffic in women". Art. 1 obliges State Parties to punish:

Any person who, in order to gratify the passions of another person, procures, entices or leads away, even with her consent, a woman or a girl of full age for immoral purposes to be carried out in another country.

As for the "traffic in women" within borders, the requirement of constraint is left intact. A state can thus tolerate on a national level what it condemns on an international level.

2.2 United Nations Convention for the Suppression of the Traffic in Persons and of the Exploitation of the Prostitution of others (1949)

In the years to follow, the League of Nations - later the United Nations - supports the idea of integration of the previous international conventions. On December 2, 1949 the General Assembly of the United Nations adopts the Convention for the Suppression of the Traffic in Persons and of the Exploitation of the Prostitution of Others[7], which replaces all the preceding treaties. Whereas, according to the preamble, "prostitution and the accompanying evil of the traffic in persons for the purpose of prostitution are incompatible with the dignity and worth of the human person and endanger the welfare of the individual, the family and the community", art. 1 of the new convention obliges State Parties to punish any person who "to gratify the passions of another":

1] Procures, entices or leads away, for purposes of prostitution, another person, even with the consent of that person;

With this paragraph the previous distinction between international and national "trafficking" disappears: in both cases now "trafficking" is punishable even with the consent of the woman concerned. Moreover, in the following articles the scope of the convention is broadened to include the exploitation of prostitution by calling State Parties to punish anyone who:

2] Exploits the prostitution of another person, even with the consent of that person;

3] Keeps or manages, or knowingly finances or takes part in the financing of a brothel;

4] Knowingly lets or rents a building or other place or any part thereof for the purpose of the prostitution of others.

The extension to exploitation of prostitution is one of the reasons why a number of states who were party to the preceding conventions, do not accede to this new convention. In fact the convention was ratified by less than half the UN member states (66 out of 160). The grounds for refusal to ratify which were indicated vary from constitutional incompatibility to criticism of the basic assumptions of the text (van Hemeldonck, 1996).

6 International Convention for the Suppression of the Traffic in Women, Geneva, Switzerland, October 11 1933.

7 Resolution 317, UN Treaties Series, Vol. 96, p.271, no. 1342, came into effect on July 25 1951.

2.3 Post-war developments in the UN

After a period of silence, the issue of "trafficking" becomes a topic again at the UN level as well as the European level during the 1980s. Different reasons may be given for the resurfacing of concern, such as the strength of the women's movement and the feminist concern with addressing questions of female exploitation and/or the global concern with the spread of AIDS[8].

Apart from the initiatives of organizations as the United Nations, the International Organization for Migration (IOM) and the International Labour Organization (ILO), the issue is addressed in a number of world conferences.

UNITED NATIONS GENERAL ASSEMBLY AND COMMISSION ON HUMAN RIGHTS

The early eighties see "trafficking in women" resurface on the agenda of the United Nations. In 1991, the prevention of "traffic in persons and the exploitation of the prostitution of others" is the main topic at the sixteenth session of the Working Group on Contemporary Forms of Slavery. This results in a Draft Programme of Action for the Prevention of Traffic in Persons and of the Exploitation of the Prostitution of Others[9]. In its 48th session (1992) the Commission on Human Rights endorses the need to launch a concerted programme of action and decides to transmit the Draft Programme to Governments and other concerned organizations for their comments[10]. However, only a few replies are received and no further action is taken by the Commission either in its 49th session (1993) or in its 50th session (1994). Eventually, in April 1996, the Draft Programme of Action is adopted by the Commission on Human Rights[11].
An explanation for the lack of enthusiasm towards the adoption of the Draft Programme of Action could be the lack of innovative elements as compared with the contents of the 1949 Convention (Zegveld, 1995).

Meanwhile, in 1994, the UN General Assembly adopts a resolution on "traffic in women and girls" [12], which condemns:

The illicit and clandestine movement of persons across national and international borders, largely from developing countries and some countries with economies in transition, with the end goal of forcing women and girl children into sexually or economically oppressive and exploitative situations for the profit of recruiters, traffickers and crime syndicates, as well as other illegal activities related to trafficking, such as forced domestic labour, false marriages, clandestine employment and false adoption.

8 Many other reasons might have played a role as well, such as the fear of the western states for migration flows from developing countries. An analysis of the factors that made "trafficking" a concern in the first place and why it resurfaces on the political agenda in the 1980s, would require more research.

9 E/CN.4/Sub.2/1991/41, annex I.

10 Commission on Human Rights resolution 1992/36.

11 Draft Programme of Action for the Prevention of the Traffic in Persons and the Exploitation of the Prostitution of Others (E/CN.4/Sub.2/1995/28/Add.1) adopted by Commission on Human Rights in its resolution 1996/61 entitled *"Contemporary Forms of Slavery"*.

12 Resolution 49/166 of the General Assembly of the United Nations (A/Res/49/166), adopted December 23 1994.

In its report[13] to the 50th session of the General Assembly in 1995 the Secretary-General refers to this resolution, commenting that:
While focussing on international dimensions of trafficking, the Assembly goes beyond a narrow view of trafficking only for the purpose of prostitution to incorporate other aspects of forced labour and deceptive practices.

Continuing in paragraph 17:
Trafficking across international borders is by definition illegal... The question must be asked, however, whether trafficking is the same as illegal migration. It would seem that the two are related, but different. Migration across frontiers without documentation does not have to be coerced or xploitative. At the same time, persons can be trafficked with their consent. A distinction could be made in terms of the purpose for which borders are crossed and whether movement occurs through the instrumentality of another person. Under this distinction, trafficking of women and girls would be defined in terms of 'the end goal of forcing women and girl children into sexually or economically oppressive and exploitative situations' and the fact that it is done 'for the profit of recruiters, traffickers and crime syndicates'.

At about the same time, in 1994, the Chair of the Human Rights Commission announces the appointment of Mrs. Radhika Coomaraswamy as Special Rapporteur on Violence Against Women, including its causes and consequences, for a period of three years[14]. Her mandate includes "traffic in women and forced prostitution".

In 1996 the Commission on Human Rights adopts a resolution[15], calling on governments to implement the Platform for Action of the 1995 Fourth World Conference on Women by "considering the ratification and enforcement of international conventions on trafficking in persons and on slavery" and by:
Taking appropriate measures to address the root factors, incl. external factors, that encourage trafficking in women and girls for prostitution and other forms of commercialised sex, forced marriages and forced labour in order to eliminate trafficking in women.

Convention on the Elimination of all forms of Discrimination Against Women

The 1979 Convention on the Elimination of all forms of Discrimination Against Women[16] specifically deals with the human rights of women, obliging State parties to take all appropriate measures to eliminate all forms of discrimination against women. The Women's Convention is a broad non-discrimination treaty, structured to commit governments to remove obstacles and

[13] Traffic in women and girls, Report of the Secretary General. A/50/369, 24 August 1995.
[14] Commission on Human Rights resolution 1994/45, entitled *"The question of integrating the rights of women into the human rights mechanisms of the United Nations and the elimination of violence against women".*
[15] Commission on Human Rights resolution 1996/...Traffic in women and girls (E/CN.4/1996/L.29), adopted April 19 1996.
[16] U.N. Convention on the Elimination of all Forms of Discrimination Against Women (CEDAW), 10 December 1979.

provide conditions for women to exercise all their human rights in all fields (Miller, 1995). Embedded in this broader non-discrimination principle, article 6 contains a provision with respect to "traffic in women" and prostitution, requiring States "to take all appropriate measures to suppress all forms of traffic in women and exploitation of prostitution of women".

An important issue in the drafting of article 6 was the question of whether prostitution as such should be combated or merely the exploitation of prostitution. However, according to the "Travaux Preparatoire", the rejection of Morocco's proposal to include the combat of prostitution in all its forms indicates that the intention of the adopted text of article 6 is not to combat prostitution as such, but rather forms of exploitation of prostitution (Haveman & Hes, 1994). A definition, however of what should be understood by "traffic in women and the exploitation of prostitution" is missing.

World Conference on Human Rights, Vienna 1993

Undoubtedly, one of the important results of the 1993 World Conference on Human Rights - following years of intensive lobbying by women's organizations - is the recognition of women's rights as human rights and thereby the extension of state accountability to violence against women in the private sphere. As the Vienna Declaration and Programme of Action, adopted by the World Conference on Human Rights on 25 June 1993, states:
The human rights of women and of the girl-child are an inalienable, integral and indivisible part of universal human rights.

The Declaration urges the elimination of violence against women in both the public and private spheres. It addresses the issue of "international trafficking" as a form of gender-based violence and calls for its elimination through international co-operation in economic and development fields and through national legislation.

World Conference on Women, Beijing 1995

Whereas the Forward Looking Strategies of the third World Conference on Women in 1985, are limited to "traffic in women for prostitution and forced prostitution" as a form of slavery[17], the Platform for Action of Beijing in 1995, goes beyond the notion of "trafficking" for purposes of prostitution only, and incorporates other contemporary forms of "trafficking and slavery-like practices". Under actions to be taken[18], governments of countries of origin, transit and destination as well as regional and international organizations are called upon to:
Take appropriate measures to address the root factors, including external factors, that encourage trafficking in women and girls for prostitution and other forms of commercialised sex, forced marriages, and forced labour in order to eliminate trafficking in women, including by strengthening existing legislation with a view to providing better protection of the rights of women and girls and to punish the perpetrators, through both criminal and civil measures.

[17] Forward Looking Strategies, paragraph 290 and 291, Nairobi 1985.

[18] Platform for Action, Strategic Objective D 3, paragraph 130b, Fourth World Conference on Women, Beijing, 1995.

Both documents call for the elimination of "traffic in women and forced prostitution", and not for the elimination of prostitution as such. Yet, the texts still contain ambiguities. For example, paragraph 122 of the Platform for Action[19] stresses the need to review and strengthen the implementation of the 1949 Convention. Both documents implicitly focus solely on the "traffic of women" over international borders, giving no special attention to the equivalent practice within national borders.

2.4 Post-war developments at the European level

European Parliament

In April 1989 the European Parliament adopts its first resolution on "the exploitation of prostitution and the traffic in human beings"[20]. The resolution condemns both prostitution as such and "trafficking" for prostitution and calls for measures to eliminate both practices. Since then, two more resolutions have been adopted, which, unlike the 1989 resolution, distinguish between "trafficking" and prostitution as such. The first resolution, adopted in September 1993, addresses "traffic in women" for prostitution, calling for international co-operation and the improvement of the position of victims[21]. In the second, most recent, resolution, adopted January 1996, several new developments and trends are reflected[22]. Here, for the first time, the European Parliament goes beyond the traditional concept of "trafficking" for purposes of prostitution only, taking the term "trafficking in human beings" to mean:
The illegal action of someone who, directly or indirectly, encourages a citizen from a third country to enter or stay in another country in order to exploit that person by using deceit or any other form of coercion or by abusing that person's vulnerable situation or administrative status.

Considering that "the offences of the traffic in women are not always clearly defined in national legislation or international conventions, thereby leading to confusion which makes it more difficult to fight these crimes", the resolution calls on member States to:
Provide a clear definition of the concept of trafficking in human beings, and to identify trafficking as a violation of human rights and a serious crime.

Acknowledging "force" as the crucial factor, the European Parliament calls upon the Commission and the member States to:
Take action at an international level to draft a new UN convention to supersede the obsolete and ineffective Convention on the Suppression of Traffic in Persons and of the Prostitution of Others (1949); any new convention should focus on coercion and deception.

With regard to internal preventive measures a link is made with the informal labour sector. Paragraph 14 of the resolution welcomes:

19 Platform for Action, Section D: Violence against Women, paragraph 122.
20 OJC 120, May 16 1989, p.352.
21 Resolution on Trade in Women, OJC 268, October 4 1993, p.141.
22 Resolution on Trafficking in Human Beings, A4-0326/95.
Plan of Action against traffic in women and forced prostitution, by Ms. Michèle Hirsch. EG (96) 2, Strasbourg, 9 April 1996.

The ILO and the WHO initiatives to draw up standards for the informal economy and believes it is advisable to draw up legislation on unregulated work in the Union, too, in order to reduce the vulnerability and lack of rights of persons working in this sector, and to ensure access to health care, social services and insurance.

Council of Europe

At about the same time the Council of Europe takes up the issue. In 1991 a seminar on Forced Prostitution and Trafficking as Violations of Human Rights and Human Dignity is held in Strasbourg. It is the first time that - although very limited - a number of representatives of prostitutes' organizations is invited to participate in the debate at a governmental level. Following the conclusions of the seminar, the Steering Committee for Equality between Women and Men (CDEG) establishes a Group of Specialists to draw proposals for action to be taken in member States within the framework of the Council of Europe. On the basis of the recommendations made in the final report of this working group, the CDEG asks an outside expert consultant to draw up a plan of action against "traffic in women and forced prostitution". In the resulting Plan of Action[23] the following definition of "trafficking" is proposed:
There is trafficking in women when a woman is exploited in a country other than her own by another person (natural or legal) for financial gain, the traffic consisting of organising (the stay or) the legal or illegal emigration of a woman, even with her consent, from her country of origin to the country of destination and luring her by whatever means into prostitution or any form of sexual exploitation.

"Forced prostitution" then would be:
The act, for financial gain, of inducing a person by any form of constraint to supply sexual services to another person.

Based on the Plan of Action and other inputs, a document is prepared for the oncoming meeting of the Presidents of Steering and other Committees of the Council of Europe[24]. However, "given the fact that the distinction between prostitution and forced prostitution seems to create some problems in the different member States", the Secretariat chooses "to limit the document to questions related to trafficking in human beings, with special emphasis on trafficking in women for sexual exploitation". In the section on "definition and causes of trafficking in women", reference is made to the fact that:
Trafficking in human beings, of which trafficking in women for prostitution or various forms of other sexual exploitation is an important part,...takes various forms, from the recruitment of individuals to work in degrading conditions (e.g. in the building industry, domestic work, etc.) to forced marriages, and involves both women and men; however, it concerns predominantly women being used for purposes of prostitution and pornography.

23 Plan of Action against traffic in women and forced prostitution, by Ms. Michèle Hirsch. EG (96)2, Strasbourg, 9 April 1996

24 Steering Committee for equality between women and men, 11th meeting. CDEG (96)6 rev., Strasbourg, 10 may 1996.

Subsequently the definition of "traffic in women" as formulated in the Plan of Action is accepted, yet stating in a footnote that the "CDEG should discuss and possibly amend this definition".

European Commission

In 1996 the European Commission, in collaboration with the International Organization for Migration (IOM), takes the initiative to organise a European Conference on Trafficking in Women in Vienna, resulting in a Communication from the Commission to the Council and the European Parliament on Trafficking in Women for the purpose of Sexual Exploitation (COM (96)).
The Communication is limited to "trafficking in women" for the purpose of sexual exploitation, defined as:
The transport of women from third countries into the European Union (including perhaps subsequent movement between member States) for the purpose of sexual exploitation.

Continuing:
Trafficking for the purpose of sexual exploitation covers women who have suffered intimidation and/or violence through the trafficking. Initial consent may not be relevant, as some enter the trafficking chain knowing they will work as prostitutes, but who are then deprived of their basic human rights, in conditions which are akin to slavery. The Communication does not however seek to address the question of women who are not put under duress by a third party to travel to work as prostitutes over borders, nor does it address the questions of black market labour in other sectors of the European Union.

2.5 Developments in other regions

At the (inter)governmental level, most regional developments concerning "traffic in women" take place in Europe. In 1992, a South Asia Regional Workshop on Protecting the Rights of Women and Children with special reference to "international trafficking and migration" is held in Dhaka. "Trafficking" is here defined as:
All acts involved in capture and acquisition of persons for trade and transport with the intent to sell, exchange or use for any illegal purpose.

2.6 International Organization for Migration (IOM)

In the 1990s, under the influence of increasingly restrictive immigration policies of especially the rich countries, "trafficking in women" becomes more and more an issue of illegal or "disorderly" migration. This development is most evident in definitions originating in Western Europe, the United States and Canada, which tend to equate "trafficking in women" with the "smuggling of aliens", also named "alien trafficking" or "trafficking in migrants".
This development is among others reflected in the IOM taking up the issue of "trafficking". In his statement for the Preparatory Meeting on Traffic in Women[25] in December 1995, Mr. Marco Gramegna (IOM, 1995c), addresses the definitional issue as follows, after having referred to the 1949 Convention:

25 Preparatory to the Vienna Conference on Trafficking in Women in June '96.

Since the adoption of the Convention, migrant trafficking has not only grown in scale, but also taken a greater variety of forms, such as forced marriage and labour. (.....) NGOs typically define trafficking in women in very broad terms and focus on abuses suffered by trafficked women, while immigration and police authorities generally focus more on trafficking as an organised crime problem involving sophisticated criminal networks.

Whereas the IOM is in the process of refining their definition to "adequately reflect the reality of trafficking in women", Gramegna remarks that there first is a need for more clarity as to what constitutes migrant trafficking as such:

As it relates to international migration, we consider 'trafficking' to exist if:
- an intermediary - the trafficker- is involved
- money (or another form of payment) changes hands
- an international border is crossed
- entry and/or stay in the country of origin or destination is illegal.
However, we also realise that trafficking in women has some special characteristics that are not commonly found in other forms of migrant trafficking. For example, kidnapping of persons for purposes of trafficking them and selling or trading migrants into prostitution or forced marriage commonly occur within the context of trafficking in women. Therefore we tentatively define trafficking in women as any illicit transporting of migrant women and/or trade in them for economic or other personal gain. This may include the following elements:
- facilitating the illegal movement of migrant women to other countries, with or without their consent or knowledge
- deceiving migrant women about the purpose of the migration, legal or illegal
- physically or sexually abusing migrant women, or financially exploiting them en route and/or in the country of destination
- kidnapping or coercing migrant women for the purpose of trafficking them
- selling women into, or trading in women for the purpose of, employment, marriage, prostitution or other forms of profit-making abuse.

The same trend is reflected in the conference itself in Vienna, June 1996, organized by the European Commission in collaboration with the IOM. An overwhelming number of the documents prepared by governments and international organizations are headed "trafficking in migrants" or "trafficking in aliens" (though what is understood by these terms vary) and predominantly address questions of illegal migration[26].

2.7 International Labour Organization (ILO)

Until recently the International Labour Organization has not been very active in the field of "traffic in women", in the narrow meaning of "trafficking" for prostitution. However, over the last few years the ILO has taken some initial steps to include women's work in the informal labour sector as a part of its mandate. An illustration could be taken from their studies on the situation of foreign domestic workers and entertainers (Weinert, 1991, and Colectivo loé, 1991).

[26] For example, the pleading for a European Convention on Prevention and Suppression of Alien Smuggling (see Austria, 1994).

3 Developments & themes

A review of the various definitions and their historical development identifies a number of trends and themes. Some of them run parallel, others merge.

3.1 From "recruitment" to "exploitation"

The traditional concept of "trafficking", as expressed in the earliest treaties at the turn of the century, focuses exclusively upon the process of (forced) recruitment and transport of women (i.e.: "entices or leads away"). Underlying concern is the protection of "innocent" women from being lured into brothels. Coercive conditions inside brothels (i.e.: "the case of the retention, against her will, of a woman or girl") are explicitly not addressed as this is a "question of internal legislation".

The 1949 Convention, for the first time, combines "trafficking as procurement" with "prostitution as exploitation". Whereas the first article addresses the enticing and leading away of women and girls - and in that sense only summarises the previous treaties - the two following articles broaden the scope of the treaty to the "exploitation of prostitution" (defined particularly by financial management or rental of premises for the purpose of prostitution). Although still addressed in separate articles, "trafficking" and "exploitation of prostitution" are mentioned in the same breath; the distinction between the two more or less disappears. Illustrative is the legislation that is drafted pursuant to the 1949 Convention. For example, contrary to what its title suggests, the Indian Immoral Traffic (Prevention) Act targets the exploitation of prostitution rather than "trafficking".

The disappearance of the distinction between "trafficking" and "exploitation of prostitution" may also be seen in other post-war international definitions. Whilst some contemporary definitions address predominantly the procurement aspect as in to the traditional concept of "trafficking" (e.g. the IOM definition, though the emphasis here is on illegal migration), other definitions include the situation in which women end up, be it by coercion or with their consent. In many definitions this merging of "trafficking in women" and "exploitation of prostitution" leads to confusion; it is not clear what is meant, which situations are being addressed exactly and how these should be characterised.

3.2 From "coercion" to "even with her consent"

The first treaties are clearly limited to compulsive forms of procurement. They do not address situations in which no coercion, abuse or deceit is used. In this sense the 1910 Convention can be considered a "minimum agreement treaty": although individual states are allowed to penalise non-compulsive forms of procurement, international agreement obliges punishment only in cases of "fraud or the use of violence, threats, abuse of authority, or any other means of constraint".

It is only in 1933 that the condition of restraint is removed: from then on procurement is punishable "even with her consent". This trend continues after World War II. The 1949 Convention explicitly addresses all forms of procurement and exploitation for the purpose of prostitution, with or without the consent of the woman involved.

In the 1980s, the question of consent resurfaces on the political agenda. A number of the more recent definitions re-introduces coercion or force as a crucial element in defining the crime of "trafficking". However, to what "force" or "consent" exactly are referring is another source of confusion.

Relatively clear is the view in which "force" refers to both the conditions of recruitment and the conditions of work (i.e. the way the work is organized). Here, the central question is under what conditions one may speak of forced recruitment or forced working conditions, as distinguished from forms of recruitment and working conditions based on mutual agreement. "Forced prostitution" here is the equivalent of forced labour in prostitution.

A more traditional interpretation of the free/forced dichotomy - and one which is still very common - is the one in which the distinction between free and forced is understood as referring to the recruitment process only. Free or forced in this interpretation does not address working conditions, but the way a woman came to be a prostitute: as the result of a free choice or forced by others. "Force" here refers solely to the recruitment process, i.e. to force "innocent" women into prostitution. "Forced prostitution" here is the equivalent of forced recruitment. From this perspective, once a woman works as a prostitute, it is of no importance under which conditions she is working. "Force" defined in this way excludes those women who agree to work as prostitutes, but who are subject to force in the course of their work or who are promised other working conditions than those in which they find themselves: "The abuses she undergoes are considered to be the natural consequences of her willingness to be a prostitute". Underlying is "the idea that it is wrong to force an innocent women to be a prostitute, but a guilty one can be mistreated with impunity" (Doezema, 1995).

Especially confusing is a second view in which prostitution itself is seen as violence against women. From this perspective any distinction which refers to the will or consent of the woman involved, is irrelevant. Neither do the conditions of recruitment and/or work bear any relevance as a criterion of "forced". In this view, any distinction between forced and free prostitution is a false one, as prostitution, by definition, is forced.

The difference between the two views mentioned may become more transparent when compared to the discussion about domestic labour. In the case of domestic labour, the activity as such is never regarded as inherently exploitative or "forced". It is the way the work is organised - in terms of both the recruitment and the working conditions - that can make domestic labour "forced" (as is the case in all modern forms of slavery-like practices). However, in the case of prostitution it is the activity as such that in the eyes of some makes it "forced".

It is not always clear which of these views is referred to in the discussion about "traffic in women" and "exploitation of prostitution".

3.3 From "violence against women" to "violation of human rights"

The last two decades have shown a move from the conceptualization of women's problems solely as a private issue or as violence against women, to the perception of violence against women as a violation of human rights, for which states are accountable, not only as far as the public sphere is concerned but also in the private sphere. Illustrative of this development are the 1993 UN World Conference on Human Rights and the 1979 Convention on the Elimination of all forms of Discrimination Against Women (CEDAW). Accordingly, "traffic in women" and "forced prostitution" are recognized as a violation of human rights.

However imperative it is to approach "traffic in women" and "forced prostitution" as a violation of human rights, here also it is of crucial importance how the issue is defined. An example may be taken from the report of J. Fernand-Laurent (1983), UN Special Rapporteur on the "suppression of the traffic in persons and the exploitation of the prostitution of others".
In his report Fernand-Laurent approaches "traffic in women" and "exploitation of prostitution" from a human rights perspective. Yet for him this implies that prostitution itself is a form of slavery[27]: "While it is true that not all are tortured, all are nevertheless subjected to the most degrading and destructive form of slavery"[28]. In addition, he argues that it is important that states cooperate with social organizations, including organizations of prostitutes, that is to say, as long as they do not ask for the recognition of prostitution as a profession[29].
This view exemplifies the confusion between nature and conditions of labour: for him, it is not the working conditions but the nature of the activity that makes it a form of slavery. Compared to other forms of slavery, this is a unique situation. The abolition of slavery deals not with the abolishment of a certain type of work, but with the abolition of a certain type of power relationship - namely ownership - which is considered a violation of human rights. After the abolition of slavery, people still work in the cotton-fields and domestic work is still being done. Only when the discussion is about prostitution, the aim moves to the abolishment of the activity as such, rather than the abolishment of certain power relationships in prostitution. The comparison with other (modern) forms of slavery makes it clear that it is not the activity as such, but the conditions in which this activity takes place, that must be the focal point. The human rights that are violated are the rights of women as workers.

3.4 From "trafficking in women" to "illegal migration"

In some of the more recent definitions, especially those that are strongly influenced by the western-European countries in their attempts to counteract migration, "trafficking in women" is equated to the smuggling of aliens, also called "aliens trafficking" or "trafficking in migrants" (e.g. the IOM definition). In other definitions illegal entry or stay are at least considered a necessary component of "traffic in women".

Though it is a fact that in a substantial number of cases of international "trafficking", women are brought into the country illegally or lack a valid residence permit, just as many cases are known

27 J. Fernand-Laurent, 1983, paragraph 17.
28 op cit paragraph 35.
29 op cit paragraph 74.

in which women enter the country in a completely legal way, e.g. as tourists, brides, maids or artists. Their stay in the country may, in fact, be completely legal, that is to say, as long as they do not remove themselves from the power of their husbands or employers, as in many countries the staying permit of migrant women is dependent on the husband or employer. This shows clearly that as far as international "trafficking in women" is concerned, illegal border-crossing is definitely not a necessary component, nor are the two the same. Of course this is self-evident when "trafficking" takes place within national borders, for instance from rural to urban areas as in Thailand. Then there is no border-crossing at all, let alone the illegal crossing of a border.

Possibly the greatest objection is that within this approach the focus moves from violence against women to illegality. When "trafficking" is defined by illegal migration or residence, both the element of violence and abuse and the gender specific character of "trafficking in women" disappear from sight. The crime then becomes illegal entry or residence, i.e. infraction of state laws, rather than violence against women, i.e. violation of woman's rights. In this perspective, rather than the women, the state is the "victim", namely of migrants who want to enter the country illegally and of smugglers who help these migrants. It thus transforms the women concerned from victims who need to be empowered in relation to "traffickers" into collaborators with these "traffickers". Here, it is not the fact that women are forced, abused or deceived that is defined as the basic problem, but migration itself, whether legal or illegal.

When "trafficking in women" is equated with "trafficking in aliens", measures will primarily aim at combating illegality and illegal aliens, thus "protecting the state", instead of the women. Rather than preventing and combating violence against and abuse of women, such measures risk - even if they primarily target the recruiters and exploiters - further marginalization and criminalization of the women concerned.

A further confusion resulting from the equation of "trafficking in women" and smuggling of aliens arises in the context of "consent". It is true that many women choose of their own accord, within the options available to them, to migrate from one country to another or from rural to urban areas. If one equates "trafficking" with (illegal) migration, one may say that "a woman is trafficked with her consent". However, although she may consent to migrate for work or marriage, this does not mean that she consents to violence and abuse.

3.5. From "prostitution" to "(informal and unregulated) labour"

In the last fifteen years new manifestations of "trafficking" have become visible, such as the "traffic in women" for marriage or the trade in domestic workers. This development is reflected in more recent definitions of "trafficking", which go beyond the view of "trafficking" for the purpose of prostitution only, and incorporate other contemporary forms of "trafficking and slavery-like practices", whether this be in prostitution, in domestic labour, in marriage or in other situations (see e.g. the UNGA Resolution 1994, and the Beijing Platform for Action, 1995).

One common element in all the above stated situations is the aspect of forced labour and deceptive practices: women and girls are recruited by means of deception, violence or abuse of authority and subjected to slavery-like conditions, in which they are denied fundamental human rights and freedoms.

The second common element in these contemporary forms of "trafficking and slavery-like ractices" is that they invariably occur in those areas that traditionally, and even still today, are considered "women's work": domestic labour and sexual services. Moreover, they are not only considered women's work, but they are in fact the only areas in which work is available to women, and even more so during times of economic deprivation. These are the activities to which millions of women are relegated to earn an income. As stated by Coomaraswamy in relation to prostitution:
A discussion of prostitution must accept the premise that prostitution as a phenomenon is the aggregate of social and sexual relations which are historically, culturally and personally specific. The only common denomination - shared by the international community of prostitutes - is an economic one: prostitution is an income generating activity, marked by a degree of commercial indifference between client and worker (Coomaraswamy, 1994).

Women's work in the informal sector is mostly invisible, and since it takes place on the verge of the private and public domain, until today often not considered an area of state responsibility. Consequently, women's work did and still does not develop parallel to the sectors of labour in which men traditionally work. Labour laws and regulations, as evolved from the beginning of this century until the present day, pertain in particular to what is considered to be men's work, and which thus has become normal and regulated forms of labour. Women's activities, despite generating income for millions of women and their families, are often not regarded as work, and even when considered as such, labour laws and regulations only apply in very restricted ways.
Significantly, "trafficking and slavery-like practices" predominantly occur in these informal, unregulated and unprotected labour sectors: prostitution, entertainment, domestic labour and, related to this, the commercial marriage market.

3.6 Summary

The debate on "trafficking in women" and the "exploitation of prostitution", from the beginning of this century until the present, has offered a range of different definitions. The first definitions in international treaties a hundred years ago limit "traffic in women" to the "procuring, enticing or leading away" of a woman by coercion for the purpose of prostitution. In the succeeding years, "trafficking" has been linked to the exploitation of prostitution, and coercion as a restraining condition is abandoned, as exemplified by the 1949 Convention for the Suppression of the Traffic in Persons and of the Exploitation of the Prostitution of Others.

In the 1980s, the discussion on "trafficking" re-opened. A diversity of definitions shows up in the various national and international bodies, such as the European Parliament, the Council of Europe, the United Nations, the International Organization of Migration and the International

Labour Organization. No definition is the same; each definition emphasizes a different aspect. Some definitions focus on coercion, others on (illegal) migration, on (informal and unregulated) labour or on human rights.
Significantly, all different definitions reflect different interests, mixing the issue with other agendas. For example, when "trafficking" is defined by illegal migration or residence, it is not the interests of the women involved but rather those of the, mainly western-European, states who are trying to counteract migration which are at stake.

The discussion has become even more confusing because some, restricting "trafficking" to prostitution, argue that it is the activity of prostitution itself that makes "trafficking" a violation of human rights, rather than the way prostitution is organised - both in terms of the recruitment and the working conditions - like in other (modern) forms of slavery and slavery-like practices.

It is beyond doubt that the debate around "trafficking in women", "exploitation of prostitution" and "forced prostitution" is characterized by many misunderstandings. This is especially so when the distinction between "trafficking" and "exploitation" becomes blurred, as is the case in almost all definitions. This lack of clarity is aggravated, when the issue is discussed in different languages with different words and different connotations.

4 Starting-points for new definitions

In order to discuss "trafficking in women" in a useful way, a clear and common definition is needed. This is needed not only for the sake of the discussion. It is particularly important when thinking about "solutions", i.e. measures to prevent or combat the problem.
The choice of policies to pursue depends to a great extent on the definition of the problem, since each definition produces its own solutions and related policies. Every policy in fact serves a particular interest, e.g. that of the state or of the women involved. Moreover, every policy will affect - whether intentionally or unintentionally - the interests of another party.
When developing new definitions of "trafficking in women", it is essential to clarify the underlying ideas and interests. Pursuant to the analysis of the developments and themes as described in the former sections and the subsequent deconstruction of the different definitions, the following section will outline the starting-points for a new definition.

4.1 Perspective of women

The perspective from which the problem is defined is an essential question. As is illustrated above, "trafficking" not only affects the women involved but is at the same time closely connected with different interests of the state - such as the interest of the rich countries to restrict immigration, or of the poor countries to encourage labour migration, or the interests of states to combat organised crime or to control prostitution.

However relevant the various state interests are, "trafficking" should first and foremost be defined by the interests and perspectives of the women involved. It is the women concerned who define what is problematic.

Secondly, each proposed solution has to be examined in terms of its effects for the women concerned, the interests which are being served, whose problems are addressed and whether or not the solution might produce more problems for the women concerned rather than solve them.

At this point, it should be added that in this report the concept of "trafficking in women" will be used rather than the gender neutral "trafficking in persons". Although cases are known of boys or men who have been subject to "trafficking", the overwhelming majority of the victims are women. Substitution of "trafficking in women" by "trafficking in persons" suggests a gender neutrality which in reality does not exist. A more practical argument is that, by using the term "trafficking in women", the danger of confusion with the smuggling of aliens seems less than when using the term "trafficking in persons".

4.2 (Informal) labour

The different definitions of "traffic in women" used over the last fifteen years illustrate that the notion is no longer restricted solely to prostitution as it was in earlier days.
It is increasingly acknowledged that prostitution has much in common with other activities that are traditionally considered "women's work" (and which often appear to be virtually the only areas in which work is available to women): domestic labour and sexual services. In these unprotected and unregulated sectors of the labour market millions of women earn an income for their families and themselves. It is not coincidental that "trafficking in women" and slavery-like practices predominantly occur: within these labour sectors prostitution, entertainment, domestic labour and, related to this, the commercial marriage market.

In defining "trafficking in women" the next logical step in this development - as far as it has not already been done - is to broaden the concept of "trafficking" to apply to any work or services, instead of limiting it to prostitution. However within the context of this report, "work and services" are restricted to prostitution, domestic work and marriage.

4.3 Coercion

As a consequence of the choice for the perspectives and interests of women the central element of a new definition has to be "force": i.e. all sorts of coercion by means of which a woman loses control over her own life, body and mind. Coercion is the only element in all definitions used until now that is indisputably considered a problem. It is in the institutionalized unequal power relation between men and women that the core of the problem has to be found and not in the activities in which women are involved as such. Not the work or services (in prostitution, marriage or domestic labour) as such, but the way those are organised (both in terms of the recruitment and the working conditions) makes it a problem to the women involved: that is "forced".

Coercion is the discriminating element which turns recruitment of women and the situations they end up in into "trafficking in women" and slavery-like practices. Therefore, coercion has to be the core element of any definition.

4.4 Migration, crossing of borders, illegality

All other elements mentioned in the different definitions - for example illegal entry or stay, clandestine work - may be elements of "trafficking" but certainly not per se. Both abusive recruitment practices and slavery-like working and living conditions are possible without the crossing of borders, legally or illegally, and with the woman in the possession of a legal staying or working permit. However, in the case that entry or stay is illegal, this illegality is not necessarily the problem for the women involved, as long as it does not serve as a means of coercion. On the contrary, illegal entry, stay or work may well be the only possibility for women to escape from slavery-like situations.

This implies that measures to prevent illegal entry or stay in a country may even be counter-productive: it increases the possibilities to put and keep women in slavery-like situations.

4.5 Recruitment and living & working conditions

As may be clear by now, a distinction will be made in this report between the aspect of recruitment and the living and working conditions women are subjected to. This is not only important for mere analytical reasons, but also because measures to prevent or combat abusive recruitment and brokerage practices are not necessarily the same as measures to prevent or combat abusive working and living conditions.

"Trafficking" refers to the aspect of recruitment for work or services, to be distinguished from the actual work or services. The two aspects are connected - abusive recruitment leading to slavery-like practices - but not per se. "Trafficking" is possible without the women involved ending up in slavery-like situations, while slavery-like practices may occur without the women involved being "trafficked". Both need to be described and addressed.

5 Conclusion

5.1 Working Definitions

Based upon the previous analysis, the following working definitions are developed in order to cover abusive recruitment and brokerage practices, as well as abusive working and living conditions, occurring in both public and private spheres:

Trafficking In Women

All acts involved in the recruitment and/or transportation of a woman within and across national borders for work or services by means of violence or threat of violence, abuse of authority or dominant position, debt bondage, deception or other forms of coercion.

Forced Labour & Slavery-like Practices

The extraction of work or services from any woman or the appropriation of the legal identity and/or physical person of any woman by means of violence or threat of violence, abuse of authority or dominant position, debt bondage, deception or other forms of coercion.

5.2 Explanation

TRAFFICKING IN WOMEN AND FORCED LABOUR & SLAVERY-LIKE PRACTICES

As has been shown in the preceding sections, the work or services as such do not form the core of the problem, but rather the abusive and coercive working conditions. This means that both forced labour and slavery-like practices as well as the way women are brought into such situations have to be addressed.

Since none of the past or present documents specific to "trafficking" offer a clear definition. Unambiguously in women interest two well-established international agreements are used as the basis fer: i.e. the League of Nations Slavery Convention of 1926 and the Supplementary Convention of 1956[30] - which condemn all slavery-like practices, including debt bondage[31] and forced marriage[32] - and the ILO Forced Labour Convention No. 29[33].

These conventions have broad international acceptance and clearly describe the situations at hand. It is worth noting that such clarity exists only in conventions that do not address gender-specific behaviour and are therefore not gender-biased.

The working definitions distinguish between trafficking - which comprises all the processes involved in recruitment and transportation of women under coercive conditions - and the situations of forced labour & slavery-like practices to which women are subjected. Although closely related, they do not necessarily go together. Trafficking can be a means to bring women into slavery-like situations, but this is not necessarily the case. On the one hand, women can be recruited and transported under conditions of coercion but not end up in a forced labour/ slavery-like situation. On the other hand, women may find themselves in forced labour/slavery-like situations without having been trafficked.

By making this distinction it is possible to visualize a broader range of forced labour & slavery-like practices to which women are subjected, and which may or may not be the result of trafficking. Taking coercion as the critical element, all working and living situations in which the personal freedom of women is curtailed, can be addressed as well as the practices which are used to bring women into such situations.

30 Slavery Convention, 1926; Supplementary Convention on the Abolition of Slavery, the Slave Trade, and Institutions and Practices similar to Slavery, 1956.

31 Article 1a of the Supplementary Slavery Convention prohibits "Debt bondage, that is to say, the status or condition arising from a pledge by a debtor of his personal services or those of a person under his control as security for a debt, if the value of those services as reasonable assessed is not applied towards the liquidation of the debt or the length and nature of those services are not respectively limited and defined".

32 Article 1c of the Supplementary Slavery Condition prohibits "Any institution or practice whereby a woman without the right to refuse, is promised or given in marriage on payment of a consideration in money or kind to her parents, guardian, family or any other person or group", or whereby "the husband of a woman, his family, or his clan, has the right to transfer her to another person for value received or otherwise".

33 ILO Convention no. 29 concerning Forced Labour, 1930.

Secondly, the distinction clarifies the relation between abusive brokerage practices (defined as trafficking) and slavery-like exploitation of women (defined as forced labour & slavery-like practices). As long as the latter practices are allowed to exist, and in some cases even are legitimised by the non-existence or non-enforcement of government policies, then recruiting agencies, intermediaries and other profit-seeking individuals and organizations will seize the opportunity to supply these sectors with new recruits. To draw an analogy: without slavery, the slave-trade could never have existed.

By means of violence or threat of violence, abuse of authority or dominant position, debt bondage, deception or other forms of coercion

The basic principle underlying both definitions is the (human) right of every woman to have control over her own life, body and mind.

In the Slavery Convention, the concept of "ownership" fundamental to slavery, is defined in article 1.1 as:

The status or condition of a person over whom any or all of the powers attaching to the right of ownership are exercised.

In article 2 of the ILO Forced Labour Convention, forced or compulsory labour is defined as:

All work or service which is extracted from any person under the menace of any penalty and for which the said person has not offered himself voluntarily.

Whereas the concept of forced labour in the ILO Convention is predominantly used for the relation between the state and the individual (see article 1), article 4.1 of the same Convention takes it to the private domain, ruling on state accountability regarding forced labour situations between individuals:

The competent authority shall not impose or permit the imposition of forced or compulsory labour for the benefit of private individuals, companies or associations.

The crucial element in both definitions is coercion, which can take various forms, including, but not limited to:

- violence or threat of violence, including deprivation of freedom (of movement, of personal choice)
- deception: with regard to, amongst other things, working conditions or the nature of the work to be done
- abuse of authority or dominant position: this can range from confiscating personal documents in order to place another person in a dependent position, to abusing one's dominant social position or natural parental authority or abusing the vulnerable position of persons without legal status
- debt bondage: i.e. pledging the personal services or labour of oneself or another person as security for a debt, if the value of those services or labour as reasonable assessed is not applied towards the liquidation of the debt, or the length and nature of those services or labour are not limited and defined.

Work or services

"Work or services" includes all domestic, sexual, reproductive or other services rendered under the above-mentioned conditions of coercion, regardless of whether these services are recognised as work, whether they take place under a work contract or whether they take place under a marriage contract and regardless of whether they are normative in the society or illegitimate.

This report will concentrate on forced labour & slavery-like practices and trafficking in women in the field of prostitution, domestic work and marriage, since these are the most commonly researched and described situations. However, the definition is not limited to these fields, leaving open the possibility to address any such practices occurring in other areas.

The appropriation of the legal identity and/or physical person

This refers to the concept of partial or total ownership as used in the Slavery Conventions. The word "appropriation" is used to denote the act of claiming ownership of a person, acting as if one owns the person. The appropriation of legal identity can range from confiscating one's identity papers or supplying a woman with a false identity to the loss of one's legal personality under the marriage contract.

3 CONTEMPORARY MANIFESTATIONS AND TRENDS

I Introduction

This chapter will examine the contemporary manifestations of forced labour & slavery-like practices ("the extraction of work or services under conditions of force or deceit" as defined in Chapter II), and trafficking in women ("the recruitment for work and services under conditions of force or deceit" as defined in Chapter II) within marriage, domestic labour and prostitution. The first part of this chapter introduces these issues within the broader context of traditional female roles, a gendered labour market and female labour migration. It continues with an overview of the prevalence of trafficking and forced labour & slavery-like practices in the three areas of our concern - marriage, domestic labour and prostitution -and points to the overall factors which contribute to such practices.

The second part reviews in depth each area separately, examining the specific characteristics, contributing factors and manifestations in the particular contexts of marriage, domestic labour and prostitution. It ends with an overview of the constraints on women to escape or change their situation, the factors which hinder them to report and press charges, and the manner in which complaints are dealt with by the authorities.

The limitations in research which have been stated in chapter I apply to this chapter.

A comprehensive analysis of the extent of trafficking and forced labour & slavery-like practices is not possible, since reliable figures are lacking. Moreover, information on specific trends and manifestations varies greatly from country to country and region to region. The mere fact that the number of examples of a specific manifestation for one region exceeds that of another does not imply that such practices do not occur in other regions. This unevenness in available data allows only the highlighting of general trends and exemplary cases.

The results of the questionnaire for NGOs[1] have been processed from this chapter on. A total of 61 NGOs, from 41 countries, completed the general sections (sections A and B) of the questionnaire. In addition, 46 NGOs filled in the specialized section on prostitution (section C), and 17 completed the section on domestic labour (section D). The absolute number of respondents is recorded per diagram. Unless otherwise indicated, respondents were requested to fill in the questionnaire according to the working definitions which have been developed for this report.

It should be emphasised that the given percentages reflect the perspective and experiences of the respondents, which in turn represent just part of the organizations working in the field. In addition, terms such as "frequently" in Thailand may mean something totally different from that in Canada. In this sense, absolute significance cannot be attached to the figures: they show trends

[1] A copy of the questionnaire can be found in annex I. For more information on the use of the questionnaire and the (methodological) limitations: see chapter I.

and not "facts". Nevertheless, in combination with the other sources employed, one can assume these figures represent relevant trends.

Since the aim is to show trends, the original six categories (very frequently/ frequently/ occasionally/ rarely/ not/ don't know) were reduced to four categories; the categories "very frequently" and "frequently", and "occasionally" and "rarely" have been combined. For the same reason, percentages were rounded off. Percentages do not always add up to 100 per cent due to incomplete questionnaires.

2 General framework

2.1 Traditional female roles

Housekeeping, caring for husbands (also sexually), caring for children, extended family members and the aged are traditionally reproductive tasks assigned to women in all societies. In addition, women - especially in rural communities - may spend many hours each day growing food and keeping livestock for family consumption and selling their own surplus produce at the market. Although these activities have considerable economic significance, they are generally viewed as outside of the cash economy.

Significantly, female labour is rarely recognised as work. In most societies, woman's role and identity as wife and mother are considered biological rather than economic and social. The work women have always done, and continue to do, is considered a "natural" aspect of being female, respectively as a "natural part" of women's responsibility to supplement family subsistence. Expectations and socialisation - including religious tenets circumscribing the role of women - oblige girls and women to fulfil their "duties" as daughter, wife and mother. Thus the work that women do every day is not viewed as work, but as the fulfillment of their natural role (Afshar, 1985).

2.2 Gendered labour market

The same cultural and political mechanisms relegate women to certain sectors of waged labour: *Girls are educated on a lower level than boys and have fewer opportunities for work in skilled professions. The occupations open to them are often limited to those considered 'suitable work' for women, such as domestic services, factory work and prostitution* (GAATW, 1996, p.13).

In general, women have less access to the formal labour sectors either in the poor or in the more developed countries. They are greatly dependent on work in the informal and unregulated labour sectors, such as domestic work, small trade, entertainment and prostitution. This means, work without rights and without protection and sometimes not even recognised as work, like prostitution. In the Dominican Republic, for example, it is reported that two-thirds of the economically active women works in the services sector or as domestic worker. These are the lowest paid jobs with hardly, if any, occupational protection (Ferreira, 1996).

Labour markets do not value male and female labour independently of gender. They operate not only to exclude women from skilled jobs, but also to down-grade jobs when they are performed by women. As Afshar points out: "It is the sex of those who do the work, rather than its context, which leads to its identification as skilled or unskilled" (Afshar, 1985).

Both the delegation of women's work to the realm of "nature" and the down-grading of women's work has been questioned by feminists at the beginning of the century (Hamilton, 1909) and, with intense vigour, during the past three decades. Women in domestic service, who have been called maids or house-girls or servants, have organised themselves to improve their labour rights as domestic workers; likewise, prostitutes organise themselves to demand labour rights as sex workers. Wives remain the most isolated and unorganised group. There are great regional differences in the plight of women, but the patterns that refuse worker status to women who perform sexual, domestic and reproductive services continue to reign throughout the world.

2.3 Feminization of migration: female labour migration

Women and children are particularly vulnerable to the present global malaise of increasing economic and social inequality, rural economic failure, rising unemployment and the growing gap between the rich and poor countries. The decline in the former socialist countries is illustrative of its impact on women. The breakdown of national economic and political systems has precipitated the hitherto unknown phenomenon of unemployment which has stricken women first and foremost. Women were the first to lose their jobs while social services, education, and medical care are no longer free. As stated in a report of the Polish Feminist Association:
The growing unemployment among Polish women, the lack of vocational retraining programmes, the very low social benefits (less than US $ 100, when the rent of a single room varies from US $ 100 to 200) and the increasingly common necessity of paying for education - it is for these reasons that ever younger women decide to try to find work in the West or in prostitution in Poland (Limanowski, 1995, p.60).

In Poland and many other countries the responsibility for the sustenance and care of dependent family members is increasingly borne by women, and by women alone in case of absence of husbands due to migration, abandonment or death. They often find themselves in the paradoxical situation of being responsible for the family income, while having neither access to well-paid jobs nor the equal opportunities for legal labour migration.

At the same time, social and political developments have raised expectations in general of what the world outside one's own communities may offer. Women everywhere aspire to a better life than that of their mothers and grandmother's. They seek opportunities to escape from traditional gender and family constraints and to find the means for an independent life.
As described in a report on violence against women in China:
Economic reform opened the gate to a new world to not only men but also to women. Suddenly appearing before women was a world that was fast, new and exciting. Human kinds natural desire for a better life and the instinct to pursue freedom led more and more women to aspire to leave the

kitchen stove and kang, from which they had served generation after generation and to leave the villages and the fields that had been their entire lives. More and more women left the path that had been set for them by their families and chose rather to elope... One may say that these women who wish to say farewell to the old world and go search for a new life are brave... The movement of women from their homes and the burgeoning desire on the part of the women to change themselves are first steps forward for women and historically significant steps at that (Harvard, 1992, p.5ff).

Not only in China, but in many places throughout the world, women seek to take their lives in their own hands:

Another factor which draws Polish women to Western Europe is the myth of independence and emancipation supposedly awaiting them in the West. After the communist regime in Poland came to an end, the new authorities, prodded by the Roman Catholic Church, have been promoting the conservative traditional model of the family, in which the only proper role for a woman is that of mother and housewife. Women are pushed away from decision making and into the margins of life. In these conditions, along with prevailing violence and alcoholism within families, women may connect their plans for a better future with employment in the West. They are drawn there not only by the myth of prosperity, but also of career opportunities, of independence and the partnership model of the family in which she will be equal to her male partner. It is not by chance that the only countries to which more Polish women than men emigrate are those countries that are considered the most 'women-friendly': The Netherlands, Germany, Belgium, and the Scandinavian countries, including Denmark (Kootstra, 1996, p.26).

The general belief ex-colonies the South that envisions Europe, the mother country, as the ideal of development and progress, promoted throughout the years of colonial domination and, more recently, by the globalization of communication, is another factor influencing women to leave to work abroad (Lim, 1996).

As a consequence, the number of women migrating in search of work and a better life or to support their families has increased dramatically during the past twenty years. Nearly half of the migrants world-wide are women, although in official policies women are still primarily considered as dependants of male labour migrants. This trend is described also by the IOM in their report on trafficking to the EU states:

One factor is the changing nature of female labour migration. Traditionally female migrants have tended to emigrate with their families or after the male head of the family has emigrated. Today, however, given the rise in single parent families, women increasingly have sole responsibility for their families and have a stronger incentive to emigrate in order to send back remittances to their children (IOM, 1996d, p.6).

According to an ILO report (Lim, 1996), approximately 1.5 million Asian women are working abroad, both legally and illegally:

The countries of origin report an aggregate outflow of 800,000 female migrant workers per year, and the number is increasing steadily... In the Philippines women account for about 60 % of legal migrant workers (excluding seafarers) and this figure rises to 94 % for those destined for Asia, excluding the

Middle East... In Thailand, women account for only about 25 % of the recorded workers leaving the country for overseas employment, but clandestine female emigration is increasing faster than that of men (ILO, 1996).

This labour division is also reflected in migration patterns, whether it be on the national or the intra-regional or the international level. Yet:
Gender remains by and large a neglected area in the field of international migration studies. Evidence from limited inquiries into the situation of female migrants in a number of OECD countries, suggested that whether legally or illegally recruited, many female migrant workers tend to be deployed in a narrow range of occupations shunned by the local female population (entertainers, sexual services, domestic workers, and semi-skilled service occupations in restaurants and hotels). Apart from the service occupations, migrant women are also engaged in floor processing lines, garments and textiles. Service occupations filled by migrant women tend to fall in the domain of sex-affective services, care taking and social maintenance of labour, commonly referred to as reproductive labour (Truong, 1995, p.2).

Wherever women go they find extremely restricted kinds of paid work: "unskilled" work on the assembly line, cleaning and cooking and caring work - either in private houses as domestic workers or in restaurants and hotels -, or as entertainers and prostitutes, usually in the "boom industry" of the 20th century: tourism with its attendant sex services (Lim, 1996). An airport survey in Sri Lanka, for example, revealed that 84 per cent of migrant workers were female; of these women 94 per cent were domestic workers (Lim, 1996).
Ironically, many women also opt to leave their country altogether in the ultimate women's role of "bride", hoping to find economic and social security, and eventually find themselves in the same gender-bind of family and home care from which they had hoped to escape.

Within a gendered labour market sexual or domestic work are two of the few income - generating options available to women, especially from poorer countries or regions, to make a living. Many women consciously enter into prostitution and domestic work and move in and out of a particular activity during their lifetime. In the Latin American region, for example, sex and domestic work have traditionally been established as "women's work" and as legitimate ways in which women earn a living, and many women move around the region and abroad in search of this type of engagement. In this sense, prostitution should be understood as an activity which for centuries has been an integral part of Afro-Caribbean female survival strategies (Azize-Vargas, 1996, p.7). In the same way Asian
organizations caution "not to equate prostitution with trafficking as for some women sex work is a valid choice and they should be given the same rights as workers in other occupations." (GAATW, 1996, p.33)
At the same time, it is these unregulated and unprotected labour markets, including the commercial marriage market, where abusive and exploitative practices flourish. As observed by the ILO:
While migration provides productive labour and an economic lifeline for millions of Asian women, the dramatic plight of unprotected female migrant workers has become an increasing source of public concern as evidence of abuses mounts (ILO, 1996, p.16).

Although there is a clear demand for these types of work in the destination countries, there are few legal and independent possibilities for women to migrate within this informal labour market and these possibilities decrease even further in view of the increasingly restrictive immigration policies of the wealthier countries. Owing to the nature of the work and the forms of migration open to them, they are forced to make use of the services of more or less dubious agencies and middlemen proliferating to meet that demand. Migrating women are thus placed in an extremely vulnerable situation.

Poor or lacking legislation and labour standards and the partially illegal or semi-legal character of the work form the basis for suppressive and exploitative working conditions, varying from humiliating treatment, low payment and extreme working hours to outright forced labour and slavery-like conditions. Women, caught in clandestine and informal sectors, are hardly in the position to protest or claim their rights.

In the case of international migration, the right of residence is usually linked to the employer or the husband and subjected to various restrictions. Foreign domestic maids in a number of Asian countries, for example, are not allowed to change jobs within two years of their employment contract. Migrant women workers are prohibited from marrying local citizens. They are not allowed to become pregnant, and some countries can even subject them to pregnancy tests every six months. Domestic service and entertainment are usually not covered by labour laws or social security regulations in most receiving countries, but even where they are, enforcement of workers' rights is difficult (Lim, 1996). Even in countries where prostitution is more or less legalised, policies often do not allow migrant women to work as prostitutes. In the case of marriage, the residence right of the wife is usually fully dependent on the husband for a considerable number of years, a bind which renders the man almost complete power over his wife.

In its *World Labour Report* 1993 the ILO describes the present day occurrence of forced labour and slavery in the tin mines, sugar plantations and forestry estates in some Latin American countries. The characteristics of these modern forms of forced labour or slavery-like practices, which can be derived from the different cases (ILO, 1993), are:

- confinement
- no pay or not enough pay
- debt bondage: parents are pre-paid for their children or workers are offered an advance that has to paid off from future earnings, but the debt is extremely difficult to pay off and often increases
- recruitment with promises of good wages and working conditions, but on arrival workers are told that wages are lower than promised. They have to pay for transport and buy food from the recruiters at higher than normal prices, all adding to the "debt" they have to repay
- physical punishment and sexual abuse for trying to escape, sometimes amounting to killings
- belongings are kept by employers
- due wages are withheld for all kinds of reasons
- they have no control over their daily lives.

Although there is no specific reference to women in this ILO report, these mechanisms which lead to conditions of forced labour, are similar to those employed to coerce and control women within the sectors of our concern.

3 General overview of trafficking in women, forced labour and slavery-like practices in marriage, domestic labour and prostitution

3.1 General prevalence of forced labour and slavery-like practices

In response to the question of whether forced labour and slavery-like practices - as defined in the working definition - occur in their respective countries, a quarter of the respondents report that forced labour & slavery-like practices do occur (very) frequently in marriage and domestic labour; about half of the respondents report these practices to happen (very) frequently in prostitution. Table 1 shows the reported prevalence of forced labour & slavery-like practices within the three areas of our concern.

Table 1

Absolute number of respondents: 61

Do forced labour & slaverly-like practices take place in your country in the context of:

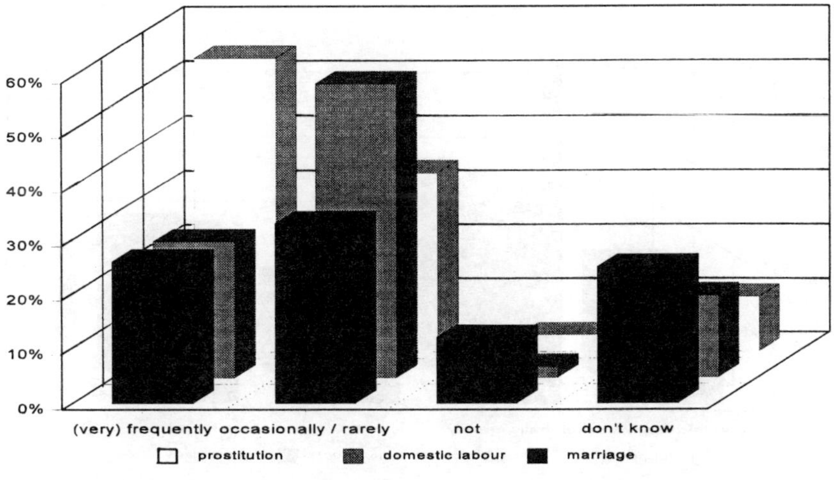

Although this report will focus on contemporary forms of forced labour & slavery-like practices in marriage, domestic labour and prostitution, similar conditions may occur in other fields, as several respondents indicate. Other situations that respondents mention are foreign exotic dancers, factory workers, garment workers, Free Trade Zone workers, restaurant workers, daily wage earners, agricultural labourers and gold and coal mining labourers (men and women). An illustration is the case of 68 Thai garment workers, most of whom were women, who were rescued in August 1995 from a sweatshop in Los Angeles. They had been deceived about working conditions and were working sixteen hour days for less than US $ 1 an hour in a closed compound under armed guard (GAATW, 1996, p.32)

3.2 General prevalence of trafficking in women

Whereas forced labour and slavery-like practices refer to the living and working conditions in which women may end up, trafficking - as defined for this report - refers to recruitment practices. Though we made a distinction between trafficking for the purpose of marriage, domestic labour or prostitution for this report, in practice these dividing lines are less sharp. Women, for example, may be recruited for marriage but then sold into prostitution by their husband.

Trafficking may take place within national boundaries as well as across borders. Although most attention until now has been paid to international trafficking, a considerable percentage of respondents report the prevalence of trafficking WITHIN national borders for as well marriage as domestic labour and prostitution. Table 2 shows the reported prevalence of trafficking in women within countries.

Table 2
Absolute number of respondents: 61
Does trafficking in women take place <u>within</u> your country.

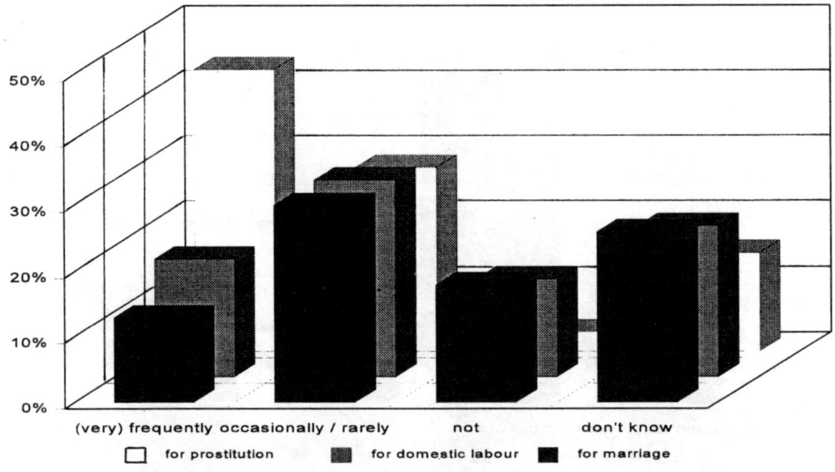

At the same time trafficking may occur ACROSS borders, whereby it should be noted that the same country can function as a sending and destination country and transit country. In relation to trafficking across borders more than 60 % of the respondents mention their own country as a sending country, about 70 % as a receiving country and about 45 % as a transit country.

When these figures are further analyzed in relation to the various purposes of trafficking, the following patterns show:

Table 3

Absolute number of respondents: 61
Does trafficking in women take place <u>to</u> your country.

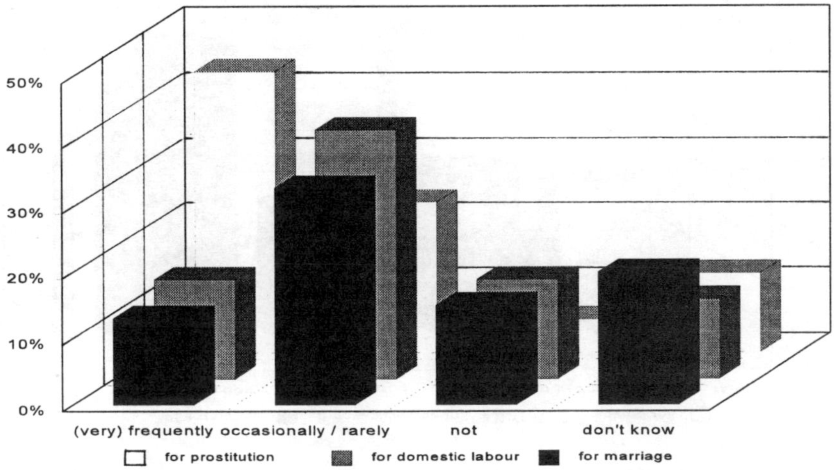

Table 4

Absolute number of respondents: 61
Does trafficking in women take place <u>from</u> your country.

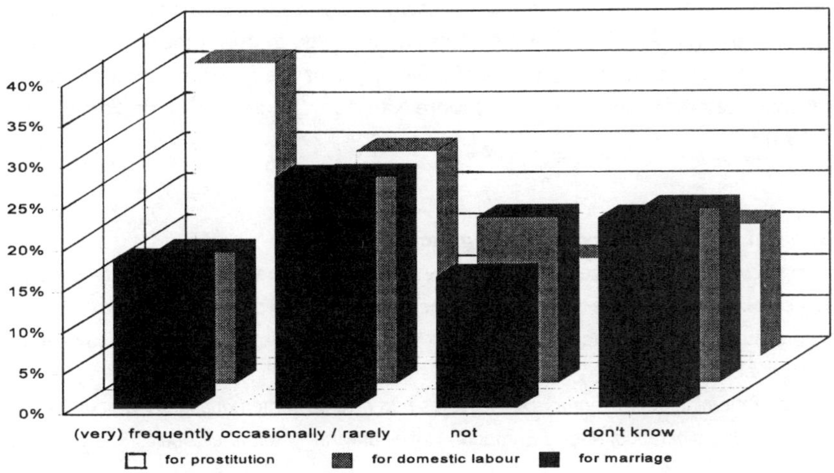

Table 5

Absolute number of respondents: 61

Does trafficking in women take place <u>through</u> your country.

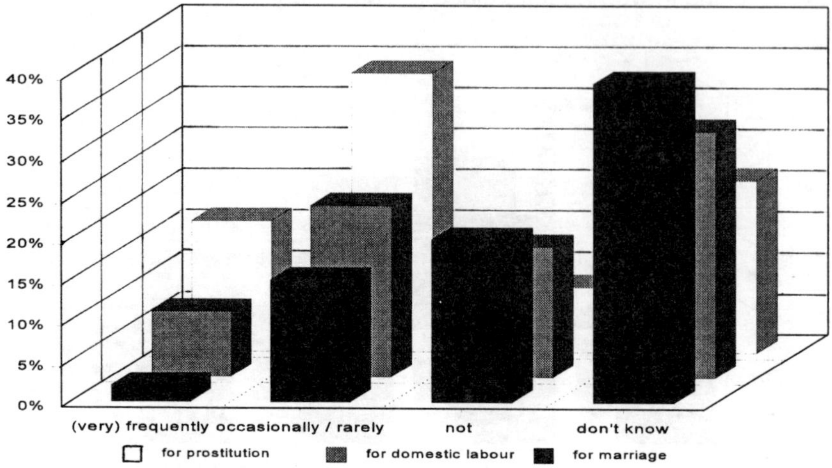

According to respondents trafficking occurs also for other purposes, such as factory labour, farm work or foreign exotic dancers.

Almost equal percentages of respondents report that trafficking occurs within, to and from their countries. This supports the contention that trafficking is not necessarily a cross-border phenomenon.

International trafficking clearly has no simple "one way" pattern. Many countries are simultaneously countries of origin, countries of destination and transit countries. Others started originally as sending countries but developed into destination countries, as Thailand. Women are trafficked from China to Hong Kong, from Vietnam to China, from Burma to Thailand and from Thailand to Japan (GAATW, 1996). Women can be trafficked through other countries as transit points, for example, from Thailand to Malaysia with Japan as the final destination, or from several South East Asian countries to Singapore with Australia as the final destination (AFP, 1995).[2]

4 General overview of contributing factors

Trafficking in women and forced labour & slavery-like practices are certainly not recent phenomena. In the Latin American and Caribbean region news of these activities dates back to the 19th century, more specifically the 1860s in Argentina and Brazil, as Donna J. Guy and others have described:

At the end of the nineteenth century Buenos Aires had a terrible international reputation as the port of missing women, where kidnapped European virgins unwillingly sold their bodies and danced the

[2] An overview of countries of origin and destination with regard to intra-regional and international trafficking for marriage, domestic labour and prostitution can be found in annex 5.

tango... By the 1860s the Continental Press reported frightening stories of women lured away by strangers with false promises of marriage or work, only to be trapped in some sordid house of ill repute... According to a Budapest newspaper, they arranged transportation and promises of marriage for women, then sold them as prostitutes in Buenos Aires... In fact, verifiable cases of white slavery were infrequent, but they did involve a system of forced recruitment by lovers, fiancés, husbands, and professional procurers... European prostitutes in Buenos Aires, for the most part, came from poverty stricken families and worked out of desperation. Marginalised by the industrial revolution, driven from their homelands by hunger or by family, political or religious persecution, they saw immigration to a new land or even a new continent as the key to survival (Guy, 1995, p.5ff).

Since this recorded history more that a century has passed, but many of the factors mentioned here are still current. At the same time new factors have emerged and old factors, such as poverty, have taken new forms.

The factors in COUNTRIES OF ORIGIN most mentioned by respondents as contributing (very) frequently to forced labour and slavery-like practices and/or trafficking, are:
- poverty/unemployment (mentioned by 89 % of the respondents as contributing (very) frequently)
- corruption of authorities (48 %)
- globalization of the economy (48 %)
- development strategies, e.g. tourism (43 %)
- laws and policies on migrant labour (23 %)
- laws and policies on prostitution (23 %)
- national or local conflict/military presence (20 %)
- cultural and religious practices (20 %)
- migration laws and policies (18 %).

Contributing factors in DESTINATION COUNTRIES that are most mentioned by respondents as contributing (very) frequently, are:
- immigration laws and policies (43 %)
- laws and policies on migrant labour (39 %)
- globalization of the economy (38 %)
- labour legislation (31 %)
- laws and policies on prostitution (31 %)
- development strategies, e.g. tourism (25 %)
- poverty and unemployment (23 %)
- corruption of the authorities (21 %).

The low status and subordinate position of women in many societies and the potential to earn substantial profits from these practices also were mentioned as overall factors.

The following section will scrutinise some of these contributing factors. "Globalization of the economy" will not be discussed here as a separate factor; aspects thereof will be addressed in the sections on poverty and unemployment, development strategies, and demand and supply.

4.1 Poverty and unemployment

A recent report by the IOM on trafficking in women to countries of the European Union states a combination of factors as the cause of trafficking:

Root causes are poverty, lack of opportunities, the disparity in wealth between rich and poor countries, and the marginalization of women in the latter countries (IOM, 1996d, p.6).

Information from NGOs as well as testimonies provided by the women concerned confirm that the absence of viable employment opportunities in their home situation coupled with the urge to improve their economic situation is one of the main reasons why women seek opportunities to work abroad.

The creation of export processing zones in countries like the Dominican Republic, Brazil, Mexico and other countries from the region, by no means constitute real economic options for women, as pointed out by, among others, Azize-Vargas in her report on trafficking in women in Latin America and the Caribbean (1996a). Low salaries, poor working conditions and instability, are among the most frequent situations faced by women in this sector. This applies not only to the situation in Latin America. In her paper on women as migrants and workers in developing countries Zlotnik notes that:

Despite the new employment opportunities created by the growth of export oriented manufacturing in many developing countries, too many unskilled migrant women are still likely to end up working as domestic servants in the informal sector. Furthermore, even when they manage to work in the formal sector, their positions are far from secure (Zlotnik, 1995, p.12).

At the same time, the economic burden of women is increasing as male unemployment rises. In many cases, reductions in demand for male labour, due to economic slowdowns in receiving countries, spur female migration. Women increasingly migrate to support their families, especially since the demand for maids and nurses continues to increase (Lim, 1996). Data from 1990 show that Latin America shares with Eastern Asia the highest percentage of female headed households (21 %) among developing countries (UN, 1995b, p.6). The Caribbean region has the highest rate of female headed households in the world: 35 %. It is estimated that women in the urban zones in the Dominican Republic constitute 40 % of heads of households (Ferreira, 1996).

According to Safa, the changes occurring in the role of women as economic providers in the Dominican Republic and Puerto Rico have altered the role of men in such a way that it can be argued that what is left is just "the myth of the male breadwinner" (Safa, 1987, p.389).
Also Azize-Vargas in her report on Latin America notes that gender roles are shifting and traditional patterns of migration initiated by men have changed:

In addition, the economic crisis has pushed more women into the informal sector activities like commercial trading and sex trade. In this sense, the search for economic survival and autonomy is the structuring principle for women's entering into the sex trade, domestic work or other working activities. Ways and strategies used by women to achieve their autonomy are becoming more flexible and varied... Sex work appears therefore as a strategy for many women to cope with painfully economic consequences of global capitalism... At another level we need to understand how global capitalism creates conditions for women to sell sexual services at far better rates of pay than the sale of another form of labour (Azize-Vargas, 1996a, p.14).

The same mechanisms apply to other regions, such as South East Asia, where great numbers of women support their extended family with their earnings. Because of the foremost priority of earning money, family or friends rarely inquire about the conditions of their work as this is the only means to improve their position within their country (GAATW, 1996).

4.2 Development strategies

A number of reports points out the use of tourism as an economic strategy to boost the economies of developing countries - often encouraged by international banks - as a contributing factor to trafficking in women for prostitution:

Although a clear difference should be established between sex tourism and trafficking in women for prostitution, several factors have been identified as fostering the relationship between tourism and trafficking of women. For instance, the transit of wealthy European tourists to poor, ex-colonial territories, where women have been portrayed by agencies as an essential part of the tourist package and sexualised exotic products, are elements identified by organizations as ways of facilitating trafficking operations (Azize-Vargas, 1996, p.12).

Butegwa mentions the same mechanism regarding Kenya:

Kenya, with its flourishing tourism industry, has not escaped the global racket of trafficking in women for purposes of prostitution. Regarding the situation of trafficking it has already been noted that young women from Uganda are lured into Kenya to serve as prostitutes for the millions of tourists who constantly flock into Kenya. There are also reports of other young women who are lured from India allegedly to work as performing musicians in Kenya, only to end up as prostitutes (Butegwa, 1996, p.4).

However, other development strategies can have similar devastating consequences for women. Human rights activists in Indonesia (Handayani, 1996), point out that the focus of the government's policy to speed up economic growth through industrialization, has changed vast areas of agricultural land into industrialised areas. As a consequence, peasant women have lost their jobs and income in rural areas and are pushed into poverty. Illegal agents come to rural areas and promise women jobs as domestic worker, secretary, and the like.

In Sri Lanka the new economic policies of the government as part of the conditions to receive loans from international financial institutions include opening up new sectors of the economy and reducing the state sectors, a move which has raised the level of unemployment. The most vibrant sectors of the economy at the moment are the Free Trade Zones, established by the government, and migration for employment. Women constitute the majority of the labour force in both sectors:

When one looks at the nature of work in both these categories, they are traditionally 'women's tasks' and highly labour intensive. When one looks at the conditions of work, they are slave-like for both categories and the women are themselves extremely vulnerable to all forms of physical and sexual abuse (De Silva, 1996).

4.3 Demand and supply: laws and policies on migration and migrant labour

While the number of female labour migrants is growing, the opportunities for legal international migration, especially to Western Europe, North America and Canada, have decreased. A great number of destination countries claim that they are no longer immigration countries. Measures have been effected to tighten asylum procedures, reinforce border control and reduce labour permits for foreign workers. However, though official policies of these countries hold that they should not allow more immigrants, these statements can hardly be maintained when it is clear that there is a apparent demand in economic terms for certain types of jobs, especially in the informal labour market, and that these jobs sustain their economies. The market for domestic workers in Europe forms an example:

Throughout Europe there has been a massive increase in demand for private domestic services, including child care and care of the elderly. In Spain it is estimated that there are over 600,000 domestic workers, and in France the Federation of Employers of domestic workers now has 900,000 members. These services are increasingly being provided almost exclusively by migrant women - and in France, by their descendants. According to migrant women's groups it is now the only employment available for migrant women in Italy, Spain, France and Greece (Anderson, 1996, p.3).

Given the demographic shift in the EU[3] and the decline of state provision of services for care of children and the elderly in Northern Europe, migrant women play an increasingly important role in providing services, which were formerly provided by the state or the extended family:

The employment of the foreign domestic worker is the new 'solution' to the difficulties arising from social and economic changes in the Union. Those workers who are providing 'live-in' care in the growth areas of care of children and the elderly are increasingly women without legal status in the country where they live. Thus the work involved around 'personal services' continues to be invisible and those workers are vulnerable to exploitation in the form of low wages, job insecurity and excessive working hours (Ibid., p.3).

In this sense the growth of migrant domestic workers provides a unique insight into the relationship between the developed and developing world:

With the ease of communication, of transport and of money transfer, emigration is becoming part of family survival strategies. While the woman migrates to do domestic service, other female members of her family, her mother or sisters, do her domestic chores and child care responsibilities unpaid. As other female family members follow the original migrant abroad, those remaining at home take on more and more domestic labours. So, the strategies of female employers in Europe to enter the labour market fully, have implications for the family structures and strategies throughout the world (Ibid., p.11).

The increasingly repressive immigration policies of the wealthier countries, clearly have their negative effects for female migrants. On the one hand, they reduce even more the possibilities for women to organise their migration independently. Spring (1992) describes this mechanism with regard to the trade with striptease dancers and prostitutes in Switzerland:

3 According to a report published by the European Commission in March 1996 Europe is set to experience a massive demographic shift, with a 50% increase in the number of people over 60 in the next 30 years and an 11% decrease in the under 20.

Border crossing presents no problem, particularly when experienced organizations are behind them, because they know exactly which stipulations have to be complied with. Women who attempt to enter the country under their own steam are frequently refused entry. They are at the mercy of these organizations.

On the other hand, they make working and living conditions more precarious. As stated by del Rosario:
...The circumstances of female migrants in the European Union countries are becoming even worse due to these countries moving towards a common, repressive immigration policy (del Rosario, 1994, p.4).

Whereas labour migration from developing countries, and recently the CEECs, in the majority of the Northern countries, is subject to massive restrictions, most of the Northern countries maintain a total ban on prostitution by migrants, even if local women are allowed to work as prostitutes. In reality, entertainment and prostitution are the few working possibilities which are tolerated for foreign women, whether this is the official policy in Switzerland[4], or as an everyday practice like in The Netherlands.

According to the IOM, the number of migrant prostitutes in many countries within the EU is higher than the number of local sex workers. In Germany it is estimated that 75 per cent of those involved in street prostitution are foreigners. In Milan, Italy, 80 per cent of the streetworkers are migrant women. In Vienna, a similar percentage of the women working as dancers/hostesses in sex clubs are from the Central and Eastern European countries. In The Netherlands, it is estimated that about one-third of the prostitutes comes from countries outside the EU, and this percentage rises to 50 per cent or more in the large cities (IOM, 1996d, p.4). These women work for cheap money, do not lay a claim on legal or social protection due to their precarious legal situation, and generate significant revenue for the state (for example, by tax imposition), private individuals and criminal organizations (Wijers, 1995). The economic importance of this sector is impressive: the profit from the sex industry in Japan, for example, is estimated to be 4.2 trillion Yen[5] annually (Yunomae, 1995). Though figures from other countries are unavailable, it may be assumed that these will be comparable.

At the same time, the work they are doing is not recognised as work and the women involved are without legal protection, either from labour laws or immigration laws. The illegal nature of the work, the resulting social, political and legal marginalization and their status as irregular, undocumented, dependent or illegal migrant can be used against them at any moment.
In countries where prostitution is prohibited, the act itself is sufficient reason for the authorities to remove a foreign woman, but:
Even when no such prohibition exists, the foreign women's illegal status automatically gives authorities of the country of migration the ground for immediately deporting her. The question of

[4] See for the trade with striptease dancers: Kathrin Spring *Gekauftes Ungluck, Frauenhandel in der Schweiz*, 1992.
[5] 100 Yen is approximately 1.19 US $, exchange rate January 1997.

trafficking may not even be raised in any of these circumstances, thereby removing the possibility of any redress for the victim. While traffickers virtually remain unprosecuted and free to continue with their trade, migrant women not only face exploitation by their traffickers but become wide open to racist immigration and police control in destination countries (del Rosario, 1994, p.4).

It is this glaring incongruency between the official no-migration policies of receiving countries and the day to day practices of prostitution, mail-order brides and domestic workers, which creatles the gap that allows organised crime to step in.

However, not all destination countries deter immigration. Some of them even have an active labour import policy for certain types of labour, as Truong (1995) cites for Japan:
"The evidence suggests that Japan has been opting for the import of foreign brides to solve female labour shortage in agriculture, and entertainers for its service sector". But also in these cases, this does not mean that the women involved are protected by the law. Rather they are seen as needed, but undesirable aliens.

From the interest of sending countries, the export of (female) labour has become an increasingly crucial source of foreign exchange. As stated by GAATW (1996, p.34): "There is a demand for migrant labour from richer countries, but the benefit accrues also to poorer countries in remittances from overseas workers". In the Philippines, for example, overseas workers are required to send home a minimum percentage of their pay. If they do not, the government can withdraw their permission to travel abroad. (Enloe, 1989, p. 188). In the Dominican Republic, the more than 100,000 women working as prostitutes in foreign countries form one of the most important sources of foreign exchange. Government policies may actively encourage labour migration for economic profit and unemployment reduction, as is the case in Indonesia, the Philippines, Thailand and Sri Lanka.

The increasing rate of unemployment and poverty as well as the large debts of the majority of the labour exporting countries are, among others, engendered by what Enloe refers to as "international debt policies":
International debt policies has helped create incentives for many women to emigrate, while at the same time it has made governments dependent on the money those women send home to their families. The International Monetary Fund, which serves as a vanguard for the commercial banking community by pressuring indebted governments to adopt policies which will maximize a country's ability to repay its outstanding loans with interest, has insisted that governments cut their social service budgets. Reduction of food-price subsidies are high on the IMF's list of demands for any government that want its financial assistance. Keeping wages down, cutting back public works, reducing the number of governments employees, rolling back health and education budgets - these are standard IMF prescriptions for indebted governments (Enloe, 1989, p.184).

Receiving and sending countries thus share a common interest in maintaining a cheap labour force and therefore both have an interest in preserving the status quo (Skrobanek, 1994).

Since poor, unskilled women have few opportunities to travel independently and to work legally in the destination countries, they are heavily dependent on recruiting agencies and brokers, and thus at risk of falling victim to criminal networks. It could be said that restrictive immigration laws work indirectly in favour of traffickers, who will always find ways to circumvent laws, while they increase the dependence of the women who want to migrate - again, a favourable situation for criminal networks.

In general "trafficked" women, be it for domestic labour, prostitution or marriage are regarded principally as undesired aliens, regardless of a repressive immigration policy or an active labour import policy of the countries of destination. Under current aliens policies of most countries, the status of "victim of trafficking or slavery-like practices" is irrelevant subordinate.
In this situation it is almost impossible for migrant women to ask for protection in case of violence or abuse.

4.4 Corruption of authorities

Numerous reports attest to the incidental and structural, small and large scale involvement of officials on both the local and the international level[6]. This seems to be a theme that runs through all reports. We cite a few examples from the report on trafficking in Nepal, India, Bangladesh, Hong Kong, Taiwan and Japan, compiled by GAATW (1996):
On the Bangladesh/India border the price paid to immigration officials is reportedly around 50 Rps (US $ 2,63). Honest officers are transferred away from the border (GAATW, 1996, p.3).

Many women report being recruited by officials, like 19 year old Yai:
Yai worked in a department store in the south of Thailand. She was promised a job in a clothing factory in Taiwan where she would make good money to save for her future, much better money than she could ever earn working in her current job. Her recruiter was a high ranking Malaysian police officer. She arranged her passport and gave it to him as he was to arrange her visa for Taiwan. As they were landing in Taiwan he gave her a fake Malaysian passport with her photo in it and told her to use it. She never saw her Thai passport again. After she passed through immigration a Chinese man met her in the arrivals hall and drove her to the hotel. That night she was raped by this man. She was then forced into prostitution serving ten to twenty clients a day. There was no way for her to leave and she was threatened with beating. She never received any money that was paid for her... Among Yai's customers were high ranking local Taiwanese policemen who received free services in return for protection (Ibid., p.16).

NGO workers in Nepal tell of the necessity to pay the local police in order to prosecute a case of trafficking. Traffickers are protected on all levels of authority, including a judiciary that is not independent and of corrupt politicians. In Japan, NGO workers relate that once the women are in the country they are basically ignored by the police, apart from two or three symbolic brothel raids each year (GAATW, 1996). In the Philippines, BATIS reports that corrupt officials conduct marriage ceremonies even without the husband presenting a certificate of legal capacity, thus permitting foreigners to practice serial marriages (BATIS, 1996b, p.4).

[6] See chapter 4 for a more structural review of involvement of officials in trafficking and slavery-like practices in prostitution .

4.5 Traditional practices

Several respondents indicate that the low social value given to girls is a contributing factor to trafficking and slavery-like practices, as the following quote of a father in Nepal illustrates:
We are very happy to have a daughter. Once she is grown up she will go to Bombay to earn money. Why are the Nepalese police having headaches for sending or selling our daughters? Why do they prosecute or imprison us? What have we done wrong to the government? (Poudel, 1994)

Trafficking and slavery-like practices may be encouraged by or may even be part of traditional and/or religious practices. A series of representations submitted to the Working Group on Contemporary Forms of Slavery by Anti-Slavery International in the last three years documents various forms of ritual slavery, such as the devaki, devadasi and trokosi systems (ASI, 1995a/b).

In India for example, women are married to the gods through the Devadasi system and are then unable to marry a man. They are used by the priests of the temple and go into prostitution to survive economically. Young girls who are devadasis are sometimes sold by the priests to brothels. A similar practice is the Deukis or Devaki system in Nepal: women are endowed to a patron God against requests for favours. Recent practice is that rich families buy a young girl from poor rural families and adopt her as "daughter" to offer her to the temple. They cannot marry, which means that only a life as "kepts" (kept wives) or prostitutes remains for them. Many government officials working in the area keep them as "kepts" and leave them when transferred. Parents who refuse to sell their daughters are refused being hired as wage labourers and have to face various accusations before court or police. In 1992 there was an estimated number of 17,000 girls endowed as Deukis in Nepal (Poudel, 1994).

Although women in China officially enjoy the legal right to free marriage for 40 years now, the institution of arranged/forced marriages as an economic transaction is still a widely accepted and legal practice, rooted in feudal, traditional culture. Though the law prohibits the kidnapping and sale of women as a wife, it does not prohibit arranged marriages and its related violence:
In fact these arranged marriages are the disguised sale of women. It is just that this sale is at this time in China legal. This legal practice prepares the ground and provides public support for the illegal activities of slave traders (Harvard, 1992, p.13).

Reports (HRIC, 1995/Harvard, 1992) document that the most common form of violence against women in China occurs in relation to arranged marriages or within marriages. Yet, this type of violence is considered by society, including women, to be a private, family matter and perfectly normal.

Especially with regard to marriage and religious practices, there are strong undercurrents of tension between cultural obligations, sanctioned by the concerned community, and trafficking in women and slavery-like practices.

4.6 High profits

Trafficking and slavery-like practices hold relatively few risks but afford considerable financial gain. Its illegal nature and attractive financial benefits encourage involvement of well-established criminal syndicates. In Japan, for example, links with the Yakuza have been reported, and in Hong Kong Triad connections have been reported in reports from NGOs and newspapers (GAATW, 1996). In Europe, criminal groups from the Central and Eastern European countries have entered the business (IOM, 1996d).

Profits can be huge. In Poland, the police estimate that for each Polish woman delivered to a brothel, the trafficker receives 1,000 DM (US $ 700). In Berlin, the police calculate that a foreign woman in a brothel typically earns 500 DM (US $ 350) a day, of which she is eventually allowed to keep 20 DM (Wall Street journal, 1996). A 1988 assessment of the Australian Federal Police estimates that a minimum of 200 Asian women[7] are working illegally as prostitutes in Australia at any one time. Calculations based on 200 prostitutes grossing A $ 4,800 per week each, suggest possible overall cash flows of up to A $ 900,000 per week. A substantial part of this money is forwarded overseas. Financial investigations in 1994 identified 280 transactions, totalling over A $ 1.3 m. related to movements of funds to South-east Asia. These funds reflect both the forwarding of prostitutes' earnings to their country and the payment to organisers and facilitators in these countries (AFP, 1995).

Penalties are in general fairly light. Although sentences may be posed incidentally, it is extremely difficult to obtain successful convictions. In the case of international trafficking, most countries simply expel migrant women before they have the opportunity to report or give evidence against the offenders. Few of the victims are prepared to testify since no protection or very limited protection is guaranteed to them. Moreover, in many countries women risk arrest should they turn to the police for help.

4.7 Civil and military conflicts

Military conflicts and civil wars may be contributing factors in several ways. An illustration of this is the situation in Burma, where people throughout the country are forced to work as "porters" or to perform other forms of forced labour by the Burmese military. Women forced to serve as porters in military columns are raped or forced to serve as sexual counterparts for the soldiers. Many women prefer to leave the country to work in the sex industry in Thailand, rather than serving the SLORC[8] soldiers without payment. Others go to work as sex workers in Thailand in order to earn money for their families so they can buy-off forced labour by paying "porter's fee" to the SLORC authorities (Images Asia, 1995/6). In Thailand they risk arrest, detention and expulsion as prostitutes and illegal immigrants. Many fear arrest on return to Burma for leaving the country illegally, not to mention the social stigma of having worked in a brothel. If they are found to be HIV positive, they risk prosecution by the Burmese government as a result of their HIV-positive status. It is in this context that trafficking of Burmese women, especially women from minority groups, to Thailand and their exposure to conditions of forced

[7] This seems to be a very conservative estimate.

[8] SLORC: State Law and Order Restauration Council.

labour must be understood (Simm, 1996).
The following sections will examine each area separately.

5 Trafficking in women and forced labour and slavery-like practices in marriage

5.1 Characteristics

It is a documented fact today that families are not an undisputed safe haven for women and children. In her report to the Commission on Human Rights in 1995 (Coomaraswamy, 1995) the special Rapporteur on Violence Against Women presented the many forms of violence that take place in the family context. A pattern which places the wife at a disadvantage in relation to the husband, is present in both traditional and modern forms of marriage - a position which embodies potential dangers of forced labour & slavery-like practices as well as trafficking in women for marriage.

In her study on servile marriages Taylor (1993) identifies a number of factors, which in certain combinations, might be said to constitute a servile marriage. These are marriages, in which the wife:

- enters marriage in exchange of goods or money with significant economic as well as ritual value, over which she has no control, especially where virginity carries an economic price
- is not consulted over the choice of spouse and may not refuse to marry him
- is below the age of majority when she marries, especially where her husband is older, or where she is expected to reside with her in-laws
- is prevented by her husband or his kin from controlling her fertility
- has reduced parental rights over the children of the marriage
- has less control of, access to, or rights to inheritance of family income or property
- is subject to being raped, beaten or murdered without recourse to law or society for protection or redress
- is subject to arbitrary authority and routine humiliation by her husband, which is condoned by society, on the basis of her assumed inferiority
- is secluded, prevented from earning an income, or otherwise restricted in her behaviour according to rules which do not apply to her husband
- is intimidated by threat of violence, divorce or the withholding of food or money into working longer hours than her husband
- is forbidden to leave the marriage or intimidated into staying by violence, threat of violence, threat of penury, or extreme social disapprobation

Under such conditions, the husband effectively "owns" the wife. Such a servile marriage relationship can be termed "slavery" to the extent that the husband exerts his power as "owner" within the marriage. At each stage of the marriage, on entrance, during and on ending of the marriage, the woman is subjugated to the will of those controlling the whole process: mostly of the husband and other male members of the family, but often also with the complicity of her

mother, who herself is probably party in a servile marriage.
Regardless of how a woman has entered such a marriage, she is likely to be subjected to exploitation, intimidation and seclusion, comparable with slavery. Furthermore she can be made to work without pay, may not decide the number of children to have and is threatened with the loss of her children if she disobeys. She is threatened physically or emotionally and punished for not complying to the wishes of her husband, she is kept dependent on her husband and his family, she is forbidden to leave the marriage or to earn an independent income outside the home, or if she does earn, is not allowed to dispose of it.

Servile forms of marriage take place predominantly in societies where women's status is low. The wife-to-be tends to be viewed as a chattel by her own family, as a source of potential costs and benefits, to be controlled by them while under their jurisdiction and disposed of as they see fit. Once she is married, the young wife is seen as a source of labour and children by her husband and his kin. Here too, she is viewed as someone who must be controlled to ensure that she continues to labour and produce the appropriate number (and sex) of offspring. If she fails to do these duties, she may be punished or be disposed of as he or they see fit (Taylor, 1993).

5.2 Contributing factors

One of the crucial factors determining the position of women is the denial of women's right to property. According to a study on servile marriages, conducted in Nepal, Pakistan, Tanzania, the Gambia and Lesotho, the issues of property rights and inheritance rights are fundamental to women's autonomy. Denying women the right to property and, in particular, land amounts to far more than economic discrimination; it may deny women independence, mobility and legal autonomy (Yudkin, 1996).

Another related factor is women's legal identity. In many countries all over the world (married) women have no full legal status or are considered minors under customary, religious or secular law. This implies that she possesses no independent legal capacity to enter into contracts, is not able to sue or to be sued in her own name, or to enter into employment contracts or to start a business of her own. She is unable to acquire property or have access to credit unless assisted. This makes her totally reliant on the co-operation of her husband or a male guardian (Yudkin, 1996).

Laws on marriage, separation and divorce can put women at greater risk of abuse and violence. In Uganda and Kenya, for instance, a court will not consider a petition for divorce within the first three years of marriage. Even after this period, a woman petitioning for divorce or judicial separation must have proof of grounds for divorce in accordance with the terms laid down by the Divorce Act. The woman must prove that her husband has committed adultery and deserted her for at least two years or committed adultery and has been cruel.
Many women, who are trafficked for marriage, are kept as virtual prisoners and are unlikely to have evidence of adultery, which is the key to getting a divorce. Moreover, divorce may not be the solution since the right of residence in the country is often dependent on the marriage (Butegwa, 1996).

These factors, which form the basis for a continuing pattern of servitude of women, range from diverse forms of traditional servile marriages to contemporary forms of forced or arranged marriage and vary from the direct buying and selling of women between individual men or agents and their family members to the organised matchmaking business.

5.3 Contemporary manifestations and trends

The scope of this report does not allow a comprehensive overview and analysis of the different contemporary manifestations of trafficking and forced labour/slavery-like practices in marriage. However, from the available material some patterns can be distinguished:

- kidnapping and sale of women for marriage
- forced/arranged marriages
- pretended marriages
- the mail-order bride system

We will shortly discuss these patterns and present some exemplary cases.

KIDNAPPING AND SALE OF WOMEN FOR MARRIAGE

Reports (Harvard, 1992/HRIC, 1995) from CHINA document that since the mid-1980s the incidence of the kidnapping and sale of women as wives in certain rural areas has increased at an extra-ordinary scale. Although official statistics have always been kept secret, public security offices from all of China reported 11,698 cases of kidnapping and sale of human beings in the first ten months of 1990. These numbers are probably not complete and conservative since public security officials in the single province of Shandong found 13,958 women who had been bought and sold, freed 3,966 enslaved women and children and arrested 1,690 people on charges of slave-trading in that same year. In some villages kidnapped and sold women account for two-thirds of all young married women in the village (Harvard 1992).

Several reasons are given for this increase. One of them is the shortage of women across the nation, but especially in the rural areas. The majority of women are sold as wives to remote and poverty stricken parts of the country. Another contributing factor is the traditional Chinese belief in maintaining the family line, which means families want their sons to marry no matter what. Those who have difficulty finding wives - as well as the poor, older men, the ill-favoured, the sick, the disabled and the mentally retarded - might consider buying a woman as the easiest way of getting a wife. Furthermore, it is cheaper to buy a wife than to marry one due to, among other factors, the still prevailing practice of betrothal gifts:
Despite a great deal of criticism in the official press of lavish weddings and betrothal gifts, these are very popular and even required, especially in the country side. This exchange also reflects the traditional view of women as property for whom payment is made (HRIC, 1995, p.13).

Most of the women trafficked are from rural areas and are generally abducted when they are travelling away from their native places. Some of them leave their village to escape arranged marriages, others want to see the world and search for a new life. Traffickers approach these young women under the pretences of showing them the way, getting them jobs as domestics or nannies or training in technology or handicrafts, or finding them good husbands, or being their travelling companions. Many women who are kidnapped and sold are beaten and raped, or gang raped while in the hands of slave traders. Most of the cases of kidnapping by gangs involve the repeated sale and resale of each woman.

After sale many of the women suffer cruel and inhuman treatment from the men who purchased them as wives and extreme violence may be exercised to prevent women from running away and to punish them for doing so:
Because in the past many women had escaped from slavery or committed suicide the farmers in the county locked up or tied up their women during the daytime. In the evening, after venting their sexual desire, they removed all of the women's clothing so that they could not run away. A young woman named Wu Yan was sold to a forty year old man. She could not endure her mistreatment and ran away. She was caught, brought back, strung up and beaten... Other women who are caught trying to run away are not only beaten but are burned or cut. In some cases their ears are cut off... Some who tried to run away had the tendons in their feet cut... (Harvard, 1992).

Twenty-two years old Tang was sold for 2,900 yuan to a man who locked her into a room for eight months to prevent her from running away. His mother and sister took turns watching Tang, and she was not even allowed to leave the room to use the toilet. Desperate Tang attempted suicide three times and repeatedly tried to escape which resulted in fierce beatings. When she was rescued, Tang's body was covered with scars (HRIC, 1995, p.10).

Although the Chinese government has paid considerable attention to the problem of kidnapping and sale of women and has put some effort into fighting the practice, the results have been scanty and short-lived:
Until recently, the authorities have not prosecuted men who purchase women as wives; thus the trade has continued unabated. Official action to rescue victims of trafficking is generally initiated only if a complaint is made by the woman or her family. Local officials turn a blind eye, even formally register marriages into which the woman has been sold (China Human Rights Fact Sheet, 1995).

In **Taiwan** poor farmers, the handicapped and elderly pay intermediaries around $ 3,000 for a young Vietnamese wife (News Report, 1996).

In **Vietnam**, there is a growing traffic in smuggled brides on the Vietnamese border; ethnic Chinese girls from dirt-poor North Vietnam cross into China to marry men from women-starved villages (Newsweek, 1996).

In **Mozambique**, refugee women from the war-torn countryside are sold as concubines and wives to South African men. Referred to simply as "stock" by the traders, the girls/women are lured over the border with offers of work, and then sold to men in the townships (Taylor, 1993, p.36).

In **Italy**, over 5,000 Nigerian prostitutes, aged between sixteen and thirty are reported to have been sold as wives to farm workers in the south of the country (Taylor, 1993, p.36).

Forced/arranged marriages

The institution of mercenary arranged marriages is still a flourishing and legal practice in many countries today. In China figures indicate that depending on the county/village, 30 to 90 % of the marriages are forced marriages (Harvard, 1992).

Arranged or forced marriages can take different forms:

- the exchange of wives: the family of the prospective groom pays a bride price (money or other goods) to the family of the prospective bride in the marriage arrangement
- the extended exchange of wives: the exchange of unmarried daughters between two or more families as brides for their sons. These marriages are based on the exchange of brides that are "equal", which means that if one marriage fails they all fail. Therefore in this kind of marriages the women are more or less hostages. Families are not likely to allow women to run away or file for divorce:

On New Years Day 1989 in Linsu County in Shandong Province, sixteen years old Liu Xuelan was married to a man twenty-six years her senior. After the wedding she tried to run away, but each time was caught and tied up and beaten by her husband. He drove needles under her fingernails. She was bruised and bloodied from head to foot and her arms were swollen to the size of her thighs. When people from the county women's federation arrived to save Liu, her husband ran out and yelled "What do you think you are doing? She is mine. I got her in exchange for my little sister (Harvard, 1992, p.10).

Very few options are open to women who find themselves in the conditions described. She may try to run away, risking even more severe violence when caught and brought back. She may try to file for a divorce, but even in cases of severe abuse the court may deny her divorce. If she runs off with a man who does not beat her, she commits the crime of bigamy and runs the risk of prison sentence:

Jin Fengqin, a peasant woman of 39, was sentenced to two year-jail for bigamy. When she had filed for divorce, the court had Jin and her husband go through three different counselling sessions, during each of which Jin showed her wounds to court officials, and each time her husband beat her even more severely when they got home. He stripped off her clothing and forced her to kneel, almost unconscious from the pain, on broken light bulbs. She lost the use of one of her arms but still was unable to win her divorce. In the end she ran away and moved in with a man who did not beat her (Harvard, 1992, p.24).

However, the practice of forced or arranged marriages is not confined to China. In her study on servile marriage Taylor (1993), describes various traditional forms of arranged marriages in a number of African countries, such as Nigeria, Senegal, Burkina Faso and Gambia.

In **Kenya**, Indian women are brought into the country for marriages that have been negotiated without their consent. Once negotiations are complete, they are sent to Kenya to meet their husbands and new in-laws. Their husbands impound their passports which in effect prevents them from leaving the country should the marriage fail. Hindu women are kept in bondage which is reinforced through their children whom they are not willing to leave behind.

Forced marriages are not rare in Kenya, especially within pastoral communities, which marry off young pubescent girls without their consent (Butegwa, 1996 p.5).

In **Iraq** the provision of the law outlawing forced marriages actually encourages rape of unwilling brides by ruling that "marriage under duress shall be null and void if consummation has not taken place" (Taylor, 1993, p.21).

A somewhat different practice is reported in Japan where women from Sri Lanka were recruited as computer trainees, but forced into mass marriages:
Priyani, 27, from Sri Lanka, answered an advertisement for computer training, but found herself trapped in a forced marriage with a Japanese businessman. Upon arrival in Japan the women who applied as trainees were forced to attend group matchmaking after having their passport taken away from them. They were told that if they refuse to marry Japanese men they would have to pay airfares and other expenses, too high for her (Asahi Evening News, Feb. 1991/ International Herald Tribune, April 1991).

Pretended marriage

In Bangladesh, agents known as Ghataks (match-makers) roam the rural areas in search of girls as wives of Indian men. Many of these marriages appear to be fake since they have taken place without compliance with the necessary conditions of Muslim marriage, such as registration:
It is learnt that agents of both Bangladesh and India reach a prior agreement over a fake marriage and share of money thereof. The man who wants to purchase a Bengal girl in the guise of bridegroom agrees to pay a certain amount after much bargain. According to agreement the four parties share the amount, one portion goes to the local agent, another to the Indian agent, a third one for the female ghatak who arranges the fake marriage and manages to allure girls and their parents, and a fourth to the border agents who manage safe crossing of the border by bride and bridegroom (ACD, 1995, p.11).

When everything is settled, the pretended bridegroom comes over, completes the "marriage" ceremony and takes the girl across the border. Once at the place of destination the girl is forced to live a life under slavery-like conditions with her "husband":
They just procured young girls to work in bangle factories and with their earnings they drink, gamble and spend a life of enjoyment. The girls had no liberty, but there was every possibility of being kicked out of the house on the slightest plea or if they disobeyed their so-called husbands. Once out of house their only alternative was to accept the life of a sex worker in a brothel (ACD, 1995, p.20).

In cases where the husband sells his wife to another person or to a brothel, she may be continually transferred from one owner to another.

Mail-order bride system

In the industrialised countries there is a growing demand for women as wives for men in recent years:

Another striking feature of female international migration today is multi-cultural marriages involving a high degree of commercialization of matchmaking such as Mail-Order Brides (MOBs), often loaded with fraudulent practices (Truong, 1995).

According to Taylor (1993, p.37), the majority of women involved in mail-order bride business at present are Filipinas, but there is a growing trade in women from Eastern Europe, Colombia and several other South-east Asian countries. The agencies operate on the West European, Japanese, Chinese, Australian, Canadian and North American market. In JAPAN, for example, there are more than 700 marriage brokers importing Asian women to Japan. Matchmaking fees run as high as $ 20,000. In the USA, there are currently hundreds of companies, offering mail-order services, which an estimated 2,000 to 5,000 American men use successfully to find wives each year (Amirrezvani, 1996). Despite the remarkable growth in the industry over the last five to ten years and the potential for abuse, there is virtually no governmental regulation within the industry.

The industry primarily focuses on women from developing countries. Although marriages arranged this way may be successful, several reports document cases where women end up in violent marriages or marriages in which the sole expectation of their husbands involves the provision of domestic labour and/or sexual services. Under such circumstances, the wife is usually not in a position to enlist help from the authorities or to leave an abusive husband for fear of being deported or as a result of the lack of support systems.

The vulnerability of women in MOB marriages is increased by her legal status as a migrant on a temporary resident's permit which is dependent on the continuance of the relationship or the sponsorship of the "fiancee". Separation or divorce will lead to her deportation:
Given their vulnerability as temporary migrants, there are many reports of Filipino MOBs who have virtually become sex slaves or nurse-maids for their foreign husbands but have remained in those marital situations for fear of possible deportation. Some western husbands have been known to use this vulnerability as a weapon for threatening, even getting rid of, their Asian wives (del Rosario, 1994).

In the same way, Japanese men are reported to use the threat of portation to keep their Filipina wives in a constant state of stress, intimidation and insecurity (BATIS, 1996a/b).

In the USA, immigrant spouses are granted a conditional resident status for two years after her marriage. At the end of two years the couple must file a joint petition to the Immigration and Naturalizations Service as proof that the marriage is bona fide. If they fail to prove this, the immigrant spouse will be deported unless she can prove that one of several exceptions applies. Those exceptions include the proven existence of domestic violence. Under such circumstances, the immigrant spouse may apply for a waiver of the joint filing requirement. She can thus file a self-petition without relying on the abusive spouse. Yet, despite the exception for domestic violence, there is a lingering fear among immigrant brides that they will be deported if they report violence. This fear is often perpetuated and exploited by mail-order husbands who profit from this misinformation (Bond, 1996).

In most of the EU COUNTRIES immigrant wives are granted a dependent resident status for three years or more. If the marriage fails within this period, the wife is liable to deportation, regardless of the grounds that led to the separation. Their dependent residence status leaves women without defence against all forms of abuse, varying from battery to forced prostitution. They have no choice but to endure the abuse or to face the risk of deportation.

Some NGOs maintain that many women who marry through these commercial bureaus and other agencies come into situations where they are in fact expected to do little more than supply domestic and sexual services to their spouses. Since these men have often paid substantial amounts for the marriage to be arranged, they expect blind obedience from their wives. In Japan and Korea, for example, MOBs from other Asian countries are reported to be really "maids in disguise":

Mail-order brides placed in rural areas may find themselves in slavery-like conditions, working as domestic servants and isolated from the outside world. Some are falsely purchased as brides to work as hostesses in night clubs. Gangsters or sex industry brokers have little difficulty because there are no legal checks on the marriages. It is widely known that men in rural areas have a hard time finding wives because women have left for urban areas. Local governments see international marriages as the best way to solve this problem. Numerous mediating agencies are headed by town mayors and these lay down qualifications for the type of women they are looking for. The vice-governor of Akita prefecture said he thought that importing Filipinas was good and stated, 'I went to the Philippines last year and saw people living in poverty. If they can survive that, they can survive rural life in Japan. I also think it would bring about an improvement of breed'. Since this import of brides started, women human rights groups have formed to protest against the marriages promoted by the governments. The current trend is that where government intervention is decreasing, private agencies are stepping in to replace them (Azu, 1995).

The working methods of a typical MOB agency focus on the male customer, who is offered a wide choice of women "eager to marry him", but clearly do not consider the women as having any rights to select her own spouse:

While agencies will not admit it, the introduction is premised on the man being the client and, the woman, the subject of business negotiation between the agency and the male client.... On the part of the woman, choice - however defined - is often very limited (del Rosario, 1994).

It is the man who is the client of the agency, and the one who pays the costs. The man receives the most information, initiates contact, and exercises his choice of women at various stages.

The use of female and racist stereotypes as recruitment and advertising methods of the industry are deceptive for both men and women, and conjures up unrealistic expectations:

The main selling point is the western stereotype of Asian women, i.e. submissive, uncomplaining, sensual, exotic beauty. Worse, some agencies...even offer money back guarantees in case of dissatisfaction of their male clients (del Rosario, 1994).

5.4 Recruiting methods and agents

The methods used by traffickers to recruit women for marriage may differ, as the above indicates. The recruiting methods most mentioned by respondents as occurring (very) frequently are:

- (promise of) marriage (mentioned by 26 % of the respondents as occurring (very) frequently)
- false marriage contracts (12 %).

Other methods are: buying a woman from her parents/legal guardian (7 %)[9], kidnapping, promise of work as waitress/domestic worker (4 %), false job contracts (3 %), and buying a woman from her husband (2 %).

The recruiting agents most mentioned as occurring (very) frequently are:

- marriage agencies (mentioned by 26 % of the respondents as occurring (very) frequently)
- individual marriage brokers (23 %)
- the expected husband (21 %)
- family members (16 %)
- acquaintances of family or friends (15 %)
- friends (13 %).

6 Trafficking in women and forced labour and slavery-like practices in domestic labour

6.1 Characteristics

In its report on domestic workers to the Working Group on Contemporary Forms of Slavery (ASS, 1990), the Anti-Slavery Society documents a number of living and working conditions of overseas domestic workers in Britain, and concludes that "these conditions are those of slavery":

- debt bondage: many of the women fall into debt by borrowing at exorbitant interest rates to pay recruitment fees, or by taking an advance payment from the recruiter. Before they can even begin sending money to their families - the prime purpose of working overseas - they have to redeem these debts
- their passport is being kept by their employer
- they are not allowed off the premises except rarely and then under some sort of supervision
- they are ill-treated and humiliated: "slapping, hair-pulling, being spat upon, being called donkey, and sometimes slave are common"
- pay is withheld or given months in arrears
- they are given left-over food
- speaking to other servants is discouraged and sometimes forbidden
- heir bed may be on the floor of the children's room, in a corridor, in the bathroom or in the kitchen
- there is no respite: they are first up in the mornings and the last to go to bed at night; even

[9] Only mentioned in Africa and Asia.

then their few hours of sleep may be interrupted
- sexual harassment is usual and rape is not unknown
- they cannot legally change their jobs.

The report continues:
Those courageous women who do, and often at great physical risk, run away from their captors, immediately put themselves on the outside of the law. They cannot legally seek employment, they cannot overstay whatever period may be stamped in their passport, which in the majority of cases is in the employer's safe, and the appeal rights they have against deportation orders are very limited. In addition, they are frequently penniless and alone in a city they only know from the airport and the house they were confined to (ASS, 1990, p.110).

Although the study is limited to Britain, the report notes that the Anti-Slavery Society is aware that domestic slavery is not confined to Britain and that instances of it, in varying degrees, may be found in Middle Eastern states, in Hong Kong, in North America and in member states of the EU. Also, it leaves the exploitation of domestic workers by their fellow nationals in their home countries aside.

6.2 Contributing factors

Apart from the aforementioned general contributing factors, several reports on the trade in domestic workers and violence against women migrant workers (Anderson, 1993/1996a,b; APDC, 1989; Heyzer, 1994; UN, 1996b) pinpoint a number of specific factors which contribute to the abuse faced by (migrant) domestic workers:
- the unregulated and unprotected nature of the employment sector: domestic work is not normally covered by labour codes or social security provisions of the host countries. A worker in an employment situation where her rights are not guaranteed by law has no recourse to justice or protection.
- the legal status of the domestic: whether dependent, tying her to a employer and inhibiting her escape; undocumented, when she has been held from the beginning without legal status; or irregular, when she has contravened the immigration constraints by running away from the violent situation.
- lack of inaccessibility or inadequacy of support mechanisms and personnel to motivate and facilitate migrant women workers to escape when they are confronted with violence, and to assist them after escaping from violent situations.
- the large profits made by all parties concerned, as long as the principal - the woman migrant worker - complies with her situation. Violence, in various forms, is used to keep her in compliance.

This may be illustrated by the case of Gilly, a Nigerian woman who went to Britain as a domestic worker and who related her experiences to workers of Kalayaan:
We came here together and for the first three months everything was fine. The woman settled down and she started working herself and I got left home with the children, and to do the work in the house. The job I had signed back home was just for me to look after the children. It turned out to be a

nightmare. I had to clean the house, we live in a very big house which is four floors, do the cooking, look after all the family's needs, their children, their friends' children, about five to ten children on my own. I have to look after them all. I had to cook for them, care for them and do all sorts of work in the house. I had to clean the house, do the gardening, clean the car and also do my female employer's office. I have no day off, no time off for me. She held my passport. I was not allowed to see my passport and I was not allowed to speak to anyone else. She hit me several times but still I carry on this work for two years, from six o'clock until two in the morning. I had no one else to talk to. Most of the time I stayed in the house crying, hoping that something would free me from there but I know that my contract is for two years and that I will never get out from there. I was told, in this country you have no one to help you here. They said, "You'll be alone, if you go out you'll have no one to look after you, and to care for you. You'll have no friends." All these things made me really very sad. I was really upset. Then it was really terrible and I couldn't bear to stand the abuse and the shouting, screaming, calling names and stuff....I couldn't stand it any more so I decide to leave the work....and then I finally realise that I have no right to stay in this country. Once you left your employers, if the employer brought you here you have no right to work anywhere else. I came here as a worker but I was treated as a slave. That gets me really mad....(KALAYAAN, 1995).

Irregular and undocumented women workers are especially vulnerable to abuse. As stated by the UN Expert Group on violence against women migrant workers in their meeting of May 1996 (UN, 1996b):

The large flows of such workers are indicative of extensive trafficking networks within and between countries. Trafficking had placed the women migrants in very precarious employment situations, rendering them completely dependent on their employers and/or recruiters. That had resulted in substandard wages and exploitative terms and conditions of work. While both sending and receiving countries may have enacted laws to deal with the problem, many of them had proved ineffective.

The Expert group also notes that "one of the ironies of restrictive immigration and emigration policies is their tendency to push women into illegal and unsupervised channels of migration and employment".

As the most significant types of violence inflicted on women migrant workers the Expert group lists:

- charging by agents over and above established governmental rates for documentation and processing; the collection of unauthorised payments
- excessive rates of interest on loans for travel and other expenses
- non-payment or delay in payment of wages due under contract; violation of wages agreed to in contract
- living and working conditions substantially in breach of internationally and/or nationally agreed standards
- deprivation of access to social networks and social and religious facilities; enforced isolation
- onset of illnesses diagnosed as relating to living and working conditions that breach conventions
- deprivation of access to medical and health facilities

- subjection to harassment, threats, punishment, intimidation, verbal abuse and ridicule
- physical abuse and sexual harassment and abuse, including rape by agents, governmental officials, employers or others in their household
- unreasonable imprisonment, confinement or deportation
- unlawful or forced substitution of contracts
- unlawful withholding of passports and other documentation
- absence and/or breach of contract.

Whereas overseas domestic workers are especially vulnerable to various forms of abuse due to their status as migrants, local or domestic workers may suffer similar abusive conditions due to the unprotected and unregulated character of the work.

6.3 Contemporary manifestations and trends

In order to analyse the contemporary forms of trafficking and forced labour/slavery-like practices in relation to the specific groups of domestic workers, the following categories were distinguished for the purpose of this survey[10] :

- "national domestic workers": women who are working as domestics in their own country
- "migrant domestic workers": migrant women who are working as domestic workers in a foreign country. Migrant domestic workers can be either "documented" (with a contract and/or working permit) or "undocumented" (without a contract and/or working permit).

We also asked organizations to contribute their knowledge about women from their own country working as domestic workers abroad ("out-national domestic workers").

In total 17 NGOs completed the specific section on trafficking in women and forced labour and slavery-like practices in domestic labour. These NGOs were based in Asia (Thailand, Nepal, Hong Kong, Philippines, Bangladesh, Japan, India), Latin America and the Caribbean (Peru, Dominican Republic, Ecuador), Europe (Spain, United Kingdom, Belgium), Canada and Australia.

Since the number of respondents is very small (17), the absolute number of respondents is given where applicable instead of percentages of respondents.

We will first examine working and living conditions and subsequently review recruiting methods and agents.

Living and working conditions

Across all categories of domestic workers, respondents report the prevalence of abusive living and working conditions - which in combination may lead to conditions of forced labour and slavery-like practices - in the following order of frequency[11]:

1 psychological abuse (threats, name calling, shouting insults)
2 more than twelve hour workdays
3 denial of time off

[10] See the specific section on domestic labour (Section D) of the Questionnaire for NGOs (annex 1).
[11] Listed are the conditions which are mentioned as occurring "frequently" or "very frequently".

4 constant fear of police arrest
5 sexual assault or rape (inc. attempted and threatened harassment); not paid regularly and/or paid less than contracted; no access to medical/health services
6 not having a proper bedroom (forced to sleep in hallway, kitchen, bathroom, store room); no regular food (given left-overs, regularly denied food, insufficient food); lack of respect for cultural/ religious customs and beliefs
7 physical abuse (hitting, shoving, spitting, kicking, beating etc.); illegal confinement (movements controlled and restricted, no permission to leave household, or allowed out only with chaperon); isolation (prohibited from normal social contacts, interception of letters/ phonecalls)
8 identity papers/passport confiscated by employer and not obtainable on departure from employment
9 debt bondage; not having a bed or nothing to sleep on
10 threat of reprisals against family/relatives; false identity papers
11 personal belongings taken away
12 compulsory HIV/AIDS testing.

If we examine the prevalence of these conditions in relation to the specific groups of domestic workers as distinguished for this survey, the following trends show:

According to respondents, national domestic workers suffer most from:
- more than 12 hour workdays normally (mentioned by 8 respondents as occurring (very) frequently)
- psychological abuse (7)
- denial of time off/denial of holidays (5)
- sexual assault or rape; not having a bedroom (4)
- not paid regularly/less than agreed; no access to medical and health services; not having a bed/nothing to sleep on; no regular food; lack of respect for cultural/religious customs and beliefs (3).

Documented migrant workers suffer most from:
- psychological abuse (mentioned by 6 respondents as occurring (very) frequently)
- more than 12-hour workdays normally; denial of time off (5)
- not paid regularly; not having a bedroom; no regular food; lack of respect for cultural/religious customs & beliefs (4)
- physical abuse; illegal confinement; isolation; threat of reprisals against family/relatives; identity papers confiscated; no access to medical and health services; constant fear of police arrest (3).

Undocumented migrant workers suffer most from:
- psychological abuse; constant fear of police arrest (4).

Organizations of countries of origin report overseas domestic workers to suffer most from:
- more than 12-hour workdays (5)

- psychological abuse; sexual assault or rape; constant fear of police arrest (4)
- physical abuse; illegal confinement; isolation; debt-bondage; identity papers confiscated; no access to medical and health services; denial of time off (3).

Respondents say that they know the least about the situation of undocumented migrant domestic workers and of domestic workers from their own countries who have left to work overseas ("out-national domestic workers"). In these categories there is a high score of "don't know".

As several reports document, forced labour and slavery-like practices in domestic labour are not limited to certain regions, but occur throughout the world.

In her study[12] on working and living conditions of overseas domestic workers in the EUROPEAN UNION, Bridget Anderson (1996a), concludes that there is evidence that live-in domestic work is a boom area of employment. It is developing in a largely unregulated fashion and the demand is principally being met by third country nationals, usually undocumented. Since such a large proportion of those working in domestic service is undocumented, it is impossible to make an accurate estimate of their numbers. However, in most EU countries, domestic work is the only work available for migrant women, apart from prostitution.

Undocumented workers enter countries to work for specific employers. Some accompany their employers, like this domestic worker in Athens, who entered Greece with her Indian employer: *They kept my passport. I came in on a three month tourist visa. They wrote something on my passport, but the man negotiated it. I don't know what it is because I can't read and write. I worked there one year and three months for nothing* (Anderson, 1996a).

Others are called to work for employers but are instructed to enter on a tourist visa and promised that their employers will sort out their papers on arrival. Sometimes papers are falsified by agencies or employers:
Vicky, a registered nurse from the Philippines, arrived in Barcelona airport. A person designated by her agency met her and took all her money, $50, in return for a train ticket to the town centre.
Her employer met her at the station. He told her that she was carrying a fake passport, but that she should not worry, he would fix her papers and settle all her problems. After three months working Vicky was still not given her wages. When she approached her employer, she was informed that she was paying in service the amount she owed for him sorting out her documents. Yet she was not allowed to see her papers. In fact, she was not even allowed out of the house, and often kept locked in a room for fear that she might escape....After six months she found the courage and the opportunity to escape. She is now working without papers, afraid of being caught by the police or her old employer (Anderson, 1993, p.75).

In Italy and Spain some domestic workers have managed to take advantage of regularization

[12] This study was conducted for STV/GAATW in the framework of this report. The following part on migrant domestic workers in the European Union is largely based on Anderson's study.

measures. However, there continue to be people entering in these ways, and regularizations have been presented as "one offs", so undoubtedly the number of domestic workers trapped into irregularity through no fault of their own will continue to increase.

Domestic workers in the EU represent a wide range of nationalities. Though Filipinas tend to be the most visible, they by no means constitute the majority of domestic workers. In France, Italy and Spain women from Morocco make up a significant proportion of domestic workers; in Spain, Peruvians and Dominicans and in Greece and Italy, Eritreans and Ethiopians. Increasingly women from Eastern European countries are entering the European Union to do domestic work.

Although the educational level of the workers varies widely, a significant proportion is highly educated and professionally qualified. They may be doctors, lawyers, teachers, scientists.
As expressed by this domestic worker from the Dominican Republic:
I keep my professional qualifications hidden because there is no way my employer would keep me if she knew I was a lawyer...when I came here (Spain) my cousin taught me how to be subservient, tricks like, don't cross your legs in an interview because it looks too assertive (Anderson, 1996a, p.4).

Different states have different immigration laws pertaining to domestic workers, but the majority are not recognised as workers and so work illegally. In this situation, workers have no recourse to the police whatever abuse they suffer, because of fear of imprisonment, fines and deportations.

Whereas abuse within the home is notoriously difficult to prove - especially when the abuser is wealthy and influential and the abused is isolated and poor -, it is even more difficult in circumstances where the abused has a problematic immigration status and risks deportation should she come to the attention of the authorities. An illustration forms the case of Helen Samuels, a Nigerian domestic worker in the UK:
Helen ran away from her employer after enduring years of malnourishment, physical abuse and exploitation. At the moment of her escape she weighed about six and a half stone and was suffering from malnutrition. There were whip marks and cuts and scratches all over her body. She successfully brought a case against her employers for assault, but was then served with a deportation order as an overstayer. She had only been given leave to stay for three months, and her employers had kept her for over three years. She was an illegal overstayer and thus liable to immediate deportation (Anderson, 1993, p.55).

In **Greece** women who overstay must pay a penalty of 500.000 drachmas for every year they have overstayed. This sum represents a small fortune for migrant workers, and the impossibility of paying means that they have to remain in the country even if they want to return home.

The living and working conditions of especially live-in domestic workers are generally extremely poor. The level of payment is very low, workers are commonly not given any days off and expected to be available 24 hours a day. Food is often a serious problem: employers do not provide food for the worker and expect them to survive on left-overs, refusing to let them cook their own food. Women may be seriously brutalised by employers or their children, but unable to pursue claims against them because they are undocumented. Confiscation of passports is common as is non-payment. Employers often withhold money in order to prevent women from leaving them. Mental health is a serious problem for overseas domestic workers. In Greece for example a pastor tells:

There were two Ethiopian girls in the mental hospital. I went to ask for a doctor so I could pray with them. He told me I could not and I would have to pay for them to leave the hospital. He said, 'if you do not, we will deport her to Ethiopia'. But she was sick and she had none in Ethiopia. She had worked here for five years, and she had one shirt only...She was sent back to Ethiopia (Anderson, 1996, p.10).

Lack of sickness pay, no compensation for injuries at work and instant dismissal on pregnancy, even in cases where the woman is pregnant by her male employer, are other problems:

M. was consistently raped by her employer until she became pregnant when she was thrown out. She delivered her baby on the streets. Some weeks later, while still homeless, the child was taken from her by some officials, she did not know who. When I (Anderson) met her she was clearly mentally ill, living on the streets and still unemployed (Anderson, 1996, p.19).

Common problems for all overseas domestic workers, regardless of their country of origin or the European country they are working in, include lack of job description (resulting them in doing "everything" in the house), long hours and 24 hour availability, lack of privacy, low pay, sexual harassment, physical abuse, constant prioritising of employers over workers' needs, lack of sickness benefit and dismissal if sick or pregnant.

The important variables in terms of living and working conditions of domestic workers are firstly if they live in or live out, and secondly whether or not they have legal status. Forced labour and slavery-like practices are most often described by undocumented women living in with their employers. The key-issue is the freedom to change employer. Those who can change employer can move if their employer maltreats them, but undocumented workers often have to tolerate non-payment, extreme demands and no free time. These kinds of problems are also experienced by workers whose legal status is dependent on their employer.

Exploitation and abuse are also mediated by racism and stereotypes. The employment market for domestic workers is ruled by a "hierarchy of nationalities", often based on crude racist stereotypes and perpetrated by the informal agencies that act as intermediaries for employment. Under this hierarchy workers can expect different rates of pay and different kinds of job depending on skin colour and nationality.

Domestic service is also one of the most available of employment opportunities for women migrating from the countryside to the city. Internal migration can be a precursor to international migration. For example, a large number of Indian domestic workers now enter Britain with Indian employers.

KALAYAAN and the Commission for Filipino Migrant Workers, two NGOs working directly with overseas domestic workers in BRITAIN, documented in detail more than 2,000 cases of ill-treatment and extreme abuse of migrant domestic workers. (KALAYAAN, 1995) These included confiscation of passports, enforced change of contract, including the withholding of wages, a sixteen to twenty hour workday seven days a week, deprivation of food and malnourishment, no access to medical and health services or compensation for injuries, virtual or literal imprisonment in the home of their employer, prohibition of engaging in normal social contacts, including talking to the other staff or outsiders, the interception of letters from their families, physical abuse, sexual harassment and actual, threatened, or attempted rape.

In an article on West-Indian domestic workers in NEW YORK Shellee Colen (1993) describes the same conditions of mentally and physically exhausting work, low pay, no health care or securities and dependence on the "sponsorship" of the employer because of immigration regulations. Although a number of guidelines on working conditions exist, neither the Labour Department, the Immigration and Naturalization Service, nor any other agency monitors compliance: "This can lead to a form of state-sanctioned, indenture-like exploitation: the worker is obliged to stay in the sponsored position until the green card (legal permanent resident status) is granted (often two or more years) in spite of any abuses to which she may be subjected" (Colen, 1993, p.173).

On the sponsored job, the material and emotional exploitation potentially present in all domestic jobs is exacerbated by the workers' dependence on their employers for green cards. They are thus vulnerable to employer manipulation and are less likely to quit an intolerable situation.

However, the central issue, which was raised by all women interviewed, is the "lack of respect" in the attitude and behaviour of employers towards the domestic worker. This is manifested in various ways: name calling, not giving enough or good quality food, not allowing the worker to eat at the same table, condoning disrespect from children towards the worker.

Similar to sex work, migration for domestic labour has a long history in the LATIN AMERICAN AND CARIBBEAN REGION. Although domestic work may include living expenses like room and food and thus may help women to save money more quickly than in other kinds of employment, their unprotected and often undocumented position of migrant workers leaves them vulnerable to abuse. Research on women from the Dominican Republic doing domestic work in SPAIN (Weinert, 1991/AMDE, 1992) documents frequent violations of their rights as workers in relation to salary, working schedules and payment of benefits like social security. Given the fact that many of them are not registered as legal migrants, they have very little power to negotiate fair working conditions.

But also national domestic workers have to deal with extremely poor working conditions. In COLOMBIA, household workers who started to organise themselves in Bogota in 1977 (later to become SINTRASEDOM, National Union of Household Workers) express their problems as:

- *The fact that there is no minimum wage for working as a household employee. The exploitation of minors who are not paid because it is thought that young girls do not have the necessary capacity or the knowledge to work at a job.*
- *The fact that many of our companions become old with their health ruined; they are oppressed, working in one or more homes, with no compensation, pension, social security and without legal protection.*
- *The fact that young girls are brought from the countryside to be kept as slaves; they are paid with second-hand clothes or low salaries, and they are mistreated. The patronas take advantage of them.*
- *The fact that many household workers can neither read nor write; they are not given time to study, or to go out, and that is why few can prepare themselves for the future* (SINTRASEDOM, 1993, p.372).

In their first national meeting domestics shared common problems: workdays of twelve, sixteen, or eighteen hours, salaries very much lower than the legal minimum salary recognised by the government, lack of social benefits, discriminatory labour legislation, lack of respect, authoritarian and humiliating treatment and violation of the right to privacy. While domestic service has been considered a non-productive activity, the worker is given no protection by the labour code and is abused and fired without just cause (SINTRASEDOM, 1993).

In **Africa**, young Kenyans are recruited to Saudi Arabia where they are taken to work as house-helps and baby sitters. They are recruited through employment bureaus to which they pay thousands of shillings as commission to take them to Saudi Arabia. However, many of those who have returned tell stories of harassment by employers, who also beat, underpay and sexually abuse them (Butegwa, 1996).

In all the countries in Asia where large numbers of women from other Asian countries work as domestic workers (Japan, Hong Kong, Malaysia, Singapore) the same litany of abuses is summed up: over-work due to long hours of work and insufficient rest periods, heavy physical work, non-payment or under-payment of wages, lack of privacy and own space, lack of sufficient and adequate food, confiscation of passport by employer, psychological and physical abuse and ill-treatment, sexual harassment and rape. In some cases domestic workers are obliged to clean the houses of the families of employers or clean their offices and workplaces (Singapore and Hong Kong), working far beyond the already heavy workload of caring for one family (Heyzer, 1994).

In **Cambodia**, women form the majority of the population, but are the minority in the formal labour force. Women occupy lower positions and receive lesser salaries compared to men, especially in the "traditionally female" sectors of employment, such as sewing, weaving, secretarial work, taxi-girls, sales and vending. Economic changes in Cambodia have prompted substantive growth of the informal economic sector. Although this sector contributes significantly to the economy, there is no adequate protection from abuses and other violations of human rights, and no monitoring of working conditions:

One group in the informal sector that has been largely ignored but where slave-like working conditions prevail is, domestic workers. Their marginalization in society and law, because of the hidden nature of their work and due to their low social position, is one, if not, the major impediment to their enjoyment of basic human rights (CWHR, 1996, p.4).
Due to among other factors, the lack of protection by labour laws, women are denied basic rights: the right to just wages and humane working conditions, the right to due process and to fair and just trial, the right against inhuman and degrading treatment and unusual punishment, the right to be heard and air grievances, including the right to complain without the threat of physical or verbal abuse or withholding of salary, and the right to recreation and social security. Domestic helpers are generally looked down upon by law-enforces when they try to complain about maltreatment by their employers. They lack access to counselling, legal and social services (CWHR, 1996).

In the **Gulf states** there are an estimated number of 1.2 million female domestic workers. Domestic workers comprise about 20 per cent of the estimated six million migrants upon which the Gulf states are completely dependent. The women are predominantly from Sri Lanka, Indonesia, India and the Philippines. They live in with their employers and work for long hours and low wages. Domestic workers are explicitly excluded from labour legislation, which means that even the minimum protection granted to workers is not applied to them. They are regarded, not as workers, but as members of the household. Excluded from any protection by labour laws, domestic servants have no holidays, no time off and no limit to the hours they have to work. As well as their passport, their wages are withheld at least until the employer has recouped the agency fees, if not longer. Because of the highly personalised context of domestic work, domestics are extremely vulnerable to physical and sexual abuse. Buttressed by immigration legislation and lack of labour protection, encouraged by state practices and policies to regard all migrant labour, and female domestic labour in particular, as inferior and deserving of less respect than citizens, employers subject their housemaids to a range of mental and physical cruelties (Anderson, 1993).

Migrant domestic workers caught in situations of armed conflict and/or political and social turbulence in countries of destination may suffer traumatic experiences. Set aside by employers, many women suffer rape, abuse and hardship in their attempts to secure their safety.
Their premature return to their home countries is difficult because they often face the burden of huge debts and in some cases unwanted pregnancies (UN, June 1996b, p.10).

Recruiting agents and methods

Women may be recruited for domestic work through different methods. Whereas some of these may operate bona fide, others are characterised by deceit, cheating, over-charge, falsepromises and debt bondage, and can be classified as trafficking, according to the definition for this report.

The forms of constraint used by traffickers vary. In relation to national domestic workers deception with regard to conditions of work scores highest[13]; in relation to documented migrant domestics abuse of authority and deception regarding conditions or nature of work; in relation to undocumented migrant workers use of violence or threat with violence.
Organizations in countries of origin of overseas domestic workers report debt bondage and deception regarding conditions of work as the most frequent forms of constraint their fellow country-women working as domestics overseas are subjected to.

The recruiting agents most mentioned by respondents are employment agencies, friends and acquaintances of family or friends.

In most cases women are recruited explicitly for domestic work. However, some of them may be promised other types of work only to find at arrival that the employer gives them no choice but domestic service, or rather the non-choice of returning home immediately at their own expense (ASI, 1990). Others are recruited under false job-contracts. The following story is just one of the many familiar stories among domestic workers in the Gulf states:
Alice, a twenty-five years old Filipina and a qualified engineer, turned to a recruitment agency advertising posts as civil engineers. The agency's fee for finding a professional post was 21,000 pesos (some $ 450), half of which had to be paid immediately. Alice's parents mortgaged their small patch of land, and she undertook to repay the rest on taking up her position. Interviewed and accepted she left for Kuwait. On arrival at the recruitment office in Kuwait City, she was abruptly informed that she could not work as a civil engineer: "for Filipina the work here is domestic". Not being able to pay her airfare back or to pay the agency the fees she owed, she had no choice but to sign the contract as domestic worker. In the two and a half year she worked for her employers, members of the Kuwaiti royal family, she had to work day and night without a day or time off (Anderson, 1993, p.13).

There are many ways in which women become a domestic worker in a foreign country.
With regard to the EUROPEAN UNION Anderson (1996a) lists the major trends as follows:
- through advertisements placed in newspapers in their countries of origin
- "chain migration", whereby a friend/relative of the potential migrant working in the host country invites them to work for a friend/relative of their employer. In this method and the one above the employer often encourages the worker to enter as a tourist and promises to arrange their papers on arrival. However, this later proves to be impossible, bothersome or unbeneficial to the employer.
- recruitment agencies, which assist in the evasion of immigration controls without explaining to the migrant what is happening or the consequences of illegal entry for their living and working conditions. They often operate illegally and fees can be excessive. Women are taken on by the agency and "loaned" money to pay the fee, airfare, and the like. They must repay the agency from their earnings. The agency withholds her passport as security against the loan. As with chain migration, the women who use agencies often are ignorant of immigration legislation, visa

[13] Listed are the forms of coercion which are most mentioned by respondents as occurring "frequently" or "very frequently".

requirements etc. before it is too late.
- some migrants enter Europe as tourists or students, then overstay their visa to work.
- in practice all European Union countries admit domestic workers accompanying their employer into the country. There are a variety of regulations and schemes permitting this. In general it seems that such workers are admitted as tourists or as a worker with the name of their employer written on their passport. The worker cannot therefore change their employer. Should they leave their employer - common in the face of abuse and exploitation -, they become undocumented workers.

Many employment agencies are unlicensed and uncontrolled by any state regulations. They often operate quite openly, with or without government collaboration. Once having been drawn into the recruitment network, women are faced with the payment of a bewildering variety of fees. Agents charge excessive placement fees and costs of fake or tampered travel documents and certificates of employment (for example, in Hong Kong and Singapore), requiring women to borrow large sums of money, to sell or mortgage land or to take loans or advance payments of the agents. In the Philippines, for example, agents may charge an initial service fee to process the necessary employment papers, then a placement fee for finding an employer, the officially prescribed placement fee, followed often by additional charges, including expenses incurred before the recruits departure, such as the cost of transport, accommodation and food (Heyzer et al., 1994).

This vicious circle of debt ties women to their employer. Middle East Watch, for example, found many cases in KUWAIT where women's salaries had been withheld by employers, allegedly to settle their debts:

The women workers appeared to have no say in the amount attributed as lent to them or in the decision regarding salary proportions to be deducted towards their debt. In many cases we investigated, debt had the effect of placing women in bondage to their employers. It was used as a means of forcing the women to endure prolonged working hours, inadequate food and sleep, no days off and no time to attend a place of worship for fear of never getting paid or losing their jobs (Anderson, 1993, p.35).

The recruitment networks in the sending countries link up with the placement networks of agencies in the receiving countries. Some women tell they had to pay agents on both sides or had to pay fees that have to be borne by the employer, all adding up to the indentureship of the women.

In *The Trade in Domestic Workers* (Heyzer, 1994, p.52), a number of problems are listed that arise from the recruitment process in the sending countries:
- misinformation which can amount to false advertising and fraud
- imposition of exorbitant fees by agencies through a monopoly of overseas jobs
- lack of government regulations over the recruitment process, with regards to the accuracy of the information provided and the fees charged
- illegal modes of smuggling workers into receiving countries, set up by agents in order to evade

government charges for processing legal documents and the official exit fee
- risks of imprisonment and even death through dangerous modes of illegal migration
- indebtedness of the individual recruit and her family to agents, subagents, money-lenders, pawnshops, banks and others
- loss of assets and savings through the sale of land, property, jewellery and other valuables, in order to raise funds to pay the agents
- impoverishment of already poor villagers and the enrichment of relatively rich agents and sub-agents, money-lenders, pawnshop owners, banks and others
- family pressures on women to migrate in the expectation of their earning big money to support unemployed and under-employed male relatives, the young and the elderly
- flow of funds out of the country from agencies in the sending country to agencies in the receiving country in the form of commissions.

Some states have tried to impose some control on the activities of the agencies. But according to Heyzer, strict rules and regulations, such as selection regulations and deposit of guarantee to the state for licensing, are due not to work because there is no protection of the migrant worker who complains of abuses.

In **SAUDI ARABIA**, for instance, there are but few laws concerning workers' protection. When migrant workers report abuses to the Saudi Arabian Office of Labour Affairs, there is a long waiting period during which women are kept in holding rooms together with criminals (UN, 1994a).

6.4 Constraints to escape

Several factors inhibit women from escaping once trapped in abusive recruitment practices and/or forced labour conditions. Across all categories of domestic worker, the following "barriers to escape" are mentioned in order of frequency[14]:

1 lack of alternative employment
2 lack of knowledge of the law and her rights
3 dependence of family on her income/not wanting to return empty-handed
4 having no money
5 fear of deportation; movements are controlled by traffickers/ employers
6 fear of arrest by the authorities; violence by traffickers/ employers; having no identity papers or false papers
7 debt bondage/fear of retribution against her family for not paying her debt
8 fear of reprisals by traffickers/employers against family, friends or herself
9 involvement of own government/embassy.

If we examine the prevalence of these factors in relation to the specific groups of domestic workers, the following trends show:

According to respondents the main barriers for national domestics are:

[14] Listed are the factors that are mentioned by respondents as occurring (very) frequently.

- lack of alternative employment (mentioned by 6 respondents as occurring (very) frequently)
- lack of knowledge of the law and her rights (6)
- dependence of her family on her income (5)
- having no money (5).

The main barriers for migrant documented domestic workers are:
- lack of alternative employment (mentioned by 7 respondents as occurring (very) frequently)
- not wanting to return home empty-handed (7)
- dependence of family on her income (7)
- fear of deportation (5)
- lack of knowledge of the law and her rights (5).

As the main barriers for undocumented domestic workers respondents mention:
- fear of deportation (mentioned by 5 respondents as occurring (very) frequently)
- dependence of family on her income (5)
- not wanting to return empty-handed (5)
- lack of alternative employment (5)
- fear of arrest by the authorities (4).

Organizations in countries of origin of overseas domestic workers report having no money (7), lack of knowledge of the law and her rights (7), having no identity papers (6), not wanting to return home empty-handed (6) and lack of alternative employment (6) as the main factors that hinder women to leave abusive situations.

In general, domestic workers are extremely reluctant to leave their employers because of the difficulty of finding another job and having no surplus to tide them over a period of unemployment, not to speak of the risk of deportation.

Running away from an abusive employer does not solve the problems and clearly requires tremendous courage, not to speak of the practical difficulties: bolted doors, locked windows, security guards or dogs patrolling the premises. Many women are not allowed out of the house, and have no idea of where to go or how to get there. They have no money, no papers, no friends, no belongings:
My leaving was very frightening although at that point I did not care what happened to me or what the situation might be like out there because they (the employers) always said to me that this country is very dangerous, you cannot meet anybody who will help you, that people mind their own business, people don't care about you, even if you're walking there on the streets somebody can just kill you or shoot you (Anderson, 1996, p.25).

Escaping brings practical problems: where to live, how to survive, obtain clothes and get some money. The worker has no prospects of receiving support from the state and has no more means of redress for unfair employment practices than she did previously. Fear of being discovered is a constant source of stress:

Because of my situation, fear is with me constantly and I even give false names to my employers. They do not know about my real situation. I'm longing to have a holiday back home, but I can't do it because of my illegal position. Sometimes in the middle of the night I just lie awake thinking that one day the immigration officer will come and get me. Worst of all, I can't even trust a friend, thinking that they might tip off the immigration authorities about me (Anderson, 1996, p.25).

Women with dependent permits lose their legal status the moment they run away. In the UK, for example, women who leave their employers are not allowed to work. Within a few months they are overstayers without rights to either work or reside in the UK (Anderson, 1996a). The same applies to MALAYSIA where change of employer is not allowed under government rules. Women, who leave their employer because they are subjected to abuse and ill-treatment or because the employer breaches the terms stipulated in the contract, are usually repatriated. They have no chance to seek another employer except in extreme cases and depending on whether they are willing to pay the agent another fee. No compensation is made for loss of future earnings: "The maid goes home even poorer than she was prior to coming to Malaysia" (Tharan, 1987, p.281).

Whether women are recruited by legally or illegally operating agencies, there is little chance of "protection" from them. In case of violent or abusive employers, they can not expect support or reimbursement from the agency.

Some countries do not allow women to leave because of specific regulations, as in GREECE, where undocumented workers are fined for every month they have been in Greece in an irregular situation. As a result, workers are unable to leave the country even if they want so because they do not have the money to pay the fine. The story of this Filipina domestic worker is exemplary:
J. came in 1974 on papers falsified by her employers. They told her to destroy all documentation relating to her entry: "I had no knowledge of cheating. I had lived a very neat life until then, so I did what I was told." In 1981 her then employer, a government official, managed to get her a work permit. This enabled her to bring over to Greece her husband and children. Then, in 1991 her permit was taken away from her "it was because of Maastricht". Her children could not renew their residence permits. J., her husband and her children continue to accrue fines of millions of drachmas because they are unable to leave the country (Anderson, 1996, p.15).

In the **GULF STATES** possibilities of escape from abuse are negligible:
Women have no chance of repaying debts incurred by recruitment fees if they leave the Middle East. It is difficult for women to change employers, and virtually impossible without permission of her current employer. Those who opt to change employers without consent are in the worst situation of all. Posters offering rewards with photographs of runaways appear on billboards and on television. Very few run the risk of leaping out of the frying pan into the fire (Anderson, 1993, p. 25).

6.5 Barriers to report to the authorities

Not surprisingly, very few women report to the authorities. As the main barriers to report, respondents mention:

For national domestics:
- financial dependency of family (mentioned by 8 respondents as occurring (very) frequently)
- lack of knowledge of her rights/the legal system of the country (6)
- lack of confidence in the legal system (5)
- lack of knowledge of/access to support mechanisms (4).

For migrant documented domestics:
- lack of confidence in the legal system; lack of knowledge of their rights/ the legal system of the country (6)
- fear of losing visa sponsorship; fear of deportation; fear of reprisals by the agents; fear that she herself will be punished/arrested; outstanding debts; financial dependence of her family; lack of knowledge of/access to support mechanisms (5)
- language barrier (4).

For migrant undocumented domestic workers:
- fear of deportation; lack of knowledge of her rights/the legal system of the country; lack of knowledge of/access to support mechanisms (4).

According to organizations of countries of origin, the main barriers to report for women of their country working overseas, are:
- fear of deportation (8)
- lack of confidence in the legal system; lack of knowledge of her rights/the legal system; lack of knowledge of/access to support mechanisms (7)
- fear that she herself will be punished or arrested (6)
- fear of losing visa sponsorship; outstanding debts; financial dependence of family; language barrier (5).
- attitude of law-enforcers (4).

In almost all countries there are no governmental provisions to facilitate or encourage women to report trafficking or slavery-like practices to the authorities, such as confidential counselling, safe shelters, free legal aid, legal residence during investigations or assistance in returning home.

If women nevertheless file a complaint, this almost never leads to a serious investigation or a conviction. Almost one-third of the respondents says that women are not or rarely believed, and that complaints are rarely or not taken seriously. According to half of the respondents, complaints are never or rarely investigated or result in prosecution. According to more than half of the respondents complaints never result in a conviction of the offender.

Almost one-third of the respondents states that victims of trafficking or slavery-like practices risk ill-treatment by the authorities, such as harassment by the police, expulsion, harassment by immigration officers, arrest or detention for having false or no identity papers, refusal to give back identity papers or issue new papers or arrest as prostitute.

When any support is available, this is provided by NGOs. When respondents are asked about what services are provided by NGOs to domestic workers, almost half of the respondents mention legal and social assistance. Around two-thirds mention medical assistance, safe shelters and return programmes. Other services provided by NGOs are financial assistance and witness protection.

Most services are available to local domestic workers. Social assistance, safe shelters and legal assistance are the most frequently provided services by the NGOs to migrant domestics. The least amount of services are available for undocumented migrant domestics.

Respondents propose a range of measures that would help women to escape abusive conditions or improve their situation:
- legal protection under labour and immigrant laws, including the right to change employers/ security about their stay and work; legal rights on escaping abuse, including the right to legal assistance; laws that regulate contracts for overseas domestic workers
- information on prevailing laws, procedures, terms of contracts, labour and human rights as workers and how and where to obtain help when necessary
- education and training to enhance skills and increase chances for jobs
- support services, such as counselling, shelters and legal assistance; support to organise themselves; raising self-esteem and dignity
- economic measures to improve the economic situation of women; opportunities for savings.

6.6 Returning home

As the main problems women face on returning home, respondents mention in order of frequency[15]: lack of alternative employment, breakdown of family relationships, shame for coming home empty-handed, no housing, psychological and medical problems and lack of skills/ deskilled.

A range of measures is proposed that would support women on returning home:
- economic measures, such as financial support, alternative means of survival with full social respect and acceptance, opportunities for (self) employment, alternative employment
- education and training to develop new skills for alternative employment and self-sufficiency
- information about support and educational services available before returning; media work to highlight human right aspects of the issue
- social and political measures, such as providing health services, shelters and counseling for returnees and their families; support of NGOs in home countries

[15] Listed are the problems that are mentioned by respondents as occurring (very) frequently.

- legislation to secure the right to return to the host country to work, free legal assistance and police cooperation to charge and prosecute traffickers and abusive employers; establishment of minimum standards of responsibility between sending and receiving countries, including guaranteed fair wages.

7 Trafficking in women and forced labour and slavery-like practices in prostititution

7.1 Characteristics

In *The Globalization of Trafficking in Women* Skrobanek (1994) documents a number of human rights violations, involved in the international trafficking in women for prostitution.
These violations pertain as well to the recruitment processes as to the working and living conditions women are subjected to:

- women do not know the conditions of their employment before migration. They are sold and resold and forced to pay back debts fixed by their owners
- women are forced to work in slave-like conditions as bonded labourers in order to pay back the debts incurred in getting them to the receiving countries. As they are undocumented workers and they fear being arrested, women do not have the freedom to escape the enslaved situation
- economic exploitation: women are forced to work, whereas the income generated by their forced labour is appropriated by others. Many women work for years to pay back their debts
- women are denied the right to choose clients and conditions of selling sex as well as methods to prevent themselves from sexually transmitted diseases and AIDS
- women are denied the right to access to medical treatment and social assistance. HIV tests are forced upon women and the resulting information is withheld from them
- migrant women in some of the receiving countries are the target of racial discrimination and prejudice. They are subject to many forms of physical and psychological violence
- by enforcing immigration laws, women are subject to arrest on charges of overstaying and deported
- being transported with false documentation makes women become stateless people. They are subject to prosecution in both sending and receiving countries
- when seeking assistance from authorities such as police, women encounter other forms of sexual violence such as rape and sexual harassment
- in pursuing a court case women are required to testify usually in public and are therefore denied their right to privacy. Giving evidence, often of very personal things, is very traumatic for the women
- children born from migrant women are denied to have nationality in some receiving countries.

Although the article pertains especially to the international trafficking of women in the context of prostitution, many of the abuses mentioned are faced by prostitutes in general, both in their home countries and abroad.

Trafficking practices not only take place from South to North or from East to West, but also within regions and within countries, for example from rural to urban areas. In Colombia, for example, some trafficking networks concentrate on the internal trafficking of women, recruiting and distributing women for the local, regional and national demand. Other networks provide Colombian women to the markets in countries from the same continent, like Venezuela, Ecuador and Panama, whereas international networks provide for the markets in European countries like Spain, Greece, Holland, Germany and Belgium, in the US and in the Asiatic continent, especially Japan (Polania Molina, 1996).

Trafficking routes, sending countries and countries of destination may change quite quickly due to political or economic changes. For example, since the fall of the Berlin Wall in 1989 and the resulting political and economic changes, there has been an alarming increase in the traffic in women from Central and Eastern European countries.

In the same way, forced labour and slavery-like practices are not confined to some countries or some groups of prostitutes. Many women - migrant or local, trafficked or entering prostitution of their own accord- work as prostitutes under appalling conditions, be it in Europe, Asia, Latin America or elsewhere.

7.2 Contributing factors

In addition to the aforementioned general factors, a number of factors especially contributing to the abuse faced by prostitutes can be pinpointed. The main are:

- the clandestine and/or illegal nature of the work
- the illegal immigrant status of women working abroad
- the marginalization, stigmatization and criminalization of the women involved
- the extremely large profits that can be made, among others, as a result of the above mentioned factors.

The social, political and legal stigmatization of women who are working in prostitution puts them in an even more vulnerable position for abusive practices than women in other sectors of female-designated labour. As noted by the Czech organization ProFem:

The criminalization of all women who work in prostitution, including those who work independently and voluntarily, creates a perfect opportunity for traffickers to operate without being bothered by social control. The Czech policy towards prostitution is to hide it away from the official image of the city and to restrict it to certain areas. In Prague, a big public campaign was initiated by the authorities, according to which prostitution is moved to the city's periphery. As a result, the prostitutes are more and more brought under the control of pimps and traffickers. The public does not need to see what does not fit in their image of society. As Interpol in Prague reported, victims of trafficking are increasingly recruited in the sphere of prostitution, meaning that women who are working there form the most endangered group of getting trafficked (Profem, 1996, p.41).

Once in an abusive situation, women are further trapped by the prevailing stigma which favours traffickers and abusive employers. This mechanism is among others described by GAATW in its

report on Asia:
A woman who has been trafficked into prostitution is seen as 'in need of rehabilitation'. Her morals need to be corrected. Prostitutes are considered 'bad women' and as 'deviants' they are not accorded the same rights as 'good women' (GAATW (1996, p.21).

In Bombay, for example, the police arrested 447 sex workers in raids on brothels. They were taken from the brothels without their belongings and, in some cases, without their children. Though prostitution in itself is not illegal in India, the women were kept in detention. They were tested for HIV and other sexual diseases without their consent but were not given any medical treatment. Those who wanted to go back to work were not released: "If these women were in different occupations, there would have been considerable public outrage about this abuse and violation of rights" (GAATW, 1996, p.22).

The same mechanisms are worded in a report from Bangladesh:
In a patriarchal society, the women in an occupation which is polluting and is stigmatised and looked down upon by the society are easily vulnerable to all forms of violence and abuses. Again, because of this very low status of their occupation, the women are left helpless to defend or assert themselves against indiscriminate exploitation and oppression which is a regular feature of their lives in the brothel (Khan, 1992, p.123).

Whereas migrant prostitutes are especially vulnerable to abuse, due to their status as (illegal) migrant, migrant and national prostitutes alike may suffer severely abusive conditions due to the clandestine, unprotected and stigmatised nature of their work.

7.3 Contemporary manifestations and trends

In order to analyse the contemporary forms of trafficking and forced labour/slavery-like practices in relation to the specific groups of women working in prostitution, the following groups were distinguished for the purpose of this survey[16]:
- "national prostitutes": women who are working as prostitutes in their own country
- "migrant prostitutes": migrant women who are working as prostitutes in a foreign country. Migrant prostitutes can be either "legal", i.e. in possession of a valid staying permit, or "illegal", i.e. without a valid staying permit.

We also asked organizations for their knowledge about women from their country working as prostitutes in foreign countries ("out-national prostitutes").

In total, 46 NGOs completed the specific section on trafficking and forced labour/ slavery-like practices in prostitution (Section C). Of these NGOs, 17 came from Asia (Bangladesh, Nepal, India, Thailand, The Philippines, Japan, Hong Kong, Vietnam, Taiwan, China), 2 from Australia, 17 from Europe (Germany, Belgium, Denmark, Finland, The Netherlands, Italy, Spain, Switzerland, Slovenia, Bulgaria, Ukraine, Czech Republic, Poland, Turkey), 7 from Latin America & the Caribbean (Curaçao, Dominican Republic, Peru, Mexico, Ecuador), 3 from North America &

[16] See the specific section on trafficking in women and forced labour & slavery-like practices in prostitution (Section C) of the Questionnaire for NGOs (annex 1).

Canada. No NGOs in Africa completed this section.

It must be noted that the category "legal migrant prostitutes" does not exist in many countries because prostitution or prostitution by migrants is by definition illegal. In general, respondents knew the least about the situation of legal migrant prostitutes. This implies that in relation to this group, a high percentage of respondents answer either "not applicable" or "don't know" to the various questions.

Table 6

Absolute number of respondents Europe: 17
Absolute number of respondents Asia: 17
Absolute number of respondents Latin America & the Caribbean: 7

Forced labour & slavery-like practices occur (very) frequently in relation to.

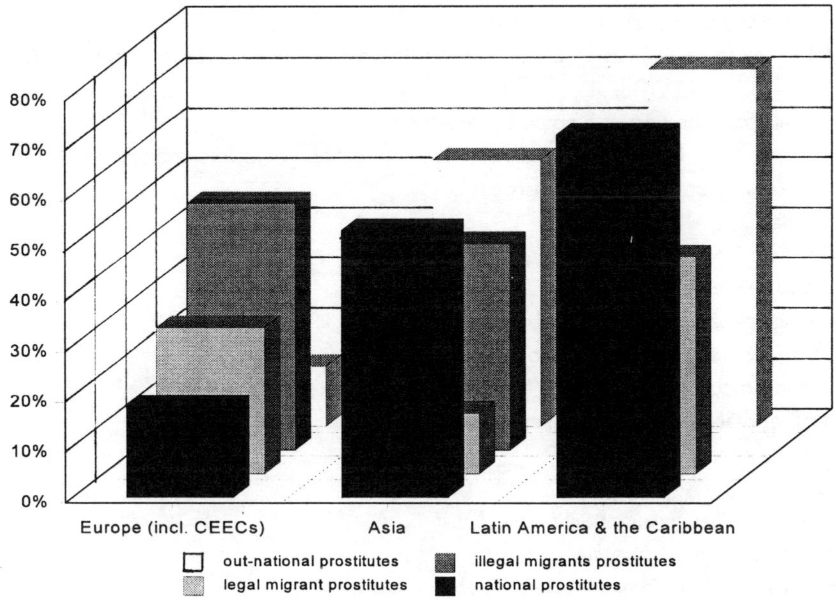

Forced labour & slavery-like practices, as defined in the working definition, are reported to occur among all groups of prostitutes, national and migrant women alike: 41 % of the respondents report forced labour and slavery-like practices to occur frequently or very frequently in relation to national women, around 25 % in relation to legal migrant women and around 55 % in relation to illegal migrant women.

Table 6 shows the reported prevalence of forced labour & slavery-like practices in relation to the different groups of prostitutes in the different regions:

For the other regions the number of respondents is too low to draw any conclusion.

Around 12 % of the respondents in Europe, mainly from the CEECs, report the occurrence of forced labour & slavery-like practices among women from their own country working abroad in prostitution, against 53 % from Asia and 71 % from Latin America and the Caribbean.

In order to discuss contemporary manifestations and trends we will first look at living and working conditions and subsequently the recruiting methods and agents.

Living and working conditions

Across all categories of prostitutes, respondents report the prevalence of abusive living and working conditions - which in combination may lead to conditions of forced labour and slavery-like practices - in the following order of frequency[17]:

1 psychological abuse (threats, name-calling, insults, humiliation etc.)
2 physical abuse (hitting, kicking, beating, threatening with violence, etc.)
3 constant fear of police arrest
4 illegal confinement (movements controlled/restricted, no permission to leave the working place or allowed only under supervision)
5 no right to refuse certain customers or forced to have a certain number of customers per day
6 sexual assault or rape (incl. attempted or threatened)
7 isolation (prohibited from normal social contacts, interception of letters and/or phone calls)
8 not paid regularly or paid less than agreed
9 debt-bondage
10 denial of time off/holidays
11 no right to refuse certain sexual acts
12 identity papers/passport confiscated
13 more than twelve hour workdays normally
14 no access to medical/health care
15 threat of reprisals against family/other relatives
16 false identity papers
17 not paid at all
18 forced abortion/dangerous abortion practices
19 personal belongings taken away
20 not having a bedroom/forced to sleep in working place
21 no right/opportunity to use condoms
22 compulsory HIV/AIDS testing
23 no regular food
24 not having a bed or nothing to sleep on
25 forced to recruit sisters/girl friends into prostitution.

If we examine the prevalence of these conditions in relation to the specific groups of women working in prostitution as distinguished for this survey, the following trends show:

According to respondents national prostitutes suffer most from:
- psychological abuse (mentioned by 48 % of the respondents as occurring frequently or very frequently)
- constant fear of police arrest (39 %)

[17] Listed are the conditions which are mentioned as occurring frequently or very frequently.

- sexual assault or rape (37 %)
- physical abuse (35 %)
- illegal confinement; no right to refuse certain customers and/or forced to have a certain number of customers per day; not paid regularly and/or paid less than agreed (33 %)
- debt bondage (31 %).

Legal migrant prostitutes suffer most from:
- psychological abuse (mentioned by 28 % of the respondents as occurring frequently or very frequently)
- physical abuse (26 %)
- constant fear of police arrest; no right to refuse certain customers/ forced to have a certain number of customers per day (22 %)
- more than twelve hour workdays normally; sexual assault or rape; illegal confinement (17 %).

Illegal migrant prostitutes suffer most from:
- constant fear of police arrest; psychological abuse (mentioned by 57 % of the respondents as occurring frequently or very frequently)
- illegal confinement (54 %)
- isolation (48 %)
- physical abuse; no right to refuse certain customers/forced to have a certain number of customers per day (46 %)
- denial of time off/denial of holidays; debt bondage (41 %)
- identity papers/passport confiscated; sexual assault or rape (44 %)
- not paid regularly or paid less than agreed (43 %)
- no right to refuse certain sexual acts/certain customers (39%)
- no access to medical and health care (37 %)
- false identity papers (36 %)
- more than twelve hour workdays normally (35 %)
- threat of reprisals against family/relatives (33 %)
- personal belongings taken away; not paid at all (30 %).

Although it is evident that illegal migrant prostitutes are in the worst position, abusive conditions are frequently reported for national prostitutes too. Legal migrant prostitutes seem to be in a better position, but it should be noted that many respondents say that they know little about the situation of legal migrant prostitutes. Also, in many countries it is per definition impossible for migrant women to work legally in prostitution. With regard to the situation of women from their own countries working abroad as prostitutes, about 40 % of the respondents reports the (very) frequent occurrence of psychological abuse, about 30 % reports illegal confinement, physical abuse, isolation and debt bondage to occur (very) frequently. However, also here there is a high percentage of respondents answering "don't know".

If we examine the prevalence of these conditions in relation to the different regions, the most frequently reported abusive conditions are[18]:
In Asia:

[18] Across all categories, in order of frequency.

1 no right to refuse certain customers/forced to have a certain number of customers per day
2 constant fear of police arrest
3 not paid regularly/paid less than agreed; psychological abuse
4 isolation; no right to refuse certain sexual acts
5 illegal confinement; debt bondage; denial of time off.

In Latin America and the Caribbean:
1 psychological abuse
2 physical abuse
3 no right to refuse certain customers/forced to have a certain customers per day; sexual assault/rape; constant fear of police arrest
4 illegal confinement; debt bondage; no right to refuse certain sexual acts; dangerous abortion practices/forced abortion.

In Europe, including the CEECs:
1 psychological abuse
2 constant fear of police arrest; physical abuse
3 illegal confinement; not paid regularly/paid less than agreed
4 isolation; sexual assault/rape
5 more than twelve hour workdays normally
6 debt bondage; identity papers confiscated.

At the moment of writing this report, little information was available regarding the situation in North America and Canada. However, according to Sanghera's report on Canada (Sanghera, 1995), the following conditions occur (very) frequently in all categories of prostitutes in Canada:
- psychological abuse
- debt bondage
- not paid regularly/paid less than agreed
- no access to medical or health care
- forced to sleep in working space
- more than twelve hour workdays normally
- denial of time off
- constant fear of police arrest
- forced drug addiction.

A striking difference in conditions seems to exist between national and illegal migrant prostitutes in the European countries: here, the reported incidence of abusive conditions is four times higher among (illegal) migrant prostitutes than among national women. In the other regions, the conditions between the various groups seem to be much more alike.

Reports from many NGOs all over the world document abusive working and living conditions in prostitution, amounting to forced labour and slavery-like practices. Some examples are given below.
According to a report of Anti-Slavery International on slavery in BRAZIL (Sutton, 1994), there is

a systematic traffic of women and girls from other parts of Brazil to work in brothels in towns near mining camps and large civil construction project in a.o. Amazonia. Even when women have not been tricked into working in prostitution, they are still trapped in these remote areas, and further immobilised by having debts chalked up against future earnings as soon as they arrive. Transport costs into the area have to be repaid, but in addition, women and girls often have to pay off their own "price" charged to the brothel owner by the intermediary, who has effectively sold them on. As one twenty-two year old women working in one of the mining camps in Itaituba told:

The brothel debts (the transport costs) I paid off quickly, but now I have to pay off my own price. She (the brothel owner) paid the (intermediary) and now I have to pay her. Payment for sexual services is handed over directly to the brothel owners who hold the money against the women's debts (Sutton, 1994, p.6).

Another form of indebtedness comes with treating malaria:

Just when a girl thinks she is free of her debts, she unexpectedly contracts malaria, which leaves her cast down in bed, unable to work and without funds for treatment. She has to borrow again. Thus malaria contributes to exacerbate a situation of dependency (Sutton, 1994, p.96).

With no access to the money they have earned and high transport costs out of the area, their freedom to leave is severely curtailed. They may succeed in escaping the brothel but remain immobilised in the area. If a woman flees her debt is transferred to those left behind. Women report being physically coerced and confined, complain of ill-treatment, beatings and imprisonment, and say that those trying to flee were killed or tortured. They also allege that the local police connive in holding them in these conditions, arresting and ill-treating those trying to flee. In a letter a woman, seeking help, writes:

Here the owners beat us with electric wires folded over four times. When they don't beat us they send the police to beat us, and we're only released when they want it (Sutton, 1994, p.97).

Another form of coercion, apart from physical violence, is to starve women of food unless they do what they are told.

These practices are by no way exceptional. Debt bondage or indentureship - in which the woman has to pay back the recruiter, brothel owner, or agency the sum for which she is purchased and/or an uncontrollable sum for travel, documents, food housing and other services - are among the most frequently used methods to bind women. Many reports from all over the world document these practices. Some examples are given below:

In **Thai** brothels Cambodian women are locked up and guarded until they have paid back their purchasing price. They are not allowed to shop on their own, instead the brothel owners do all the shopping and charge them exorbitant prices. They are over-charged for everything they need, so the "debt" increases instead of being paid. Earnings are also deducted for bribes. In the end women even lose their investment capital. The brothel owners keep their earnings for safe-keeping, so they never know how much they really earn (CWHR, 1996).

Burmese girls are recruited for brothels in Thailand by agents who pay an amount up to A $

500 to the girl's family. This becomes the basis of debt bondage for the girls who must pay back this amount and any other expenses they incur while living in the brothel. They receive little or no payment. The common scenario is a girl serving six to eight clients a day, 25 days a month, earning for the owner between A$ 600 and A$ 2.500 per month of which they pay the girls approximately A$ 1 per day or A$ 25 per month. They usually stay in the brothel network for at least two to three years. Conditions inside the brothels are appalling, including barbed wired and electric fences (Australia - Parliament, 1995).

Women trafficked to JAPAN must repay the inflated debt before they can earn anything. They are also made to pay for any other expenses such as food, accommodation and medicines:
Pung came to Japan after signing a contract with a canning factory. At first she was suspicious but she felt reassured by the formal contract. She was taken to a snack bar in Yamanashi Prefecture, where her Taiwanese mamasan told her she owed 3.8 million yen (US $ 38,000) and the only way to pay it back was to work as a prostitute. She was penalised 15,000 yen (US $ 150) for working without make-up, 1,500 yen for a broken glass and 10,000 yen for every minute she was late returning from servicing a customer. All of these were added to her debt (GAATW, 1996, p.15).

Women from the DOMINICAN REPUBLIC borrow money or mortgage the family home to pay recruiters to help them with (false) papers and travel arrangements. They are then bound by this debt to continue working until they have paid it back. (IOM, 1996a). These debts can run up to thousands of dollars: one Dominican woman had been required to pay US $ 5,000 for tickets and visa to Austria. Another was charged on credit US $ 2,900, for which she had to pay back US $ 5,400. Many women had to pay for their transfer within Europe in addition to their plane ticket from the Caribbean. Upon arrival they were picked up by a Dominican man and woman who demanded exorbitant prices for transfer services for a train ticket to Austria and a room for one night (IOM, 1996d).

Women from UGANDA, who come to Dubai and Europe, are secured loans for visas, tickets and accommodation. They are unable to get out of the arrangement until they have paid their debts. Freedom of movement and personal choice are further curtailed by the fact that their passports are retained by the airline as security for the debt (Butegwa, 1996).

In ITALY, women from Latin America, Eastern Europe, Albania and Nigeria work the streets to pay back a debt contracted with international agencies that organised their migration to Italy. Irrespective of their conscious or forced entry into prostitution they are subjected to the power of their traffickers/protectors by debts based on agreements which have been made with the traffickers before their departure to Italy. These debts must be repaid with huge interests during the first month that the women spend in Italy (IOM, 1996c).

Underpayment, extremely poor working conditions, physical abuse and constant fear of arrest are common problems for women from developing countries working in the sex industry abroad. In her article *Exotic, subservient and trapped: confronting prostitution and trafficking in Southeast Asia* Skrobanek (1992) describes the following conditions:
- third World women working in the sex business in Europe are usually paid 40 % of their total

earnings, the rest goes to the bar owners[19]. The women who work for pimps hardly earn anything at all. It is reported that in Japan, 38 % of the women who have entered the country illegally to work as hostesses, striptease dancers or prostitutes receive no payment in turn.

- women working as prostitutes in a foreign country are largely dependent on their employers since they are unable to communicate in the native language. This disadvantage allows little bargaining power. They may be shifted from one city to another. In Japan, some women are not allowed to telephone or to venture outside their workplace unaccompanied. They have to work 10-12 hours a day.
- it is common for women to be physically abused by their agents or employers. Others are threatened when they refuse to pay protection fees to the local Mafia. For example, a woman who rents her place to work not only pays double the average rent, but she is also forced into paying protection money. If she refuses, then both her safety and her property are at risk. In Switzerland, Mafia members may earn US$ 200 to 500 a night in protection money.
- women who are sent abroad through illegal means obviously run the risk of being arrested and deported. Illegal entry into a country or illegal employment give the women little grounds to seek the help of police or other governmental agencies for fear of being arrested. In some cases, state officials themselves are the ones who take advantage of the women.

Physical violence, rape and force to serve a certain number of customers per day or earning a certain amount of money per day are frequently reported:

Violence reported in NEPAL against prostitutes includes physical assault, starvation, forced use of drugs and alcohol, burning with cigarette buns, rape, isolation in dark rooms, beating with a hot iron, forced abortion and threats by thugs (GAATW, 1996).

In **HONG KONG**, reports state that women are drugged and forced to receive up to 38 clients a night (GAATW, 1996).

In **INDIA**, women who become pregnant are forced undergo an abortion, usually under illegal and dangerous conditions. Brothel owners reportedly sell babies of prostitutes for adoption (Poudel, 1994).

In *One Year La Strada* (a joint Polish-Czech-Ukraine-Dutch programme on prevention of traffic in women in the CEEC's) some of the forms of violence exercised on Eastern European women working in THE NETHERLANDS are described:
Rape seems to be a favourite among traffickers. As much as fourteen women reported to us that they were raped during their ordeal. Often, the argument was that the woman 'had to learn the tricks'. We suspect that even more women were forced to have sex with their perpetrators, but would not describe this as rape, since they did not physically fight him at the time. The withdrawal of passports and money is still popular too, although some traffickers gave their victims a small amount of money

[19] According to a European sexworker this is true for the majority of sex-workers - migrant and non-migrant - in brothels in Europe.

to control them even more. Among other violence and pressure used are debt binding, isolation, beatings, very poor living conditions (sharing a bed with three other women in the same room where during the day worked) and the use of drugs... Also, women were threatened to be sold to another trafficker, whereas eight clients indicated that they were actually resold (Kootstra, 1996, p.21).

Women often get nothing or just a fraction of their earnings and are kept isolated to prevent them from escaping, like this Kenyan woman, who met a woman who assured her she could earn well in **GERMANY**:

On reaching Germany, she realised that this was not to be when the brothel owner took away her passport. She only got a pinch of her daily earnings. She had to live like a prisoner because the woman ensured her that all her movements were monitored to avoid escaping or 'making business' else where. The brothel owner would also intercept her letters. When her visa expired, she was told that it would only be renewed if she found another Kenyan woman to replace her (Butegwa, 1996, p.7).

According to Hummel (1991), the conditions of foreign prostitutes in Germany are characterised by the absence of legal protection, isolation and extreme financial exploitation. In most cases women work in brothels during the time their visa is valid. Then they are substituted by other women, who already stay in Europe. Brothel keepers prefer foreign women because they have less legal protection and therefore can be better controlled.

In **KENYA**, foreign girls are brought in to work in massage parlours, which are registered to offer massage services, but in reality offer sexual services. Police and newspaper reports indicate that most of the foreign girls are paid up to 25 % of their daily earnings and are expected to work 24 hours (Butegwa, 1996).

Not only agents, intermediaries, protectors, keepers of brothels commit extortion, the police may be part of these practices as well:

A report on prostitution in BANGLADESH (Khan, 1992), documents various forms of police repression. Police officers force women to give free sexual services or act as babu (regular customer/protector) of "wealthy" prostitutes from whom they extract large amounts of money. Apart from this, policemen are found to forcefully and violently extract the earnings of women whom they find to have many clients:

Often the police rounds up women with their clients from the brothel on some pretext for extorting money from them. In such cases they also beat up women and manhandle their clients. Protesting prostitutes are taken to the police station where the physical abuse increases and the rates of fines go up.

An investigation of the Chamber of Commerce in Bogota, COLOMBIA reveals that 10.3 % of the prostitutes interviewed report abuse by the police as their main problem. Extortion and abuse by the police is mentioned by 50 % of the girls aged eleven to fourteen, and by about 25 % of the women aged fifteen to forty. Three per cent of the women report not being allowed to leave the scene and 1.5 % report abusive exploitation by the brothel managers (Cámara de Comercio de Bogotá, 1992).

Various reports document violations of human rights, experienced by Latin American and Caribbean women working abroad as prostitutes (COIN, 1995/ Azize-Vargas, 1996/ IOM, 1996a):

- no freedom of movement: passports are withheld, women are locked up in their work place. Sometimes women are threatened not to talk to anybody.
- irregularities in the payment of women's salaries: women are, for example, frequently obliged to work for a certain period without payment before they start to get some pay.
- no right to refuse clients.
- obligatory consumption of alcohol: women are obliged to maximise the profits of club-owners by encouraging the client to consume large quantities of expensive drinks and by drinking together with the client. Under the pressures of this consumption pattern, which is prevalent in Switzerland, for example, women invariably become alcoholics.
- sexual violence.
- ometimes the owners of clubs deliberately report women to the police so they don't have to pay them and they will be deported (cases from Spain and Greece).
- sometimes women are actually sold.

According to a report of the IOM, women trafficked to **Greece** report that they had to work as dancers/prostitutes for the first three months without any pay, which meant that during this period they incurred debts for accommodation, food, clothes, and the like. Then, for the following three months they were allowed to keep 25-30 % of their earnings from which their debts had to be settled. They were rotated every week to different cabarets and had one day off per week. All of them suffered physical violence and were told not to reject any client (IOM, 1996a).

In *Purchased Unhappiness* Karin Spring (1992) describes the working and living conditions of women from South East Asia, Latin America, Africa and the former Eastern bloc countries, coming to Switzerland for work:

With a suitcase and the hope of a better life, women from the Third World arrive daily in Switzerland, either at the airport or at the border. Most of them are heavily in debt, due to their inability to pay cash for the employment agency fees, the necessary formalities and the journey. And - apart from very few exceptions - many of them do not know that our country only provides one opportunity for work - as striptease dancers in bars. Border-crossing presents no problem, particularly when experienced organizations are behind them, because they know exactly which stipulations have to be complied with. Women who attempt to enter the country under their own steam are frequently refused entry. They are at the mercy of these organizations... Dependent on the club, a striptease dancer must perform three to four times and ten to twelve times a night. Between performances she has to 'entertain' the guests, including encouraging them to drink champagne... If the owner of a night-club does not like the woman or her striptease routine, or if she does not sell enough champagne, her contract can be canceled within the first three days without further ado...A work permit for a striptease dancer in a night-club is limited to eight months. The women are transferred by 'their' agency to a different club each month. After eight months they have to leave Switzerland...

Because of the limited duration of their residential and work permits, the women are highly dependent on night-clubs and agencies. They have no opportunity to defend themselves against poor working conditions, fraudulent settlements of accounts, humiliating treatment or violence, if they want to continue working as dancers. Most of the women working in night-clubs earn extra money from prostitution...Wherever possible, they are financially exploited: by the artist agency, by night-clubs, by real estate agents, by pimps and customers. 'The attitude towards us is always the same', said a dancer from Brazil 'we should be pleased that we're even here. Here, we're better off than at home. This is why we can be used and exploited as they want. And if we stand up to them, they threaten us with expulsion'.

Sometimes women are forced to marry a national, like this Thai woman:
Because the Thai woman was living illegally in Switzerland, she was forced into a marriage on paper with a man she did not know. For this legalization of her stay, 20,000 Swiss francs was demanded of her (Spring, 1992).

Recruiting methods & recruiting agents

Trafficking practices, as defined in the working definitions, are reported to take place in all groups of prostitutes, though the lack of a legal status clearly makes illegal migrant women the most vulnerable group. Around 35 % of the respondents to the questionnaire say trafficking occurs frequently or very frequently in relation to national prostitutes, against 52 % in relation to illegal migrant prostitutes, and 24 % in relation to legal migrant prostitutes.

Table 7 shows the reported prevalence of trafficking in women in relation to the specific groups in the different regions:
Traffickers may use different methods. In all categories, deception regarding the conditions of work, wages etc. scores highest: 61 % of the respondents reports this to happen frequently or

Table 7
Absolute number of respondents Europe (incl.CEECs): 17
Absolute number of respondents Asia: 17
Absolute number of respondents Latin America & the Caribbean: 7
Trafficking in women occurs (very) frequently in relation to

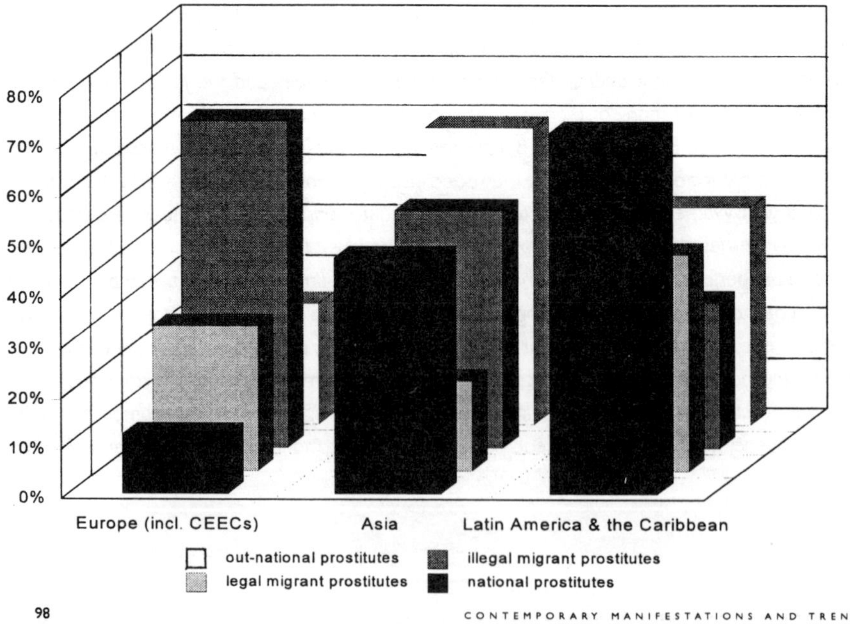

very frequently in relation to illegal migrant prostitutes, against 52 % for national prostitutes. The next mentioned forms of coercion are[20]:

For national prostitutes:
- violence or threat with violence
- deception regarding the nature of the work
- abuse of authority or dominant position.

For legal migrant prostitutes:
- violence or threat with violence
- abuse of authority or dominant position.

Evidently, illegal migrant prostitutes are the most vulnerable to coercion. Almost 50 % of the respondents report the (very) frequent use of:
- violence or threat with violence
- deception regarding the nature of work
- debt bondage
- the use of false papers
- abuse of authority.

Organizations in countries of origin mention deception regarding the conditions of work as the most frequent abusive recruitment practice to which their fellow country-women are subjected.

That most cases of deception concern the conditions of work rather than the nature of the work promised, indicates that a substantial number of women do know that they are recruited for prostitution and agree to the work itself. They are, however, clearly unaware of the conditions under which they will be forced to work.

Other women are deceived about the nature of the work. They are recruited under promises of jobs as waitresses, cleaners, dancers, entertainers or domestic workers. Sometimes traffickers make use of false job contracts. Some women are promised marriage or false marriages are arranged.

The recruiting agents most mentioned by respondents[21] are acquaintances of family and friends, friends, strangers/accidental meetings, job agencies and impresarios/artist agencies. Respondents in Europe (incl. the CEECs) mention acquaintances of family or friends, impresarios/artist agencies and friends as the most frequent recruiters; respondents from Asia job agencies, acquaintances of family or friends, strangers/accidental meetings and expected husband; respondents from Latin America and the Caribbean acquaintances of family and friends, impresarios/artist agencies, family members and friends; respondents from Africa acquaintances of family and friends.

20 Listed are the forms of constraint which are mentioned as occurring "frequently" or "very frequently.

21 Listed are the recruiting agents which are mentioned by respondents under the category "frequently" and "very frequently".

In her report on trafficking in women in LATIN AMERICA & THE CARIBBEAN, Azize-Vargas (1996) identifies several recruiting strategies:

- recruitment by procurers: nationals who work in the country act as middle-men/ intermediaries or "travel organisers" to recruit women
- recruitment by other sex workers or "dancers": frequently, women already abroad are paid money for every woman they can attract to the business
- recruitment by informal networks of relatives, friends, village and local community persons
- through a real or false marriage
- through artist or dancer contracts or under the guise of a folk dance company or to work as models.

According to a survey conducted by COIN in the DOMINICAN REPUBLIC (COIN, 1993), 29 % of the women that travel abroad are helped by friends, 15 % by relatives and 19 % by "travel organizers". Such agencies offer women help with documents and passports, "show money" to go through customs, travel arrangements, visas, birth certificates, transportation, and the like. The first contact is often made through friends (male of female) who "know a woman who organises trips" or a Dominican or foreign "impresario" who is looking to create a dance troupe to go overseas. Both in cities and in beach resorts, there is a combination of local and foreign entrepreneurs. Once the girl establishes contact, she is engaged as a dancer, barmaid or other and has to pay a fee (usually US4 400-1,000) to cover initial expenditures of certificates, passport, visa, air ticket, and contract. Financial help usually comes in the form of loans to be paid back once the woman starts work (COIN, 1993 and 1995/ IOM, 1996a).

False promises about the nature or conditions of work are also used to recruit women from the CEECs for WESTERN EUROPEAN COUNTRIES. As described in *One Year La Strada*:
Some women thought they would be waitresses, nannies or domestic servants. Others knew the job was to be in prostitution, with enormous profits to be made (up to D-Mark 3,000 a month). Little did they know about the real circumstances in which they had to work and that the profits would not go to them, but to their perpetrators (Kootstra, 1996, p.14).

Marriage as a recruiting method is regularly reported, especially in the countries where traditional practices of servitude of women are still common.

In the case of trafficking to PAKISTAN, Bengal traffickers marry girls, or force them to marry others of their network, before bringing them to Pakistan to work in brothels in order to protect themselves from being prosecuted under Islamic Hudood laws. However 2,500 Bangladeshi women and children are being detained in various jails in Pakistan under the same laws and charged with illegal entry and having "illegitimate sex" (Human Rights Watch, 1995).
In **NEPAL**, young men pay the "bride price" for a young girl and then sell her to a brothel. Such traffickers go back several times to a village and "marry" again and again. Also, it is reported that "35% of roughly 100,000-160,000 Nepalese girls working in different Indian brothels have been abducted to India under the pretext of marriage or good jobs" (Poudel, 1994).

According to Butegwa trafficking in KENYA is mostly done under the guise of marriage, friendly invitations and jobs. Most girls are taken to Germany, probably because there are many German tourists who visit Kenya. They casually incite the girls to Europe for a visit, or ask them to marry them. Later they send tickets and the girls go. On reaching Europe the girls end up in brothels or are abused by their husbands, who force them to prostitution by confiscating their passport or simply locking them up in the house (Butegwa, 1996).

In **NIGERIA** women are recruited by a special type of intermediary: this person, a woman, usually called Madam (or Mama-Loa meaning "priestess") acts as a go-between for girls/women and the organization preparing their migration. Trafficked girls/women will make references to her, even after their migration (especially to Italy, as far as known). Money will be sent to her in order to pay back the debt with the organization or to pass to the girl's family. The following case illustrates how Nigerian women are typically recruited for prostitution in Italy:
My story is very similar to the ones of many women from my country... I was born 25 years ago in a small village in the country-side, near Kaduna, in northern Nigeria. My family is a very big one and my parents are peasants...I decided to go with a few girlfriends to Lagos. There I met some persons in a discotheque, and they suggested that I could go to Europe to work and study. I paid a lot of money to an agency which organises trips to Italy. The money was not enough and so I signed a contract where I promised to work as a maid for a family in Naples, and I soon understood that my job was another one..I was threatened, and they said that I had to pay otherwise my family would have been threatened too... (IOM, 1996c).

Some parents sell their daughters into prostitution for financial gain, as in INDIA:
Bina was sold by her family to a brothel in India. She refused to co-operate and was beatenseverely. She still refused and finally men from her village were brought to the brothel. Once they saw her she could not return home, as her village would have known she was in a brothel as prostitute (GAATW, 1996, p.9).

7.4 Constraints to escape

Once trapped, many factors inhibit women to escape or change their situation. Although there are similarities between the different groups, illegal migrant prostitutes are evidently in a particularly difficult position to change their situation.

The main constraints for illegal migrant prostitutes are (mentioned by 45-55 % of the respondents as applying (very) frequently):
- fear of reprisals or arrest by the authorities
- fear of deportation
- lack of alternative employment
- their movements are controlled by the criminal network
- no money
- their family is dependent on her income
- no or false identity papers

- violence by the criminal network
- not wanting to return home empty-handed
- fear of reprisals
- debt bondage/fear of retribution against her relatives for defaulting her debt.

Other barriers, mentioned by about 35 % the respondents, are involvement of own government/ officials, fear of rejection by her family, and rejection or moral condemnation by society.

The main barriers for legal migrant prostitutes are (mentioned by 20-25 % of the respondents as applying (very) frequently):
- lack of alternative employment
- not wanting to return home empty-handed
- no money.

As the main barriers for nationals - mentioned by 35-50 % of the respondents as applying (very) frequently - are reported:
- family is dependent of their income
- lack of alternative employment
- no money
- movements are controlled by the criminal network
- not wanting to return empty-handed
- violence by the criminal network
- fear of rejection or moral condemnation by society.

The best chances for women seem to lie in trying to gain more independence through ones own efforts as the IOM report on trafficking to Italy (IOM, 1996c) notes:
The interviews conducted revealed some significant differences between nationalities concerning the degree of exploitation suffered and the degree of freedom allowed to the women. With time, women from some national groups, who were initially deceived, managed to regain some decision-making ability... particularly women from Latin America and Eastern European countries. This is mainly due to the fact that these women are on an average older than those of other national groups, and are thus capable of negotiating with the protector/trafficker more successfully. This capacity is strengthened with time, leading, in some cases, to a definitive detachment from the protector or at least to the transformation of a subordinate relationship into a more equal one.

7.5 Barriers to report to the authorities

Traffic in women mostly takes place in a network-like structure and is based on violence. This has many consequences. Even if existing policies allow women to report to the authorities, only few women will do so, for various reasons[22].

[22] See chapter V for a review of the risks for women, which are attached to the choice for a penal approach.

As the main barriers to report to the authorities respondents mention:
For national prostitutes:
- lack of confidence in the legal system (mentioned by 46 % of the respondents as applying (very) frequently)
- lack of knowledge of her rights/ the legal system of the country (39 %)
- need to financially support her family (37%)
- fear that she herself will be punished or arrested; fear of moral condemnation; need to financially support the family (35 %)
- attitudes of law-enforcers (33 %)
- no access to legal assistance; fear that her situation will become known to her family/ community; shame; (30 %).

For legal migrant prostitutes:
- need to financially support her family (mentioned by 30 % of the respondents as applying (very) frequently)
- lack of knowledge of her rights/the legal system of the country; lack of confidence in the legal system (26%)
- fear of reprisals by the criminal network (24 %)
- outstanding debts (22 %).

For illegal migrant prostitutes:
- fear of deportation; fear of reprisals of the criminal network; fear that she herself will be punished or arrested (mentioned by 54% of the respondents as applying (very) frequently)
- lack of knowledge of her rights/the legal system of the country (52%)
- language barrier (48 %)
- need to financially support her family (44 %)
- no access to legal assistance (43%)
- lack of confidence in the legal system (42 %).
- attitudes of law enforcers (39%)
- outstanding debts (37%)
- fear for moral condemnation; shame (31 %)
- fear that her situation will become known to her family/community (30 %).

In general women have no reason to have confidence in the police or any other authorities: in most countries, prostitutes are continually at risk of imprisonment, harassment or abuse by the police[23]. Migrant illegal women not only risk arrest as prostitutes, but also as illegal foreigners: any contact with authorities puts them directly at risk of deportation. Many migrant women view deportation as an even worse perspective than the situation in which they find themselves, and try to survive in the hope that at some point they will succeed in realising their original aims for migration.

Moreover, if women report to the police - by their own decision or because they are

[23] See chapter IV for an extensive review of national laws on prostitution and the opportunities they allow women to take legal action in case of violence and abuse.

arrested -, they take a serious risk of reprisals without being offered any official protection or support. Apart from a few exceptions, governments hardly provide any provisions to encourage and facilitate women to report trafficking or slavery-like practices to the police, such as confidential counselling, safe shelters, witness protection, free legal aid, specially trained police-officers, compensation for damages, provisions against deportation, legal residence during investigations, assistance in returning home, support programmes for returnees and legalization of residence status if victims can't return home. An exception is formed by The Netherlands and Belgium, where women who file charges are entitled to a temporary staying permit, legal aid and social, medical and financial assistance during criminal proceedings.

If women nevertheless file a complaint, this almost never leads to a conviction. Around 30 % of the respondents say that women are (very) frequently believed and that complaints are taken seriously and are investigated. However, according to about 20 % of the respondents, complaints result (very) frequently in prosecution; 30 % answers that complaints rarely or never result in prosecution. Only 10 % of the respondents say that prosecution results (very) frequently in a conviction; 40 % says that prosecution never or rarely results in a conviction.

Almost 65 % of the respondents say that victims of trafficking and forced labour and slavery-like practices suffer ill-treatment by the authorities.

National prostitutes suffer most from harassment by the police and arrest or detention as prostitutes (mentioned by about 35 % of the respondents as occurring (very) frequently).

Illegal migrant prostitutes suffer most from expulsion, arrest and detention as illegal alien, harassment by the police and arrest or detention for having false or no identity papers (mentioned by 33 % - 40 % of the respondents as occurring (very) frequently). In addition, about a quarter of the respondents mentions arrest or detention as prostitutes and harassment by immigration officers to occur (very) frequently.

Other mentioned forms of ill-treatment are compulsory admission in rehabilitation centers or reform camps, refusal to return identity papers or issue new documents and compulsory testing on HIV/AIDS. In some cases women are sent or sold back to their captors or brothel keepers if they turn to the police. This is reported in India and Pakistan, for example.

When any support is available, this is provided by NGOs. When respondents are asked about what support services are provided by NGOs, 74 % mentions counselling, almost 60 % legal and medical assistance, 51 % safe shelters, 38 % financial assistance, 34 % return programmes and 21 % witness protection. Most services are available to national prostitutes; the least number of services are available for legal migrant prostitutes.

A range of measures is mentioned by the respondents which would help women escape abusive conditions or change their situation. The most important are:
- access to alternative employment opportunities, access to education and training
- decriminalization of (migrant) prostitutes, access to legitimate and independent working

permits/visas for work in prostitutio
- possibilities for women to lay charges without fear for deportation or arrest, honest police officers, active prosecution of the offenders, better police co-operation and better co-operation between sending and receiving countries
- access to support systems, such as safe shelters, legal assistance, social services.

7.6 Returning home

All migrant women who have become victim of trafficking and/or forced labour & slavery-like practices face severe problems when they return home; yet illegal migrant prostitutes are in the worst position. As the main problems for illegal migrant prostitutes respondents mention:
- no earning/employment possibilities (mentioned by 48 % of the respondents as applying (very) frequently)
- psychological problems (46 %)
- medical/health problems (39 %)
- debts that cannot be paid off (35 %)
- stigmatization/ rejection by society (33 %)
- rejection by her family; reprisals by the criminal network against herself or her family/relatives; no medical care; left to prostitution because of no other possibilities; caught again by traffickers; no housing (28 %).

As the main problems for legal migrant prostitutes respondents mention:
- psychological problems; no earning/ employment possibilities (mentioned by 28 % of the respondents as applying (very) frequently)
- debts that cannot be paid off (26 %)-no medical care; left to prostitution because of no other possibilities; reprisals by the criminal network against herself or family/ relatives (20 %)
- medical and health problems (19%)
- stigmatization/ rejection by society (18 %).

The following story of this 22 years old Nepalese woman may serve as an illustration:
When I came back to my own country it was very difficult for me because the Indian police had handed me over to the Nepalese police and the Nepalese police kept me in custody and summoned my family. I only have one older brother and sister. Both my parents have died. After four months the police officer called my brother and wanted to hand me over to him, but he didn't accept me. When I said I needed his help, he said you are a prostitute, so I don't want to take you home. Even he didn't inform my sister about me. In this way I spent two years in custody. I wanted to die because I was rejected by my family and I was totally helpless (Poudel, 1994).

The most important measures that would support women on returning home are according to respondents:
- educational and training opportunities
- job opportunities
- shelters and confidential social, psychological, medical and health care
- legal and police support to prosecute the offenders

- protection against reprisals
- financial support
- no criminalization in their home countries when deported.

8 Regional Specificities and Commonalities

Owing to the different conditions and different historical developments within particular regions, a number of specific trends along with general ones for each region can be identified. Below we will discuss some of these regional specificities and commonalities. These observations, however, are tentative and subject to further research. Moreover, there is no information available on the situation in countries of the Middle East, such as Libanon and Saudi Arabia, though it is clear that considerable numbers of women from Asia, Africa, Latin America and Eastern Europe migrate to these countries, both for domestic work and prostitution.

8.1 Europe

Since the fall of the Berlin Wall in 1989 NGOs in Western Europe have started to register Central and East European women among their clients. In the Netherlands in 1995, the Dutch Foundation against Trafficking in Women (STV) received 125 women from the CEECs of a total of 166 clients. Among them were women from Ukraine, Russia, Belorussia, Poland, Bulgaria, Rumania, Lithuania, Bosnia, Croatia, Latvia, Hungary, the Czech Republic and Slowakia.
Similar trends are seen within the context of marriage and domestic labour, for example Polish women are recruited by agencies for marriage with German or Dutch men.

Several reasons account for the shift in trafficking in women from Asia, Latin America and Africa to women from the CEECs. The most obvious one is the breakdown of the national economic and political systems which was accelerated by the events of 1989. With the increasingly restrictive immigration policies of West European countries and the heightened police control of illegal immigrants, women of illegal status are most at risk of criminal or exploitative individuals or organizations, even if they initially came independently.

Reports from Germany relate the practices of malafide marriage agencies which transport women from the CEEC's to Western Europe for large sums of money (to get into Germany women pay DM 1,000 - 2,000 for a working permit and an additional DM 6,000 - 8,000 to get married to a German citizen). Swiss sources report that Hungarian women, who were promised summer jobs as waitresses in Germany were transported to Germany with false documents and were forced into prostitution. Likewise, the STV in The Netherlands meets many women who were offered jobs in restaurants or bars by malafide employment agencies that attract many women through their advertisements in newspapers or posters in official employment agencies. Other women agreed to work in prostitution, but did not have a clue about the conditions under which they would be forced to work.

The breakdown of the old regime in the former Socialist countries engendered the fear in Western European countries that they would be "flooded" by illegal immigrants and by criminality. This perspective is strongly reflected in their current policies on trafficking in women, which focus increasingly on combating illegal migration (closing borders) and organized crime (strengthening criminal laws).

8.2 North America & Canada

Little research on the issue of our concern has been done in North America. Organizations addressing the issue are scarce; information is difficult to obtain.

The available information reveals that the marriage and mail-order bride market seems to be a growing phenomenon. This is indicated, for example, by the increased advertising for brides on Internet.

Laws on trafficking form a major piece of federal legislation. An example is the MANN act, which prohibits trafficking (defined as procuring) for prostitution into the country and across state borders. In practice, the Act is used as an instrument to prosecute prostitutes rather than abusive recruiters and employers.

Anti-immigrant sentiments felt in Western Europe are similarly found in North America. Criminalization of illegal immigration is a shared tendency among all the wealthier countries: North America, Western Europe, Japan, Singapore, Australia.

Racism pervades all manifestations. This phenomenon is reflected by stereotypes of African women slaves and of exotic, subservient Asian women.

8.3 Asia

The cultural diversity in Asia relative to other regions is extremely great. This enormous spectrum of countries encompasses a heterogeneous assortment of culturally different backgrounds, ideological and religious notions and connotations which influence trafficking in women and forced labour and slavery-like practices. At the same time, different ethnic marginalised groups, living on the fringe of society, make Asia a large reservoir for recruiters.

Another distinction is the extent of economical disparities. Asia has the largest number of poor people but also books the highest rates of economic growth. Because of this heterogeneity and the growing diversity between poor and rich within and between countries, the demand and supply factor may be stronger than in other continents. Countries with explicit labour importing policies, like Malaysia, Singapore and Thailand (import of Burmese workers) are found along with countries with explicit labour exporting policies.

The enormous scale of intra-regional trafficking in women within Asia is possibly related to these factors.

Also the notion of the State may differ from other regions. Many Asian States (e.g. China, Singapore, Indonesia and Sri Lanka) claim a role as spokesperson of moral values, including the

area of sexuality, female roles, etc.
In some regions, prostitution is somehow accepted. Historically, women in prostitution are not always scorned like in Christian society; they sometimes might even be considered holy.
In the olden days in India, prostitutes had a certain position in society. Also, some traditional practices, such as the Devadasi system, gave the women some status in society. The current conditions of women in prostitution are changing for the worse, partly as a result of the growing contempt for prostitutes, indicating a congruency between social stigma and conditions of life and work. More research is needed into the relation between religion, traditional practices, stigmatization and the relation to sexwork.

8.4 Latin America and the Caribbean

Prostitution and migration for sex work has been historically established in the Latin American and Caribbean region as "women's work" and a legitimate way in which women earn a living. As early as 1950 - with the establishment of Campo Alegra on Curaçao to serve Dutch marines, US military troops and migrant workers for the oil industry - women from the nearby region were given legal working possibilities in prostitution. The workings of the system is designed to rely on women's migration within the region to do sex work, and, at the same time, guarantee the control over women's work. Though not meant to do so, it simultaneously and inadvertently laid the foundation for the empowerment of sex workers (Kempadoo, 1995).
It established a conscious view of sex work as work and a legitimate economic alternative for women. The higher degree of organization of sex workers relative to that of other regions attests to this fact.

It laid also the foundation for a significant migratory movement of women from the region to Western Europe to engage in sex work, particularly starting in the mid-80s, when the Latin American and Caribbean economies showed definite signs of crisis. As of the Eastern European women, the educational level of Latin American women in Europe is quite high, making clear that women's access to education is just one step and does not guarantee women's access to work.

Also, domestic workers are showing signs of more organization among themselves, both at home and abroad, for instance in Spain. They seem to be less isolated than other groups. However, the degree of organization is clearly influenced by the conditions in a particular country. In the Arab countries, for example, any form of organization is blocked owing to the fact that women are not allowed to go out on the street alone.

8.5 Africa

Although there is a great lack of systematic research, trafficking in women seems to occur in all three areas of our concern on the national level and on the intra-regional and international level. Recruiting agents seem to operate predominantly on a personal and small scale level, though cross-border recruiting agents appear to be more commercialized. Forced labour & slavery-like practices in marriage and in domestic work occur frequently, and are at least partly rooted in traditional practices. Especially the domestic labour market is known to be very exploitative and

uses many children. Laws exist in all three areas of our concern, but are not enforced.
A form of debt bondage that seems typical for the African region is connected with the custom of airlines selling tickets on credit. Travel agencies have stepped into this market by arranging tickets and visa on credit and taking the woman's passport as a security on arrival at her destination. To retrieve her passport and return ticket, the woman has to earn enough money within three months to pay for the ticket and the costs of the agent, increased with interest. Especially for muslim countries, women are dependent on travel agencies to arrange a visa, since these countries do not issue visa for single women. Travel agencies make use hereof by arranging visa for women as companion to a male. The disfunctioning of administrative systems (getting papers and so on) seems to be another factor, along with corruption of officials, that make women dependent on agencies to process papers, since they are not in a position to process them themselves.

4 NATIONAL LEGAL CONTEXT

1 Introduction

As is shown in chapter 2, the debate on trafficking in women is characterised by a persistent confusion about definitions. Old and new definitions show inconsistencies, contradictions, conflicting interests, failure to pinpoint violence and abuse, and a tendency to deny female self-determination. These trends are reflected in the various definitions and concepts used in national legislation.

A review of the particular laws regarding trafficking in women and forced labour & slavery-like practices in domestic labour, prostitution and marriage from the perspective of the women, reveals those laws to be only part of the legal apparatus that affects women in these situations. Laws that determine whether a woman will be "protected", penalised, sent home or sent to prison, allowed or prohibited to work, etc. are tied to the contexts of prostitution, domestic labour and marriage. For this reason it is necessary to look both at specific laws on trafficking in women and forced labour & slavery-like practices (if they exist in a particular country) and to look at the general framework of laws governing prostitution, domestic labour and marriage.

Significantly those laws are attached to very different social frameworks. Marriage laws fall under civil codes, invariably enmeshed in gender discriminatory traditions and institutions. Laws on domestic work fall under civil and labour codes whereas laws on prostitution fall within state control, often the criminal justice or public health departments.

A considerable amount of research and action has been undertaken in the realm of trafficking in women and forced labour & slavery-like practices related to prostitution. However, much less has been done where it is related to domestic work, and very little on the most normative context of such abuse, namely marriage. This chapter reflects that imbalance, although it is our purpose to challenge it and call for attention to abusive recruitment for marriage and domestic labour as well as forced labour & slavery-like practices within these contexts.

Though some research has been carried out on the various laws regarding trafficking and forced labour & slavery-like practices in the contexts of marriage and domestic labour, within the limitations of this report it has not been possible to review the various national legal systems and their impact in relation to all three areas of our concern. We will therefore restrict ourselves to the realm of prostitution.

This chapter will examine the different laws and state policies on prostitution, as well as those on trafficking, forced labour and slavery-like practices within the context of prostitution.

The different legal systems on prostitution are analysed in terms of prohibitions and regulations, aimed at the different activities and parties involved. Those prohibitions vary from a total ban on prostitution as such, criminalising all activities and all parties involved, to prohibitions which criminalise only certain activities or certain parties. Some prohibitions come under special laws on "trafficking". However, what is defined as "trafficking" in particular national laws varies widely and the same type of prohibitions may come under very different headings.

Successively we will discuss what exactly is prohibited by the different laws, how these prohibitions are enforced, and what their impact is on the working and living conditions of local and migrant women engaged in prostitution, especially in relation to violence and abuse.

In line with the working definitions on trafficking and forced labour & slavery-like practices as developed in chapter 2, we will analyse what protection the law offers women against violence and abuse and whether it enables women to take legal action, formally and actual, both in relation to abusive recruitment processes (trafficking, as defined in the working definition) and abusive working and living conditions (forced labour & slavery-like practices, as defined in the working definition). Special attention is paid to prohibitions and regulations regarding migrant prostitutes in the light of international trafficking in women for prostitution.

Finally: within this chapter prohibitions and regulations relating to clients will not be discussed. Very few countries have laws that penalise clients and where such laws exist they are seldom enforced. Also, we will not discuss prohibitions related to minors in prostitution. In (almost) all countries any act involving minors in prostitution is against the law. In some cases the law contains specific prohibitions relating to minors, in other cases the minority of the victim acts as an aggravating circumstance. Within the context of this report, however, we will not review this type of prohibition, as the prostitution of minors requires a separate approach.

2 Prohibition of prostitution as such

In a prohibitionist legal system prostitution as such is a criminal offence[1]: all activities related to prostitution are legally prohibited and all parties involved are criminalised, including the prostitute. Yet, most countries, with some exceptions, ignore the clients.

[1] Countries which qualify as prohibitionist are: USA (except Nevada), Philippines, Japan, Burma, Sri Lanka, Vietnam, Nepal, Uganda, Namibia, Tanzania, Mali, Iceland, Malta, Slovenia, China, Romania. This list is based on the respondents' answers to the questionnaire and various other documents. Almost 40% of the respondents define the legal system of their country as prohibitionist, defined in the questionnaire as "all prostitution is legally prohibited and all involved parties, incl. prostitutes, are criminalised". Due to, amongst other things, inconsistencies and ambiguities in the law and its application, in some cases respondents from the same country gave different responses to questions pertaining to the legal system in their country. For example: some respondents define the legal system in Thailand as prohibitionist, others do not. An explanation might be that officially prostitution as such is not an offence in Thailand, but in practice virtually everything related to prostitution is criminalised, amounting to a system of absolute prohibition.

In Slovenia, for example, prostitution is covered by the Law on Offences against Public Order and Peace, which penalises any person who is engaged or assists in prostitution, allows or supports prostitution, or organises, prepares or supports practices of "sexual immorality", with the exclusion of clients.

In Malta, prostitution itself is an offence under the 1930 Order for the Suppression of the White Slave Traffic. The same Order prohibits to prostitute another for financial advantage or to manage an establishment for prostitution. In Sri Lanka, prostitutes are prosecuted under the Vagrants Ordinance and the Brothel Ordinance (De Silva, 1996). In Uganda "any person who practices or engages in prostitution" may be sentenced to up to seven years imprisonment. In Japan, the Prostitution Prevention Law prohibits anyone to commit prostitution or to be a client of a prostitute (Rayanakorn, 1995).

Prostitutes may be sentenced to fines, imprisonment (Uganda: seven years!), forced rehabilitation or even, as in Iran, the death penalty (van der Vleuten, 1991). A revealing example of how sanctions against prostitutes can be exploited is the following:

In the Haman Island...when the provincial government launched its infrastructural construction, it lacked capital for building a highway. So the government decided to conduct a clean-up campaign. Women who were caught faced a penalty of Rmb. 2.000 and six months labour reform. During the period of reform labour they were sent to build a highway (Lin, 1996, p.4).

Although this type of prohibitionist legislation purports to eliminate prostitution, there is no evidence that countries where prostitution is outlawed have been even remotely successful in achieving this aim. This may be illustrated by the report of the Slovenian government to the Council of Europe (Council of Europe, 1994b), in which it is noted that the prohibition of prostitution does not implicate that brothels do not exist. Rather it means that brothels "are illegal and operate under alternative names, mainly as massage parlours". The same mechanism was seen in Aruba, where during the fifties the government tried to outlaw prostitution. The result was an increase in illicit prostitution activities, which led to the reintroduction of permits for sex workers in 1957 (Kempadoo, 1995).

The extent to which the law is actively enforced makes no significant difference to the position of prostitutes. It is sufficient that the law exists and can be used against her at any arbitrary moment. The illegality of prostitution as such renders prostitutes fully dependent on third parties. Since they have no legal protection at all - for they themselves are liable to arrest and prosecution - they may find themselves in the power of on the one hand brothel owners and middleme, and on the other hand police officers and court officials who are willing to turn a blind eye in exchange for money or free sexual services. This can make prostitution a very lucrative source of revenue for all involved parties, including the police, except the prostitutes themselves.

In case of violence, coercion or abuse - be it from the side of traffickers, brothel owners, police officers, other law-enforcement officials or clients - there is no authority, not even hypothetically, to which women can turn. Any contact with law-enforcers will expose her as a prostitute and put her at risk of being arrested and jailed. As stated by Butegwa, commenting on the legal situation in Uganda:

...Since prostitution is outlawed and not regarded as legitimate employment, pimps and traffickers would be able to victimise prostitutes. The latter would not be able to report their grievances to the police since they would be doing something illegal. Therefore it would appear that the traffickers can even use the law to keep the women enslaved and in slave-like conditions by threatening them with exposure. The women would then have no choice but to give in to all the demands and conditions set by traffickers.... In such a situation even women who were not originally trafficked find themselves in situations where they have little or no say at all regarding their work and what is expected from them. The people who use their services also know that these women are not protected by the law and therefore they can treat them carelessly (Butegwa, 1996, p.11).

Migrant women are in an even more vulnerable position. They are not only liable to arrest as prostitutes but also to arrest and deportation as illegal foreigners.

It may be concluded that, rather than "protecting women" or being in the interest of women, the prohibition of prostitution generates considerable profits for anyone but the prostitute, facilitates and sanctions control and abuse by third parties, and leaves the women with no legal means whatever to defend themselves against violence, coercion or abuse.

3 Prohibitions on third party involvement and activities related to prostitutions

In the majority of countries, prostitution in itself is not an offence[2]. Yet this does not necessarily mean that prostitutes are not liable to punishment. In Denmark for example, it is not illegal to provide sexual services for money and goods, but only as long as sex work is not the main source of income for the prostitute. The police otherwise might arrest her on charges of vagrancy (Pheterson, 1995). In Hungary, prostitution per se is not longer a crime since the modification of the Criminal Code in 1993. However: "parasitical offences (i.e. no proof of legitimate employment) connected with prostitution, are much more seriously prosecuted and punished than before" (Fehér, 1995). In Thailand, anyone found in a brothel for the purpose of prostitution is liable to punishment. In practice, this is only enforced on prostitutes but not on the clients (Rayanakorn, 1995).

[2] Almost 40 % of the respondents define the legal system of their country as abolitionist, defined as "prostitution is not an offence in itself, but any involvement of third parties/ any exploitation of the prostitution of others is prohibited". Another 15 % of the respondents define the legal system of their country as regulationist, defined as "prostitution is officially recognised and regulated through different forms of registration and other forms of control in the interest of public order and public health". The following countries qualify as predominantly abolitionist, according to information from the questionnaire and other documents: Thailand, Bangladesh, Hong Kong, India, Ukraine, Poland, Czech Republic, Lithuania, Bulgaria, Finland, Denmark, Italy, Spain, Portugal, France, Belgium, UK, Ireland, Canada, Nigeria, Mali, Cameroon, Dominican Republic, Colombia. Countries which qualify predominantly as regulationist are, according to the questionnaire and other document: Turkey, Peru, Ecuador, Curaçao, Greece, Switzerland, Australia, Germany, Austria and The Netherlands.

In all countries the practice of prostitution is controlled and regulated through an extensive range of prohibitions, restrictions and regulations. These are partly aimed at prostitutes themselves and partly at third parties. We will first discuss the prohibitions aimed at prostitutes, followed by a review of the prohibitions aimed at third parties. Separate attention will be given to prohibitions and regulations aimed at migrant prostitutes, as they run through all the other types of prohibitions and regulations.

3.1 Prohibitions and regulations aimed at prostitutes

Many of the legal prohibitions and regulations surrounding prostitution are aimed at prostitutes themselves. If women breach these prohibitions or fail to comply to the regulations they may be sentenced to imprisonment, fines or forced "rehabilitation". Female offenders in India, for instance, can be sentenced to detention in a corrective institution for a minimum of two and a maximum of five years. Release after six months is possible "if there is a reasonable probability that the offender will lead a useful and industrious life" (Immoral Traffic (Prevention) Act).
In Bangladesh arrested prostitutes can be sent to rehabilitation centres. However: "these not only prove to be ineffective, but also serve as a recruiting place for new entrants, as do the jails" (Khan, 1992). In Vietnam prostitutes may be sent to education camps (Quy, 1994). Whereas prostitution is seen as a social vice that must be eradicated, prostitutes are considered victims, who should be rehabilitated through receiving assistance to become respectable citizens and "reintegrate in their communities where they could be living amid the love of their countrymen" (Vietnam, 1996).

Asked whether it is possible to work in prostitution on a legal basis - and if so, under what conditions - 57 % of the respondents answer "yes" for national women and 41 % answer "yes" with respect to migrant women. The conditions mentioned by the respondents can be categorised in prohibitions and regulations pertaining to:
- mandatory registration
- mandatory medical control
- areas/places where to work
- soliciting and related activities
- taxes
- nationality, residence and work permits

In the following part we will review these prohibitions and their impact on the situation of women one by one. As mentioned before, prohibitions and regulations pertaining to migrant women will be addressed separately.

Mandatory registration

In many countries prostitutes are obliged to register: 33 % of the respondents answer that prostitutes are subjected to special registration, whilst 26 % answer that prostitution without registration or licence is prohibited[3]. In Bangladesh for example, although prostitution is officially prohibited, women in at least a proportion of the brothels have to register with the police at their entry and pay for an affidavit. This affidavit functions as a sort of licence that allows them to live in the brothel areas, though without giving them any official status or rights or even protection against arbitrary arrest (Khan, 1992). In Turkey also, prostitution is formally prohibited[4], however "women who have proved to prostitute themselves and who insist on carrying out this activity are registered as prostitutes and can only work as licensed prostitutes in brothels". Foreign women can not register, and are deported (Council of Europe, 1994a). In Greece, non-registered prostitutes are considered guilty of an illegal act; they are arrested, tried and imprisoned (Europap, 1995).

One of the objections raised against registration is that, due to the stigma on prostitutes, it leads to severe social and economic isolation. Moreover, forced registration creates a distinction between "legal" and "illegal" prostitutes. Figures show for example that in Athens there are 400 registered prostitutes, whilst an estimated 5,000 more prostitutes are not registered. Similarly, in Germany 50,000 prostitutes are registered, but a further 150,000 women are estimated to work in prostitution (Europap, 1995).

Many women do not want to register for fear of the stigma attached to being recognised as a prostitute. Other women cannot register because of their illegal residence status, like most migrant prostitutes. As a result, many women will try to avoid registration, which not only makes them liable to prosecution, but also relegates them to an illegal circuit with all the negative consequences this entails. It encourages women to hide from the authorities and functions as a barrier against taking legal action in case of violence, abuse or coercion.

Mandatory registration may also make it more difficult or impossible for women to quit working as a prostitute. Around 35 % of the respondents in countries with mandatory registration say that prostitutes can de-register, but that records will be kept and that these can be used against her. This may be illustrated by the case of Turkey. If a woman has been found to be practising prostitution, she has to be formally registered as a prostitute. Her normal identity card, carried by every Turkish citizen, is withdrawn and replaced by a prostitute's identity card giving her name, her working pseudonym, age, place of birth, place of residence and place of work. Registered women are supposed to inform the police when they move from one area to another and they are not allowed to marry. It is possible to de-register, but records may be kept and made available on demand to, for instance, a prospective husband or employer. As expressed by Anti-Slavery International in its report on forced prostitution in Turkey : "once a prostitute is registered and working within the Genelev system[5] she is seldom able to re-enter the outside world and pursue other employment" (ASI, 1993).

[3] Countries where prostitutes are subjected to special registration are (according to the questionnaire and other documents): Bangladesh, Thailand, Australia, Curaçao, Peru, Mexico, Ecuador, Dominican Republic, Turkey, Greece, Austria, Switzerland. Countries where prostitution without licence/registration is prohibited (based on the questionnaire and reports): Australia, Thailand, Turkey, Greece, Switzerland, Curaçao, Peru, Ecuador, Mexico, Slovenia and Belgium.

[4] At least according to the Turkish government in their report to the Council of Europe (Council of Europe, 1994a) In reality Turkey has a legal and highly regulated prostitution system: see ASI report, 1993.

[5] Licensed walled brothel complexes, with only one permanently guarded door. Genelevs may only employ registered prostitutes.

Mandatory medical control

In most countries where prostitutes are required to register, registration is combined with mandatory medical checks. This is for instance the case in Curaçao, Peru, Dominican Republic, Ecuador, Greece, Austria, Switzerland, Germany and Turkey. Their frequency varies from once a month (Dominican Republic) to biweekly (Greece and Turkey). Failing to attend mandatory medical screening may make women liable to prosecution, like in Greece.

In Turkey, for example, prostitutes are subjected to mandatory medical controls under the Rules governing Prostitutes and Brothels and the Regulations on Combating Contagious Venereal Diseases which can be transmitted by Prostitution. In addition to the prostitute's registration card, women are issued a certificate of examination with similar information but containing pages to stamp the biweekly medical examinations she is required to take. If a woman does not turn up for her scheduled examination or treatment, she can be brought in by force (ASI, 1993). In Curaçao, women who do not report for the weekly medical exam and an update of their health card[6], are reported by the doctors to the police department, which in turn is supposed to track down the offender (Kempadoo, 1995).

The system of mandatory medical controls can be criticised for a number of reasons. With an eye to the prevention of contagious diseases the results of such controls are seriously limited. Clients who infect women are not traced, which not only makes controls quite useless, but also stigmatises the prostitute one-sidedly. Almost always medical control is limited to the detection of STDs in the interest of protecting the client or "public health", disregarding other illnesses who are "only" detrimental to the women's health but can not damage the client. Moreover, they create a false illusion of safety among clients, which encourages the demand for unsafe sex.
This clearly is detrimental as well for the health of the women concerned as for the prevention of the spread of STDs. Moreover, health care facilities and STD prevention activities are only accessible for registered prostitutes, which is ineffective in public health terms[7]. Women who cannot register, for example, because they are illegal, are excluded from health care services.
In most countries, if women are found to be infected they are prohibited from working, which means that they have no source of income. This can be a reason not to seek medical attention, even if women are in need of medical care.

Areas/places where to work

In many countries the law prohibits working outside permitted areas[8]. In other countries it is only permitted to work in licensed brothels. Some countries impose restrictions on certain types of prostitution, like street or window prostitution. In Turkey, for example, women are only permitted to work in licensed brothels or in specific areas alone in an apartment (ASI, 1993).
In Hong Kong women are only allowed to work in "one-woman brothels", though according to

[6] All registered sex workers are ordered to have in their possession a health card, commonly referred to as "the pink card".

[7] See for an extensive description of the effects of mandatory health controls: Europap, 1995.

[8] The following countries prohibit prostitution outside permitted areas (according to the questionnaire and other documents): Canada, Bangladesh, Nepal, India, Thailand, Hong Kong, Peru, Mexico, Ecuador, Australia, Turkey, Belgium, Switzerland, Germany, The Netherlands and Slovenia.

a respondent to the questionnaire: "even then the police usually find some reason for arresting them". In Hungary, it is prohibited to rent a building or other place for the purpose of prostitution (to be punished with a maximum of three years imprisonment), though prostitution per se is not a crime (Council of Europe, 1994a). In The Netherlands window and street prostitution are only allowed in designated areas. Many countries do not allow prostitution in the vicinity of public places (e.g. India) or in the vicinity of schools (e.g. Germany).

Local regulations can have a major effect on the way prostitutes are able to organise their work. These regulations may be used to move prostitutes from one area to another, making it more difficult for health workers to maintain contact with prostitutes. Banishing prostitutes to certain restricted areas or remote places may contribute to their isolation and make working conditions more dangerous. In Paris, for example, local regulations have been used to close down apartments and hotels in the traditional prostitution district around Rue St. Denis. As a result "sex workers were forced to move to the town outskirts where they are more isolated and working conditions more dangerous" (Europap, 1995). In Germany, most cities have zones where prostitution is prohibited and areas of tolerance, where prostitution is found in super brothels and Eros centres. Only certain sex workers are tolerated: "Those who do not fit in, such as migrant workers, are expelled to isolated areas, where working conditions are more dangerous and access to health and social services may be difficult" (Europap, 1995).

Soliciting and related activities

Even though prostitution is not an offence in itself, in most countries the law criminalises attracting clients: around 45 % of the respondents say that the law prohibits soliciting, loitering and related activities[9]. The exact content of this type of prohibition may vary. In the UK for example, "the law seeks to prevent the serious nuisance caused to the public when prostitutes operate on the streets through a prohibition on soliciting, loitering and kerb crawling" (Council of Europe, 1994a). Norway prohibits "indecent behaviour" and in Belgium "soliciting, taking someone to or bringing someone away from a place for the purpose of prostitution and promoting vice in public places by words, gestures, signs or publicity" is prohibited (Europap, 1995). Other countries penalise soliciting in a public place, as is the case in e.g. the Czech Republic, Cyprus, Kenya, Thailand and India.

In India the Immoral Traffic (Prevention) Act prohibits prostitution, seducing and soliciting in, or in the vicinity of, a public place. In the case of prostitution in (the vicinity of) a public place all parties, including the prostitute and the client, are punishable. However, in the case of soliciting in (the vicinity of) a public place only the prostitute is liable to punishment. For a female prostitute the maximum penalty may vary from six months to one year imprisonment, but "provided that where an offence under this section (i.e. seducing or soliciting for prostitution) is committed by a man, he shall be punishable with imprisonment for a period of not less than seven days but which may extend to three months". Female offenders can also be sentenced to detention in a corrective institution for a period of two years up to five years.

[9] The following countries criminalise soliciting, loitering and related activities (according to the questionnaire and other documents): Japan, Bangladesh, India, Thailand, Hong Kong, Philippines, Australia, Canada, Curaçao, Mexico, Uganda, Kenya, Norway, Italy, Belgium, Switzerland, Ireland, UK and Slovenia.

According to the Thai Restriction of Prostitution Act "any person who loiters or solicits in public places for the purpose of prostitution is liable to a term of not more than three months imprisonment or a fine of not more than two thousand baht or both". The same Act gives the General Director of the Welfare Department discretionary power to send prostitutes to a rehabilitation centre for medical treatment or skill training up to a maximum of one year:
In practice however, most prostitutes would escape on bail to avoid being rehabilitated. This is so despite the fact that they would normally be sentenced to a fine of 200 to 500 baht, a sum less than the amount of the bail money forfeited which is usually around 1,000 baht. The reasons behind this are mainly economic reasons. One year in a rehabilitation centre would mean severe hardship both for the prostitutes themselves and for the family they are supporting. Besides, skills training is of little use if there is no likelihood of finding employment after the training (Rayanakorn, 1995, p.21).

Normally a prostitute is bailed out by a brothel keeper, which means that the amount of bail money forfeited will be deducted from her future earnings. Yet many prostitutes prefer this cycle, rather than being sent to a rehabilitation centre.

In Japan, prostitutes sentenced for soliciting, loitering or inducing a person to be a client, may be placed under "guidance disposition" and detained in a Woman's Guidance Home for rehabilitation for a period of six months.

Though soliciting is prohibited by the Penal Code in Kenya, prostitutes are usually charged under other Acts:
Prostitutes in Kenya are usually charged under the Vagrancy Act and the General Nuisance by-laws which seek to control vagrancy and loitering within urban areas. The Public Health Act is also applied in cases where commercial sex workers fail to seek medical treatment for sexually transmitted diseases. The police do not prefer the Penal Code charges, due to factors such as burden of proof cast on the prosecution. Usually the evidence is insufficient to proof an offence (Butegwa, 1996, p.14).

By restricting the ways that prostitutes can meet customers, they are canpelled to rely on third parties to make business contacts. In many cases such restrictions lead to unsafe working circumstances and an increased risk of violence by clients. This may be illustrated by the case of Ireland, where soliciting by both prostitute and client is an offence. Since 1993 the police may also summon a person suspected of loitering in a street to leave (making it an offence when the person fails to comply). A survey on the health needs of women engaged in prostitution in Ireland reveals the following effects:
For the majority of the women interviewed the new legislation has meant a decline in their working conditions. Because they are constantly being moved on by the Gardai (Irish police) they are having to work longer hours to make the same amount of money as previously. Also, because of greater Gardai presence there has been a decline in the number of clients seeking services. Thus many of the women have experienced a drop in their income. For some this has meant increasing pressure with regard to payment of bills, etc.... The increased pressure to maintain a certain level of income is leading to greater risk taking on the part of the women... Risks are also being taken in relation to choice of clients in that women are getting into cars more quickly with no time to study prospective

clients... [as one woman says] "before you had to look out for clients, now you are looking out for the Gardai as well (O'Connor, 1994, p. 17)

If a woman is charged with an offence she may incur heavy fines which necessitate her working extra hours to earn money to pay the fine. Also, the role of intermediaries becomes more important, as well for providing contacts with clients, as for providing protection and paying bail in case of arrest.
The same applies to England and Wales, where the law against kerb crawling by prospective clients has reduced the time prostitutes have to assess clients and negotiate safe sex. In other cases women may avoid breaking the law by officially working as waitresses, like in Belgium.
In some countries even the possession of condoms can be used as evidence of soliciting, as in California[10].

Taxes

In quite a number of, especially Western, countries, e.g. The Netherlands, Germany, Belgium, France and Austria, the state imposes tax payments on prostitutes, even though the profiting from prostitution is legally prohibited. The attitude of the French government may be called exemplary for this "dual morality":
This ambiguous legal stance also characterises the attitude of the tax administration. For the French tax department, prostitution is a source of income just like any other activity and should therefore be liable for tax (Europap, 1995, p.63).

In Belgium, several city councils impose local taxes on "waitresses" or "performing artists" in bars, clubs and cabarets. The local police are charged with registering the number of such workers and ensuring they pay taxes. In Germany, taxes on income from sex work are in general imposed in the category "other income", which is much higher than the usual tax rate, within the regular tax categories for self-employed businesses. At the same time, prostitutes are not entitled to the same tax deductions as other self-employed businesses are entitled to, since the Civil Code prohibits them to register as a business.

Paying taxes, however, does not imply that prostitutes have rights to social insurance or cannot be arrested at the same time, like in the UK:
..As prostitution businesses are not regarded as legitimate, prostitutes cannot legally make a living. Therefore prostitutes are denied rights in relation to state benefits and pensions. Prostitutes have been presented with tax demands for their earnings, but denied the right to form businesses and claim expenses against tax (Europap, 1995, p. 127).

Also in Turkey registered women pay tax, but are denied normal social security rights, such as pension and sick-pay. Recently a number of registered prostitutes joined the Trade Union, trying to procure better rights within their work. The initial aim was to get normal social security rights

[10] See for an extensive description of the effects of restrictions on soliciting with regard to safe sex: Europap, 1995.

for the genelev workers, who already pay tax. A test case is underway: a genelev prostitute demanded a pension from her former employer but was refused. The case is now with a higher court[11].

Other prohibitions

It is worth noting that most laws implicitly or explicitly make the assumption that prostitutes are female. In Turkey this is even obligatory: prostitutes must be Turkish, female, over the age of 18, and singles. All laws prohibit the involvement of minors in prostitution, though the age of consent may vary from fifteen to twenty-one.

Prostitutes organising themselves

Over the last years prostitutes have started to organise themselves to defend their rights and improve their working and living conditions. However, not in all countries are prostitutes permitted to do so. Around 35 % of the respondents say that prostitutes are not allowed to have their own organisations[12]. But, even when they are allowed to have their own organisation, it does not mean they are allowed to form their own labour or trade unions or join any existing ones as a specific population of workers. In general, prostitutes are denied union rights.

Prohibitions on aiding, abetting or living off immoral earnings may also make it effectively impossible for women to organise themselves or even to co-operate: in Cyprus for example any woman aiding or abetting another woman to prostitution is punishable (Council of Europe, 1994a). In France the very wide legal definition of procuration is the cause of many problems among prostitutes, especially those who are working in flats and who, according to the law, are forced to be the owner:

If they rent their work place, the owner can be immediately prosecuted for brothel procuration. Similarly, two prostitutes cannot become co-owners of the same flat, for in legal terms one of them is automatically considered as the tenant and the other as the owner and can therefore be prosecuted for procuration. Finally, this law prevents any true solidarity between prostitutes, since any loan or financial donation from one person to another can be considered procuration (Europap, 1995, p.62).

3.2 Prohibitions and regulations aimed at third parties

The majority of prohibitions and regulations concerning prostitution are aimed at third parties, varying from a complete ban on any form of third party involvement to various forms of regulation of third party involvement.

Parallel to the distinction between "trafficking" and "forced labour & slavery-like practices", prohibitions and regulations with regard to third parties can be roughly divided into two main categories:

[11] Information from a current research project "Defining Prostitution as Commercial Sexwork on the International Agenda", conducted by Anti-Slavery International.

[12] The following countries don't allow prostitutes to have their own associations (according to respondents to questionnaire): Nepal, Thailand, Philippines, Vietnam, Taiwan, China, Peru, Mexico, Bulgaria, Poland and Slovenia,

- prohibitions pertaining to recruiting women for or bringing women into prostitution ("recruitment" prohibitions), and
- prohibitions pertaining to the managing, organising or profiting from prostitution, traditionally referred to as the "exploitation of the prostitution of others" ("employment" prohibitions).

If the criminal law contains specific provisions prohibiting "traffic in women", these are mostly - but not always[13] - related to the process of bringing a person into prostitution. However, what exactly is understood by "traffic in women", or which conditions have to be fulfilled to make up the crime of trafficking, varies substantially. At the same time, legal provisions on trafficking are not always exclusively linked to prostitution but may cover also recruitment or "exploitation" for other purposes. Legal provisions concerning other crimes (for instance kidnapping and abduction) may also be applied to trafficking situations. Moreover, not all countries have specific legal provisions on trafficking in women.

In section 3.3 "recruitment" prohibitions will be discussed, followed by a review of "employment" prohibitions in section 3.4 . We will do so, irrespective of the title under which specific prohibitions appear, since what is called "trafficking" in one country may be called recruitment, pimping, procuring or exploitation in another. A review of prohibitions with regard to migrant prostitutes is given in section 4.

Section 5 concludes with a summary of the current legal definitions of "traffic in women", followed by a critical assessment of the different laws on prostitution and "trafficking" and their impact on the working and living conditions of women engaged in prostitution. The leading question is to what extent the existing legislation is in the interest of women and what protection it offers women against violence and abuse, both in relation to abusive recruitment processes (trafficking, as defined in the working definition) and abusive working and living conditions (forced labour & slavery-like practices, as defined in the working definition).

3.3 Recruitment and mediation for prostitution

Although the exact content and wording vary widely, the Criminal Codes of most countries contain a vast range of provisions with regard to bringing another person into prostitution. The variety in language probably may be partly due to the different treaties on "trafficking in women" on which the provisions are based. Terms that are employed are: recruit, induce, entice, instigate or lead a woman into prostitution, encourage or cause prostitution, make a person to prostitute herself, tempt a person to prostitution, promote, facilitate or incite prostitution. In a number of countries also taking a person to, or bringing a person away from, a place for the purpose of prostitution is separately penalised. This is for example the case in Canada, where section 211 of the Criminal Code penalises anyone who "takes, transports, directs or offers to take, transport or direct any person to a common bawdy-house" (Sanghera, 1996).

[13] In some countries provisions on "trafficking" (also) cover the "exploitation of the prostitution of another person".

In some countries the law provides for a general ban on all acts relating to bringing another person into prostitution, including any mediation for prostitution, with or without consent. The use of violence, the age of the woman involved or the relationship with the offender may constitute aggravating circumstances. This is for example the case in Turkey, India, Bangladesh, Canada, Uganda, Hungary, Portugal, UK and Nicaragua.

In Turkey, though it has a licensed brothel system, any encouragement to and mediation in prostitution are criminal offences. In addition forced prostitution, defined as forcing somebody into prostitution (not as abusive or coercive employment) constitutes a criminal offence. The severity of it is determined by the age of the person forced into prostitution and whether or not she is married. If the offender is a family member, husband, teacher, etc., heavier penalties are imposed[14]. In its report to the Council of Europe (Council of Europe, 1994a), the Turkish government considers that "in comparison to other countries prostitution and trafficking in women are not serious problems in Turkey". In sharp contrast to this opinion of the Turkish government, Anti-Slavery International reports a widespread practice of selling women into genelevs (closed brothels):
One of the more common ways of selling a woman appears to be for her boyfriend to invite her to live with him for a few weeks before he takes her to a genelev and after that he usually disappears. Often the women are no more than teenagers when they are initially trapped. A number of the prostitutes interviewed emphasised that "once a very young woman finds herself abandoned by her man inside a genelev she immediately feels it is impossible for her to escape - there is, after all, only one door by which she could leave and that is always guarded by the police or security officers" (ASI, 1993, p.21).

In India, inducing a person "to go from any place, with the intent that she/he may, for the purpose of prostitution, become an inmate of, or frequent, a brothel" or taking a person for the sake of prostitution with or without consent, including (attempting to) "take a person or cause a person to be taken from one place to another for the purpose of prostitution", is prohibited by the 1959 Immoral Traffic (Prevention) Act. (If this happens against the will of that person or in case of a child the maximum punishment is increased from seven years to fourteen years and lifelong imprisonment respectively.) The Act penalises at the same time procuring, living off the earnings of prostitution, brothel keeping and detaining a person in premises where prostitution is practised, with or without consent. In practice, the law is not or inadequately enforced. According to police-officers in Calcutta, if a case is filed it can take ten years to reach a conclusion. After such a delay, witnesses have gone or memories have dimmed. There is ample opportunity to intimidate the trafficked women and their families (GAATW, 1996).

The same prohibition on inciting a person to go from any place with the intent that she/he, for the purpose of prostitution, becomes an inmate of, or frequent a brothel is found in the

[14] Current Turkish law covering prostitution is embodied in Decree 5/984, entitled Statutes Concerning the Prostitutes, Regulations which the Brothels will comply with, and the Prevention of the Infectious Venereal Diseases resulting (sic) from Prostitution, and in Chapter II (Abduction of Girls) and III (Instigation to Prostitution) of the Turkish Penal Code (ASI, 1993).

Bangladesh Suppression of Immoral Traffic Act, which likewise penalises simultaneously any third party involvement.

The Penal Code of Uganda prohibits to procure any woman or girl for her to become either in Uganda or elsewhere a "common prostitute", to leave Uganda with the intent that she may become an inmate of or frequent a brothel elsewhere, or to leave her usual place of abode in Uganda (such place not being a brothel!) with the intent that she may, for the purpose of prostitution, become an inmate of or frequent a brothel either in Uganda or elsewhere. Here too, the law is rarely or never enforced. One of the reasons is the provision that no person shall be convicted of any offences in this section upon the evidence of one witness only, unless that witness be corroborated in some material particular by evidence implicating the accused (Butegwa, 1996).

The Canadian criminal law defines "trafficking in women" as either transporting or procuring. Under the heading of "procuring or living on the avails of prostitution" the Canadian Criminal Code prohibits the inducement of women into prostitution. Procurement includes "procuring or soliciting a person to become, whether in or out of Canada, a prostitute or to have illicit intercourse with another person", "procuring a person to enter or leave Canada for the purpose of prostitution" and "on arrival in Canada taking or causing a person to be taken to a common bawdy-house". According to Canada's paper for the EU Conference on Trafficking in Women for Sexual Exploitation in 1996, "these offences are designed to prevent persons from being forced into prostitution" (Canada, 1996). Special attention should go to para. b and e of this section - not mentioned in Canada's paper - which penalise, respectively, inveigling or enticing a person "who is not a prostitute or a person of known IMMORAL character to a common bawdy house or house of assignation for the purpose of illicit sexual intercourse or prostitution", and procuring "a person to leave the usual place of abode of that person in Canada, if that place is not a common bawdy-house, with the intent that the person may become an inmate or frequenter of a common bawdy-house, whether in or out Canada"(Sanghera, 1996).

In Nicaragua, art. 203 of the Penal Code penalises, under the heading of "Trafficking in Human Beings", any recruitment of persons for prostitution within or outside the republic, with consent or by means of deception or threat, including bringing persons into the country for the purpose of prostitution.

Apart from general prohibitions, in most countries the law also provides for specific prohibitions, penalising recruitment or mediation under certain conditions, for example:
- when deception or coercion is used
- when borders are crossed
- when in relation to a certain category of victims, e.g. "chaste" women or foreign women.

In some cases recruitment is only punishable under these conditions, in other cases provisions on selling and buying women, kidnapping, etc., are additional to general prohibitions on recruitment, like in Bangladesh.

Buying, selling or purchasing women for prostitution

Under the chapter "Trafficking in Women", the 1983 Cruelty to Women (Deterrent Punishment) Ordinance of Bangladesh prohibits "importing or exporting, selling, letting to hire or otherwise disposing of, or buying, hiring or otherwise obtaining possession of any women of any age with intent that such woman shall be employed or used for the purpose of prostitution or illicit intercourse with any person or for any unlawful and immoral purpose". The Women and Child Repression (Special Provision) Law (1995) contains almost identical provisions, but provides for heavier penalties.

However, according to several reports (Shamin, 1995/LHRLA, 1991/Shahid, 1990/BNWLA, 1995/Khan, 1992), the successful implementation of the aforementioned acts and laws is questionable. This is due, amongst other things, to the inter-regional character of trafficking and the lack of international legislation which has been accepted by all the countries involved. Other factors that are mentioned are: lack of proper and timely prosecution, the vulnerability of the victims under the legislation of the receiving countries that penalises the victims themselves, the existence of strong vested interest groups and lack of state intervention in this regard.

Kidnapping and abduction

Provisions on kidnapping and abduction for the purpose of prostitution can be found in, for example, the criminal codes of Thailand, Bangladesh, Japan and Uganda.

In Thailand, both the 1960 Restraining of Prostitution Act and the Penal Code penalise any person who abducts a woman for "acts of indecency", along with other aspects related to prostitution (Rayanakorn, 1995).

In Bangladesh, the Penal Code prohibits "kidnapping, abducting or inducing a woman to compel her to marry any person against her will, or to force or seduce her to illicit intercourse", and "kidnapping or abducting in order to subject a person to grievous hurt, slavery or unnatural lust". Both provisions are aggravated forms of the general prohibitions on kidnapping and abduction. These general prohibitions on kidnapping and abduction include "conveying any person beyond the limits of Bangladesh without the consent of that person or of some person legally authorised to consent on behalf of that person" (kidnapping from Bangladesh), and "compelling a person by force or inducing any person by any deceitful means to go from any place" (abduction). In addition, the 1993 Cruelty to Women (Deterrent Punishment) Ordinance prohibits kidnapping or abducting any woman of any age with the intent that "such woman shall be employed or used for the purpose of prostitution or for any unlawful or immoral purpose, with the intent that such woman may be compelled to marry any person against her will, or in order that such woman may be forced or seduced to illicit intercourse".

Paragraph 225 of the Japanese Penal Code prohibits kidnapping another person by force or allurement for the purpose of profit or engagement in sexual activities or marriage. In case of kidnapping a person with the purpose to transport the person out of Japan, defined as "trafficking", the minimum punishment is raised to two years. The same applies to persons who buy or sell another person for the purpose of transporting the same out of Japan. Nothing is said about kidnapping, transporting or buying or selling a person for transport into Japan (Kawamura, 1996).

The same kind of provisions are found in the Penal Code of Uganda, where the law prohibits "kidnapping or abduction of a person in order that such person be subject to slavery or unnatural lust".

Deceit, abuse and coercion

Special provisions penalising the use of deceit or coercion can be found in, amongst others, the Penal Codes of Japan, The Netherlands and Germany.

In Japan the Prostitution Prevention Law prohibits making a person prostitute herself by deception, embarrassment, taking advantage of the influence through kinship, threats of violence, or by according money, goods or any other financial benefit. In case of receiving or demanding (part of) the earnings of the resulting prostitution the penalty goes up to a maximum of five years and a fine.

Under the title "Trafficking in Persons", art. 250ter of the Dutch Penal Code prohibits "inducing another person to engage in prostitution by means of (threat of) violence, abuse of ascendancy derived from actual relations or by deception". Abuse of authority is assumed if a woman is found to be in conditions which are "not equivalent to the conditions under which an independent and emancipated prostitute in The Netherlands normally works". Special directives were formulated concerning the tracing and legal action against traffic in women. It is worth noting that in relation to non-EEC subjects, recruitment is criminalized regardless of the use of violence or deceit. In the case of migrant women the way they are recruited, i.e. the will of the women involved, is no criterion, though in practice prosecution only takes place in case of violence, abuse or deceit. However, in spite of all this, there are yet many obstacles.
The directives are not consequently implemented and many women are still deported without further investigation (Boer, 1994). Often women do not dare to press charges, for example because they are afraid of reprisals. As long as they are in The Netherlands they can be offered help and protection, but when the criminal proceedings are completed, they again face deportation. Back home they are unprotected against reprisals by their traffickers or the authorities and risk rejection by their families.

Under the heading of "Trafficking in Human Beings", the German Penal Code penalises anyone who, for profit, induces a person into prostitution or keeps a person in prostitution by abusing the circumstances of that person or "exploiting the helplessness connected with being in a foreign country". There is aggravated traffic in human beings when threat, force or deceit is used or when the victim is abducted. The law also recognizes less serious forms of trafficking, less severely penalised, in the case that the victim knew she was recruited for prostitution or when deceit is used towards a person, who is "not far from prostitution"[15] (Studzinsky, 1996).

[15] "die der Prostitution nicht fern steht".

In practice the criminal procedures, requiring that witnesses are cross-examined directly and in person by the court, in combination with biased judicial attitudes towards women victims make it extremely difficult to punish those involved in trafficking. An example of the difficulties which women victims encounter, if they press charges, is provided by the research conducted on a trial on trafficking of Thai women in 1990 (Niesner, 1991). The trial which concerned the recruitment and coercion of Thai women into prostitution ended after eleven months with the acquittal of the defendants on the charge of trafficking. The defendants were found guilty of promoting prostitution and procuring, offences that are considerably less heavy punished.

Two of the women involved gave evidence that they were recruited in Thailand to work in a bar in Germany with the promise of 2,000 DM a month to be earned exclusively by go-go dancing and encouraging guests to drink. On their way to Germany they were made to marry a German man in Denmark before entering Germany. When they arrived at the bar in Germany, they were told that they had 15,000 DM in debts to pay and this much money could be earned only by prostitution. The other women were taken to Germany under similar conditions with slightly different details. One was promised to work as a waitress and another as nanny. The women's passports were taken away. From the beginning of the trial, the judge showed reluctance in pursuing the case by complaining about the expected length of the trial and the multitude of cases awaiting the court's attention. Throughout the proceeding, he was friendly towards the defendant and the defence counsel while obviously sceptical towards the prosecutor and the plaintiff's counsel. The trial judge shared the defendants view in not believing in the helplessness of the women, even though it was clear from the evidence that the women were left with little alternative. In addition, the judge regarded the past records of the women in Thailand as relevant in deciding whether they could be victims of trafficking under Art. 181. During the cross-examination at the trial, every effort was made to attack the credibility of the women's evidence. This strategy was shared by the judge who on several occasions prejudged the issue and equated the women's past status to a prostitute. Ignorance of Thai culture plus translation difficulties added to make the evidence given by the women seem less credible. It is worth noting that the Thai government showed no interest in the case, even though the women victims were Thai. Successive calls for evidence and key-witnesses from Thailand were ignored and a Thai police officer could not be questioned because the higher authorities refused to give their consent (Rayanakorn, 1995, p.36).

Crossing borders

Some countries have special provisions addressing cross-border recruitment, like Thailand, Japan, Colombia, Peru, Brazil, Paraguay, Uganda, the UK and the United States.

In addition to the Penal Code, the Act on Prevention of Traffic in Women and Children (1928) in Thailand penalises "any person who brings women or girls into Thailand or sends them for the purpose of having sexual intercourse with other persons, and any person who is involved illegally in the trading of women or girls brought into the country for such purposes" (Rayanakorn, 1995). In spite of the Prevention of Traffic Act several reports bear witness to the failure to combat trafficking as defined in this Act. Exemplary of such failure is the crackdown on

prostitution and trafficking in women in 1991:
During a number of raids many prostitutes were arrested. Approximately 30 - 40 % of the women and children arrested appeared to come from Burma.

As a result of the crackdown the women were deported or sent to penal reform institutions... Collusion, bribery and immunity from prosecution have undermined the government's intentions to stop trafficking. For all the efforts of the Government of Thailand, Asia/Watch has concluded that the trafficking of Burmese women and girls to Thailand continues, virtually unchecked. Moreover, despite clear evidence that the Thai law enforcement and immigration officials remain directly involved in the flesh trade, not a single officer has been prosecuted or punished for such abuse. Brothel keepers, pimps and procurers have been largely exempt from punishment. In fact the main targets of the crackdown on forced and child prostitution have been the victims themselves (Australia - Parliament, 1995, p.50).

Under the title "Trafficking in Women and Minors" the Penal Code of Colombia penalises "promoting or facilitating the entrance to or the exit from the country of a woman or a minor of both sexes, to practise prostitution". Additionally foreigners can be expelled from Colombia in case of "proxenitism". However, several reports (Polania Molina, 1996/Acosta, 1996), state that, apart from lack of juridical or legal instruments which allow bringing traffickers into court in case of international trafficking, corruption with the police and judicial authorities lead to a systematic lack of protection and rampant impunity. According to a report of Polania Molina (1996), bribing of the authorities by trafficking networks "to achieve that legal procedures are suspended or that the verdict is changed" is common practice.

Under the similar title "Traffic in Women" the Penal Codes of Brazil and Guatemala penalise any person who "brings on or encourages the entry or exit of a woman for the purpose of prostitution", whereby the use of violence or deceit acts as an aggravating circumstance. Similar provisions are found in the Criminal Code in Argentina under the section Offences against Morality and under the section Proxenitism in the Penal Code of Peru (Domingo Traspasso, 1996). Here, too, it is reported that, in spite of this prohibition, corruption and lack of interest on the part of the authorities result in de facto impunity, as is illustrated by the case of Ydelsa Margarita Ramirez Rodas:
Ydelsa, a young Peruvian woman, was trafficked to Italy and murdered during an attempt to escape her traffickers. Despite desperate efforts from her family to have the case properly investigated, the case was disposed of as suicide and no further investigations were made, nor by the Peruvians, nor by the Italian authorities (case described by Domingo Traspasso, 1996).

The Penal Code of Paraguay prohibits the trade or transport of adult women to another country, with or without consent, with a view to bringing them into prostitution, in addition to a general prohibition on the recruitment of women for prostitution, also under the title of "Trafficking in Women" (Acosta Vargas, 1996).

In Belgium, the Penal Code prohibits since May 1995 to "contribute to the entry or residence of a foreigner, making use of deceit, violence, threats or any other kind of force, or misusing the especially vulnerable position in which a foreigner might find her/himself due to an illegal or precarious administrative situation or due to pregnancy, illness or physical or mental disorder or disability" (Centrum voor Gelijkheid, 1996).

In the UK, "to procure a woman to be a prostitute in another country" makes up a separate offence, though the provision is rarely used. According to the UK government report to the Council of Europe:
There is no convincing evidence of the existence of one or more networks trafficking in women. However, there is evidence of the presence of prostitutes, particularly in some ports.

Amazingly, the report continues:
Malaysian, Chinese and Thai women whose occupations as given in their passport are beauticians, hairdressers, etc., are brought into the UK as part of the business activities of Triad-organised crime syndicates... Malaysians and Chinese are rigidly controlled by Triad members...In many cases it is difficult to obtain the information required, as some women, mostly Malaysian and Chinese, will not talk for fear of retribution from the Triads (Council of Europe, 1994a, p.49).

Under the White Slave Act, more commonly known as the Mann Act, Federal law of the United States prohibits transportation of "any individual in interstate or foreign commerce, or in any Territory or Possession of the United States, with intent that such an individual engage in prostitution, or in any sexual activity for which a person can be charged with a criminal offence". Punishable is also anyone who "knowingly persuades, induces, entices, or coerces any individual to travel in interstate or foreign commerce, or in any Territory or Possession of the United States" with the above mentioned aim.

Certain categories of women

In quite a number of countries the punishability of inducing a woman to prostitution is defined by the "virtue" of the woman concerned rather than by the acts of the offender. This is for example the case in most Latin American countries, Japan, Canada and Uganda.

An illustration is provided by Colombia, where the Penal Code only prohibits to induce a "persona honesta" to prostitution. Even the use of violence (i.e. to force a person into prostitution) is allowed as long as it does not concern a "chaste" woman[16]. The same type of discriminatory sanction can be found in the Penal Codes of many other Latin American countries[17]. In El Salvador, for example, abduction is viewed a less severe crime if the victim is a prostitute[18] and in Brazil "abduction with the use of violence, threats or deception with a view to illicit sexual acts" is only punishable if perpetrated against a "chaste" woman.

16 Art. 308 of the Penal Code prohibits to induce a "persona honesta into prostitution; art. 309 to force a "persona honesta"to prostutution.
17 See for an extensive review of discriminatory character of the laws on prostitution and trafficking in women in the criminal codes of the Latin American and Caribbean countries, Acosta Vargas, 1996.
18 Art. 202, Penal Code El Salvador.

The same phenomenon is seen in Japan, where art. 182 of the Penal Code penalises any person who for the purpose of obtaining profit induces a female person "not habitually licentious" to commit fornication. In Uganda the law prohibits procuring a girl or woman by causing her to leave her usual place of abode in Uganda "not being a brothel" with the intent of prostitution (Uganda, 1950/1990). In Germany, as is described above, the law views it a less serious form of trafficking, with a lower penalty, when the victim knew she was recruited for prostitution or when deceit is used towards a person, who is "not far from prostitution" (Studzinsky, 1996).

Other prohibitions

In some countries the criminal code contains special provisions prohibiting the sale and purchase of human beings for any purpose, defined as "trafficking".

In Nepal, the Trafficking in Persons Control Act 2043 (1987) prohibits the sale and purchase of a human being for any purpose, as well as taking a person to foreign countries for the purpose of trafficking. A special paragraph prohibits "involving a woman in prostitution by enticing or alluring, by undue influence, fraud, threat, force or by any other means". In addition to the Trafficking in Persons Control Act, the New Muluki-Ain (1963) prohibits in the chapter on "Trafficking in Persons", "alluring persons to cross the border with intent of trafficking or striking a deal in this regard" and "enslaving persons or striking a deal regarding human trafficking". Buyers, sellers and traffickers are subject to the same punishment (Poudel, 1994/Sangroula, 1995). However, since the promulgation of the Trafficking in Persons Control Act in July 1987 only approximately 117 cases were brought to the notice of the authorities (Sangroula, 1995). According to a report from WATCH (Poudel, 1994), no serious attempt has been made to take action against the perpetrators: usually traffickers get off with a light punishment and continue their practice. Only some low level traffickers are prosecuted, though they must be connected with high influential networks. The police and the local administration may have information on such networks but they keep quiet, either to safeguard their part of the profits or under pressure of "somewhere". An illustration is the case of Ms. XZ:

Ms. XZ was trafficked to India by an elder uncle of her, a month after the birth of her first child. After ten years she managed to escape. Through the help of a Nepalese working as policeman in India she managed to reach home again. Her mother filed a complaint at the police-station. The trafficker was arrested but released after a few days: "As I heard the issue was politicised and he was protected by the ruling party. Also the local administrative authority threatened my mother just because of the complaint she made for me. They were saying that I was not her daughter." After a long argument the police took him in custody again, but again he was released from custody after 26 days with the pressure of the political party: "Many times I tried to put the case to court but always they said you don't have enough document to prove it. I don't know what they mean by enough document, because myself a case was there. So, my case is still in the local government office, but I do not have hope for justice with this case" (Casestudy prepared by WATCH/ Poudel, 1994).

One of the problems with controlling trafficking in Nepal is police behaviour and their working style, as a Senior Superintendent of the Nepalese Police pointed out. The police are neither trained to deal with crimes against women nor in appropriate ways to assist women. They do not take complaints seriously enough. There have been recent attempts to remedy this, such as establishing women police units and training police in how to investigate crimes against women. However, there are no government-run shelters, victim compensation or witness protection schemes. Women complainants are further intimidated by formal and bureaucratic procedures. Very few cases have resulted in convictions. In rural areas there are the additional constraints of isolation. For example, the Himalayas of Nepal are difficult to get into, the villagers are often scared of the police and there is no follow-up system to ensure the victim is secure.

Apart from offences incorporated in laws on prostitution, a range of other offences may be associated which can lead to prosecution, though in practice this seldom happens.
A report, for example, of the Australian Federal Police in 1995 (AFP, 1995) regarding groups engaged in the international recruitment and movement of South East Asian women to Australia for prostitution, describes a number of offences involved: organised crime groups make multi-million profits, much of it untaxed and moved offshore, forgery of documents, use of fraudulent documents, money laundering, official corruption, involvement of international criminal networks, health risk to Australian community, illegal immigration, kidnapping, violence. The report further states that there are indications of links to Triad societies, involved in drugs smuggling. Prostitution provides groups involved in drugs smuggling with finance, criminal associates in drug source and transit countries, transport via the frequent movement of prostitutes and their escorts, and access to distribution networks via organised crime contacts in Australia.
One of the problems in law enforcement that is mentioned is the ability of criminal syndicates to change their methods of operation to counter law enforcement efforts. Focusing of law enforcement and tightening of visa procedures in one region results in organisers finding other sources and methods of operation; they move, for example, to different countries for obtaining women. Another problem is the complexity of the cases, which makes prosecution difficult.

In theory, general provisions on violence could be applied to prosecute coercive recruitment practices. In Cambodia for example the UNCTAD law on criminal procedures penalises "any one who without orders from the judicial authority, arrests, detains or illegally confines a person". Such provision could be used to address trafficking, as illustrated by the case of Sokha, who was sold by her aunt in law to a brothel for $ 20 dollar. The accused was sentenced to two years imprisonment under art. 35 of the UNCTAD law, by lack of specific legislation on trafficking. Although some cases may be prosecuted, the "inadequate skills of both the judiciary and law-enforcers on dealing with the issue, the lack of specific legislation and uncertainty or ignorance on how to use the existing laws" prevent an effective approach of trafficking in women. Moreover, fears of prosecution of influential people who are allegedly involved in the sex trade further undermine every attempt to combat the practice. Police authorities state that they are powerless because both high ranking military and civil government officials are behind the business (Cambodia, 1996).

In different cities arrested traffickers are released after being warned not to do it again and asked to compensate the parents of the woman. Some cases are amicably set by courts and police authorities outside the legal framework of the law by compensation of the victim's parents. Another problem is the lack of complaints by the victims, due to the absence of legal provisions to protect and guarantee the safety of complainants and witnesses (Cambodia, 1996). It should be noted, that the fact that it is the parents of the woman who are compensated rather than the woman herself, reflects the concept of ownership of the woman.

In Zambia the law penalises any recruitment or transportation of women within or across national borders for work or services which, according to the Employment laws, do not comply with the regulations, holding that any contract of foreign service must be applied for. If a woman is trafficked with or without her consent for whatever service, the fact that this was not an approved contract of service by the relevant authorities, makes it an offence under the Employment laws. This includes the use of Zambian women for transporting drugs, prostitution, etc. There is no indication whether or not this provision is used in practice, nor if it is used to prosecute traffickers, or to prosecute the women involved (Zambia, no date).

3.4 Managing or organising prostitution

Prohibitions and regulations of this type may be classified into two categories:
- prohibitions relating to procuring, pimping or living off the earnings of prostitution, and
- prohibitions related to keeping, operating, managing or owning a brothel, making available premises for prostitution or furnishing a place for prostitution.

We will examine both categories one by one, with special attention to prohibitions relating to violence or abuse. In some cases prohibitions on violence act as aggravating circumstances to general prohibitions, in other cases organising or profiting from prostitution is only punishable when violence or abuse is used.

In some countries the law prohibits all prostitution-related activities or the organising of the prostitution of another under the heading of "Traffic of Women". This is for example the case in Malta, where under the Order for the Suppression of the White Slave Trade (1930) all forms of prostitution, accosting on a public highway, procurement and brothel keeping are an offence.
In Portugal any organising of the prostitution of another is defined as "trafficking" (Council of Europe, 1994a).

Procuring, pimping or living off the earnings of prostitution

In almost all countries procurement is criminalised: around 75 % of the respondents say that the law in their country prohibits procurement or pimping per se[19]. Prohibitions on procurement may criminalise "procurement", "pimping" and/or "living of the avails of prostitution".

19 The following countries prohibit procurement/pimping per se (according to the questionnaire and other documents); Canada, Australia, France, Belgium, Germany, UK, Switzerland, Italy, Spain, Norway, Finland, Bulgaria, Hungary, Slovenia, Ukraine, Poland, Czech Republic, Lithuania, Japan, China, India, Bangladesh, Thailand, Vietnam, Peru, Ecuador, Mexico, Bolivia, Brazil, Costa Rica, El Salvador, Guatemala, Nicaragua, Dutch Caribbean, Uganda, Kenya and Zambia

Especially prohibitions on living off the earnings of prostitution reinforce the social isolation of prostitutes through making it difficult for them to live with other persons, as these may be charged with procurement and living off the earnings of prostitution. This may be illustrated by Canada, where the Criminal Code penalises "procuring or living on the avails of prostitution", including partners, room mates and children who share a dwelling with a woman who works as a prostitute. Even if another source of income can be proven, the simple fact that one member of a household works as a prostitute can be held against any other member of that house as "living off the avails of prostitution":
While this law should have been intended to be used against pimps/procurers who parasitically exploit prostitutes for financial gain, it has been enforced frequently against innocent family members and friends of prostitutes (Sanghera, 1996).

In France, the very wide legal definition of procurement prevents any prostitute from living with the person of her choice as a partner:
One of the direct effects of the law is to reinforce the social isolation of prostitutes and to make them outcasts...However, a recent modification of the law was introduced in March 1993. Now, a man living with a prostitute and who can demonstrate sufficient independent income, is no longer considered as a pimp (Europap, 1995, p. 63).

In the UK, any adults who share a prostitute's income are subject to prosecution. In Italy, the "exploitation of prostitutes" is illegal, but unfortunately the family of prostitutes is also included in this category. The same applies to Belgium, where the husband of a prostitute may be prosecuted if he profits from her revenue, despite the fact that he has a job and his own income (Europap, 1995). At the same time, as we have already seen, prostitutes who work together may risk prosecution for procuration or pimping, as in France or Cyprus.

In India and Bangladesh living off the earnings of prostitution and procuring are prohibited under the Immoral Traffic Act. In India, living off the earnings of prostitution is presumed, until the contrary is proved, "when any person is proved to be living with or to be habitually in the company of a prostitute".

In most countries factors as the involvement of minors or persons under one's care, kinship relationships, the use of force, threat, deception or violence, and making a habit or profession of procurement, act as aggravating circumstances.

Keeping, managing or operating a brothel

In the majority of countries the criminal code contains an absolute ban on keeping, managing, operating, letting or hiring or furnishing a brothel/premises/a place for prostitution, though again the exact content and wordings may vary[20]. The use of coercion, illegal detention or violence

20 The following countries prohibit brothel-keeping per se (according to the questionnaire and other documents); Bangladesh, India, Thailand, Japan, Hong Kong, China, Vietnam, Philippines, Dutch Caribbean, Mexico, Peru, Uganda, Kenya, Hungary, Poland, Slovenia, Ukraine, Finland, Norway, Spain, UK, Italy, Cyprus and Canada.

and the involvement of minors, are generally viewed as aggravating circumstances, which are more severely penalised. In some cases brothel-keeping falls under provisions on "trafficking", as in India and Bangladesh, where brothel-keeping and detaining a person in premises where prostitution is carried on, with or without consent, is prohibited under the Immoral Traffic Act.

It is worth noting that in some countries procuring or living off immoral earnings is more severely penalised than brothel-keeping, as for instance in the UK. Here, the maximum penalty on living off immoral earnings or controlling prostitutes is seven years, on procuration two years and on brothel-keeping six months.

The fact that brothels are prohibited does not mean that they do not exist. On the contrary, in many countries brothels are simultaneously prohibited and highly regulated and controlled through different laws and state agencies, such as the police, courts and local administration. The situation in Bangladesh could be taken as an illustration. Though brothels are prohibited, various reports relate about the police exercising control over the brothel activities, directly as well as indirectly through the brothel managers and agents, or as regular clients. Connections between brothel owners and the local and national level politics are common:

Both the brothel business of prostitution and its affiliated businesses are "prohibited", therefore necessitating a special linkage with state agencies as well as with local level politics. The interests of the brothel business are safeguarded through the owners by regular contracted payments to the police at higher, middle and local levels and also by such regular payments to the customs and excise department. Also we have found that the house owners are very closely connected with the local and national level politics (Khan, 1992, p.47).

Police violence and abuse are common in brothels, varying from extortion of money to psychological, physical and sexual violence (kicking, beating, rape) and extortion of free sexual services:

Josna, a twenty-seven years old prostitute in Tanbazar, narrated various forms of police torture and extortion that she faces and had to face. Police often raid the brothel on the pretext of picking up underage girls. Apart from this the police indiscriminately picks up prostitutes on different excuses and extorts money and sexual gratification from them. Josna was picked up six times in a period of two months and was used sexually by policemen, in addition to having to spend up to Tk. 6,000 to Tk. 7,000 for getting "released". Josna and others often have to accept policemen as customers who do not pay for the services received (Khan, 1992, p.66).

Women are regularly harassed by the police and forced to pay considerable amounts of money in order to escape arrest or being sent to the police station where even worse abuse can take place:

If the "arrested" women fail to pay or fail sexually to gratify the policemen, they are taken to the police-station where again they are subjected to physical and sexual torture. Failing to satisfy the authorities in cash or in kind leads to a transfer to the courts for confinement and punishment. Usually the court decrees confinement for brief periods of seven to ten days. In the courts, the prostitutes or their pimps have line-ups with the "muhuri". On payment, the "muhuri" arranges for the release of the women or for shorter terms in jail. On an average, a prostitute has to spend about taka 300-400 on the police and around taka 100 on the "muhuri" for release from police custody (Khan, 1992, p.211).

Where active attempts are undertaken to ban brothels, they result mainly in brothels going underground and arbitrary arrest of the prostitutes, as the following example from the Philippines illustrates:

The City Major in Manila banned clubs, bars and massage parlours in the City. As a result the owners and operators moved to nearby places. The vacated places in Ermita are now occupied by prostitution establishments disguised as beer gardens. The City Ordinance has been circumvented by the owners and operators, who always remain scot-free whenever policemen conduct law enforcement operations. The women victims are the ones usually caught, penalised and jailed (BATIS, 1996a). *Some City officials in the National Capital Region are actively enforcing the laws against prostitution. The raiding operations they conduct in night spots, beer-gardens and massage parlours apprehend only the women and not the operators and the owners* (BATIS, 1996b).

Also Thailand has not been very successful. According to a report of Images Asia, action is restricted to periodic crackdowns on the child sex industry and placing temporary restrictions upon the operators of brothels:

Following these crackdowns, brothels have merely changed their surface appearance, and have continued to function as before. Some put up the thinly veiled facade of being karaoke restaurants, teashops, pubs etc....Such establishments still have to maintain connections with local Thai officials who still ask for bribe money to allow illegal Burmese women to work there...Central government policy simply becomes an excuse for local Thai officials to ask for "protection money" to guard the security of unlawful business (Images Asia, 1995, p.9).

The brothel owners in their turn use the payment of "protection money" as a reason for cutting the income of the sex-workers.

Reports from Kenya (Sunday Standard, 1996/East African Standard, 1996), relate of country-wide police crackdowns on prostitution, aimed at curbing the increasing number of prostitutes in towns, "resulting in the arrest of 3,000 suspects" (that is: prostitutes). Many of them were subjected to forced STD tests. Most of them were charged with various offences including prostitution, loitering with immoral intentions and failing to seek medical treatment.

Other charges were dependent of the outcome of the medical tests. Those found to be STD positive were arraigned in court. However, no action was taken against the (massage parlours) licensing department, parlour/brothel owners or any of the men involved. Brothel operators easily manage to escape the police. When the pressure is strong and making buy-outs impossible, they go underground for a while or change locations (Weekend Mail, 1993). All in all, "there seems little reason to believe that the incidence of prostitution has been seriously reduced by the criminal law enforcement, although the forms in which it is conducted have altered" (Kenya, 1996).

Despite prohibitions on brothels, it is generally the prostitutes who are caught and detained. In Peru, thousands of women working clandestinely are detained monthly, without any action taken against the brothel owners (Domingo Traspasso, 1996). The same mechanism is reported by NGOs in various other countries, like in Colombia and the Dominican Republic. According to a report of the Dominican NGO COIN, it is only the prostitutes who are suppressed, but not prostitution itself, the clients, the middlemen or the brothel owners:
For the law-enforcement authorities, the tourist industry, the rum & cigarette trade and prostitution form part of a lucrative business. Impunity of violence and abuse of prostitutes characterise the official policies (Ferreira, 1996, p.9).

At the same time, prohibitions on brothel keeping necessarily criminalise the relationship between a prostitute and a brothel manager, forcing them to deny their business relationship, and denying prostitutes any workers' rights, including the right of access to social and medical services. Prostitutes cannot sue the brothel manager (or the client) when they are not paid according to agreement, since in many countries any legal contract is considered as offending good morals and therefore invalid. The situation in Germany may serve as an example:
In contrast to the civil rights afforded to other professional businesses, no similar protection is given to the profession of prostitution in Germany. The business' fundamental premise - the agreement to provide a sexual service in return for payment - offends the moral basis of the rules of the German Civil Code and is, therefore, not regarded as valid. Conflicting criminal laws also mean that it is not possible to conclude regular employment contracts. This leads to the total absence of social security (Europap, 1995, p.99).

In some countries any contract regarding prostitution is explicitly criminalised, like in Japan, where the law prohibits any contract to make a person prostitute herself.

For migrant women it is even more difficult to get paid according to agreement, due to their illegal status. An illustration forms the situation of Burmese sex workers in Thailand:
Unfortunately, they can seldom get a proper income from their work because the income depends on the whims of the brothel owners, not on a law or contract. Interviews with many Burmese sex workers, as well as those of other nationalities working in Thailand, make it clear that it is almost impossible for sex workers to speak with the brothel owners about their rightful income. No Burmese sex worker can get the full of her rightful income because the brothel owners do not feel obliged to give them more than a "Burmese" (i.e.: lower than Thai women) income (Images Asia, 1995, p.8).

In many countries brothel-keeping is formally prohibited, but in practice more or less regulated or legalised, for example through paying taxes or through a more or less formalised licensing system, as in Colombia, the Dutch Caribbean, The Netherlands and Germany.

Laws may be established on different levels and be contradictory. In Colombia, laws and regulations laid down on national, departmental and municipality levels, present various contradictions. The National Code of Police of Colombia does not prohibit prostitution and authorises other institutions on regional level to regulate it. However the District Code of Police prohibits in any part of the national territory establishments "which nature is principally or secondarily to practise prostitution", whilst at the same time the Planning Department of the Districts Council of Bogota accepts the existence of brothels and permits them officially in certain areas. Such contradiction in laws is the reason that prostitution is practised under the camouflage of bars, canteens, residences, hotels, cafes, saunas, dancings, motels and apartments (Polania Molina, 1996).

In some countries brothels are regulated through an official licensing system, like in Turkey and in Curaçao. In Curaçao, prostitution is controlled through various regulations. In Campo Alegre registration and control of women takes place under the supervision of a special police department, in conjunction with the Public Health Departments and the Immigration Department. Non-national women can apply for a licence to work in Campo Alegre for a certain period. In St. Martin special regulations exist for the "Japanese Club", whereas other prostitution houses for the local population operate clandestinely. According to Kempadoo, describing the situation in the Dutch Caribbean, brothels are tolerated as long as they do not cause any nuisance or disruption to the broader society, while turning a blind eye to malpractice and coercion in the business (Kempadoo, 1995).

DECEIT, ABUSE AND COERCION

In some countries the law contains special provisions on abusive or coercive procurement. Such is the case in Uganda, where - apart from the provision on living off the earnings of prostitution - para. 126 of the Penal Code provides against "procuring the defilement of or carnal connection with a woman by threats, intimidation, false pretences or false representations, or by applying or administering to or causing to be taken by any woman any drug, matter or thing with intent to stupefy or overpower, so as thereby to enable any person to have unlawful carnal connection with such woman". However, the provision also imports the requirement for the evidence of one witness to be corroborated, which makes prosecution under this provision extremely difficult (Butegwa, 1996).

In a number of countries-brothel keeping as such is not an offence, but the law prohibits brothel keeping with the use of coercion, deception or violence, as in Germany. In other countries brothel-keeping is formally an offence, but prosecution only takes place in case of coercion, deceit, violence or other abusive practices, as in The Netherlands.

In Germany brothel-keeping is an offence only when a person is kept in personal or economic dependence. In The Netherlands, operating a brothel is tolerated as long as no coercion, violence or deceit is used, though the Penal Code officially still prohibits brothel-keeping as such[21]. Some municipalities require brothels to have a kind of informal licence, in other cities they are tolerated as long as they comply with regulations on public order, etc. In Belgium any exploitation of prostitution is prohibited. In practice, legal action is only taken where there is

[21] A bill to remove the absolute ban on brothel-keeping from the Penal Code, to be replaced with a provision that prohibits any form of managing a prostitution business with the use of coercion, violence or deceit, is in preparation.

evidence that the landlord seeks to make a profit from this commerce by charging an excessively high rent, whereby the definition of excessive gain depends on the police department involved (Europap, 1995). Remarkably enough, the Antwerp City Council provides itself with a substantial source of revenue from prostitution through the application of a so-called "rendezvous tax" on bars, clubs, cabarets, windows, rooms and rendezvous hotels (hotels used by street workers). Officially this tax has to be paid by the operators of the place, in practice it is paid by the prostitutes, either directly or through the bar owners who charge the them for the "extra costs" they have to make. Nonetheless, paying taxes does not give the women any rights nor safeguards them against the risk of being arrested, e.g. for soliciting [22].

In some countries the law provides against "illegal detention with sexual intent", as in Uganda. Section 129 of the Penal Code Act prohibits illegal detainment for the purpose of sexual intercourse, stating that "a person is deemed to have unlawfully detained another person when he, with the intent to induce him or her to remain in that place or brothel, withholds from a person any wearing apparel or other property belonging to the person detained, or where wearing apparel has been lent or supplied by that person, such person in any matter threatens the other person if he or she takes away the wearing apparel".

Other prohibitions

Non-prostitution (and non-gender) related provisions on illegal confinement, compulsion, extortion, debt bondage, slavery, etc., which would apply to the situations of forced labour & slavery-like practices as defined and described in this report, can be found in the criminal codes of all countries. Moreover, in many countries, the law contains special provisions on forced labour and slavery. However, there is no indication that such provisions are used to combat such practices in prostitution.

The Japanese Penal Code for instance prohibits compulsion, defined as "intimidating a person with threat or injury to his life, person, liberty, reputation or property or using violence against another in order to force him to perform an act which he is not bound to perform or obstruct him from exercising a right to which he is entitled". Art. 5 of the Labour Standard Law prohibits forced labour in general under penalty of one to ten years imprisonment: "an employer shall not force workers to work against their will by means of violence, intimidation, confinement, or any other unfair restraint on the mental or physical freedom of the workers". The article is based on article 18 of the Constitution, which says that anyone should be free from slavery-like confinement and forced labour. However, the article does not apply to forced labour in prostitution. Forced prostitution is separately prohibited by the Prostitution Prevention Law, defined as "forcing another person to engage in prostitution by intimidation or violence"[23] and is strikingly enough much less severely punished than forced labour (maximum three years).

22 Personal communication of a worker of the Belgian support organization Payoke to the authors.
23 Apparently it does not address conditions of forced labour in prostitution, but only forcing somebody to enter prostitution.

In Bangladesh, the Penal Code prohibits slavery and forced labour, defined as "importing, exporting, removing, buying, selling or disposing of any person as a slave or accepting, receiving or detaining against his will a person as a slave". In Mexico, the Constitution prohibits slavery, defined as forcing another person to render personal services without proper reward and without his consent.

Also the Constitution of Uganda prohibits the holding of any person in slavery or servitude, whereas the Penal Code Act prohibits the trade in and export or import of persons for purposes of slavery:
Where women are made to work in slave-like conditions or are denied the right to choose their conditions of work, s. 243, which makes it an offence to compel a person to labour against their will, would be very useful (Butegwa, 1996, p.12).

In practice, most of the provisions in the Penal Code related to trafficking and slavery-like practices are merely in the statute-books without much practical relevance:
In most cases, no prosecutions, let alone convictions have arisen out of them, mostly due to the nature of the offences and the evidence needed to prove cases...Complaints are in most cases dismissed or ignored as rubbish, or investigations are discontinued when the police realise what the complainants do for a living (Butegwa, 1996, p.12).

A major obstacle in the application of the various provisions in both the Penal Code and labour laws, is the fact that prostitution is not regarded as legitimate employment. As worded by Butegwa:
Generally it is believed that were prostitution not outlawed, then some of the Penal Code Act provisions could be used by women who are trafficked or who work in slave-like conditions to their benefit or redress (Butegwa, 1996, p. 11).

4 Prohibitions and regulations aimed at migrant women

Within this section we will review more extensively the situation of migrant women working in prostitution. In some countries it is not possible for migrant women to work in prostitution on a legal basis. Other countries provide legal possibilities under certain conditions. In some countries migrant women who are married to a national are allowed to work in prostitution, other countries allow prostitution by migrant women under a tourist or artist visa, or issue working permits for prostitution. At the same time, most countries have provisions which penalise illegal entry and/or stay, whereas in some cases (especially in the former Warsaw Pact countries) the illegal exit from the country is also penalised. Since the impact of these regulations and prohibitions is directly related to the position of migrant prostitutes and their possibilities to defend themselves against trafficking and forced labour & slavery-like practices as defined for this report, we will successively discuss the various conditions, followed by a separate section pertaining to their impact.

4.1 No possibility to work on a legal basis

Almost 55 % of the respondents state that it is not possible for migrant women to work on a legal basis [24].

In Turkey for example, though it has a legalised brothel system, migrant women are not allowed to engage in prostitution, since Turkish citizenship is required for prostitutes (ASI, 1993). Foreign women working as prostitutes in Turkey are deported, as is any foreigner encouraging or mediating in prostitution (Council of Europe, 1994). Migrant women found working as prostitutes in the UK, are liable to deportation under the power of the Immigration Act relating to Unauthorised Employment: any person, who "gains entry to the country lawfully, but who subsequently overstays her leave or breaches conditions attached to it, or who takes unauthorised employment, may be deported". If they entered the country illegally, they may be removed as illegal entrants. (Council of Europe, 1994a).

In Thailand, there are two methods for Burmese to get permission from local Thai officials for a temporary stay in Thailand:

In 1994 the Thai Ministry of Labor and Social Welfare guaranteed work permits for Burmese working in ten Thai border provinces. Laborers associated with a Thai firm can get documents for a year-long temporary stay in Thailand, as long as their boss, or the business official concerned, guarantees the continuation of their job in that particular firm or industry. However,

In most cases, sex workers do not have any kind of direct connection with the Thai officials or any access to identity documents to state that they are Thai, or that they can legally work in Thailand. On behalf of the sex workers, brothel owners and agents create an understanding with the officials by giving them bribe money, which is calculated in accordance with the number of sex workers in an establishment. Five hundred Baht ($20) per sex-worker per month, is a common "fee". However, the understanding is not made between the sex-workers and the officials, which is why the sex-workers may be arrested if there is a crackdown on brothels. Sometime the brothel owner or agent even asks the police make the arrests. This kind of arrest happens often when the owners or agents do not want to give the sex-workers the money that they owe them (Images Asia, 1995, 4/5).

Some countries like the US, Japan, Turkey and Cyprus, explicitly exclude prostitutes from legal emigration or immigration. In Cyprus the Aliens and Immigration Law provides that "any prostitute or any person living on the proceeds of prostitution are prohibited immigrants and are not permitted to enter the country. These persons having entered the country, are ordered to be deported" (Council of Europe, 1994a). In Turkey prostitutes are barred from entering the country under the Passport Act (Council of Europe, 1994). Also in the United States foreign women with a prostitution record can be refused entry (Pheterson, 1996). In Uganda, the Immigration Act prohibits certain classes of immigrants from entering Uganda. These include prostitutes and those living off the earnings of prostitutes. The same Act provides for the deportation of such prohibited immigrants. Contrary to the cardinal rules regarding burden of

[24] Countries where it is not possible for migrant women to work in prostitution on a legal basis are (based on the questionnaire and reports): Nepal, Pakistan, Japan, Thailand, Philippines, Vietnam, Taiwan, Canada, Ukraine, Italy, Turkey, Spain, Mexico, Bulgaria, China, Belgium, Slovenia, Poland, Cyprus and UK.

proof, the onus is put on the prohibited immigrant to prove that she or he is not a prostitute or was not living on the earnings of prostitution prior to entry in Uganda (Butegwa, 1996).

4.2 Possibility to work on a legal basis under certain conditions

Around 40 % of the respondents answer that it is possible for migrant women to work in prostitution on a legal basis under certain conditions[25]. The conditions mentioned by respondents pertain to:

- marriage
- tourist or artist visa
- work permit

In a number of countries, amongst others Finland, The Netherlands, Switzerland, Germany and Australia, migrant women are allowed to work in prostitution if they are married to a national, which entitles them to reside legally in the country. In such cases, the authorities may check if the foreign woman lives together with her husband. When it is found otherwise, the woman can be deported. Her residence permit is (at least during three to five years) dependent on the marriage. In case of divorce she will lose the right to stay and risk being deported.

Some countries allow women to work in prostitution for a maximum period of three months on a tourist visa, although it is formally prohibited to work on a tourist visa. This is for instance the case in some cities in The Netherlands.

Another possibility is working on an artist visa. Generally, the visa is officially issued to work as a dancer or model, but this often acts as a cover for prostitution. Sometimes this is completely illegal, sometimes the authorities are acquainted with this construction but allow it unofficially. For example in Switzerland cabaret dancers are entitled to obtain a residence permit for eight months per calendar year. In December 1992, there were 1,239 cabaret dancers resident in Switzerland, often recruited by artist agencies in different countries (Council of Europe, 1994a).

As far as is known, only in the Dutch Caribbean are working permits issued for sex work.
In Surinam, for example, foreign women entering the country to work as prostitutes are given a six month work permit. In Aruba, bar/hotel owners are legally allowed to employ two or three non-Aruban female sex workers up to three months. Registration with the police department and weekly medical controls are mandatory. Curaçao has set up a well-developed application and work permit system to allow foreign women to work for a limited period in Campo Alegre. The permit is issued for six months. To be allowed to work, women must be in possession of a valid passport/visa, a health report, four photographs, a return ticket and work permit. They must register with the police as a prostitute immediately on arrival. Registration with the police and

25 The following countries allow migrant women to work on a legal basis in prostitution, according to respondents of the questionnaire: Hong Kong, Curaçao, Mexico, Ecuador, Peru, Dominican Republic, Switzerland, The Netherlands, Germany, Finland, Czech Republic, Australia. In some cases, respondents from the same country are of a different opinion regarding this question, as in Bangladesh, India, Canada, Italy and Mexico.

weekly medical checks are obligatory. Campo Alegre is exclusively for non-Antillian women. Local women are allowed to work in a number of hotels in Willemstad, but not in Campo Alegre. Women must apply to the Immigration Department. The administration, screening and selection of candidates, and the issue of work permits is done by the police. This is free of charge and dependent of available places. Since the mid 1980's however, the existence of recruiting agents is signalled, who charge the women for their services or who add costs to other expenses and debts owed by the women to the club owners (Kempadoo, 1995).

4.3 Crossing borders illegally

In many countries not only the third party organising, aiding or abetting the illegal entry (and/or the illegal employment) of another person, but also the illegal alien him or herself is liable to punishment. This is the case in most European countries, North America and Canada (IGC, 1995). Due to the desire of the rich countries in particular to deter "illegal migration", and to combat "alien smuggling" or "trafficking of aliens", migration laws and policies[26] have become more and more repressive over the last years. Migrants who enter or stay illegally may be punished with imprisonment and/or fines, varying from six months imprisonment (Denmark, The Netherlands, Norway, UK) to one year (Belgium, France, Germany) or two years (Canada, Italy).

Not only illegal entry into the country may make women punishable, in some countries it is also against the law to leave the country without permission from the relevant authorities or valid documents. One example is Burma, where the Immigration and Manpower Act prohibits illegally leaving the country. Also in Poland and in a number of other former socialist countries, it is against the law to leave the country without a valid passport. For migrant women this means that they are not only punishable as illegal foreigners in the destination countries, but also on return to their home country for having departed illegally. This happened for example to Joanna, a Polish girl, who was trafficked to The Netherlands when she was seventeen, along with three other girls:

After pressing charges Joanna went back to Poland. On her arrival at Warsaw airport, she immediately was interviewed by the police on charges of having left the country illegally on a false passport. They let her go, but told her that they would come back to call her to account. Later, the police visited her relatives a number of times, looking for her. For fear of the police as well as her (Polish/German) traffickers, and lacking any support from her relatives, Joanna fled back to The Netherlands. After a long procedure and initial rejections, she obtained a Dutch residence permit on humanitarian grounds. However, even after four years she still has no identity papers. The Polish Embassy refuses to issue her a passport, because she has committed an offence according to Polish law. The fact that, at the moment of her departure from Poland, she was convinced that the passport the agent had arranged for her was a valid one makes no difference[27].

[26] Also called "trafficking legislation": see for example IGC, December 1995, "Summary description of legislation on aliens trafficking". This document contains an overview of legislation in the fifteen participating States of the Inter-Governmental Consultation (IGC) to deter illegal migration, i.e. provisions on alien smuggling, aiding and abetting illegal entry, the production of fraudulent documents, employers sanctions for hiring illegal workers, carrier sanctions for transporting illegal aliens, and confiscation and for feiture of prosperity used in connection with alien smuggling.

[27] Personal experience of one of the authors in her capacity as worker of the Foundation Against Trafficking in Women (STV) in The Netherlands.

4.4 Impact

Policies concerning immigration and possibilities for obtaining a legal residence or work permit, strongly influence the living and working conditions of migrant sex workers, their vulnerability to violence and abuse and their control by criminal networks. As concluded in the evaluation report of a transnational project on AIDS/STD prevention among migrant prostitutes in Europe: *These differences (in immigration policies) also increase their marginalization, and facilitate possibilities for exploitation, dependency, and control by criminal organizations. In particular, the severity of regulations enacted in Europe against non-Europeans directly influences the basic living and working conditions of clandestine migrant sex workers. Those who are clandestine and work in closed prostitution (apartments, window brothels, sex clubs) remain constantly within the same milieu. Since they rarely, if ever, have an opportunity to leave the context of work of the sex industry, their lifestyle is one of severe isolation and marginalization, with damaging consequences to physical and mental well-being... The possibilities for sex workers to have optimal control over their sexual services and the promotion of their health in general, is determined more by the control they have over their working and living conditions, and by their legal status in Europe, than by their cultural and national background* (Brussa, 1996, p.7).

A woman who works in the EU on a marriage-based residence permit is, at least during three to five years, fully dependent on her husband. In case of trafficking or forced labour, she has no means of escape, since leaving her husband implies that she loses her right to stay and risks deportation. In many countries, especially in Western Europe, marriage with a national is in fact the only way for women to acquire a legal residence permit. As a result they may be made to pay large amounts of money for sham marriages, either to their "husbands" or to middlemen. If a woman refuses to pay or to subject herself to abuse, the "husband" can simply threaten to report her to the Aliens police. Another common trick is to threaten the woman to "leave" her just before the end of the three or five years period, unless she is willing to pay again and again considerable amounts of money. Laws to combat sham marriages, introduced in many European countries over the last ten years, have mainly resulted in driving up prices women are charged and in criminal organizations finding other ways to bring in women.

In the same way, women who work illegally on an artist or tourist visa, expose themselves to arrest and expulsion the moment they seek help from the police in case of violence or abuse. Even when they work on a legal visa, as in Switzerland, the women are highly dependent on nightclub owners and agencies, because of the limited duration of their residential and work permits. According to Spring (1992) "they have no opportunity to defend themselves against poor working conditions, fraudulent settlements of accounts, humiliating treatment or even violence, if they want to continue to work as dancers".

In most countries, illegal migrant women have no access to health or social services, whether in Europe or in other parts of the world. Images Asia for example reports Burmese women in Thailand to be afraid to seek medical help for fear that someone might inform the police to arrest her (Images Asia, 1996).

Lack of access to an independent residence and working permit makes women not only dependant of traffickers, husbands and abusive employers, but also of border and law enforcement officials, who co-operate with agents and brothel- keepers, as is illustrated by several reports from India, Bangladesh, Thailand, Pakistan and Burma:
Indian agents have good networks in both Bangladesh and Nepal and extremely well organised rapport with police and the judiciary. Law enforcement officials, border security and police take bribes. If women or children are caught in raids, they are generally released to false parents or family members coming from the agents, which take custody with the help of police and lawyers, to be brought back to the brothels (Action for Reach Out Newsletter, 1995).

In Bangladesh the leader of one of the trafficking networks in the border areas is reported to make all the required arrangements with border forces. Women and children are divided in small groups and brought to a secret hiding place. From there they cross the border to India by night and are handed over to the Indian agents:
If disagreements with border officials arise or when they are not sufficiently paid in advance, arrests are made, but the worst victims are usually the women and the children. They are the ones subjected to police harassment, while the agents escape in the meantime, being well aware of the situation (Shamin, 1995, p.13).

A 30 years old woman from Bangladesh, who was trafficked to Pakistan when she was twenty-seven, relates how she, along with 50 to 60 girls and 25 to 30 men from different parts of Bangladesh, was brought to Pakistan:
We were taken to a secluded place in the jungle before crossing the border to Pakistan under police custody. The border officials kept the girls who were pretty and sexually abused them until the other lots of girls came, then the previous ones were released (LHRLA, 1991).

In Pakistan various brothels have been discovered in the slums in Karachi, where trafficked women and children are confined:
At times police raid these dens, usually when their bhatta or protection money is stopped by the den operators. It is alleged that the border security forces of all the three countries - Bangladesh, India and Pakistan - are involved (Shamin, 1995, p.14).

Burmese and Thai officials are reported to connive at or even to be involved in trafficking of Burmese women to Thailand and to protect practices of forced labour in Thai brothels, as documented in a report of an Australian Government Committee with regard to the situation in Burma:
Agents have very sophisticated arrangements with the Thai police. In many instances, the girls could document instances of being transported into Thailand with policemen in uniform, armed and often in police vehicles. Once in Thailand the brothels are under protection and had the patronage of the police. One of the girls tells that *she saw the police in all the brothels where she worked.
They seemed to know the owners very well and were often around with their uniforms, guns and walkie-talkies. They also often took the girls to the rooms or out for the whole night. In Klong Yai the police had special arrangements with the owner and could take the girls for free* (Australia, 1995, p.49).

The report continues:
Women and girls from Burma who are victims of trafficking are arrested as prostitutes or illegal immigrants, detained in penal servitude in reform institutions. They suffer mistreatment, abuse and extortion in detention and are deported with little concern for the consequences of their return to Burma (Australia, 1995, p.50).

When women are arrested, they are either deported or jailed. This way, thousands of women end up in jails, often under appalling circumstances, sometimes for years and without hope of release. If they have no identity papers, they may be denied citizenship of both their country of origin and the country to which they were trafficked. In some cases, agents and pimps make use of the immigration policies to dispose of women that are unruly or to avoid payment.

Reports of the Bangladesh National Women Lawyers Association (BNWLA), mention several cases of victims of trafficking who, after being arrested by the police - either before they were brought out of the country, or on their return from India or Pakistan to Bangladesh - are taken into so-called"safe custody":
Safe custody prisoners are usually victims that are kept in jails because the court or any other competent authority decides it to be in their best interest. However, while safe custody prisoners are ideally supposed to be kept separately from convicted or under trial prisoners, this is not practices in reality. Many victimised women and children are thus further abused by being kept in overcrowded prison cells, subjected to supervision by male officials and guards trained to manage criminals, and exposed to the detrimental influence of criminals (BNWLA, 1995, p.3).

Also in India thousands of Bengal and Nepalese women are held in jails and shelter homes in different parts of India. One of them is Hamida, a twelve year old Bengal girl, who was trafficked to India when she was ten. In addition several policemen raped her repeatedly till she was able to escape from her trafficker two years later:
Hamida now is detained at Tihar jail in Delhi "in safe custody" for already two years. The young girl would like to leave the place but cannot find a way out. The five policemen have been released on bail. So far they have not been prosecuted. The trial against two of the three traffickers is repeatedly obstructed, amongst other things, due to the repeated absence of the public prosecutor.
Meanwhile Hamida's interpreter and sole support was removed as translator for 'developing a sympathetic corner for the victim' and is not allowed contact with Hamida any more following a Court order. Arrangements to send her back to her parents can only be made after instructions from the Home Ministry. Just two years ago, the Bengal high commission refused to admit her as their citizen. Now they admit she is from Bangladesh (The Times of India July 25, 1995/ reports of BNWLA, 1995).

In Switzerland and Italy, hundreds of Dominican women are detained in jail. Dominican women whose residence permit is expired are arrested by the Italian and Swiss police during raids on night-clubs and detained (El Nacional, 1995). According to the IOM (IOM, 1996a), the majority of women is given a false identity in legal certificates and passports as a strategy used by traffickers to avoid legal problems both in the country of origin and the country of destination.

Women cannot make a complaint legally or ask to be repatriated because they are using a "non-existent" identity. In case of disappearance, the false identity will facilitate things for the trafficker. Other Dominican women are deported from Spain and Greece to the Dominican Republic after being caught by the police or reported by the traffickers themselves in order to avoid payment to the women. Many trafficked women cannot return because they do not have the financial means, are drug or alcohol dependent or are in prison.

In countries where prostitution is an offence in itself, as in Pakistan and Japan, women can be arrested and detained both as illegal alien and as prostitute. Even if laws are formally designed to criminalise procurers and pimps, they end up in being used to arrest the women instead of the offenders.

According to reports from Pakistan more than 2,500 Bengal women and children are held in different jails in Pakistan under the Hudood Ordinance and Illegal Entry Act, whilst their offenders go free (BNWLA, 1995). Most of them are between twelve and thirty:

When there are police raids, many women and children are arrested, while the main culprits are left behind. The victims are sent to jail under the Immigration Act and Hudood Ordinance and are detained. The pimps with the help of jail authorities meet these victims and assure them that they are their only saviours and no one would come to their rescue. But once they are released they have to obey the pimps. Victims who have been released on bail through these pimps are again trapped in the same vicious circle. Some detainees are further detained, despite completing their detention period (Shamin, 1995, p.16).

Powerful brokers and agents make it difficult for anyone else to get these women and children out of jail. In December 1989, the Lawyers for Human Rights and Legal Aid, prepared a list of 62 Bengal women detained in Karachi Central Jail (LHRLA, 1991). Most had been in prison for more than three years and were facing charges for illegal entry, border crossing and illegal stay in Pakistan. Among them were many minor girls and children, all in the most horrific of situations:

The majority of the women did not have any lawyers to represent them and there was no external support to deal with their cases or provide them with basic necessities in jail. They were incessantly under pressure of touts who were very influential and having support of the local police, compelling them to come out with their effort to involve them after release again in prostitution (Shamin, 1995, p. 16, based on a report of Shahid and Khan, 1990).

In Japan, immigrant women are charged under the Prostitution Prevention Act, given a suspended sentence and deported. The Prostitution Prevention Act was enacted to fulfil Japan's obligations under the 1949 Convention and criminalises soliciting, procuring of a client for a prostitute, deceiving or forcing someone into becoming a prostitute and profiting from prostitution (GAATW, 1996). In its application, the law punishes trafficked women and ignores the syndicates:

Lea worked as a prostitute in Manila. A recruiter approached her and offered her a job in a club in Japan. In Japan she was sold to the YAKUSA and forced to work without pay. When one day she refused to have sex with her employer, he locked her up for two months and denied her enough food. During her detainment she was gang raped. Finally she managed to escape and reported to the police.

The police invited her employer to the police-station for questioning, but after a few minutes he left the station again. Lea saw her employer giving money to the policemen. The police reported Lea to the immigration for overstaying and she was deported (BATIS, 1996a).

Women, arrested by immigration control authorities on charges of immigration law violations (e.g. overstaying visa, working illegally, not possessing proper travel documentation) are deported from Japan under compulsion. During the procedures they are kept in detention. Due to the immigration policy, which stipulates that an alien must bear his or her own departure expenses, detention may be extended over an indefinable period of time until the alien acquires sufficient funds to return to his/her country of origin. The Japanese Immigration Review Taskforce reports several human rights violations against foreign nationals during their detention (Onitsuka, 1995). Protection of the rights of foreigners who undergo criminal investigations or interrogations is extremely insufficient. Sexual harassment, rape and sexual assaults by officials against detained foreign women in detention centres are reported frequently.

In most countries, illegal migrant women are deported without any investigation and regardless of whether or not they are a victim of trafficking or forced labour & slavery-like practices.
An illustration forms this interview with a representative of the Canadian Immigration Department:
"If any illegal migrant prostitute were involved in any activities prohibited by any laws (civil, criminal or otherwise) and a complaint or arrest was placed, then that person would be deported". When asked about the circumstances, for example whether, if the woman was trafficked, abused or violated in any way while in the country, she could press charges, the answer was a clear no: ""any involvement" includes being victim of a crime - she would be deported" (Sanghera, 1996, p.8).

In Taiwan migrant women are arrested and charged with illegal entry under the Disruption of Social Order Act and criminal law. No effort is made to find out if they are trafficked, or to prosecute the traffickers (GAATW, 1996).

In the UK, the development of a "system to identify migrant women as possible prostitutes at the border" and the removal of prostitutes under the immigration legislation, is viewed as a way to contain the problem of trafficking:
The Immigration Service points out that, in the case of prostitutes working for the Triad, it is difficult to obtain evidence against brothel managers and secure convictions [....]. It is for this reason that joint police/Immigration Service operations have been thought to be the best way of containing that particular problem. By removing prostitutes under the immigration legislation, the UK has been able to contain the problem to an extent. Greater international collaboration by all enforcement agencies working in this field might lead to prostitutes being identified and refused entry at the ports (Council of Europe, 1994a, p.53).

Exceptions to the policy of automatic expulsion are found in The Netherlands and in Belgium, where as a result of intensive NGO lobbying, women who press charges of trafficking are entitled to a temporary staying-permit during criminal proceedings. In The Netherlands, according to a special ruling in the Dutch Immigration Law a woman should be allowed time to consider pressing charges in the presence of the least indication of trafficking. When she has done so she should be allowed to stay in The Netherlands until the whole juridical process has been completed (Aliens Circular, Chapter B17).

In Australia, according to the report of the Committee on Foreign Affairs of the Australian Government, 120 illegal prostitutes were apprehended between 1992 and 1995, although "figures are in no way representative, since women evade detection". The women are in breach of immigration laws and therefore they are liable to visa cancellation, removal, deportation or prosecution. Those who are detained under the Migration Act are accommodated in Immigration Detention Centres, where medical assessments and female interpreters are supplied: "Those being deported are only held for a couple of days while travel arrangements are made. If women apply for a protection visa, they are not held in detention and they receive a bridging visa and are usually granted permission to work" (Australia, 1995, p.52).

Even when prostitution is "legal" for local women, its practice by foreign women may be ground for expulsion, as is the case in Germany, where a foreign woman may be deported on grounds of prostitution unless she is married to a German national. Comparable double standards regarding prostitution by nationals and by migrant women are applied in The Netherlands. As a result of the changing view on prostitution as work, the police in most cities now require migrant women to have a work permit, where before they accepted women to work on a tourist or artist visa. At the same time, however, it is prohibited by law to issue work permits for prostitution. Consequently, women who fell victim to trafficking and/or forced labour & slavery-like

practices but wish to continue working as prostitutes cannot turn to the police without giving up their source of income. Moreover, they still risk deportation the moment the penal proceedings have finished.

In general it must be concluded that, with no legal residence and working permit and the constant risk of arrest and expulsion, migrant women are compelled to work in the worst conditions, without defence against abusive agents, brothel-keepers and corrupt officials. Their position doesn't allow them to lodge a complaint in case of trafficking and/or forced labour & slavery-like practices. If they nevertheless dare to do so, they face immediate deportation (with the exception ofThe Netherlands and Belgium) or arrest and detention as illegal aliens or prostitutes. Even women who independently migrated for prostitution are, by virtue of their illegal status, forced to rely on malafide or criminal organizations. The risk of arrest, either as prostitute or as illegal alien, makes it virtually impossible for women to defend themselves against violence and abuse and to notify the police or to press charges in case of trafficking or forced labour & slavery-like practices.

5 Summary of legal definitions of 'trafficking in women'

In the preceding sections we examined the existing prohibitions with respect to prostitution and their applicability to situations of abuse and violence in prostitution, regardless of whether or not these prohibitions came under the heading of "trafficking" or whether they were specifically addressing prostitution. We will change perspectives now and take the heading "trafficking" as the starting-point to see what is understood by the term in the various national laws.

It can be concluded that huge differences exist between countries as to what exactly is prohibited under the heading "trafficking in women". Acts which are prohibited under trafficking laws in one country, may be prohibited under laws on morality, public decency, pimping, procuring, abduction or exploitation of prostitution, etc. in another country[28].

In the following section we will list the various legal definitions of "trafficking in women", as can be derived from the preceding sections. For each definition some examples will be given of countries where this definition is in use.

Legal definitions of trafficking in women

trafficking in women = prostitution and prostitution related activities

Malta: Under the 1930 Order for the Suppression of the White Slave Traffic all prostitution, accosting on a public highway, procurement and brothel keeping are an offence.

trafficking in women = all third party involvement

India: Under the 1956 Immoral Traffic (Prevention) Act, all third party involvement is prohibited. In some cases penalties are more severe if the offence is committed against the will of the woman involved.
Bangladesh: Suppression of Immoral Traffic Act, 1933. Ibid.
Portugal: Under the heading of "Traffic in Women", Art. 217 of the Penal Code penalises anyone organising the prostitution of others.

In India and Bangladesh the law prohibits "trafficking in persons and the exploitation of the prostitution of another person", without it being clear what is understood by "trafficking" and what is understood by "exploitation". De facto "trafficking in women" is equated with any form of third party involvement, be it recruitment, procuring, living off the earnings of prostitution or brothel keeping. This type of definition is especially found in countries where legislation on

28 The following countries have specific provisions on "trafficking in women": India, Bangladesh, Malta, Portugal, Thailand, Japan, Colombia, Peru, The Netherlands, Germany, Switzerland, Dutch Caribbean. Some countries which have no special provisions on "trafficking in women" are: Norway, Finland, Lithuania, Hungary, Slovenia, UK, Turkey, Cambodia, Taiwan, Australia and Mexico.

prostitution is provided in accordance with the '49 Convention, like India and Bangladesh. Not only activities related to third party involvement, but also activities relating to the prostitute, such as soliciting or loitering, are penalised under the title of "trafficking".

In other countries similar prohibitions may be incorporated in general prostitution laws or specific provisions on prostitution in the Penal Code. Examples are the Prostitution Prevention Law in Japan, and the 1960 Restraining of Prostitution Act and sections 282 -286 of the 1956 Penal Code in Thailand.

trafficking in women = buying, selling or obtaining possession of a woman for prostitution

Bangladesh: Separate sections of 1983 Cruelty to Women (Deterrent Punishment) Ordinance and the 1995 Women and Child Repression (special provision) Law, prohibit "trafficking in women", defined as the importing or exporting, or selling, letting or otherwise dispose of, or buying, hiring or otherwise obtaining possession of any woman for prostitution or any other unlawful or immoral purpose.

trafficking in women = any recruitment for prostitution

Nicaragua: Art. 203 of the Penal Code penalises, under "Trafficking in Human Beings" any recruitment of persons for prostitution within or outside the country, with consent or by means of deception or threat, including bringing persons into the country for the purpose of prostitution.

trafficking in women = bringing a person/woman into prostitution in another country/ promote or facilitate the entrance to or exit from the country of a woman to practice prostitution

Thailand:The 1928 Act on Prevention of Traffic in Women and Children penalises anyone who brings women or girls into Thailand or sends them for the purpose of having sexual intercourse with other persons, and any person who is illegally involved in the trading of women and girls brought into the country for such purposes.
Japan: Under "Traffic in Persons", art. 225 & 226 of the Penal Code prohibit the kidnapping of a person with the purpose to transport such person out of Japan, buying or selling another person with the purpose of transporting the same out of Japan and transporting a kidnapped or sold person out of Japan.
Colombia: Under "Trafficking in Women and Minors", art. 311 of the Penal Code prohibits to promote or facilitate the entrance to or exit from the country of a woman or a minor to practice prostitution.
Peru: Ibid. Colombia, but also including the transit through the country (Art. 182 Penal Code).
Austria: Under "Trafficking in Human Beings", section 1 of par. 217 of the Penal Code prohibits leading someone into or recruiting someone for prostitution in a country other than the person's own (citizenship) or that where the person normally resides.

United States: The White Slave Act, commonly known as the "Mann Act" prohibits transporting someone "in interstate or foreign commerce" to engage in prostitution or to induce or coerce someone to travel "in interstate or foreign commerce" to engage in prostitution.

With regard to the Japanese provision on trafficking, it is worth noting that it only addresses women trafficked out of Japan, but does not say anything about trafficking into Japan.

trafficking in women = bringing another person into prostitution
by violence, deceit, or abuse of authority or circumstances.

Nepal: The 1987 Trafficking in Persons Control Act 2043 prohibits "trafficking", defined as involving a woman in prostitution by enticing or alluring by undue influence, fraud, threat, force or any other means.
Austria: Section 2 of par. 217 of the Penal Code prohibits under "Trafficking in Human Beings", recruitment for prostitution in another country by means of deceit or violence.

trafficking in women = bringing or keeping a person in prostitution
by abuse of circumstances and/or violence, deceit or abuse of authority

Germany: Under the heading of "Trafficking in Human Beings", the German Penal Code penalises any one who, for profit, induces a person into prostitution or keeps a person in prostitution by abusing the circumstances of that person or exploiting the helplessness connected with being in a foreign country.
The Netherlands: Under art. 250ter "Trafficking in Persons", the Penal Code penalizes anyone who recruits a person for prostitution or organizes/manages the prostitution of others by means of violence, deceit or abuse of authority[29].

trafficking in women = punishable without further
description of what is to be understood by trafficking in women

In some countries, like the Dutch Caribbean, the law simply prohibits "trafficking in women" without providing a definition.

trafficking in women = sale and purchase of a human being for any purpose

Nepal: The 1987 Trafficking in Persons Control Act 2043 prohibits "trafficking", defined as the sale and purchase of a human being for any purpose. Taking a person to a foreign country for

[29] This interpretation of the current article 250ter PC is laid down in the Special Directives of the Procurator General concerning the Tracing and Legal Action Against Trafficking in Women.

the purpose of trafficking is prohibited by the same law. In addition the 1963 New Muluki-Ain prohibits under the chapter on "Trafficking in Persons" to allure persons to cross borders with the intent of trafficking, enslaving persons or striking a deal regarding human trafficking.

6 Conclusions

It can be concluded that legal control of prostitution targets the outward appearance rather than the conditions in which women find themselves. On the whole, governments are far more anxious about public order and public health than about abuse and violence. An example is Turkey, where the government reports, after having stated that trafficking in women and forced prostitution are no problem in Turkey:

However, according to the unofficial information from the Black Sea region, foreign women involved in traffic have relations with married men. As a result, some Government departments have expressed their concern about the wives, as they rather constitute a potential high risk if no preventive measures are taken with respect to sexually transmitted diseases, including AIDS (Council of Europe, 1994a).

Laws on prostitution and trafficking are seldom designed to target abuse and violence. On the whole, no distinction is made between abusive or coercive situations and situations where no deceit, abuse or violence are involved. All forms of recruitment, mediation, profiting from, organising or managing prostitution are criminalised, regardless of whether or not abuse or violence are involved.

Provisions on "trafficking" predominantly address the recruitment aspect, their main concern being to prevent "innocent" women (contrary to "guilty" women) from being lured into prostitution. Insofar they define trafficking as bringing a person into prostitution in another country, they generally do not target force, but refer mainly to the migration aspect, rejecting and denying prostitution as a survival strategy for the women involved.

Once women are working in prostitution, they are, irrespective of the manner of entrance, more or less outlawed and deprived of all protective mechanisms to which other citizens are entitled. Insofar as specific provisions against violence and abuse exist, they tend to apply exclusively to the category of "innocent" women, that is to say "non-prostitutes": women who were not prostitutes before, did not know they would work as a prostitute, do not aim to continue working as a prostitute and whose virtue on the whole is "undisputed". According to this interpretation,
prostitutes, i.e. any woman whose virtue is "disputed", cannot be subject to trafficking.

Hardly any specific provisions addressing forced labour and slavery-like practices in prostitution are found. Non-prostitution and non-gender related general provisions, penalising for example illegal confinement, kidnapping, debt bondage, extortion, compulsion, etc., are seldom applied or - again - only in case of "innocent" women. The over-all result is that women working in prostitution are deprived of all legal protection, no matter how they entered prostitution.

Although violence is seldom defined as a discriminating factor, in all countries the "virtue" of the woman concerned is so used. Sometimes this is explicitly worded in the law, as in Colombia. The same concept of a "scale of female chastity", deciding the seriousness of the crime, is found in the criminal codes of a number of other Latin American countries, for example in Venezuela, El Salvador and Paraguay, where the penalty for rape is reduced by one fifth if the victim is a prostitute[30]. In the same way abduction is less heavily penalised in Paraguay if the victim is a prostitute or when done with the intent of marriage (!). Another example is provided by the German law on trafficking, which defines trafficking a less serious crime if the victim knew she would work as a prostitute or when she "is not far from prostitution".

Usually, however, the virtue of the woman is not mentioned as an explicit criterion in law, but it plays -implicitly or explicitly - a crucial role in the interpretation and enforcement of the law. In trafficking cases, as in other cases of sexual violence, it is by no means exceptional that the victim stands trial instead of the accused. An illustration is the case of Lisa[31], a Filippine woman who was trafficked to The Netherlands in 1981. After years of struggling to have her traffickers brought to trial, in 1988 the Dutch Court sentenced the Dutch suspect to two and a half years imprisonment. However, the man who recruited her on the Philippines, a chief prosecutor of the Court of Justice in Lisa's village, was acquitted by the Philippine Court, with reference to the alleged immoral character of the victim:

...considering her glaring immoral conduct manifested by her unusual inclination for illicit sex, she will have no qualms in fabricating situations to pursue her ends in bringing the accused to public ridicule [...] what amazed the Court is why the authorities [...] relied on the sole uncorroborated testimony of Lisa M., whose penchant for lying is so manifest and whose moral background is more than questionable [...], despite the declaration of the accused whose character is beyond reproach and whose public life remains unblemished (STV, 1991a, p. 10/11).

The fact that a woman's alleged character and sexual history is relevant in deciding whether or not she can be a victim of trafficking exemplifies the widespread and deep-rooted notion that only "decent", that is "innocent" or "chaste", women can claim protection against violence, rape or abuse.

Also in other ways, the interpretation of the law and its enforcement is often discriminatory towards women. Actions against trafficking tend to be limited to raids on prostitutes. In Thailand, for instance, in practice only women are prosecuted under the article that penalises anyone found in a brothel. Whereas violence against prostitutes goes unpunished, women using violence against their captors face severe punishment, as illustrated by these stories of Thai women trafficked to Japan:

30 In Paraguay the penalty is reduced when the victim is a prostitute, no matter the age of the girl involved.

31 See for an extensive review of both the lawsuit in The Netherlands and the Philippines: "From the other side of the sea, Lisa's story" (STV, 1991a).

Sometimes, the only way left for women to escape is to kill their captors. Three Thai women who had been forced into prostitution, killed their "mamasan" to escape. She had kept them, withheld their passports and never paid them. They were sentenced to ten years imprisonment. Another group of five Thai women killed a Singaporean night club owner in Japan. They had been forced into prostitution and saw the murder as their only way out. They were sentenced to terms of between four and six years. In this last case a NGO initiated a private action against the husband of the night-club owner. He was arrested but released after 21 days on paying a fine of approximately US $ 250 (GAATW, 1996, p.28).

On the whole, existing legislation offers few if any possibilities for women to take legal action against their violators due to their illegal or socially marginalised status as prostitutes. In the case of migrant women, common policies of expulsion not only hamper women to press charges, but also make prosecution virtually impossible since the main witnesses are deported.
Even when the law enables women to press charges, many women will choose not to do so. One reason is the lack of protection the law offers against retaliation. Moreover, in many countries officials themselves are involved in trafficking or profit from the slavery-like conditions women are subjected to.

When laws against trafficking exist they are seldom enforced. Even when they are enforced their objective of lessening trafficking in women is rarely achieved.

Existing laws on prostitution do not help in deterring women from prostitution, neither do they protect the fundamental rights of women working as prostitutes. Rather they lead to various forms of exploitation and oppression:
Paradoxically, although it is these women's income that gives the whole range of male functionaries in the brothel their living, the women are totally under the dominating control of these men. This can be done because of the fact that the whole issue of brothel prostitution is viewed as an aberrant behaviour of sexuality, which is not permitted in society. As a result it has been made into an exclusive institution, the operation of which necessitates male control through the intervention of the state (Khan, 1992, p.48)

Although being a prostitute as such is not against the law in most countries, working as a prostitute is de facto prohibited or subjected to an extensive range of legal prohibitions and regulations. In most cases these are predominantly designed to control prostitutes - be it in the interest of public order, public nuisance, public health or tax imposition - and contribute very little to the well-being of the women themselves. On the contrary, they expose women to arbitrary arrest and render the police an extraordinary amount of power over prostitutes, against which prostitutes can hardly defend themselves. They may lead to unsafe working conditions and increased dependence on third parties, and act as an effective barrier to escape violence or seek help and take legal action in case of trafficking, forced labour or slavery-like practices.

Existing laws on prostitution lead to a profoundly ambivalent legal position for prostitutes: they are allowed to be prostitutes (either because they are a "victim" or a "necessary evil"), but working as such is prohibited. The law itself deprives prostitutes of crucial means of assuring an income, e.g. facilities to recruit clients, to advertise, to hire accommodation, or to be employed, and relegates them to an illegal and criminal circuit.

In general the various prohibitions and regulations contribute to the stigmatization of prostitutes and lead to their marginalization and isolation. Regulations on mandatory registration not only stigmatise prostitutes, they may also force them to stay in prostitution or make it much more difficult to take up another job if they so wish. Prostitutes who are in breach of the law may be sentenced to fines or imprisonment. In some countries they can be sentenced to forced detention in rehabilitation centres, like in Japan, India, Vietnam and Thailand.

Migrant prostitutes risk being arrested as illegal aliens and deported. With the exception of Curaçao it is not possible to obtain a legal work permit for prostitution. This implies that women are either relegated to middlemen and husbands to provide for a legal status as artist or wife, or condemned to a life as illegal alien without any rights or access to legal, social or medical services. In both cases pressing charges in case of violence or abuse will mean deportation, with the exception of Belgium and The Netherlands, where women are entitled to a temporary staying-permit during criminal proceedings.

All prohibitions and regulations are based on the premise that prostitution is morally to be condemned. This legal standpoint leads to a social and legal attitude towards prostitutes according to which they are primarily seen as "victims of their situation" or "compliant in their situation", instead of autonomous individuals and carriers of rights.

Prostitution itself is considered either a moral evil that should be eradicated, or an inevitable evil that has to be tolerated but kept under control. The first position is supported by moral arguments, holding that prostitution is incompatible with the dignity and value of human beings and "endangers the welfare of the individual, the family and the community"[32] or - a more contemporary feminist argument - that prostitution per definition represents sexual violence. Within this view, all prostitution in essence is trafficking in women. Laws to combat trafficking are directed towards the elimination of prostitution, criminalising either all involved parties, including prostitutes, or any "third party" with the exclusion of prostitutes, who are considered victims. Within the second position prostitution is just as much considered to be morally unacceptable, yet impossible to eradicate from society. As Kempadoo notes, discussing the regulation of prostitution in the Dutch Caribbean:

Regulations were thus constructed to facilitate the sale of female sexual labour to men, premised on several assumptions. First, that heterosexual intercourse was necessary for male health and well-being. A second was that homosexuality led to moral degeneracy and a third, that sexually transmitted diseases were most harmful to the working and fighting power of men (Kempadoo, 1995,p.1).

32 Preamble 1949 Convention.

Prostitution is thus considered not only an inevitable, but even a necessary evil. To protect society against the dangers of this "necessary evil", prostitution is controlled through the introduction of regulations and various state sanctioned measures in the interest of public order, public health, masculine needs, the need to protect "decent" women, tax payment, public nuisance and visibility. The women, however, are not given legal rights as workers, neither does the state take responsibility for working and living conditions of prostitutes.

Whereas in reality all states tolerate or legitimise prostitution as long as this does not cause nuisance or disruption to the broader society, all legal systems based on the "immorality" of prostitution simultaneously outlaw prostitutes - regardless of whether they are viewed as victims or as deviants - simply because they are prostitutes. As formulated by Khan and Arefeen in "Prostitution in Bangladesh":

The state proclaims prostitution illegal on the basis of its immorality, while its law and its administration by the courts allows women to operate as prostitutes. The police uphold this legal position by "protecting" the prostitutes in the brothel and outside. This contradictory role of the state not only perpetuates this institution and the socio-religious ideology which creates it in the first place, but also creates opportunities for the exploitation and oppression of women in it (Khan, 1992, p. 243).

Existing laws do not in any way depart from the views and interests of the women concerned. Prostitutes are objects of the law that either have to be "rescued" or made "harmless" (i.e. not dangerous to public health or order). They are not subjects accorded with rights. Even where the law does not criminalise prostitutes, it does not encompass legal rights for women engaged in prostitution, whether as workers, as citizens, or as persons, thus depriving them of both workers' rights and human rights.

5 CURRENT STRATEGIES

1 Introduction

The variety of current strategies employed by both governmental and non-governmental organizations to address traffic in women and forced labour & slavery-like practices reflects the diversity - and divergence - of the various definitions and interests attached to those phenomena, as have been discussed in chapter 2. Different solutions - that is, measures to prevent or combat "trafficking in women"- are drafted, dependent on the conceptualization of the problem to be solved and the corresponding analysis of its causes. Some definitions focus on what is felt as the problem by the aggrieved party. Other definitions target particular aspects that have great significance for other parties, or for society as a whole. Others again concentrate on what are considered to be the causes of the problem. Each definition produces its own solutions and each solution is connected to a certain definition of the problem; if "trafficking in women" is predominantly viewed as a problem of poverty, then different solutions will be proposed than if it is viewed as a problem of morality or of (organised) crime.

Any analysis - and its matching solutions - carries its own value. Given the complexity of the issue, strategies are necessarily many faceted. More than one strategy is appropriate and any one approach is not by definition good or bad. Significantly, the situation of the women concerned is determined by many factors: their position as woman, as prostitute/ domestic worker/ wife, as migrant, migrant worker, victim of (organized) crime and so forth. All those positions are reflected in the different approaches as developed by both governmental and non-governmental organizations: each strategy addresses a different aspect. Adherence to one particular definition and its consequent solutions may be hazardous, since other - and possibly more effective - solutions then easily disappear from view.
Therefore, when thinking about strategies against "trafficking" it is important to have a clear view of what one understands by it and what exactly one wants to address. If the issue is ill-defined, objectives become blurred and measures may well be more harmful than good for those who should benefit from the actions.

From the array of current strategies six main approaches can be separated: "trafficking in women" as a moral problem, as a problem of (organised) crime, a migration problem, a public order problem, a labour problem and as a human rights problem. Within each approach, two modes of strategies can be distinguished: repressive strategies, aimed at suppressing "undesirable behaviour", such as criminality or illegal migration, and empowering strategies - used primarily by NGOs - geared towards supporting women and strengthening their position. Although repressive strategies can be of value, they run a major risk of turning against women, for example by restricting women's freedom of movement or by using them as witnesses against organized crime without appropriate protection. At the same time, such strategies appeal to governments by their simplicity and their congruence with different state interests, such as immigration control.

This chapter examines each of the aforementioned approaches and their corresponding strategies, as employed by both governmental and non-governmental organizations.
Leading question in assessing those strategies is their impact on the women concerned; does a given strategy help to prevent and combat abusive conditions of recruitment and work (trafficking in women and forced labour & slavery-like practices as defined for this report) or does it actually target another problem? Whose interests are served by a particular strategy and whose problem is addressed?

2 A moral problem

The basic principle within a moral framework is the moral rejection of prostitution. Here, the problem is prostitution as such, without regard to conditions of coercion or consent[1]. "Trafficking" is seen as a phenomenon which inevitably accompanies the "evil of prostitution"[2]. Within this framework strategies designed to prevent and combat "trafficking" are directly related with strategies to combat prostitution as such. When prostitution is seen as morally reprehensible, any assistance given by other persons to work in prostitution will be similarly reprehensible. Women working in prostitution are considered either "victims" who need rescue, or "deviants" who must be re-educated or punished.

2.1 Governmental policies

Corresponding governmental strategies include criminalization either of all parties involved in prostitution (as in a prohibitionist system), or of any third party (as in an abolitionist system).

Within an abolitionist approach, prostitution is considered "incompatible with the dignity and worth of the human person and endangering the welfare of the individual, the family and the community", as expressed in the preamble of the 1949 Convention. Any involvement of the authorities is rejected, as it would encourage moral decay. Even when in words the "problem" of prostitution is put in other contexts, for example a human rights or feminist context, the underlying notion is a strong moral rejection of prostitution as such (and thus the idea of prostitution as legitimate work), with all its (negative) consequences for the women involved[3].

[1] Evidently, morality always plays a role in defining the (un)desirability of certain behaviour, but when sexuality is at stake, moral arguments seem to gain extra weight, often obscuring the discussion and sometimes becoming the problem itself.

[2] As formulated in the Preamble of the 1949 Convention "Whereas prostitution and the accompanying evil of the traffic in persons for the purpose of prostitution are..."

[3] As a matter of fact, the same is true in a prohibitionist system (in which prostitution as such is prohibited) and a regulationist system (in which prostitution is tolerated as a necessary evil and some aspects are regulated in the interest of public health or public order).

According to this view the prostitute should not be penalised, as she is a victim, but all other aspects remain a crime. All third persons who are involved in prostitution are exploitative by definition. No distinction is made referring to the will of the women involved; all prostitution is "traffic in women", without regard to conditions of consent or coercion. Prostitutes are basically seen as passive victims of the social and economic system who need to be rescued, thus negating individual choices and denying women the status of subjects capable of assuming individual agency and responsibility. Yet, many cases are known where no legal proceedings have been initiated against traffickers under a abolitionist system because the woman did not reflect the stereotyped image of a victim of trafficking, for instance because she agreed initially to work as a prostitute.

Though unintentional, the impact on women is invariably a combination of isolation, stigmatization, marginalization and criminalization. Moreover, any third party is compelled to operate illegally, which puts the women concerned at greater risks of violence and abuse. Even improvement of working conditions may be seen as a form of "trafficking", as exemplified by recent court rulings in Germany:
In recent legal cases some rulings go so far as to construe all forms of good working conditions in brothels, or brothel-like businesses, such as good sanitary equipment, internal social arrangements, and even the supplying of condoms, as a promotion of prostitution" (to be punished with a term of imprisonment up to three years, or with a fine (art. 180a STGB). 'The background to this is the idea that good working conditions are not conducive to turning women away from the 'deviant' way of life they have entered' (Europap, 1994, p.102/103).

The prohibitionist system goes one step further; here, not only the procurer but also the prostitute is liable for punishment, as is any third party. And although in theory all parties involved in prostitution are criminalized, in most cases, the primary target for law enforcement is the female prostitute, not those who profit from her income. In case of violence or abuse, there is no authority, not even hypothetically, to which women can turn, as they themselves are punishable by law.

In both systems, prostitutes may be seriously hindered in organising themselves, if it is not totally prevented:
Numerous attempts to organise have been blocked by violence or social control. In Ireland, for example, a prostitute who tried to organise her colleagues was killed; fire was set to her house and she was burnt to death. In Thailand, a few women tried to organise a kind of union called 'Thai Night Guard', but they failed because of family pressure, police harassment and threats from their managers. In Ecuador, brothel managers purposely rotate prostitutes each week to prevent them from grouping together and expressing their grievances about ill-treatment and bad working conditions (Pheterson, 1992).

Evidently, this does not mean that women don't organise. Even under adverse conditions, prostitutes increasingly manage to organise and to fight for their rights.

2.2 NGO strategies

Non-governmental organizations direct strategies primarily against moral judgements and their negative effects on women. They work against discrimination, stigmatization and social exclusion of prostitutes. They campaign for better legal protection of the women concerned and for the development of employment alternatives. They fight prejudices against prostitutes and question the division of women into "good" and "bad", "innocent" and "guilty":

Many strategies have been applied in fighting against this form of violence against women....some actions are spontaneous, for example, the demonstrations at airports. Others involve a long process requiring broad-based co-operation... The obvious lesson we learn from all the cases is that prejudice against women victims of international trafficking and sex tourism is very strong. The division of 'good' versus 'bad' women is strongly pronounced. There is no legal protection for 'fallen women' because society believes that prostitutes cannot be victims (Skrobanek, 1992).

Over the last few years an increasing number of groups - both prostitutes' organizations and women's organizations working with prostitutes- advocate taking a non-abolitionist route and approaching prostitution from the point of view of the workers themselves. Here, the basic principle is the appreciation of women as independent citizens who are able to exercise the same freedom as men, but also expect the same protection from violence and from subjection to various forms of servitude. Strategies then aim at the decriminalization of prostitution and at moving the focus of the debate from moral positions to working conditions. According to this view, any policy should be based on the rights of the women concerned to self-determination and the protection of their rights as workers. Moral judgement against prostitution should not be the principle motivation in drafting policies, because of the danger of marginalising and stigmatising prostitutes. It is rather believed that trafficking in women, coercion and exploitation can only be stopped if the existence of prostitution is recognised, and the legal and social rights of prostitutes are acknowledged and guaranteed. Policies should aim at improving working conditions on the one hand and fighting abuse and violence on the other hand, through the same mechanisms applied to other labour sections, i.e. labour laws and civil laws. Within this perspective, the concept of "trafficking" is expanded to include other forms of exploitation of women's work in the informal sector, such as domestic work and, related to this, the commercial marriage market. Obligations, such as in the 1949 Convention, to take measures to rehabilitate the "victims of prostitution" and to achieve their social "adaptation" obviously do not fit into this view.

Connected to this debate is the question of the role of the state in "solving" the problem. Based on the "harm to others" principle as formulated by John Stuart Mill[4], it is believed that the state is only entitled to intervene in the life of its citizens when the behaviour in question is harmful to others (as is the case with force, deceit or violence). Moral rejection on its own is not a sufficient reason for state-intervention. State- intervention with regard to behaviour that is not harmful to others but only to the person itself is rejected as paternalistic. This principle leads to the notion that the state is not a moralist, at least not through the criminal law. This does not necessarily mean that prostitution or profiting from prostitution are not considered

[4] In his essay *On Liberty* in 1859.

moral problems; it mainly implies that there is no role for the state in promulgating morality. This notion is contrary to the obligation in, for example, the 1949 Convention to penalize profiting from prostitution of others, including adult and independent women who have given their consent to this by their own volition. Not the stimulation of morality by criminal law, at which the treaty apparently aims (and many states with it), but the protection of those who work under involuntary or coercive conditions should be the object of penal policy.

Many of the other strategies which will be described in the following sections, also address, in addition to other aspects, also problems that arise from the moral rejection by society of prostitution.

3 A problem of (organised) crime

"Trafficking in women" may also be seen as a criminal problem. This is currently one of the more dominant approaches, especially in Western countries, which is consistent with the generally increased popularity of the criminal law as the instrument to solve any kind of societal problems. Traffic in women is defined as a problem of the criminal law and the criminal justice system.
In many countries, both governmental and non-governmental organizations call for more stringent criminal laws and heavier punishments to combat trafficking and forced labour & slavery-like practices. The underlying idea is that, if the state does not evoke action by the criminal justice system, the problem is not taken seriously.
For states also, a criminal approach is appealing. Criminalising certain behaviour provides states with the opportunity to demonstrate that they address the problem. At the same time it releases them from taking other, and maybe more effective, measures. As described in chapter 4, states have criminalised "traffic in women" and related acts in the context of prostitution extensively and in many different wordings.

3.1 The interest of the state vs. the interest of women

The choice for a penal approach is not without risks. Addressing a particular problem in the context of the criminal law means transforming the problem in such a way that it can be mastered by the criminal law and the criminal justice system. Facts and circumstances that are irrelevant in the criminal context are precluded. The criminal justice system operates in terms of concrete offences committed by identifiable individuals. The context in which a certain event takes place, is reduced to a specific act by a specific individual; only that is relevant for the criminal justice system. A criminal approach necessarily focusses on individual perpetrators of crime and individual victims, whilst leaving aside structural causes of complex problems.

In practice, criminal laws on trafficking seem to have, above all, a mere symbolic value, since they are seldom enforced. In the words of one NGO: "we don't need new laws, we need application of existing laws". Another general complaint by NGOs is that criminal laws are mostly used against the women concerned instead of against their violators.
Often, it even seems to be of no importance whether or not the criminal law is effective. In fact,

experiences of women point out the opposite. Penal approaches run a major risk of turning against the women whom they are officially supposed to "protect", as has been abundantly illustrated in the previous chapter. Several reasons contribute to this ineffectiveness and counter-productiveness of a criminal approach.

Traffic in women and forced labour & slavery-like practices are rooted on violence and often take place in a network-like structure. This has several consequences. Even if existing policies allow women to report to the police, which is often not the case, many women do not consider doing so a viable route for escape or for improving their situation.

Most women have no confidence whatsoever in the police and the criminal justice system. They have often had negative experiences with the police, such as arrest, harassment or, for migrant women, expulsion. Corruption and abuse of power are frequent in numerous countries. In the majority of countries prostitution is prohibited or illegal. Many migrant women are undocumented or become so the minute they leave their husbands or employers, meaning that any contact with the police exposes them to arrest and expulsion.

Although at first glance expulsion could appear as a way of escaping an abusive situation, the reality is more complicated. Many women consider expulsion an even worse alternative than trying to cope with the situation, in the hope of finding ways to improve conditions on their own. Often, they have borrowed money to pay for the costs of middlemen. They can be indebted to their own family, but also to agencies or individual recruiters. In many cases, the family is relying on their income. If women are deported, they return home with empty hands: without money and with debts they will never be able to pay off. When they have worked as prostitutes, and this becomes known, they face moral condemnation or rejection by the community or their families.

If women report to the police, they take a considerable risk without proper protection against reprisals. There is no country in the world where a woman is adequately protected against the consequences of acting as a witness, assuming that her complaint is taken seriously in the first place. By pressing charges she also runs a higher risk that her plight will get known in her own community, for instance when the criminal investigation involves gathering information in her home situation. In many cases women are threatened with reprisals if they dare to escape or go to the police. These threats do not lose their effect when the police gets involved, even if the police is understanding and motivated to support them, which is obviously not the rule. Moreover, their families and children at home are easy targets for reprisals.

All women involved in sex work are very aware of the prevailing attitudes towards prostitutes. This is one of the reasons why they do not want other people to know that they have worked as prostitutes. Apparently common opinion holds that once a prostitute, a woman loses all her rights and is no longer entitled to protection against violence, exploitation, abuse, blackmail or being held prisoner, as other citizens are. Unfortunately, these attitudes are all too familiar to the women involved. This also explains their lack of motivation to report to the police: a decision to report to the authorities is always based on the conviction that you have certain rights and that you have a claim to protection in case of violation of these rights. Needless to say that these attitudes towards prostitutes work clearly in favour of the criminal networks and very much against women.

Although the interest of the state in a criminal approach, i.e. combatting (organised) crime, is rather clear, the interest of the women involved is much less clear. The criminal justice system serves fundamentally other interests than those of the victims of a crime. That applies to crimes in general, but is certainly true here. Whereas the position of the victim is a general problem in criminal proceedings, this is evidently so in cases of trafficking and forced labour & slavery-like practices. While the court case itself can be rather incriminating for women, it can also lead to reprisals or harassment either by their violators or the authorities, and to stigmatising exposure at home. As yet a criminal approach seems to increase women's problems and even create new problems, rather than solve them. This does not mean that women have no interest in the criminal system at all. Trafficking in women and forced labour & slavery-like practices definitely violate, apart from many other things, the sense of justice of the women involved. Prosecution of the offenders sets a norm and means a certain recognition of the wrong that has been done. As stated by a Philippine woman who fought for many years to get her traffickers convicted: "I'm not only doing this for myself, but also to give courage to other victims of trafficking, proving to them that there is a way to win justice". (Lisa, 1991). But the criminal system does not guarantee rights for the women involved, and that is what they need most of all.

As far as criminalization of traffic in women, forced labour & slavery-like practices can be useful in preventing and combating those practices, at least the law has to be implemented as it is meant to be done, i.e. addressing the offenders instead of the victims. And, if women are to be encouraged to report violations to the authorities, at least some basic services have to be provided, partly to counteract the problems which are created by the criminal system itself.

3.2 Governmental policies and NGO strategies

Where "trafficking" is seen as a criminal problem, government policies lean towards more punitive legislation with longer and heavier penalties, increased national and international police cooperation, and a more active prosecution of offenders.

Corresponding non-governmental strategies are directed towards supporting individual women with legal aid, safe shelters, medical care and counselling. Advocacy groups provide and organise legal assistance and give information about rights and legal procedures. They help women in filing complaints, provide support during police interrogations, court proceedings and cross examinations, and work to counteract attempts to discredit women's testimonies. They try to prevent immediate expulsion and work to get women discharged from prison.

NGOs offer education and training for police and judicial personnel to increase awareness of the phenomenon and the consequences for the women involved, and to change attitudes

towards women in general and victims of trafficking specifically. They carry out awareness campaigns for the general public and lobby for recognition of trafficking in women as a crime, for getting complaints taken seriously and for better co-operation between different governmental institutions and between states to more effectively prosecute the offenders.
In some countries NGOs work to expose the involvement of corrupt officials in trafficking and slavery-like practices.
Most central however, they lobby for an improvement in the position of the victims, such as the right to a (temporary) staying permit, the right to an interpreter, legal aid and adequate witness protection during legal proceedings, the right to state aid and safe shelter in the place of arrest and detention, the right to compensation for damages, and the right to permanent residence on humanitarian grounds or, when appropriate, political asylum according to international guidelines. It should be noted that lobbying for more rights is not everywhere without risks.
In some cases organizations advocating migrants rights are themselves exposed to prosecution[5].

Some NGOs plea for stricter criminal legislation and higher penalties, but most respondents mention in their questionnaires that first of all those laws currently in place should be implemented.

4 A migration problem

"Trafficking" may also be seen in the context of migration. Here, attention is focused on the aspect of border-crossing, namely on illegal border-crossing and illegal stay. Trafficking and forced labour & slavery-like practices occurring within countries, when no borders are crossed, remain out of sight. Depending on the perspective of the party, that is, for which party "trafficking" is seen as a problem, solutions vary. Two different strategies can be distinguished.

4.1 Trafficking as a problem for the state

In many of the economically advanced countries, particularly the Western and Northern states, migration flows from the poorer regions are increasingly seen as a problem for society, such in contrast with the situation during the 1970s and 1980s when cheap labour from developing countries was in demand in the industrialized countries. To protect the state against alleged "uncontrollable flows of migrants", increasingly restrictive immigration policies are put in place.

Corresponding governmental policies to combat "trafficking in women" aim at obstructing illegal or "unorderly" migration. Measures include tightening visa policies, limiting the number of residence and labour permits, bringing in more instruments for detention and expulsion of persons without residence permits, stricter control of foreigners on the national territory, closer supervision of "mixed" marriages and criminalization of third parties who facilitate illegal entry or stay (and sometimes of the migrant her or him self).

An illustration of this approach, in which "trafficking" is actually defined as a problem for the state

5 For example in Asia: The case of Tenaganita, Malaysia; AMB (Asia Migrant Bulletin): "Government crackdown on migrant's rights advocates."

rather than for the women involved, could be taken from the discussion paper prepared by Mr. R. Veijalainen for the Working Group on Migration Policy at the joint EU/IOM Conference on Trafficking in Women held in Vienna in June 1996. In this paper, "trafficking in women" is repeatedly linked with "illegal migration". The basic concern is how to control borders and the legal status of "aliens" in the European Union:

The control of EU's external borders is the keystone as far as the arrangement of the actual travel and entry into the country is concerned ... it is justified that all activities striving for illegal import of persons be subjected to sanctions as such in all states ... an alien who has been engaged in prostitution in Finland will find it difficult to get a new visa, because it is possible to apply certain waiting periods to her ...

The paper concludes by reiterating the (real) interest of the EU in addressing "trafficking", which is obviously not the protection of women's rights:

The members of the Reflection Group of the 1996 Inter-govern mental Conference of the European Union have said in their report that the Conference should strengthen the Union's capacity of protecting its citizens against terrorism, drug trafficking, money laundering, exploitation of illegal immigration and other forms of organised crime. So there is a growing need for **PUBLIC SECURITY** *that cannot be met by states acting alone.*

In its final recommendations for the prevention and repression of "trafficking in women", the above-mentioned Working Group takes prevention to mean "to prevent the entry of possible victims". This should be done through scrutiny by Embassy officials in countries of origin in the issuance of visas "to reveal suspected cases before the visa application of the victims are concluded, with the aim of combating organised trafficking in the countries of origin", and through raising public awareness about the "opportunities, limitations and rights of individuals in the case of legal migration and the risks linked to illegal migration on the other hand" (European Commission, 1996a).

Similarly, the Asian Migrant Bulletin reports that Japan is considering an amendment to its Immigration Laws to abolish "entertainment visas", on the assumption that foreign "entertainers" work actually as "hostesses", which has been termed as a euphemism for prostitutes (AMC, 1996).

However, not only destination countries seek to counteract "trafficking in women" by obstructing migration, especially of women. The Indonesian government, for example, announced that its citizens will no longer be allowed to work overseas as maids (domestic workers) by the year 2000, due to the increasing numbers of Indonesian workers being maltreated overseas (AMC, 1996).

Another illustration is Bangladesh, where the Government carried out restrictive measures against its own citizens, following incidents of women workers who had been abandoned by recruiters and then turned to prostitution, who had been imprisoned as illegal migrants, or had been tricked into prostitution. Rather than taking measures to strengthen the position of women workers against the trickery of recruiting agents and corruption of officials, the government issued a directive prohibiting the issuance of No Objection Certificates (NOCs) for low and semi-skilled women. Significantly, the ban was worded such that the women were blamed for their own condition: "These women (...) have low moral standards and can easily be seduced to be engaged in immoral activities" (Sobhan, 1992). In her report, Sobhan relates cases of women who, being financially desperate and having no opportunities of job advancement at home, managed to find employment overseas through clandestine means and after paying bribes. The cases she describes not only show that there are ways to get around official bans, but above all they illustrate that, precisely because of the restrictions imposed on them by their own government, women were actually compelled to run greater risks of exploitation and abuse.

In case of prostitution, measures tend to become even more repressive. As discussed in chapter 4, some countries explicitly exclude (alleged) prostitutes from legal emigration or immigration. Frequently such measures are legitimised by arguments of combating "trafficking in women", as in the UK, where the development of a "system" to identify migrant women as possible prostitutes at the border and the removal of prostitutes under immigration laws is presented as a means to contain the problem of "trafficking" (Council of Europe, 1994a). Other countries categorically forbid migrant women to work in prostitution under penalty of detention and expulsion, even if they permit nationals to do so.

It may be concluded that such measures, though purporting to combat "trafficking", aim in fact at protecting the state against (illegal) migrants, rather than at protecting those migrants against violence and abuse, thus serving the interests of the state rather than those of the women. Moreover, repressive migration policies and the resulting illegal status of women in the destination countries make migrant women more dependent and more vulnerable to various forms of abuse and violence, and thus tend to promote rather than repress trafficking and forced labour & slavery-like practices.

4.2 Trafficking as a problem for women

The interests of women oppose those of the state. For women, it is exactly their illegal status, the lack of legal migration possibilities (in combination with the demand for work in the informal sector) and the lack of viable employment opportunities at home, that make trafficking such a highly profitable business and that force them into an illegal circuit without protection against violence and abuse.

As has been argued before, women are to a great extent dependent on the informal, unprotected and unregulated labour sectors. Migration patterns reflect this labour division which relegates women to the national and international markets for female domestic workers, for marriage partners and for the sex and entertainment industry. Since there are practically no legal and independent ways for women to migrate within these informal labour sectors - even if there exists a clear demand for these types of work in the countries of destination - women cannot but make use of the services of dubious agencies and exploitative middlemen, and only more so as immigration policies in the wealthier countries become more restrictive.

Moreover, owing to their illegal status as worker and/or as migrant, women who are trafficked or are forced to work in slavery-like conditions have no access to legal recourse in order to bring the perpetrators to justice. In the majority of the destination countries, those who are found to be illegal will be deported immediately. They are not legally protected by any national or interstate policies.

The following observations exemplify some of the fundamental questions that need to be raised with respect to measures aimed at restricting migration and the rigorous way in which states are implementing them. As formulated by Claude- Valentin Marie, French migration expert, in his discussion paper for a IOM seminar on trafficking in migrants,
Given the substantial means (legislation, regulations and institutions) set up in recent years to restrict all entries by nationals of third countries and to limit admissions of asylum seekers, is there not a (serious?) risk that potential migrant flows may be diverted to totally illegal access channels? Does not this trend towards 'criminalization' of individual movements of migrants have the paradoxical consequence of promoting the development of organised trafficking in persons? (Marie, 1994)

Since all countries rationalise the adoption of more stringent immigration policies by referring to the "threat to or disturbance of law and order", two questions should be asked according to Marie:
Is it the traffic, associated with the acceleration of international mobility, which constitutes this threat? Or is it the mobility itself which is conceived as a disturbance of law and order?

In the first case, the migrant is seen as a victim of numerous forms of ill-treatment and those who exploit his/her precarious situation should be penalised. In the second case, the migrant is seen as "troublemaker" and it is his/her very mobility which constitutes the "corpus delicti". In the opinion of Marie, almost all the measures devised by states to curb population movements place responsibility on the migrant him/her self, who is the one who is finally penalised. The result of this misconception of the "real" threat is a continuous building up of controls aimed more at identifying (and punishing) the person who is "subject" of the traffic than at taking action against the causes of the traffic and those who profit from it. The basic question that should be asked with regard to state migration control mechanisms is about the tension between control and democracy, and the risk that interests of the state may override the rights of individuals.

The questions raised by Marie echo a report of the Committee on Civil Liberties and Internal Affairs of the European Parliament, released one year earlier, on immigration from Central and Eastern Europe. The Rapporteur, Mrs. Claudia Roth, concludes her report with the following:
Raising barriers around the European Union is unrealistic and it does not comply with the Western European countries' humanitarian principles, which are based on freedom of movement. It must be assumed that both refugees and people in search of better living conditions will continue their efforts to settle in the European Union in the future, possibly in greater numbers...Faced with this situation the European Union must not become a fortress...The EU should, moreover, pursue a policy that tackles the causes of migration...(EP, Roth, 1993).

Similar questions arise where the countries of origin are concerned, for example Bangladesh, which sends abroad huge numbers of workers each year (nearly 250,000 in 1993) through formal, officially sanctioned channels, mainly to the Middle East (IOM, 1994). In an interview, the Counsellor at the Permanent Mission of Bangladesh to the UN, Mr. M. Quayes, observes that restrictions on migration create distortions in the labour market, of which "migrant trafficking" is but one. He warns against repressive anti-trafficking approaches which target migrants rather than traffickers, and expresses his fear that many countries view migrants as "troublemakers":

The problem of trafficking would be reduced if people could have access to normal channels of migration, more conducive to the market forces... When we target trafficking, it will be essential to be sensitised about the humanitarian aspect of the individual. And legislation should NOT be directed at the migrant as troublemaker (IOM, 1994).

Like Marie, he questions whether countries of destination see the "trafficking" aspect of migrant trafficking as a cause of concern, or whether or not it is migration as such which is disturbing. Bangladesh, a country with a strong tradition of labour emigration, is concerned about trafficking, he says, but supports migration: "This is where we want to emphasise our difference" from many countries of destination (IOM, 1994)[6].

Measures in view of the women's interest rather than the states' would include recognising the work of women in the informal sector and ensuring the protection of their rights as workers and as migrants, including access to legal channels of migration. As stated in the aforementioned report of the Committee on Civil Liberties and Internal Affairs of the European Parliament:

If Eastern Europeans are to be prevented from immigrating into the EU illegally, they must be offered, to a limited extent at least, legal immigration and employment opportunities. Ways of regularizing the status of illegal immigrants already living in the EU must be sought. Illegal employment at marginal wages and under poor working conditions must be counteracted; workers from non-EU countries should be employed on the same terms as EU citizens (EP, Roth, 1993)

At the same time, genuine prevention would involve addressing the causes for migration. As Marie put forward, genuine prevention involves a political, democratic choice. It presents a challenge to the developed world"

To assume responsibility for, and even more the burden of, a genuine prevention policy which benefits the poorest in the first instance. In this connection, it might be useful to restate that the first condition for the genuine exercise of freedom of movement (Helsinki) is the choice left to each person not to be obliged to use that freedom, without which it is no longer a right, but a constraint. The challenge is therefore not so much to prevent one person from entering the home of another, as to give each person the 'freedom' to stay at home...It therefore remains essential to encourage the developed States to expend, on this matter, energy at least equal to that displayed in the sophistication of controls on their common or national frontiers (Marie, 1994).

[6] However, it should be remembered that the government of Bangladesh itself enacted restrictive immigration measures for low and semi-skilled women, as described in section 4.1 of this chapter.

However, no governmental policies can be found which address trafficking in women and forced labour & slavery-like practices from the perspective of migration in any positive, non-repressive, way. Two of the few "humanitarian" rulings which are the exceptions that prove the rule, are:

- In Norway, a migrant wife is entitled to a permanent residence permit under immigration law, when it is proven that she has been abused.
- A woman trafficked for prostitution to The Netherlands or Belgium is allowed a temporary staying permit on the condition that she files charges, and only for the duration of the criminal procedures. This measure is meant to encourage women to press charges, and as such serves primarily the interest of the prosecution rather than the interest of the women concerned.

When governmental policies are directed towards the women, they aim primarily at deterring them from migration. Examples are programmes to inform women in their countries of origin of the risks of migration and the situation that awaits them in the destination countries, in the hope that this will deter them from leaving their country. In the same way, Embassies are called upon to warn women who apply for visa of the potential dangers.

NGOs question such strategies and advocate caution, since they easily lead to stigmatization of migrant women and may make it more difficult to return home, once stigmatised as "victim" or "prostitute". Moreover, they observe that policies such as scrutinising visa applications of women at Embassies, closer border checks and stricter regulations and controls on marriages involving women from "suspect" third countries, lead to humiliating and discriminatory treatment of migrant women at borders, police stations and Embassies.

4.3 NGO strategies

Contrary to governmental policies, non-governmental organizations, especially women activist and support organizations, strive for recognition of migration as a survival strategy for women, and for improvement of the legal and social position of women both in countries of destination and origin. Their strategies usually developed during and through their direct contacts with women migrants seeking help and advise and through feminist research in the field of female migration, and are essentially aimed at understanding the real issues facing women migrants in order to propose ways of enhancing women's rights and participation.

Acknowledging migration as a strategy for women to escape from poverty or traditional and social constraints, NGOs pinpoint the many barriers which hinder women from achieving their ambitions. For example, immigration restrictions and the prevailing climate of discrimination and racism in destination societies do not make migrant women feel welcome, even when they are legally married to nationals of these societies and are therefore "legitimate"; women who deliberately embark on temporary migration for work are limited to choices within the informal sector and must take on low paid, unskilled or marginal jobs like domestic work and prostitution, regardless of their educational and professional qualifications.

NGO strategies within the context of migration include documentation and research, information and support programmes, campaigning for improvement of the legal situation of migrant women and the creation of alternative income and employment opportunities.

Documentation and research

In order to gain better insight into the mechanisms which put women into "risk situations", NGOs research and analyse the legal and social conditions and mechanisms which hold migrant women (workers) in forced labour and slavery-like situations. They investigate questions like: are there indeed women at risk or is every woman a potential "victim" (Latin America)? Are there certain migration patterns to be recognized (Thailand)? How organised is trafficking in women in the region (Africa)?
NGOs - in particular feminist groups - set certain standards for methodology of research into issues concerning women, and for research into the complexity of issues involved in trafficking in women. They develop participatory and action-oriented research methods, based on feminist principles.

Information programmes

Information programmes developed by NGOs generally acknowledge the need and right of women to work and to migrate. Apart from the more fundamental questions raised in section 4.2, NGOs have learned that there is no way to stop women from leaving their country when they have made up their mind to try their luck elsewhere, if only because there are no viable employment alternatives which can compare to the expected earnings of even the lowest paying jobs overseas, or to the projected opportunities which are portrayed as within reach.

Strategies of NGOs in countries of origin rather aim at "empowering" potential migrants before they embark on their journeys. Programmes are in operation to provide general information about migrants' rights, cultural differences and expectations, as well as more specific information about laws, work options and working and living conditions in destination countries, validity of contracts and addresses where help is available when necessary.
Printed information is also placed at strategic localities: embassies, airports, railway stations, public health offices, schools, etc.

Information packs sometimes contain warning materials, illustrating poor working conditions, physical injuries and police raids on foreign prostitutes aimed to warn women in risk groups of the dangers awaiting them. But in general NGOs that are involved in solidarity work with migrants avoid approaches that stigmatise migrant women abroad as "victims", "enslaved" or "forced". Such images lower chances of a safe return and social acceptance. They also undermine the self-esteem of migrant women, who have consciously chosen an economic strategy - even at the risk of abuse - to build a better future for their children or families by working overseas or marrying into a socially more secure society.

Support services

Both in countries of destination and of origin, NGOs offer support services, run safe shelters, provide counselling and medical care, organise or give legal assistance in case of abuse or threat of expulsion, and support women throughout legal proceedings. They provide all sorts of practical help, from introduction into culture and language classes to assistance in obtaining the correct papers and negotiations with the authorities. They support women to leave or alter abusive situations and assist them if they want to return home.

Some NGOs have initiated return programmes, aimed at supporting migrant women who return to their home countries, either because they want to, or because they have been expelled. Sometimes religious groups or churches help women to return home with financial assistance. However, in general there is little known about what happens to those women who have returned.

Advocacy and lobby

In addition to practical support, NGOs conduct information campaigns for the general public and lobby for improvement of the legal and social position of women.

Campaigns target the restricted or non-existent legal status of migrant women as one of the crucial causes that bring women into abusive situations and hold them there. NGOs lobby for independent residence permits for migrant women who have fled abusive marriages, forced prostitution or slavery-like working and living conditions. They campaign against laws that render even legal migrants completely dependent on their employers or husbands for their safety and well-being, such as the existing immigration rules, which accord legality only on the basis of these relationships without providing adequate protection against abuse and exploitation by employers and husbands.

Long term advocacy campaigns aim at securing workers' rights for migrant women workers, at a legal and independent status as workers and as migrants, and at application of international agreements related to protection of migrant workers, e.g. ratification of the International Convention on the Protection of Migrant Workers and their Families.

The advocacy for workers' rights for domestic workers is well-known. Even more difficult and controversial is the lobby for the recognition of workers' rights for women, both national and migrant, in prostitution.

4.4 International Organization for Migration (IOM)

Amongst international organizations, the International Organization for Migration (IOM), much quoted in this report, is exemplary in its strategies regarding 'trafficking in women" from the perspective of migration. IOM started to work seriously on "migrant trafficking" in response to a UN General Assembly resolution on "Prevention of Alien Smuggling"[7], in which international organizations were requested to "consider ways and means ... to enhance international co-operation to combat alien smuggling".

[7] Resolution 48/102, 1993.

Within its overall mandate to promote "orderly and humane migration" IOM devoted its 11th seminar in October 1994 to the theme of the "International response to trafficking in migrants and the safeguarding of migrant rights". This seminar marked the start of IOM efforts to address trafficking in women as a distinct issue within the wider phenomenon of "trafficking of migrants" in general. Although acknowledging the complexities and specifics of the issues involved in "trafficking in women", IOM has maintained its (basic) definition of "migrant trafficking" as comprising the following elements (IOM, 1996d)[8]:

- an intermediary is involved
- money is paid
- illegal movement is facilitated
- it is a cross-border phenomenon
- it is taking place with or without the consent or knowledge of the person involved.

With regard to "traffic in women", IOM added the following elements to the above characteristics:

- use of deception as to the purpose and legality of the procedures
- physical or sexual abuse
- selling or trading for purposes of employment, marriage, prostitution or other forms of profit-making.

From this perspective, IOM has developed an impressive package of activities to address the issue of "trafficking in migrant women" since 1994. The package consists of four components: research, information campaigns, technical co-operation, and return and reintegration assistance(IOM 1995a).

In the last two years IOM has systematised and collated data and information from both governmental and non-governmental organizations and institutions in different regions of the world, which resulted in the production of a number of useful country- and region-specific reports on the issue. They also actively co-operate with both GOs and NGOs in several forums, including co-organising the EU International Conference on Trafficking in Women for Sexual Exploitation in Vienna, June 1996.

Together with government representatives and NGOs, IOM currently develops information campaigns for the Philippines and Vietnam to provide women and children with "credible information on potential dangers and likely circumstances should they choose to migrate illegally, with aim of preventing them from being trafficked". Similar campaigns are planned for Nepal and Bangladesh (IOM, 1996e).

Most interesting current initiatives are the two IOM pilot projects for the "return and reintegration of trafficked Chinese, Cambodian and Vietnamese women and children" from Thailand, which began mid 1996 (IOM, 1996e). The projects aim at creating an effective and humane infra-structure to facilitate the return and reintegration into their home towns/villages

[8] See also chapter II.

of Chinese, Cambodian and Vietnamese women who have been trafficked to Thailand. It offers women who are practically "stranded" in Thailand - either in the government immigration detention centres or in NGO-shelters - an integrated "assistance package" - including administrative- legal assistance, transport, medical attention and psycho-social counselling, vocational training and reintegration assistance. This being voluntary return programmes, women who are eligible for the assistance must sign an undertaking for the whole programme. Success of the project will be monitored by regular follow-up visits to the returnee's towns/villages. The projects are implemented in co-operation with NGOs and government bodies in countries of origin and destination. Since those are fairly recent initiatives, it is not yet possible to evaluate the results and judge their significance as a strategy to address the needs of migrant women caught in the trafficking continuum.

5 A public order problem

Trafficking in women, forced labour & slavery-like practices may also be placed in the context of public order. Strategies then focus on the regulation of work in which (migrant) women are engaged, in the interest of public order. Also here the problem and possible solutions are defined differently by different parties. And also here the effects of such regulations on the women involved depend to a large extent on the interests that they are meant to serve: those of the authorities in preventing disorderly behaviour in public places, or those of the women involved.

5.1 The interest of the state

Government strategies generally focus on enforcement of public order through repression or control of "indecent" or "disorderly" behaviour or persons. In the interest of public order or public health regulations are enacted to ban such behaviour, or such persons, as much as possible from public life. This approach is particularly dominant with respect to prostitution.

In many countries the existence of prostitution is more or less accepted as an inevitable - or even necessary - "evil". At the same time it is considered a threat to public health or public order, for which it has to be controlled and regulated. The situation in Germany could be taken as an example. Here, prostitution is regulated by the state through different forms of registration and other forms of state control, such as mandatory medical checks, regulations with regard to permitted or forbidden areas, the residence status of the women concerned and so on, often with corresponding penalties for women who fail to comply to those regulations. Principal motivation is not the interests of prostitutes but rather the interests of the state, notably public order, public health and tax imposition. As argued in chapter 4, those types of regulations often carry negative results for women, for example because of their stigmatising and marginalising effects.

Another revealing example of similarly oriented measures is the recommendation of the European Commission in its recent Communication on "trafficking in women for the purpose of sexual exploitation" to educate potential clients on the risks of sex with migrant prostitutes:

In order to discourage potential clients, preventive work on information on health risks could be stepped up. This would also help in reducing risks to public health within the EU (European Commission, 1996).

It may be evident that women have not much to gain from regulations which are designed to ban them from public life or to control their activities in the interests of others.

5.2 The interest of women

If we start form the interests of women, public order would not be defined in terms of controlling the worker but rather in terms of controlling the working conditions. Within such an approach, regulations concerning public order could be used to regulate working conditions. For example, licences could be withdrawn when brothel-keepers fail to comply with certain standards with respect to working conditions, such as the right of workers to refuse certain clients or to refuse certain sexual acts, the right to choose one's own doctor, confidentiality of medical information etc. In the same way licenses could be withdrawn in the case of coercion or abuse. There are no current strategies which put this perspective in operation, although the Netherlands may do so in the future.

6 A labour problem

When trafficking in women, forced labour & slavery-like practices are defined as labour problems, these practices can be considered the result of the poor legal and social position of women in the areas of our concern. Within this approach the position of women as workers is the focus of change strategies. Strategies aim to achieve recognition of labour in the informal sectors as legitimate work, recognition by destination countries of the demand for workers in these sectors and labour law protection for the women concerned. Trafficking in women, forced labour & slavery-like practices then are problems which have to be dealt with by employers and employees, employees' protection laws, trade unions, the labour inspectorate etc.

In the case of prostitution for example, brothel-keepers and employers clearly are in a position of power, as long as prostitutes lack any legal protection of their rights as workers. Improvement in the social and legal position of prostitutes would impede traffic in women and slavery-like practices, and would give women instruments to defend themselves against such practices, just like workers in other labour sectors.

The power-balance between prostitutes and brothel-keepers/employers would significantly change if prostitutes could legally conclude civil and labour contracts, if they could enter into collective labour agreements as a result of collective bargaining between employers and employees, if they could insure themselves against the consequences of unemployment or illness, if they would be entitled to state benefits and pensions, if labour regulations (e.g. with respect to health and safety) would be applicable to work in prostitution, and if they could start their own business with the help of state subsidies - all measures that are common to "regular" professions.

6.1 Governmental policies

Governmental policies rarely, if ever, share this perspective and certainly not in relation to prostitution or migrant workers. Within a gendered labour market, government policies for protection of workers and improvement of labour conditions tend to be geared to the male autochthonous worker, excluding labour sectors designated to women and migrants.

Although over the last years some countries have established new laws on sexual assault and intimidation in the workplace and on equal pay for work of equal value, enforcement of these laws is often inadequate. Moreover, they are not validated in domestic work and the entertainment and sex industry. Legislation on labour migration and rights of migrant workers has not been improved for twenty years, rather has it worsened. Government policies, especially in destination countries, primarily aim at inhibiting women from migrating for work in the informal sectors, for example through "prevention" programmes in countries of origin, stressing the risks of (illegal) migration and the impossibility of getting a legal work permit. At the same time, repressive and restrictive migrant labour legislation is reinforced, even though it is clear that it is impossible (and even undesirable from an economic point of view) to stop labour migration.

6.2 NGO strategies

It is primarily NGOs which develop strategies within a labour framework. NGO initiatives include support services, self-organization, lobbying, and research and information campaigns.

In the area of support services NGOs have been starting programmes to strengthen women in their working and living situations. They organise language classes, develop courses to improve negotiating skills and to inform women of their rights, and provide information on matters relating to health and safety. They offer counselling, health care, legal resources and practical help, e.g. in sending money home. Some support women to get alternative employment or vocational training. Some of the centres or groups working with prostitutes tend to disrespect the women's profession and aim to "rescue" them. But others have programs that are in connection with the qualities women use and have learnt in their work and which can be of great value to improve their situation or indeed qualify for alternative employment.

At the same time, domestic workers, prostitutes and wives are forming organizations, often in collaboration with other NGOs, to improve their working and living conditions and to fight for their rights as workers and/or as migrants.

NGOs, prostitutes' rights and migrant workers' rights organizations lobby governments to improve the legal position and the working and living conditions of the women involved, to strengthen (migrant) workers' rights, also in the entertainment sector, and to gain recognition of prostitution as work. In some countries trade unions are urged to represent entertainers and prostitutes.

In the countries of origin NGOs work on a community level to implement prevention

programmes in combination with income generating and employment programmes.
These programmes are not primarily aimed at preventing women from migration, rather they are meant to inform women of abusive practices and of their rights in case they do decide to migrate.

Information campaigns world-wide have brought more attention to trafficking, forced labour & slavery-like practices, but according to respondents of the questionnaire public awareness of the problem still remains low. Information campaigns of NGOs for the general public and lobbying the government mostly have two aspects: the first is to ask for direct (and financial) support, the other is to raise awareness of the predicament of the women and to solicit support for measures to improve the (legal) position and the working conditions of women.

A major and shared problem for most NGOs is the lack of government support, either financial or in other ways.

6.3 International Labour Organization (ILO)

Amongst international bodies, the ILO has tentatively begun to address the issue by researching the situation of migrant domestic workers and migrant workers in the entertainment industry. The ILO could play an important role in setting standards appropriate to the informal sectors, particularly those affecting a large number of women, such as domestic work and sex work[9]. ILO conventions, such as the Convention on Forced Labour (ILO No 29) and the Convention concerning the Protection of Wages (ILO No 95) could be used to abolish slavery-like practices. Article 9 of the latter convention,for example, specifically prohibits the deduction of any payment from wages for the purpose of obtaining or retaining employment, including a recruiting agent. However, until now this course has hardly been taken.
Another instrument that might be used to strengthen the rights of migrant women workers is the Migrant Workers Convention[10]. Yet depressingly few states have shown interest in this treaty, given the small number that has ratified it.

One of the problems in the application of treaties on workers' rights is the refusal of countries of destination to recognise that they are immigration countries. If this were indeed done, international institutions argue, they would more easily implement migrants protection and promotion of welfare. Another obstacle is created by the refusal to acknowledge female work in the informal sector, particularly prostitution, as work.

7 A human rights problem

Strategies linked to a human rights perspective are predominantly used by NGOs. In this perspective, trafficking in women, forced labour & slavery-like practices are seen as violations of women's human rights, for which states are accountable, both in the public sphere and the

[9] See also: Conclusions of the Conference on Traffic in Persons, held from 15-19 November 1994 in Utrecht and Maastricht (SIM, 1995)

[10] Convention on the Protection of the Rights of All Migrant Workers and their families, adopted 18 December 1990.

private sphere. Instruments designed to protect human rights are invoked as key guidelines and used to enhance the rights of women, as well as to hold governments accountable for perpetrating or condoning violence against women in all spheres of life.

However, as previously argued, here again two different currents of analysis exist. Again the perspective from which the issue is approached and strategies are developed is crucial.

7.1 The interest of morals vs. the interest of women

For some, who define "trafficking" in the traditional narrow sense, prostitution itself is considered a violation of women's human rights equal to slavery. Such judgement brings us back to the moral approach, in which prostitutes are stigmatized as "victims" or "deviants" and denied a legitimate place in the public debate, but this time via the detour of human rights. Strategies to combat "trafficking" defined as a human rights problem in this way, will aim at the abolition of prostitution as such. It is very difficult to see how respect for prostitutes can be promoted if their work as such is seen as inherently degrading. It is equally difficult to see how the interests of women are served by excluding prostitutes' rights organizations from the political debate, as was advised by Fernand- Laurent in his report on the "suppression of the traffic in persons and the exploitation of the prostitution of others" (Jean Fernand Laurel, 1983)[11].

For others it is not the work as such that violates women's human rights, but the conditions of force, deceit, violence and abuse of authority. As argued in chapter II, it is the comparison with slavery that makes clear that it is not the type of work that is at stake, but the conditions under which work is done; in the same way as the abolition of slavery was to do with the elimination of an oppressive power relation - notably ownership by one person of another -, rather than with the elimination of a certain type of work.

From the perspective of the women involved it is coercion, abuse and deceit that violate their human rights: the right to control their own body, life and work, the right to work with just compensation under proper conditions, the right to decide on their own marriage partners, the right to migrate, to decide for themselves whether or not to work in prostitution and under what circumstances, the right to freedom of movement and the right to be free from violence and restraint. As put in Vindication of the Rights of Whores,

Human rights must include the right to migrate (also as legal immigrants or refugees), the right to work (also as prostitutes). the protection of children against sexual exploitation, and the right of all people to be protected against coercion, deceit and violence (in or out of prostitution)....Migrant rights, (migrant) prostitute rights and (migrant) worker rights are crucial to liberation struggles everywhere. Those rights call for a politics in which neither 'home' nor 'purity' are idealised and imposed (Pheterson, 1992).

Strategies from this perspective include examining structural causes and mainstreaming action

[11] J. Fernand-Laurent, 1983, paragraph 74. See also chapter II, section 3.3.

to eliminate all gender-based violence. It means shifting focus from protection to empowerment, and it means the participation and organization of the women concerned. Lobbying focuses on replacement of the 1949 Convention with a new instrument based on female self-determination, on ratification and implementation of CEDAW and adoption of the Optional Protocol, on opposition to all policies which marginalise and discriminate against women, and on extension of the definitions to the range of situations in which women find themselves in slavery-like conditions, including not only prostitution but also marriage, domestic work and other work and services.

8 Conclusion: repressive vs. empowering strategies

Within all approaches two types of strategies can be distinguished. On the one hand there are the repressive strategies, such as:

- more restrictive immigration policies: i.e. "if we prohibit foreign women from travelling, from leaving or entering the country, they cannot become victims".
- more severe penalization: i.e. "if we make punishments heavy enough, people will be deterred".
- stronger and more effective prosecution: i.e. "if we catch them more effectively, they will not get a chance to do it again".

Existing governmental policies are predominantly limited to these types of strategies, such as restrictive immigration policies and more stringent criminal action. Not only do those approaches have limited preventive effects, they also tend to eventually work against women instead of in their favour, e.g. by restricting women's freedom of movement or by using women as witnesses for combating organised crime in the interest of the state, without allowing them the corresponding protection. Significantly, repressive measures are the most obvious, easiest to implement and most appealing to governments in terms of correspondence to diverse state interests. Combating "trafficking in women" then comes to legitimise very different interests than those of the women.

On the other hand, there are the strategies against violence and abuse that rest upon a strengthening of the rights of women. This approach is mainly put forward by NGOs, next to a call for clearer criminal codes and stricter and non-discriminatory enforcement of existing laws, in combination with providing practical social, legal and medical support.
Acknowledging women's right to self-determination, NGOs take the needs, aspirations and interests of the women concerned as the basis for advocacy work and political campaigning. Participation of the women concerned is seen as essential to the development of effective change strategies. Support and lobby strategies are directed towards empowering women, enabling them to take back control over their lives, and towards facilitating their ability to speak up for their own rights. Repressive strategies are rejected, if the rights of the women involved are not at the same time clearly defined and protected. The aim is to ensure the rights of those involved, as women, as female migrants, as female migrant workers, as domestic workers, as sex workers and as wives. As long as those rights are not recognised and guaranteed, traffic in women, forced labour & slavery-like practices will continue to exist.

6 CONCLUSIONS AND RECOMMENDATIONS

1 Conclusions

A fundamental problem in responding to the issue of trafficking in women is the lack of a precise and coherent definition. The debate is above all characterised by an immense amount of confusion about what is exactly meant by the term "trafficking in women". Old and new definitions show inconsistencies, contradictions, conflicting interests, failure to pinpoint violence and abuse, and a tendency to deny female self-determination. These trends are reflected in the various definitions and concepts used in international and national legislation.

Trafficking in women and forced labour & slavery-like practices should be seen in the context of traditional female roles, a gendered labour market and the world-wide feminization of labour migration, a.o. resulting from women's increasing responsibility for the economic survival of themselves and their families. The women concerned should be seen essentially as (migrant) workers.

Women, denied equal access to the formal and regulated labour markets, are to a great extent relegated to the informal, unprotected and unregulated labour sectors. Within a gendered labour market, sexual and domestic work are two of the few income generating options available for women, especially from poor countries and regions, who seek opportunities to support their families, to escape from traditional gender and family constraints or to find means for an independent life. Migration patterns - on national, intra-regional and international levels - reflect this labour division, relegating migrant women to the national and international markets for female domestic workers, for marriage partners and for the sex-and entertainment industry.

At the same time, poor or lacking legislation and labour standards and the partially illegal or semi-legal character of these types of work create the conditions for abusive recruitment practices and exploitative working conditions, varying from humiliating treatment, low payment and extreme working hours, to outright forced labour and slavery-like practices.

Whilst the number of women wishing to migrate has grown, many destination countries have put in place more restrictive immigration policies, thereby further decreasing the possibilities for legal migration, even when there is a clear demand for certain types of labour. Diminished legal possibilities for labour migration in combination with a demand for foreign labour in the informal sector, create a considerable gap between official polices of receiving countries and day to day practices in prostitution, mail-order bridebusiness and the domestic work sector. This is where organised crime comes in: filling the gap official policies leave. Not only considerable criminal profits are at stake, the incomes of the women concerned also form an important source of foreign exchange for their home countries, while at the same time their labour contributes significantly to the economies of the destination countries.

Poverty and unemployment, development strategies, traditional practices, civil and military conflicts, corruption, high criminal profits, and lack of support mechanisms further contribute to the prevalence of the contemporary forms of trafficking and forced labour & slavery-like practices in marriage, domestic labour and prostitution.

Apart from these general factors, a number of specific contributing factors can be pinpointed in relation to the different manifestations. Laws pertaining to property and inheritance rights, laws on marriage, separation, divorce and residence rights, denying women independence, mobility and legal autonomy, act as a specific contributing factor to trafficking and forced labour & slavery-like practices in marriage. The unregulated and unprotected nature of domestic work and the lack of access to independent residence and work permits make domestic workers vulnerable to violence and abuse. The clandestine and illegal nature of prostitution as such, the (per definition) illegal immigrant status of women working abroad and the marginalization, stigmatization and criminalization of the women involved place women at the mercy of traffickers, abusive brothel keepers and corrupt officials, without the legal instruments to defend themselves.

Common to all contemporary forms of trafficking in women and forced labour & slavery-like practices is that women are denied control over their working and living conditions, and have no recourse to law or society for protection or redress.

Mechanisms of coercion may vary from kidnapping and sale of women, physical force, threats with violence, illegal confinement, withholding of passports and wages, extortion, isolation, deceit, abuse of authority and debt bondage. Within this range, deception, debt bondage and practices amounting to debt bondage seem to be the most prevalent and pervasive contemporary mechanisms of coercion within all three areas covered in this report.

Though most attention until now has been paid to international trafficking, trafficking practices take as much place within national boundaries. With regard to international trafficking, no simple "one way" pattern can be discovered. Many countries are both countries of origin and destination country, while functioning as transit country for again other countries. One can thus speak of a dynamic process, with new patterns developing in a short period of time, due to economic or political changes, as is seen in the rapid growth of traffic in women from the former socialist countries.

Where laws against trafficking exist they are limited to trafficking for prostitution. Inasfar as they define "trafficking" as bringing a person into prostitution in another country, they generally do not target force, but refer mainly to the migration aspect, rejecting and denying prostitution as a survival strategy for the women involved. Also laws typically address the recruitment of 'innocent' women, i.e. women who have never worked in prostitution, did not know they would work in prostitution and who do not want to continue to work as a prostitute.

Women working in prostitution are more or less outlawed and deprived of all protective mechanisms other citizens are entitled to, both in relation to abusive recruitment practices and in relation to abusive working and living conditions. Legal control of prostitution maintains state interests regarding public order, public health, tax payment, deterrence of immigration, etc., instead of monitoring the conditions in which women find themselves. Existing legislation almost never focusses on forced labour and slavery-like practices in prostitution, or only in relation to "innocent" women: women who can prove that they are not prostitutes and whose "morals" are also otherwise undisputed. In general, laws make no distinction between abusive or coercive situations and situations where no deceit, abuse or violence is involved.
General provisions on violence, compulsion, illegal confinement, debt bondage etc., are hardly applied or - again - only in case of "innocent" women. The over-all result is that women working in prostitution are deprived of all legal protection.

Although the law seldom defines violence as the relevant and discriminating criterion, in all countries the presumed "virtue" of the woman concerned is so used. Even when the "chastity" of the woman is not mentioned as an explicit condition in law, it implicitly or explicitly plays a crucial role in the interpretation and enforcement of the law. In trafficking cases, as in other cases of sexual violence, it is by no means exceptional that the victim appears to stand trial instead of the accused. Also in other ways, the interpretation and enforcement of the law is often discriminatory towards women. Actions against trafficking, for example, tend to limit themselves to raids on the prostitutes.
In no way do existing laws on prostitution take the women themselves, their views and interests as a starting point. All prohibitions and regulations with regard to prostitution have the moral condemnation of prostitution as a common basis. This legal standpoint leads to a legal and social attitude towards prostitutes which sees them primarily as "victims" or "deviants". Prostitutes are "objects" of the law, who have to be either "rescued" or made "harmless", they are not considered subjects accorded with rights. Even if the law does not prosecute prostitutes, it does not give legal rights to women working in prostitution, not as workers and, in many countries, not as citizens and persons.

On the whole, existing laws on prostitution neither deter women from entering prostitution, nor do they protect the fundamental rights of women in prostitution. Instead they lead to the stigmatization, marginalization and isolation of prostitutes, thus legitimising and sanctioning the various forms of abuse and oppression of prostitutes. In general it can be said that any form of legislation which marginalises and victimises women in prostitution makes them more vulnerable to violence and abuse.

Existing legislation offers few if any possibilities for women to take legal actions against their violators, due to their illegal or socially marginalised status. Migrant prostitutes not only risk arrest as prostitutes, but also arrest and deportation as illegal aliens. Common policies of expulsion act as a factual barrier to women to seek justice and make prosecution of the offenders virtually impossible since the main witnesses are deported. Even when the law enables women to press charges, many women will choose not to do so for fear of retaliation and lack of legal protection against reprisals. Moreover, in a considerable number of countries law enforcement officials, the judiciary and local politicians themselves are involved in and profit from trafficking and forced labour & slavery-like practices.

Current strategies suffer from the confusion of definitions and contradictory interests of the parties involved. Most governmental measures taken to combat trafficking, forced labour & slavery-like practices can be characterised as repressive strategies, such as stricter immigration policies, more severe penalization and stronger and more effective prosecution. It can be concluded however that especially this type of strategies tends to work against the women concerned instead of in their favour, for example, by restricting women's freedom of movement or by using women as witnesses in the interest of the state for combating organised crime, without providing adequate protection. Non-governmental organizations, on the contrary, concentrate largely on "empowering" strategies, such as strengthening the legal and social position of the women concerned, advocacy and support services.

2 Recommendations

1] New definitions need to be developed, which take the perspective and interests of the women involved as a starting point and which cover abusive brokerage practices as well as abusive working and living conditions, in both the public and private domain.
A new definition should be based on the following principles:

- Recognition of female agency, i.e. the right of women to have control over their own life and body.
- The women themselves, their views, their interests and what is problematic for them should be taken as a starting point, instead of the interests of other parties, however important they may be, such as state interests to restrict immigration or to combat organised crime.
- Coercion should be the fundamental element: violence and abuse constitute the core issue for the women involved. Coercion can take many forms, including but not limited to, violence or threat of violence, deprivation of freedom of movement, deception regarding conditions or nature of work, abuse of authority, confiscation of passports, debt bondage and practices amounting to debt bondage.
- A definition should include all work and services rendered under conditions of coercion as defined above, regardless of whether or not these services are recognised as work, whether they take place under a work contract or a marriage contract or whether they are normative in the society or illegitimate. Within this context, prostitution is one of the income generating activities open to women, which are characterised by the fact that they are unregulated and unprotected forms of labour in the informal sector.
- Both abusive recruitment and brokerage practices and forced labour & slavery-like practices should be addressed. Especially with an eye to measures to be taken, it is important to distinguish between abusive forms of recruitment and mediation and abusive living and working conditions, both within and across borders. Though closely related, they do not necessarily go together.

2] On the basis of these principles the following working definitions are developed, which can serve both as a model and a criterion to re-assess existing legislation:

Trafficking In Women

All acts involved in the recruitment and/or transportation of a woman within and across national borders for work or services by means of violence or threat of violence, abuse of authority or dominant position, debt bondage, deception or other forms of coercion.

Forced Labour & Slavery-like Practices

The extraction of work or services from any woman or the appropriation of the legal identity and/or physical person of any woman by means of violence or threat of violence, abuse of authority or dominant position, debt bondage, deception or other forms of coercion.

3] Existing national and international legislation and other instruments should be re-assessed on the basis of the developed working definitions and the principles involved.

4] The Working group on Contemporary Forms of Slavery should be mandated and adequately financed, to
- assess the usefulness of the 1949 Convention from the perspective of the definitions and principles as developed in this report
- assess the nature and extent of state responsibility for the continuing prevalence of trafficking in women and forced labour and slavery-like practices in their countries.

5] Within the framework of the UN information should be collected on women who are detained by states or are missing in the context of trafficking in women and forced labour & slavery-like practices as defined in this report.

6] Apart from a review of international and national legislation, Standard Minimum Rules for the Treatment of Victims of Trafficking in Women and Forced Labour & Slavery-like Practices, as defined in this report, should be developed which guarantee basic legal protection and possibilities for redress to victims of these practices, such as:
- the right to freedom from persecution or harassment by those in positions of authority
- access to adequate, confidential and affordable health, social and psychological care
- access to competent translators during legal proceedings
- access to free legal assistance and legal representation during criminal or other proceedings
- access to legal possibilities of compensation and redress
- provisions to enable women to press criminal charges and/or take civil action against their violators, such as a temporary staying permit during criminal and/or civil proceedings and adequate witness protection
- assistance to return to her home country if she wishes to do so
- legal permission to stay if return to her home country is unsafe
- protection against reprisals from the side of the perpetrators or from the side of the authorities

In developing such a standard, the draft Standard Minimum Rules developed by the Global Alliance Against Trafficking in Women could be taken as a model.

7] States should ensure and enhance the civil and political, economic, social and cultural rights of women as persons and workers, such as:
- safe working conditions
- freedom of movement, speech and assembly
- freedom to control their working and living conditions as domestic workers, as prostitutes and as wives
- freedom to stop working as prostitutes or domestic workers and/or change the venue of that work
- freedom of divorce

This implies the application of national and international labour regulations and conventions, such as the ILO Conventions on Forced Labour (no. 29), using Article 4; on the Protection of Wages (no. 95), Articles 3, 7, 8 and 9; and the Protection of the Rights of all Migrant Workers and their Families. Special attention should be given to the elimination of debt bondage and practices amounting to debt bondage.

States should promote strategies to improve women's access to viable employment opportunities.

8] Women should be accorded full legal status, independent of marital status, professional activity, etc.

9] The law should treat women as subjects, accorded with rights as independent persons, as workers and as migrants, instead of as objects or dependants who need to be controlled.

10] Strategies to combat trafficking, forced labour & slavery-like practices should be directed towards empowering the women concerned, as persons, as workers and as migrant workers.

Action should be directed towards enabling them to take back control over their lives, and towards facilitating their speaking up for their own rights. Strategies should be based on the recognition of women's right to self-determination and to choose, and avoid stigmatization and victimization of the women concerned.

11] Independent of the official labelling by the authorities labour should be treated as labour, the moment it actually is labour, i.e. an income generating activity.

12] Prostitution should be decriminalised. All laws specific to prostitution should be repealed and prostitution should fall under general laws and regulations pertaining to independent workers and businesses within gender neutral legislation.

13] Working conditions of women in the informal sector, including the sex and entertainment industry, should be improved by creating a legal basis which guarantees working conditions in accordance with national and international accepted labour standards.

14] Noting that self-organizations and NGOs are the main agents for change in the field as well as the main - and often the sole - source of support for the women involved, essential condition for every measure taken should be co-operation with self-organizations and NGOs working in direct contact with the women involved to ensure that the interests of the women are adequately represented. This means that part of any programme should be support and adequate finding of self-organizations and NGOs.

15] Given the lack of precise information on the mechanisms of trafficking in women, forced labour & slavery-like practices, as defined in this report, in the context of marriage and domestic labour research in these fields should be encouraged.

7 SUMMARY

TOWARDS NEW DEFINITIONS

A fundamental problem in responding to the issue of trafficking in women is the lack of a precise and coherent definition. Although the issue was addressed as early as 1885 in Paris at the first international conference on the prevention of trafficking in women, both national legislation and international conventions waver in basic conceptualizations of the crime to be combatted. Historical study reveals five major definitional shifts during the last century with corresponding confusions and tensions. Effective strategies on women's behalf require new definitions that clearly pinpoint violences against women within the scope or intent of what has been referred to as 'trafficking'. Historical shifts in definitions that beg clarification include:

1] From Physical Recruitment to Commercial Exploitation: Whereas the earliest turn of the century treaties focused exclusively upon the process of (forced) recruitment and transport of women, the still influential 1949 Convention for the Suppression of the Traffic in Persons and of the Exploitation of the Prostitution of Others combines 'trafficking as procurement' with 'prostitution as exploitation' (defined particularly by financial management or rental of premises for the purpose of prostitution). "Trafficking" referred specifically to "the purpose of prostitution"; in the words of the convention, the trafficking crime was defined as an "evil accompanying" commercial gain for the "gratification of passions". This 1949 treaty replaced all preceding agreements and remains the key international guideline on trafficking. Many states which signed earlier conventions did not sign this one due, among other things, to the extension of the definition from procurement to commercial gain from prostitution.

2] From Coercion to 'even with her consent': The first treaties are limited to compulsive forms of procurement. For example, the 1910 Convention can be considered a 'minimum agreement treaty': although individual states are allowed to punish non-compulsive forms of procurement, international accord obliges punishment only in cases of "fraud or the use of violence, threats, abuse of authority, or any other means of constraint...". In 1933 the condition of restraint is removed in a new international agreement which renders procurement punishable "even with her consent". This trend is continued after the Second World War. The 1949 Convention explicitly addresses all forms of procurement and exploitation for the purpose of prostitution, with or without consent.

Since the 1980s, the question of consent is again on the agenda. A number of recent initiatives insist upon conditions of 'force' and 'deceit' in defining the crime of trafficking. Most recently, the European Parliament Resolution adopted January 18, 1996 calls upon member states "to provide a clear definition of the concept of trafficking...[and] to take action at an international level to draft a new UN Convention to supersede the obsolete and ineffective Convention for the Suppression of Traffic in Persons and of the Prostitution of Others (1949)". "Any new convention", reads the resolution, "should focus on coercion and deception".

On a more grass roots level of national and international debate, a tension exists between those who define prostitution per se as violence against women and those who distinguish between prostitution by force and by individual decision. Those positions have become more refined and less dichotomized in recent years with the strategic recognition that women may consent to prostitution but not to slavery-like conditions in prostitution. International conventions have not yet caught up to such grass roots perspectives on women's actual experience.

3] From 'trafficking in women' to 'illegal migration': Some of the more recent definitions, especially in western Europe, equate trafficking in women with the smuggling of aliens, also called alien trafficking or trafficking in migrants. The crime then becomes illegal entry or residence. Research shows, however, that although many victims of the international traffic in women (defined by deceit and/or force) are brought illegally into a country and/or are unable to obtain a valid residence permit, just as many cases are known where women enter the country legally, e.g. as brides, maids or artists, and where women have a legal right to stay in a country, often dependent upon the guardianship of an authorized husband or employer. It must also be stressed that trafficking in women is not per definition related to international migration processes, but can and does occur within national borders.

When trafficking is defined by illegal migration or residence, the crime is no longer violence against women but rather infraction of state law. The women concerned are transformed from victims to outlaws or collaborators and are, thereby, subject to detention, penalization and expulsion regardless of the risk to their safety and livelihood. Even if, in principle, it is primarily the transporters and exploiters who are targeted by such definitions, the migrant women themselves are marginalized, criminalized and endangered by their alien status.

4] From a protectionist to a human rights perspective: The Vienna Declaration and Programme of Action adopted by the World Conference on Human Rights on 25 June 1993 recognizes "international trafficking" as a form of gender-based violence and urges its elimination in keeping with the "human rights of women". The importance of this shift is twofold: Firstly, in relation to transport, violence necessarily refers to the conditions of recruitment and travel, not to migration per se. Secondly, in relation to prostitution (given that trafficking is attached specifically to prostitution by the still operative 1949 Convention), one must either specify conditions of violence within prostitution or define prostitution per se as violence. If one defines prostitution per se as violence, then no distinction is made between a commercial transaction freely negotiated and an act of coercion, deceit or abuse. A prostitute is thereby unable to call upon state protection for abuse within the context of her trade because she is defined, a priori, as a violated woman. If one specifies conditions of violence within prostitution, then one must recognize sexual- economic transactions as work and begin to apply conventions against forced labor and slavery-like practices to the sex industry. This is exactly what non-governmental organizations around the world have been informally doing in their daily esistance to violence against women for the past few decades.

5] From prostitution only to the range of informal and unregulated labour: During the last 15 years, attention has been drawn to multiple manifestations of trafficking. This shift is reflected in more recent definitions (for a notable example, see the 1994 UN General Assembly Resolution on Traffic in Women and Girls) which include trafficking not only for the purpose of prostitution but also for the purpose of domestic labour, marriage and other work or services. It is of utmost significance that the purpose of trafficking in women is overwhelmingly tied to traditional female roles and limited survival options as wife, domestic or prostitute. Those labour-intensive activities belong to informal and unregulated sectors such as the entertainment business, household services and marital obligations. The 1979 Convention on the Elimination of all Forms of Discrimination Against Women implies that the exclusion of informal labour sectors from labour law is indirectly discriminatory to women. State accountability is thus extended from the public to private sphere, a great advance for women later made explicit in the 1993 Vienna Declaration; that extension should entail the criminalization of forced labour and slavery-like practices in prostitution, domestic work and marriage as elsewhere. However, state accountability for abuses in the private sphere, most particularly as applies to traditional female services, remains meager; in fact, state law and practice often reinforce rather than combat gender discriminatory labour imperatives.

In bringing the above definitions and their contextualization up to date on women's behalf, two fundamental guidelines are needed to guarantee both minimum agreement and respect for human rights: Firstly, since neither tradition nor law offer reliable safeguards to female self-determination, it is necessary to base all concepts of gender violence on 'women's experiences and well-being' rather than on social custom or state legislation (for example regarding migration, the family or prostitution). Secondly, only 'material criteria of violence' can reliably describe women's actual circumstances. Given the institutionalized power relation between women and men, the illegality or illegitimacy of women's economic activities in emale-designated spheres does not determine whether those activities represent an escape from abuse or a perpetuation of such abuse for the women concerned.

From the perspective of women, the violence of trafficking can operate on two equally important, but separate, levels: (1) the process of recruitment (2) the context of work or services. Those levels must be separated because one can be an act of choice while the other an imposition of force, deceit or other abuse. Drawing upon documentation of the diverse experiences of women in a wide variety of regional and cross- regional contexts, the following working definitions are proposed to distinctly cover abusive brokerage practices, on the one hand, and abusive working and living conditions, on the other, in both public and private spheres:

Trafficking in Women

All acts involved in the recruitment and/or transportation of a woman within and across national borders for work or services by means of violence or threat of violence, abuse of authority or dominant position, debt-bondage, deception or other forms of coercion.

Forced Labour and Slavery-Like Practices

The extraction of work or services from any woman or the appropriation of the legal identity and/or physical person of any woman by means of violence or threat of violence, abuse of authority or dominant position, debt-bondage, deception or other forms of coercion.

Since no past or present document specific to trafficking offers a definition unambiguously in women's interest, the above careful formulations rest upon two well-established and widely accepted international agreements: The League of Nations Slavery Convention of 1926 with its Supplementary Convention of 1956 and the ILO Forced Labour Convention no. 29. Both of those conventions bear keen relevance to the violences in question. The League of Nations Convention and its Supplement condemn all slavery-like practices including debt-bondage and forced marriage. In article 2 of the ILO Forced Labour Convention, forced or compulsory labour is defined as "all work or service which is extracted from any person under the menace of any penalty and for which the said person has not offered himself <herself?> voluntarily".
Such clarity, sorely needed in relation to violence against women, exists only in conventions that do not address gender-specific issues and are therefore free of gender-discriminatory social control corollaries.

The crucial element in both new definitions is coercion in its many forms. Violence or threat of violence includes deprivation of freedom of movement; deception refers specifically to misrepresentation of working conditions or of the nature of the work to be done; abuse of authority can range from confiscation of personal documents to abusing one's dominant social position, be it parental or state authority; debt-bondage means pledging the personal services or labour of a person indefinitely as security for a debt when the length and nature of the service is not clearly defined. "Work or services" include all domestic, sexual, reproductive or other services rendered under the above-mentioned conditions of coercion, regardless of whether those services are recognized as work, whether they take place under a work contract or whether they take place under a marriage contract. "Appropriation of the legal identity" can range from confiscating one's identity papers or supplying a woman with a false identity to the loss of one's legal personality under the marriage contract. "Appropriation of the physical person" refers to the concept of partial or total ownership as used in the Slavery Convention.

The basic principle underlying both working definitions is the (human) right of every person regardless of gender to have control over her or his own life and body. Given the gender specificity of labour in the home and the sex industry, this right is particularly critical for women in the contexts of marriage, domestic work and prostitution. The definitions are, nonetheless, applicable to a wider range of work or service sectors.

CONTEMPORARY MANIFESTATIONS AND TRENDS OF TRAFFICKING IN WOMEN AND FORCED LABOUR AND SLAVERY-LIKE PRACTICES

With the above two-part definition, conditions of recruitment and conditions of work can be studied separately and the relation between the two can be examined with precision. Although former definitions fell under the one title of "trafficking", it is the labour upon destination which gives traffickers their bargaining power. We can investigate that labour according to the categories of marriage, domestic work and prostitution but the dividing lines between those sectors are not so clear because women are often fraudulently recruited for one type of work or service and then forced into another. Given the frequency of deceitful recruitment practices, a woman might find herself in a slavery-like marriage when she had expected a position in the sex industry or she might find herself in domestic service when she had expected a marriage of standing. In fact, as becomes clear from research reports, deception together with debt-bondage are the main crimes committed by contemporary traffickers.

The problem at hand for women is neither travel nor work per se, but rather travel 'conditions' and work 'conditions'. Women from all world regions are migrating for a myriad of economic, social and political reasons. But they are denied honest, safe and equitable travel and work circumstances, also by those authorities who encourage or impel their emigration. Nearly half of the migrants world-wide are women. And whereas "traditionally female migrants have tended to migrate with their families or after the male head of the family has emigrated,..." today... women have sole responsibility for their families and have a stronger incentive to migrate in order to send back remittances to their children" (IOM, 1996d). In addition to the motive of increased imperative family responsibilities, resistance to traditional gender constraints and hopes (sometimes realistic and sometimes misguided) for greater economic and social opportunity lead millions of women to leave home. According to an ILO report on international labour migration of Asian women (Lim, 1996) approximately 1.5 million Asian women are working abroad both legally and illegally. Nonetheless, despite the massive migration of women, official policies continue to treat women as dependents of male migrants.

Trafficking takes similar forms be it for marriage, domestic work or prostitution. In all cases, agents play upon women's motives to migrate by offering travel means and employment possibilities otherwise out of reach. There are, however, important distinctions between the legal context of the three spheres. In brief, whereas the greatest obstacle to safe and just economic options for migrants in general is immigration law, the greatest obstable to safe and just economic options for women in marriages is likely to be family law reinforced by religious traditions, the greatest obstable to such options for women in domestic work is likely to be labour law and the greatest obstacle for women in prostitution is likely to be criminal law reinforced by social stigma. Those institutional distinctions, united in their refusal to recognize female labour as work, are far more operative for the women in question than are the often vague distinctions between reproductive, household and sexual labour. In relation to brokerage practices and working conditions, the same principles of social justice are appropriate and should be applied to all three labour spheres regardless of the legal umbrella under which they are classically treated.

Racism interweaves with the above factors in abusive recruitment strategies and working conditions. There is a hierarchy operating in the employment market for domestic workers based upon crude racist stereotypes under which workers can expect different rates of pay and different kinds of jobs depending upon skin color and nationality.

Wherever women go, they find themselves restricted in work options: 'unskilled' work on the assembly line, cleaning and cooking and caring work (either in private houses as domestic workers or in restaurants and hotels), entertainment or prostitution. And many women opt for the marriage market in the hope of landing on a relatively wealthy man who can provide future security if not liberty. Many women do, indeed, earn a living to support themselves and their children within such spheres. At the same time, given the institutionalized exploitation of women's labour, abusive practices are most widespread exactly within traditional female occupations. Moreover, whereas demand for women's labour is all-pervasive, it is rarely recognized in law or custom as work. Women in such informal sectors are not covered by social security and they have no legal backing for worker rights. Moreover, they may actually be criminalized by laws which forbid such labour outside of existing state regulation. Prostitution, in particular, is likely to be a crime; and even if it is legal for state residents, it is a crime for foreign women (unless recruited for state-run brothels) regardless of customer demand and considerable state revenues from the labour of migrant prostitutes. In the case of marriage, a woman's labour is viewed more as a duty, an instinct or a selfless act of devotion than as a toil determined by material conditions.

***

Trafficking in women and forced labour/slavery-like practices are definitely not a new phenomena in women's lives. For only one of many examples, at the end of the 19th century women in need of economic subsistence migrated in great numbers from Europe to South America; according to historical accounts, they faced frequent deception and coercion by traffickers taking advantage of their lack of legal or social legitimacy. The same dynamics operate today within the constraints of recent historical contingencies. Research reveals the following factors as key contributors to contemporary trafficking and forced labour/slavery-like practices:

1] Poverty/ Unemployment: Information provided by NGOs as well as testimonies provided by the women concerned confirm that one of the main reason for migrating and for being receptive to recruitment is women's urge to improve their economic situation. Absence of employment opportunities combines with an increase in economic burden to make migration a pressing alternative.

2] Development Strategies: Tourism, industrialization and globalization are often more a source of aggravation than an opportunity for women. For example:

- European men, among others, are "offered" "exotic sex" in ex-colonial territories as part of a tourism package. Tourism is, therefore, an opportunity for employment but women are denied agency to work in their own interest.

- Governments have changed vast areas of agricultural land into industrial areas, thereby eliminating the jobs of peasant women without compensation or alternative employment possibilities; agents then come to rural areas and promise those women work as domestic workers, secretaries, etc. which often results in financial profit for the agent and abusive labour conditions for the women.
- Economic policies designed by some governments to fulfill the conditions of international loans, such as in Sri Lanka, include opening up of Free Trade Zones and promoting migration for employment. Women constitute the majority of workers in both sectors which are characterized by slave-like conditions including physical and sexual abuse.

3] Migration (Labour) Laws and Policies: Whilst the number of women wishing to migrate has grown, oppportunities for international legal migration, especially to Western countries, have decreased. Looking at destination countries, a great number of them claim that they are no longer immigration countries. Measures have been taken to tighten asylum procedures, reinforce border controls and reduce permits for foreign workers. Despite such official acts, the demand for migrant workers is increasing. For example, there has been a massive increase in demand in Europe for private domestic service, including care of children and the elderly; that demand is largely filled by migrant women without legal status. The other occupation open to migrant women is prostitution. According to the IOM, a majority of sex workers in many sectors of the sex industry in the European Union are migrant women (i.e. 75% of street prostitutes in overall Germany; 80% of street prostitutes in Milan, Italy; 50% of prostitutes generally in Dutch large cities). However, the work of foreign prostitutes is not recognized as work and the women involved are without legal protection, either from labour laws or immigration laws. Migrant women are, thus, not only vulnerable to traffickers but also to police control and state punishment. Even those countries that promote and legalize the immigration of women migrants, like Japan with its policy of importing foreign brides, view migrant women as undesirable, although needed, aliens. Also countries of origin profit economically from migrant women's cheap labour, such as the Dominican Republic for whom the prostitution of women abroad is one of the most important sources of foreign exchange. Those women are extremely vulnerable to abuse because current alien policies and attitudes supersede the application of human rights charters when it concerns women in the informal sectors of domestic work and prostitution, not to mention the most invisible sector of arranged marriage.

4] Corruption of authorities: Numerous are the reports on incidental and structural, small and large scale involvement of officials in trafficking and forced labor/slavery-like practices on both local and international levels. This involvement ranges from (a) coercive or deceptive recruitment of women for work or services by police officers to (b) protection by officials of traffickers and abusive employers in exchange for financial gain or free sexual service to (c) abuse of authority by officials such as robbing women of their passports or blackmailing those in need of papers at the price of rape.

5] Traditional Practices: Trafficking and slavery-like practices may be a part of traditional and/or religious custom. For example, although women have officially had the legal right to a free marriage in China for the past 40 years, the institution of arranged/forced marriage as an economic transaction is a widespread legitimized practice rooted in traditional feudal culture. That practice then provides public support for the illegal activities of traffickers; such violence, both legal and illegal, is considered a normal, private family matter.

6] High Profits: Forced recruitment and/or forced labour of women hold relatively few risks for the guilty parties whilst providing considerable financial gain. The illegality and attractive economic benefits encourage involvement of well- established criminal syndicates such as the Yakuza in Japan. Financial investigations of the Australian Federal Police in 1994 identified 280 transactions, totalling over A $1.3 m., related to movements of funds from Australia to SE Asia. Those funds reflect both the forwarding of migrant women's earnings back to their countries, particularly of prostitution earnings, and the payment to organizers and facilitators in those countries.

7] Civil and Military Conflicts: Among the abuses incurred by women in times of war are rape and forced labour. Many women in Burma, for example, prefer to leave the country to work in the sex industry in Thailand rather than serve soldiers without payment at home. In Thailand they risk arrest, detention and expulsion as prostitutes and as illegal immigrants.

Marriage

A marital relationship can be termed servile when the husband exerts power as 'owner' over the wife. However a woman has entered such a relationship, she is likely to be subjected to labour exploitation, intimidation with (the menace of) physical and sexual violence, and exclusion - comparable with slavery. Furthermore, she can be made to work without pay; she cannot decide whether and how many children she wants; she is threatened with loss of her children if she disobeys her husband; she is forbidden to leave the marriage or to earn an independent income outside the home or, if she does earn, she is not allowed to dispose of her earnings.

Women are trapped into relationships ranging from traditional servile marriages to contemporary forms of arranged or forced marriage by a number of institutionalized gender discriminations among which the following are crucial:

- In many countries all over the world (married) women do not have full legal status and are considered minors under customary, religious or secular law. They therefore possess no independent legal capacity to enter into contracts, to sue or to be sued in their own name, to enter into employment negotiations or to begin a business of their own. This makes them totally reliant upon the cooperation of their husbands or other male guardians.
- Women are denied the right to property in many places. According to a study on servile marriages in Nepal, Pakistan, Tanzania, the Gambia and Losotho, the denial of property rights (in particular, the right to own land) and inheritance rights is the greatest obstacle to women's autonomy.
- Laws on marriage, separation and divorce can put women at greater risk of abuse and violence. In Uganda and Kenya, for instance, a court will not entertain a petition for divorce

within the first three years of marriage. And even after three years, many women trafficked for marriage are kept as virtual prisoners so that they cannot get the evidence of husband adultery which is the key to getting a divorce. On the other hand, many immigrant women cannot afford a divorce despite husband abuse because their residence permit depends upon the marriage.

***

Cross-regional research suggests the following hierarchy from the most to the least common abusive recruiting methods for marriage: Promise of marriage, false marriage contracts, buying a woman from her parents or guardians, kidnapping, false job contracts, promise of work as a waitress/domestic worker, buying a woman from her previous husband. Given the clandestinity of most of the above transactions, estimates depend upon partial documentation and observation of people working in the field. Those sources point to deceit as the major trafficking strategy. Women are eager to migrate and they are well aware of the world-wide demand for their labour. They therefore seek legitimate channels of migration; as these channels are unforthcoming, the women become vulnerable to deceptive state and criminal profiteers.

With regards to kidnapping, it is important to note that, contrary to popular mythology, current research has failed to find widespread evidence of kidnapping for the purpose of prostitution or domestic work; however, kidnapping and sale for the purpose of marriage is strikingly documented for certain rural areas of China. In some villages, kidnapped and sold women account for two thirds of all young married women in the village. Reasons for this trend nclude a shortage of women across the nation to fulfill the traditional requirement of every man to continue his family line; also, it is cheaper to buy a wife than to marry one given the cost of betrothel gifts exchanged between men in transfering "their women" from one family to another. The women who are kidnapped are generally abducted en route away from their native villages, usually in an attempt to escape an arranged marriage or simply in search of a more autonomous life. Once abducted, they may be sold and resold and subjected to cruel and inhuman treatment by the men who buy them as wives. And, because many women have attempted escape from slavery or committed suicide, men are known to lock them up, tie them down or torture them when caught on the run.

Whereas kidnapping is technically illegal, forced marriages are perfectly legal in China and as well as in a number of other countries, such as Kenya. In China, 30-90% of marriages are forced depending upon local customs. In Kenya, Indian women brought into the country for the purpose of marriage are robbed of their passports and kept in bondage. Sometimes a woman is recruited under the pretense of marriage, for example in Bangladesh, and then forced into working under slave-like conditions in factories under the auspices of a so-called husband.
In Mozambique, refugee women from the war-torn countryside are sold to South African men; referred to as "stock" by the traders, they are promised work over the border and then sold to men in the townships. In Japan, women are recruited as computer trainees from Sri Lanka and then forced into mass marriages.

In the industrialized countries, there is a growing demand for women as wives; the commercialization of matchmaking such as Mail-Order-Brides (MOBs) is often loaded with fraudulent practices. The majority of women involved are presently Filipinas, but there is also a growing trade in women from Eastern Europe, Colombia and several other South East Asian countries. The bureaus operate on the West European, Japanese, Chinese, Auatralian and North American market. There is little, if any, government regulation of the industry. Although quite a number of marriages may fulfill women's expectations, many marriages become a site of forced sexual and domestic labour. Since the women depend upon the continuance of the marriage for their legal status in most places, they may choose to remain under slavery-like conditions rather than face expulsion back to the harsh home circumstances they left in the first place.

Domestic Labour

Women are recruited for domestic work through various channels. Whereas some of those channels are bona fide, others are characterized by deceit, cheating, over-charge and debt-bondage, and can be classified as trafficking. Domestic work and prostitution are often women's only two employment options and many women opt for domestic work due to the greater stigma on prostitution. Women working in their own country report deception about the conditions of domestic work but rarely about the nature of work. Also migrant women are most often deceived about work conditions. Many professional women answer adds for domestic work because they can earn more as a maid in an industrialized country than as a lawyer or engineer in their developing home country; but sometimes they find themselves robbed of legal papers and without recourse in slavery-like circumstances. Other migrants, both professional and semi- or un-educated, are deceived also about the nature of the work; traffickers take particular advantage of uneducated migrants who cannot read or write or of educated migrants who do not know the language of official documents.

In addition to newspaper advertisements in countries of origin, migrants are sometimes ecruited by friends and family already working abroad whose employer wants additional services for himself or for his associates, a process referred to as chain migration. But often the employer backs out once the newcomers arrive, finding it impossible or too much of a bother to arrange the necessary papers; the recent migrants are then stranded and without means either to stay or to return.

Others are recruited by agencies, many of which are illegal. Those which operate deceptively manage to evade immigration controls without explaining to the migrant the consequence of illegal entry for her living and working conditions. Fees can be excessive (for example, $2,500 for a voyage from Peru to Spain); in some cases agencies withhold the worker's passport and "loan" the airfare, fees, etc. under obligation to repay the agency out of later earnings before the passport will be returned. Once drawn into the recruitment network, women are often faced with the payment of a bewildering varity of fees requiring unpaid labour, confinement in abusive conditions, loans from home and sale of possessions. This catches women in a vicious circle of debt tying them to their employer. In addition, workers may be admitted as a tourist with the name of the employer on their passports, for example in the UK; thereafter they do not have the right to change employer without becoming undocumented, that is illegal, workers.

The abuses most commonly reported within domestic work are similar around the world: Despite the massive demand for domestic workers, especially in industrialized countries, most governments do not regulate or protect this occupation any more than other private sectors of the economy. Domestic work is not normally covered under labour codes or social security provisions so workers have no recourse to justice or protection. In particular, they can take no action against employers who withhold or delay pay, who impose 12 hour work days of heavy labour or who fire them without cause. Neither do they have backing to resist psychological abuse, denial of time off, beatings, sexual abuse, confinement, or compulsory HIV/AIDS tests or to insist upon proper sleeping accommodations, access to health care and a minimum wage. Migrant domestic workers are especially vulnerable to frequent breach of contract, inadequate provision of food and disrespect for their culture and religion. Furthermore, migrants who are undocumented (a status that they may have acquired by manipulation, deceit or coercion) live in constant fear of police arrest, fines, imprisonment and expulsion. Due to the large profits made by recruiters and due to the cheap service reaped by employers, migrant women's compliance - albeit by force, confinement and intimidation - is heavily imposed. Without legal rights as workers or immigrants and without support services for escape from slavery-like practices, those workers have no recourse in the face of human rights violations. As one Nigerian woman in Britain exclaimed: "I came here as a worker but I was treated as a slave. That gets me real mad..." (Kalayaan, 1995).

***

Once trapped in coercive brokerage practices or labour circumstances, it is extremely difficult, if not impossible, for many domestic workers to escape. They may be forced to remain in the abusive situation for a number of reasons: Most critical is the difficulty of finding another job and the lack of any surplus money to tie them over for a period of unemployment.

Migrant workers are also dissuaged by their lack of identity papers, by the illegality of seeking employment with anyone other than the initial contractor, by the possibility of reprisals against themselves or their families for not paying debts, by the violence of traffickers or employers, by their knowledge of the complicity of state authorities (including their own embassies in certain cases), by possible arrest by authorities, by a lack of knowledge of the laws and their actual rights and, above all, by a reluctance to return home without money or without future hope of re-emigration to a better life. In some countries, women cannot go elsewhere because of specific regulations, for example in Greece where undocumented workers are fined for every month they have been in Greece in an irregular situation. As a result, workers are unable to leave the country even if they want to do so because they do not have the money to pay the fine.

Not surprisingly, very few women report to the authorities. In addition to all the above mentioned barriers, women stress language barriers and the dismissive or abusive behavior of law-enforcers and the involvement of officials. Indeed, a risk of ill-treatment by authorities, such as harassment by the police, direct expulsion, harassment by immigration officers, arrest or detention for having false papers or no identity papers, refusal to give back identity papers or issue new papers or arrest as a prostitute are reported in every world region. With few exceptions, governments do not encourage women to report trafficking or slavery-like practices to the authorities, as evidenced by the lack of essential supportive services such as interpretors, confidential counseling, safe shelters, free legal aide, legal residence during investigations or assistance in returning home for those who so desire. When such support is available from outsiders, it is provided by NGOs. Most important, however, is the support women give to one another in informal networks and, more and more, in initiatives for collective organization.

Prostitution

The criminal treatment of prostitution renders it even more clandestine, marginal, profitable and stigmatized than other sectors of female-designated labour. Furthermore, official criminalization of women identified as prostitutes, whether during recruitment or on the work site, functions to rationalize abusive treatment as the fault of corrupt, dangerous, bad or 'fallen' women rather than of discriminatory laws and rituals.

Trafficking practices, as defined by the working definitions, are reported for the purpose of prostitution in relation to women of every legal status ("national" women who are working in their own country, "legal migrants" and "illegal migrants"); however, illegal migrants clearly form the most violated group with nearly three times as much reported abuse as for either nationals or legal migrants. It must be noted that the category "legal migrant prostitute", unlike the category "legal migrant wife or domestic" is often meaningless since a woman is criminalized in most countries by her status as a prostitute if not be her status as an immigrant.

The most common strategy used by traffickers of women for the purpose of prostitution is once again deceit. And, as with domestic work, deception is usually about the conditions of work rather than about the nature of work. The fact that most deception is not about the nature of the work indicates that a substantial number of women do know that they are recruited for prostitution and consent to the work itself, but clearly do not know that they will end up in slavery-like conditions. Other women are deceived about the nature of the work. They are recruited under promises of jobs as waitresses, cleaners, dancers, entertainers or domestic workers. Sometimes traffickers make use of false job contracts; women may be promised marriage or false marriages may be arranged. Recruiting agents are most often acquaintaines of family and friends, friends, job agencies and artist agents; family and friends are sometimes themselves coerced into mediating for traffickers.

The relation between trafficking and forced labour/slavery-like practices is nowhere more clear than in the practice of debt- bondage: For example, a woman may be led to believe that she has a clear contract for transport and a job, perhaps knowingly in a brothel, and then find herself in a situation of unspecified, indefinite and uncontrollable debt; she is then bonded against eventual earnings to her future employer. She will have to pay back the recruiter or travel agent and the brothel owner the sum for which she was purchased (in other words, she is owned) and/or she must pay back a sum for travel, documents, food, housing, medical and other unforeseen expenses, often including a host of arbitrary fines. It is not uncommon in such situations for the debt to increase rather than decrease due to employer control of fining, over-charges and additional deductions, notably for police bribes and obligatory "savings accounts" controlled by the brothel owner. Payment for sexual services is then handed directly over to the owner who holds the money against the woman's debts. With no access to her earnings and no control over the (in)justice of her debts, women have no means to leave. Such slavery-like abuse occurs in all world regions.

Other manifestations of abusive conditions within prostitution include, in order of frequency reported: psychological abuse, physical abuse, confinement, police harassment and arrest, sexual assault, no right to refuse a customer or a mandatory minimum number of customers per day, isolation, denial of days off, no right to refuse specific sexual acts, confiscation of identity papers and/or passport, imposition of twelve or more hours of work daily, no access to medical care, forced or dangerous abortions, threats of reprisals against family members for non-compliance, confiscation of personal belongings, denial of right to use condoms, withholding of pay, no proper sleeping accommodations, compulsory AIDS testing and no access to the results, inadequate food and, incidentally, forced recruitment of sisters and friends into prostitution. According to reports, the preceding abuses are perpetuated four times more often against (illegal) migrant women than among national and legal migrant women in Europe; in other regions, the conditions for various groups are much more alike.

Escape from coercive conditions is inhibited by a fear of violent reprisals to self and family, fear of arrest, fear of expulsion (for migrants) and fear of rejection or moral condemnation by society. Indeed, escape is an act of resistance which does often elicit reprisals by both state and criminal agents and which may mean social visibility and stigmatization as a prostitute or as an abused (seen as "damaged") woman. Next to fears of physical and social punishment for insubordination, women are locked into slavery- like conditions by a lack of economic alternatives, a lack of money, no support system and no (or false) identity papers. Some women do manage to escape coercive employers and to establish themselves more autonomously within prostitution or within another occupation. Others abandon escape strategies as simply too risky, but succeed in gaining some power of negotiation with their employer and, in the best of cases, in arriving at eventual detachment from oppressive control.

Even if state policies permit women, in principle, to report abuse, few women do so because of a lack of confidence in the legal system, a lack of knowledge of their rights, fear that they will be punished or arrested, fear of reprisals by criminal networks and, for migrants, language barriers and a fear of expulsion. Most women have no trust whatsoever in the police or in any other authorities because they are continually faced with daily harassment, corruption, and physical and sexual coercion by exactly those officials. As to migrant prostitutes, a majority of them are illegal in the country of residence and they realistically expect expulsion and probably blame for the abuse committed against them if they report to the police. A forced return home may mean a return to intolerable toil and confinement, the reasons for their original departure, as well as humiliation for returning empty- handed and perhaps rejection by their own family for having worked as prostitutes; at the same time, there is no guarantee that return will avoid reprisals from criminal networks. But the bottom line inhibiting these women from reporting to authorities is their awareness that the law and law officials world-wide do not respect the person or the human rights of prostitutes. Prostitute women know, more than anyone, that their recruiters and employers have more power than they, especially if those agents are public authorities.

The support that is available, provided by NGOs as well as by prostitutes' rights organizations, includes counseling, legal advise, medical attention, safe shelters, financial assistance and witness protection. Most important among measures designed to concretely help women escape abuse or change their situation are access to alternative employment (whether or not still in prostitution), access to education and training, decriminalization by arrangement of legal papers, possibilities to take civil action against violators without fear of expulsion or arrest, and access to an array of services as listed above for legal and medical assistance and for safe shelters. For those migrants who return home, there is likewise great need for educational and training opportunities, job opportunities, financial support, shelters, services, support to prosecute offenders and protection against reprisals from agents and against state criminalization.

The above-mentioned prostitutes' rights organizations have been the most grass roots source of information, advocacy and self- organization among sex workers in diverse circumstances. As yet, those organizations are only marginally recognized by national governments and international bodies as essential partners in the struggle for social justice and self-representation.

NATIONAL LEGAL CONTEXTS

National and cross-national legal instruments governing brokerage and working conditions of women in marriage, domestic work and prostitution are complex both conceptually and practically. As stated earlier, the term "trafficking" is fraught with inconsistencies, contradictions and conflicting interests both within and between juridical frameworks such that deceit, force and violence are often irrelevant or secondary in recruitment and labour legislation pertaining to women migrants and nationals in female-designated labour spheres. In fact, the only labour sphere considered in national anti-trafficking legislation, as in international conventions, is prostitution, thus excluding a whole range of other work or service activities including those subsumed under domestic work and marriage. Some laws glue trafficking to commercial exploitation as if every (migrant) prostitute is necessarily a victim of (forced) recruitment (who must be expulsed, detained or rehabilitated "for her own good" or "for the good of society") and as if the migration of women per se implies criminal, whether or not freely contracted, labour intentions. Labour intentions are, indeed, central to the problematic at hand. From the perspective of women, the need and right to work with just compensation under proper conditions is primary, whether in one's country of origin or in a country with a demand for one's labour. However, from the perspective of the state, restriction and control of such labour is primary so that officials have more authorization to police women workers than to police working conditions.

A detailed review of pertinent legislation demonstrates the double bind of women whereby they are obliged and recruited to work in female-designated sectors due both to a lack of alternative employment and/or to gender imperatives while, at the same time, they are punished and discredited for doing so. Legal contexts framing that bind include both trafficking legislation (however defined and under whatever heading) and legislation on marriage, domestic labour and prostitution. Marriage and domestic labour laws go beyond the scope of the present report although the preceding examination of current manifestations of trafficking and forced labour/slavery-like practices reveals the need for in-depth study of the effect of those legal contexts on women's lives. The focus here will be specifically prostitution laws, both in relation to conditions of work and conditions of recruitment. How do those laws affect women? Do they guard against trafficking and forced labour/slavery-like practices according to our working definitions? Or, do those laws collude with violence, coercion and deception of women either inadvertently or by institutional design?

Documentation from all world regions based upon direct interviews, police records, surveys and case studies overwhelmingly shows the failure of the range of existing prostitution laws to support women attempting to avoid, escape, report or prosecute abusers. Prostitution laws fall into two categories, both of which deny the legitimacy of sex work and sex workers: (1) Absolute prohibition of prostitution (2) Selective prohibition and regulation of prostitution. It is important to emphasize that despite contradictions with their own legal codes, states everywhere are explicit or implicit partners in the management and exploitation of the sex industry. A review of legal practices provides a sketch of the uneasy relation between state regulations and the labour conditions imposed upon women.

The first category of prostitution laws prohibit prostitution and criminalize prostitutes.
Sex workers can be fined heavily and regularly (such as in France), arrested and imprisoned (for up to seven years in Uganda, also in Bangladesh, India, Pakistan, Switzerland and Italy), detained in so-called rehabilitation centers against their will (in Vietnam) or sentenced to death (in Iran). Although such laws pretend to eliminate prostitution, governments admit (for one example, see report of the Slovenia government to the Council of Europe, 1994) the failure of prohibitionist laws to deter either customers or their providers. Instead, the common effect of a prohibition system is to increase illicit activity at considerable profit for both pimps and police; control of prostitutes by legal and illegal third parties increases prostitute vulnerability to abuse.
Migrant women, whether or not victims of trafficking, are in an even more defenseless position than other women. They are not only liable to arrest as prostitutes but also to arrest and expulsion as illegal foreigners. Under such precarious circumstances, prostitute self-organization is all but impossible and medical, social, legal or other services are inaccessible. Prostitute clients are basically immune to punishment despite formal sanctions; even when reprimanded, their punishments are incomparable to those of their providers (for example, in India a prostitute can be imprisoned from six months to one year and her customer from seven days to three months, although his sentence is almost never imposed). It must be emphasized that periodic arrests of customers has never in any way improved the position of prostitutes; rather, it is again another push to more isolated and unsafe conditions for women.

The second, and dominant, type of prostitution laws do not prohibit prostitution per se but do legislate selective regulations and prohibitions regarding an array of behaviors intrinsic to the work. Some behaviors are those of prostitutes (and their customers) and some are behaviors of third parties. Beginning with state control of prostitutes (control of customers is secondary, at most), one finds definite enforcement of sentences for failure to register, to appear for mandatory state venereal disease checks, to pay taxes and to stay within designated work zones; in addition, prostitutes can be punished for organizing or even living with other prostitutes, and for working without a legal residence, tourist, artist, working or marital permit. In practice, the above exigencies jeopardize women's social mobility, health, safety and possibilities for escaping and reporting abuse. Specifically, women at risk of job loss, arrest, imprisonment, expulsion or lifelong commitment to a brothel by state authorities will avoid registration at all costs. For that reason, a large majority of prostitutes under a mandatory registration system prefer to work in hiding from the police despite the greater risk of violence and of police blackmail for money and sex. Prostitutes will avoid mandatory health checks for the same reasons; it should also be noted that mandatory checks deny medical confidentiality, encourage customers to insist on unsafe sex due to their illusory sense of immunity, signify arrest for unregistered/unexamined women, and fail as public health measures due to their focus on detection rather than prevention of disease and to the lack of control of the overwhelming majority of players, namely customers. As to zoning, prostitutes fearful of police control avoid prescribed areas and move to isolated, often unsafe work areas. Lastly and perhaps the most widespread prohibition, anti-soliciting laws mpose extra work hours to cover frequent fines, impose reliance on pimps for mediated contact with customers, and lead to an exhausting flight from police officers who are trained to entrap rather than protect women.

The above range of state constraints and harassments portrays the legal context to which women locked into forced labour/slavery-like practices in prostitution have recourse. How can they report abuse when their status or commercial activity as prostitute defines they themselves as outlaws? Escape would probably mean arrest by authorities and even more violence from their abusers. Many women prefer to take their chances with criminal networks than to face the public humiliation, definitive social ruin and risk of violent reprisal a turn to the law could entail. That no-win situation, whether based upon a system of absolute or selective prohibitions, operates for all prostitutes and is especially prohibitive for migrants. Migrant women are often dependent upon recruiters, border guards, employers and husbands in order to live and work legally in a country; such overseers are known to collaborate with the police by offering bribes and "free service" at the expense of the migrants. And when bribes are not paid or the authorities decide to enforce the laws, foreign women are the first to be arrested and either detained in jails (be it in Thailand, Pakistan, Netherlands or Italy) or expulsed to a situation they had originally fled for reasons of need, violence, forced labour or threat to life.

***

Next to prohibitions on women's commercial behavior in prostitution are prohibitions on third parties who recruit women for prostitution or who manage prostitution businesses.

Most anti-trafficking laws fall under prohibitions on recruitment, although some are subsumed under the heading of anti-management or anti-exploitation. Drawing upon diverse national laws, "trafficking" is currently defined in the following ways: (1) All prostitution related activities (Malta) (2) All third party involvement in prostitution (India, Bangladesh, Portugal) (3) Buying, selling or obtaining possession of a woman for prostitution (Bangladesh) (4) Any recruitment for prostitution (Nicaragua) (5) Bringing a person/woman into prostitution in another country/ promoting or facilitating the entrance to or exit from the country of a woman to practice prostitution (Austria, Thailand, Japan, Colombia, Peru) (6) Bringing another person into prostitution under conditions of violence, deceit or abuse of authority or circumstances (Nepal) (7) Bringing or keeping a person in prostitution by abuse of circumstances and/or violence, deceit or abuse of authority/ Any recruitment and/or exploitation with the use of violence, abuse of authority or deceit (Germany, Netherlands) (8) Sale and purchase of a human being for any purpose (Nepal). The above list demonstrates clearly that no examination or re-evaluation of trafficking legislation can avoid an assessment of prostitution legislation and its application. In most countries, the two terms - prostitution and trafficking - are intertwined or even synonymous.

Unlike prohibitions on women's behavior, prohibitions on third parties, whether called anti-trafficking or anti-prostitution, are not enforced against exploiters as dictated by law but are regularly enforced against prostitutes. For example, laws in most countries include a prohibition of procurement, pimping and/or living off the earnings of prostitution; prostitutes suffer under this law because anyone with whom they live (including a partner, roommate or child) can be and frequently is charged with procurement and living off "immoral earnings". Anti-pimping laws also make it illegal for women to work together in the interest of safety, social support and economic cooperation because prohibitions against female solidarity are strongly enforced. Another example of a third party prohibition that burdens women is the common ban on keeping, managing, operating, letting, hiring or furnishing a brothel or other premise for the purpose of prostitution. It is the women working in brothels who are regularly harassed by the police and forced to pay large amounts of money to escape arrest, physical and sexual torture, and confinement. Typically, bans on brothels coincide, however hypocritically, with open or undercover state complicity with brothel owners. For two of many examples: In Bangladesh brothel owners make regular contracted payments to the police, customs department and other local state agencies; in Peru, thousands of women working in brothels are detained monthly without any action taken against brothel owners. Also, prohibitions on brothels necessarily criminalize the relationship between a prostitute and the brothel owner, thus denying prostitutes worker rights including proper conditions and access to medical and social benefits. In almost all countries any contract regarding prostitution is either against the criminal law or considered as offending "good morals" and therefore invalid. And once again, the women in the weakest position are migrant women who are totally discredited both as prostitutes and as foreigners.

Discreditation of women is a central theme in relation both to the violation of women and to their denial of just recourse following abuse. Quite a number of countries explicitly disqualify women from legal protection who lack "virtue," (Canada, Uganda) "honesty" (Colombia) or "chastity" (Brazil, Japan). "Virtue," "chastity" and "honesty" are not used to delegitimize men; they refer specifically to the sexual or sexual-economic behavior of women, notably to women in prostitution. Other countries diminish sentences against the violator of a woman if she is a prostitute (El Salvador). Research has shown that countries with less explicit distinctions between worthy and unworthy women are no less likely to put a woman on trial when she accuses a man of abuse. In relation to "trafficking", the offense is considered less serious if the woman was a prostitute prior to being recruited. In other words, once a woman has worked in the sex industry, be it by consent or by force, her legal rights diminish or disappear. The reason for her disqualification is not the illicit character of prostitution because male parties, notably clients, managers, police collaborators and state regulators, do not suffer the same plight. No, the denial of rights to women in prostitution is clearly an example of gender discrimination and abuse.

A second legal disqualification of women in prostitution refers to the non-application of existing laws to female-designated sectors of the economy, in particular to prostitution, domestic work and marriage. There exists legislation in the criminal codes of all countries against illegal confinement, coercion, debt-binding, deception and slavery-like practices. Although such legislation could appropriately be applied to situations of trafficking and forced labour as defined in this report, it is never so applied. Perhaps the main reason for non- application is a refusal to recognize prostitution, the case in point, as labour despite the fact that it entails commercial exchanges of great importance that involve many profit-oriented parties, including the state, and despite the fact that millions of women depend upon earnings from sex work for their livelihood.

Returning to the question of how prostitution and trafficking laws (sometimes one and the same) affect women and whether they protect or endanger prostitutes, women who migrate with the intention of working in prostitution and women who are forced to do so, we can conclude that those laws menace rather than protect women. Most fundamentally, they refuse to grant women the status of adult subjects with human rights. The letter of the law and official practice rarely target force, deceit, violence or slavery-like practices when the victim is female and never do they honor female self-determination. In particular, women stigmatized as prostitutes or unchaste persons are controlled, fined, imprisoned, medically examined by force and commercially exploited by governments in the interest of state agents, criminal networks, brothel owners and individual husbands, pimps, customers and guardians of women.

CURRENT STRATEGIES

The diversity of current strategies employed by both governmental and non-governmental organizations to address traffic in women and forced labour/ slavery-like practices reflects the diversity - and divergence - of definitions and interests attached to those phenomena. Logically, a solution is drafted in accordance with one's conceptualization of the problem to be solved. If the problem is viewed as economic, then different solutions will be proposed than if the problem is viewed as moral or criminal. Furthermore, since the issues in question are complex, strategic responses are necessarily many faceted; the situation of women is determined by multiple positions as woman, prostitute/ domestic worker/ wife, migrant, migrant worker, victim of (organized) criminality, and so forth. More than one strategy is appropriate and any one approach is not necessarily good or bad. It is, however, possible to evaluate the impact of a given strategy on the women concerned and such has been the aim of the present report.

Six main approaches to traffic in women and forced labour/ slavery-like practices can be deciphered from the array of current strategies. Within each approach one can distinguish a repressive and a empowering strategic mode. Although repressive modes can contribute to a recognition of coercion in recruitment and work as a crime, they run a major risk of turning against women (for example, by restricting women's freedom of movement or by using women as witnesses against organized crime without protection against reprisals); significantly, repressives strategies are appealing to governments for their simplicity and congruence with a range of state interests such as immigration control. Empowerment strategies, used primarily by NGOs, are geared toward supporting women and strengthening their position.

1] A moral Problem

Within a moral framework, prostitution is viewed as the problem. Based upon the traditional definition wherein trafficking is inherently coupled with prostitution, prostitution itself is seen as evil without regard for conditions of consent or coercion. Women in prostitution are either victims who must be rescued or deviants who must be reformed/punished.

Corresponding governmental strategies include a criminalization of prostitution (either of all parties in a prohibitionist system or of third parties in an abolitionist system) and sometimes rehabilitation programmes, obligatory or not, for prostitutes. The impact on women is invariably a combination of isolation, stigmatization, marginalization, criminalization, and increased vulnerability to violence due to the illegality of their status and/or activity. Improvement of work conditions and prostitute self-organization are difficult if not impossible since either can be considered in law as facilitation of prostitution.

Non-governmental organizations direct their strategies primarily against moral judgments and the insidious effects of those judgments on women; they work to interrupt the stigmatization and marginalization of prostitutes, to interrupt the prejudices which cast victims of trafficking as fallen women and to interrupt the division of women into good and bad. NGOs plead for legal protection of prostitutes and for the development of work alternatives to prostitution.
Some organizations try to shift debates about trafficking from moral stances to a concentration on concrete work conditions and safety measures for prostitutes. They plea against state legislation of morality and against state intervention in prostitution except in cases of force, deceit or violence; they are also in favor of extending the notion of trafficking to include other forms of exploitation such as in domestic work and marriage.

2] A Problem of (Organized) Crime

In Western countries, a criminal approach is currently dominant not only in response to traffic in women but in response to societal problems in general. This approach focuses on individual perpetrators of crime and individual victims while leaving aside structural causes of complex problems. In practice, criminal laws on trafficking seem to have a purely symbolic value since they are rarely applied: As one NGO says, "We don't need new laws; we need application of existing laws." Or, another general complaint of NGOs: Crimimal laws are mostly used against women rather than against their violators.

Criminal approaches do indeed carry great risks for women. Most women have negative experiences with the police such as arrest, harassment or, for migrants, expulsion. Filing complaints can lead to stigmatizing exposure at home as well as to reprisals from t raffickers or exploiters against oneself and one's family. Governments lean toward stronger punitive legislation with higher sentences, increased national and international police cooperation and a more active prosecution of offenders. Non-governmental strategies within the criminal approach are directed toward supporting individual women with legal aid, safe shelters, counseling, medical care, help in filing complaints and during court proceedings, prevention of direct expulsion and/or advocacy for discharge from prison. In addition, NGOs train police and judicial personnel and lobby for recognition of traffic in women as a crime and for application of existing legislation against actual perpetuators of violence. Most central, NGOs lobby for an improvement in the position of the victims such that their complaints are handled seriously, their violators are indeed reprimanded, they are granted (temporary) living permits, adequate witness protection, compensation for damages, state aid and shelter in the place of arrest and expulsion, and humanitarian right to permanent residence or, when appropriate, political asylum according to international guidelines.

3] A Migration Problem

Those who view traffic in women as a problem of migration put the accent on border crossing, namely on illegal border crossing and illegal residence. Depending upon the perspective of the party, two different strategies are proposed: For the state, most particularly rich countries, fear of "uncontrolled waves of foreigners" leads to strategies geared to halt and sometime criminalize (illegal) migration from poor countries. Also sending countries impose restrictive migration legislation, such as Indonesia with its prohibition of migration for low- and semi-skilled women.

The perspective of women opposes that of the state: For women, it is exactly their illegal status, the lack of legal migration possibilities (in combination with the demand for work in the informal sector) and the inavailability of work in their own country that makes trafficking such a profitable business and that forces them into an illegal circuit without protection against violence and exploitation. Beginning from the perspective of women, NGOs strive toward (a) recognition of migration as a survival strategy for women (b) research on the legal and social conditions and mechanisms which contribute to trafficking and forced labour/slavery-like conditions (c) information programmes for women considering migration concerning laws, work options, support services, etc. in destination countries (d) organisation of support services for women in sending and destination countries (e) improvement of the legal position of women in destination countries, i.e. by lobbying for legal and independent status as workers and as migrants, for workers' rights, for application of conventions related to protection of migrant workers, for independent residence status for women married to a national (f) organisation of support for women who return home such as alternative income and employment opportunities (g) creation of viable employment opportunities in countries of origin.

In the context of migration, also the IOM has been active in forging strategies for combatting abuses in recruitment and work conditions. Four main aspects of IOM involvement are (a) research (b) information campaigns in countries of origin (c) technical assistance for women to enable their return (d) support programmes for returnees. Those are fairly recent intiatives so it is not yet possible to judge their correspondence to women's needs.

4] A Public Order Problem

Within a public order optique, strategies focus on the regulation of work. Also here the problem and possible solutions are defined differently by different parties. The state generally views public order in repressive terms whereby "indecent" or "disorderly" behavior and "illegal persons" (notably, migrants) must be banned. Public order is very much tied by governments to public health and especially to medical regulation of prostitutes. Women view public order not in terms of controlling the worker but rather in terms of controlling the working conditions; for example, employers could be penalized or disqualified for coercive or unfair practices. There are no current strategies which put this last perspective in operation although the Netherlands may do so in the future.

5] A Labour Problem

When traffic in women and forced labour/slavery-like practices are viewed as labour problems, then the position of women as workers becomes the focus of change strategies. In an attempt to improve women's poor legal and social base, strategies aim to achieve recognition of labour in informal sectors as legitimate work, legal possibilities for such work, a recognition by destination countries of the demand for workers in the informal sectors and labour law protection for the women concerned. Governmental policies rarely, if ever, share this perspective and certainly not in relation to prostitution or to migrant workers. Governments are more likely to employ strategies that inhibit women from migrating for work in the informal sectors and that reinforce repressive and restrictive migrant labour legislation. It is primarily NGOs which strategize within a labour framework. Concrete NGO initiatives include: (a) support services to strengthen the women in their working situation such as legal resources, language classes, practical help with negotiating money and sending money home, abuse counseling, etc. (b) lobbying for recognition of trafficking and forced labour in marriage, domestic work and prostitution as serious problems (c) lobbying to strengthen (migrant) worker rights, also in the entertainment sector, and to gain recognition of prostitution as work (d) lobbying to improve the legal position and the working conditions of the women involved (e) support of self-organisation (f) development of alternative employment programmes (g) research and information campaigns. Also the ILO has begun to focus on the work of women in informal sectors with research on the situation of migrant domestic workers and migrant workers in the entertainment industry.

6] A Human Rights Problem

Strategies linked to a human rights perspective are predominantly employed by NGOs. Traffic in women and forced labour/ slavery-like practices are seen within this framework as violations of women's human rights for which states are accountable. Instruments designed to protect human rights are then invoked as key guidelines. Also here there exist two different currents of analysis: For some, prostitution itself is considered a violation of women's human rights equal to slavery. That judgment of sex commerce per se brings us back to the moral approach whereby prostitutes are stigmatized (as victims or deviants) and whereby prostitute self-organisations are allowed no legitimate place in public debate. For others, the human rights violation is not prostitution itself but the work conditions of force, deceit, violence and abuse of authority. In fact, this approach makes a more real comparison with slavery than an anti-prostitution approach in that condemnation falls upon an oppressive power relation rather than upon a certain type of work; the elimination of slavery ends ownership by one person of another but it does not end farm or domestic labour. Such an analysis reflects the perspective of the women concerned who wish to keep their job but end abusive conditions.

The latter approach rests upon women's rights to control their own body, life, work and, specifically, to migrate, to decide for themselves whether or not to work in prostitution and under what circumstances, and to be free from violence and restraint. Lobbying focuses upon replacement of the 1949 Convention with a new instrument based upon female self-determination, upon ratification of CEDAW, upon opposition to all policies which marginalise and discriminate against women and upon expansion of definitions to the range of situations in which women find themselves in slavery-like conditions including not only prostitution but also marriage, domestic work and other work or services.

***

In concluding this review of current strategies, the distinction between repressive and empowerment approaches should be emphasized: Existing governmental strategies are predominantly limited to repressive strategies such as restrictive migration policies and stronger criminal action. Not only do those approaches have meager preventive effects, but they also fail to meet the women's interests in whose behalf they were supposedly drafted. However, repressive measures are the most obvious, easiest to implement and most appealing for governments in terms of their correspondence to diverse state interests. Traffic in women then comes to legitimize very different goals than those of women.

On the other side are strategies against force and violence which rest upon a strengthening of the rights of women. NGOs put forth this approach (next to a call for clearer and more enforced criminal codes) in combination with practical support (social, medical, juridical).

Starting with women's right to self-determination, the interests of women stand central and their participation is seen as essential to the development of effective change strategies. The goal is to insure the rights of those involved as women, as female migrants, as female migrant workers, as domestic workers, as sex workers and as wives. "As long as those rights are not recognized and guaranteed, traffic in women and forced labour/slavery-like practices will continue to exist."

CONCLUDING RECOMMENDATIONS

1] Research strongly supports the need for new definitions of traffic in women and forced labour/slavery-like practices based upon the perspective and interests of women. Those definitions must specify abusive circumstances attached to brokerage practices, on the one side, and working conditions in both public and private domains, on the other. The central principles underlying the new definitions are the right of women to self-determination, an exclusive focus on coercion in diverse forms and an inclusion of all work and services rendered under forced labour/slavery-like practices regardless of whether these services are recognized as work, whether they take place under a work or marriage contract, and whether they are considered legitimate or illegitimate in society.

2] Once definitions on behalf of women's rights, safety and social agency have been accepted, existing legislation and other legal instruments, both national and international, should be re-assessed.
Specifically, the Working Group on Contemporary Forms of Slavery should receive adequate financing to (1) evaluate the usefulness of the 1949 Convention from the perspective of the new definitions and their principles and (2) evaluate the nature and extent of state responsibility.

3] Within the framework of the United Nations, information should be collected concerning women who are detained by states or who are missing in the context of trafficking in women and forced labour/slavery-like practices.

4] 'Standard Minimum Rules for the Treatment of Victims of Trafficking in Women and Forced Labour/ Slavery-Like Practices' should be developed to guarantee basic legal protection and possibilities for redress to victims of these practices. The model developed by the Global Alliance Against Trafficking in Women and The Foundation for Women should be taken as a reference in developing standards for victims including:
- Right to freedom from persecution or harassment by those in positions of authority
- Access to competent translators during legal proceedings
- Access to free legal assistance and legal representation during criminal or other proceedings
- Access to legal possibilities of compensation and redress
- Provisions to enable women to press criminal charges and/or to take civil action against their offenders, such as a temporary staying permit during criminal and/or civil proceedings and adequate protection as witnesses

- Legal permission to stay if return to one's home country is unsafe or, if so desired, assistence to return
- Protection against reprisals either from the side of the violators or from the side of the authorities

5] States should address the contributing factors, including women's access to viable employment opportunities, as well as the civil and political, economic, social and cultural rights of women as persons and workers, such as: safe working conditions; freedom of movement, speech and assembly; freedom to control one's living and working conditions as domestic worker, as prostitute, as wife; freedom to stop working as a domestic worker or prostitute and freedom of divorce. The above rights imply the application of national and international labour regulations, such as the ILO Conventions on wage labour, forced labour, rights of migrant workers and their families, with special attention to clauses on the elimination of debt-bondage and practices amounting to debt- bondage.

6] Women should be accorded 'full legal status', independent of marital contract or occupation (including prostitution).

7] The law should treat women as subjects accorded with rights as 'independent persons', as workers and as migrants, and never as objects of exchange or dependents to be controlled. Strategies should be based upon a recognition of women's right to autonomy and social egitimacy rather than upon female subordination and stigmatization.

8] Decrimalization of Prostitution: all laws specific to prostitution should be repealed.

9] Working conditions of women in the informal sectors, including the sex industry, should be improved by creating a legal basis which guarantees working conditions in accordance with international accepted labour standards.

10] Noting that self-organizations and NGOs are the main agents for change as well as the main - and sometimes the only - source of support for the women involved, an essential condition for every measure taken should be cooperation with self-organizations and NGOs working in direct contact with the women concerned to ensure their interests are adequately represented. This means that part of any programme should be support and adequately funding of self-organizations and NGOs.

11] Given the lack of information on the mechanisms of trafficking in women and forced labour/ slavery-like practices, as defined in this report, in the contexts of marriage and domestic labour, research in these fields should be encouraged.

LIST OF ABBREVIATIONS

CEEC	Central and Eastern European Countries
CDEG	Steering Committee for Equality between Women and Men
CEDAW	Convention on the Elimination of All Forms of Discrimination against Women
CSW	Commission on the Status of Women
EEC	European Economic Community
FLS	Forward Looking Strategies
FL & SLP	Forced Labour and Slavery-like Practices
GAATW	Global Alliance Against Traffick in Women
GO	Governmental Organization
IMF	International Monetary Fund
IOM	International Organization for Migration
ILO	International Labour Organization
IRP	International Report Project
MOB	Mail Order Bride
NGO	Non-Governmental Organization
OECD	Organization for Economic Cooperation and Development
STV	Foundation Against Trafficking in Women (Stichting Tegen Vrouwenhandel)
TIW	Trafficking in Women
UN	United Nations
UNCTAD	United Nations Conference on Trade and Development
WHO	World Health Organization

BIBLIOGRAPHY

A

- ACD (Association for Community Development). *International Migration of Women: a Study on Causes and Consequences*. Rajshahi, Bangladesh, 1995.
- Acosta Vargas, Gladys. "La prostitución forzada como fenomeno global desde perspectiva de los derechos humanos: Caso Colombia." Paper presented at the Regional Meeting on Trafficking in Women and Forced Labour in the Caribbean, Central and South America. Puerto Rico, May 24-26 1996.
- *Action for Reach Out newsletter*. Hong Kong, December 1995.
- Afanasiev, Vyacheslav, Sven Axel Mansson, Sergei Skrobogatov. *Sexual Commerce in St. Petersburg: legislation, extent and forms of expression*. University of Göteborg, Department of Social Work, Sweden, 1993.
- AFP (Australian Federal Police). "Briefing paper on Movement of South East Asian Women for Prostitution in Australia". 1995.
- Afshar, Haleh, ed. *Women, Work and Ideology in the Third World*. Tavistock publications, 1985.
- Agence France Presse. "Comercio con el sexo". *El Nuevo Día*, 29 de abril.
- Akademie für öffentliches Gesundheitswesen in Düsseldorf. *Prostitution im Grenzland, Beratung und Hilfe jenseits fon Zwang und Aufsicht*, Gemeinsame Tagung der Mr. A. de Graaf Stichting Amsterdam und der Akademie für öffentliches Gesundheitswesen in Düsseldorf vom 20. bis 21. Oktober 1994 in Monschau/Eifel. Berichte und Materialien, Band 12, 1995.
- Akina Mama Wa Afrika. "Trafficking of African Women, the reality is Often Worse Than the Stories". *African Women, June- November 1993*. Published by Akina Mama Wa Afrika, London, 1993.
- Alexander, Priscilla. "Some ideas regarding Prostitution and Migration." In: M. Klap et al. (ed.), *Combatting Traffic in Persons*, Proceedings of the Conference on Traffic in Persons, held from 15 - 19 November 1994 in Utrecht and Maastricht. SIM Special No. 17, Institutue of Human Rights, Utrecht, The Netherlands, 1995.
- Altenberg, Juanita. "Trafficking in Women and forced Prostitution in Suriname." Paramaribo, Suriname, May 1996. Paper presented at the Regional Meeting on Trafficking in Women and Forced Labour in the Caribbean, Central and South America. Puerto Rico, May 24-26 1996.
- Altink, Sietske. *Stolen Lives, trading Women into Sex and Slavery*. Scarlet Press, London/Harrington Park Press, New York, 1995.
- AMC (Asian Migrant Center). *Asian Migrant Bulletin*, Vol. IV, No. 2, April-June 1996.
- AMDE (Asociación de Mujeres Dominicanas en España) *Dominicanas en España*. Madrid, Spain, 1992.
- Amirrezvani, Anita. "Marketing Mail-order Marriages". *The Times Union*, Albany, New York, April 16 1996.
- Amnesty for Women. *Prostitutionstourismus, Frauenhandel, Zwangsprostitution*. Hamburg, Germany, 1995a.
- *Amnesty for Women Magazine, No.4*. Hamburg, Germany, 1995b.
- *Amnesty for Women Magazine, No.5*. Hamburg, Germany, 1996.
- Anderson, Bridget. *Britain's Secret Slaves. An Investigation into the Plight of Overseas Domestic Workers*. Anti-Slavery International & Kalayaan. ASI's Human Rights Series No 5, 1993.
- Anderson, Bridget. "Living and working conditions of overseas domestic workers in the European Union." Report prepared for STV/GAATW, Utrecht, The Netherlands, July 1996.
- Anderson, Bridget. "Migrant domestic workers in Germany; a Berlin case study." Report prepared for STV/GAATW. Utrecht, The Netherlands, October,

1996.
- APDC (Asian and Pacific Development Centre). *The Trade in Domestic Helpers: Causes, Mechanismes and Consequences.* Selected papers from the Planning Meeting on International Migration and Women, Quezon City, Philippines, 30 November - 5 December, 1987, APDC, Kuala Lumpur, Malaysia, 1989.
- *Asahi Evening News*, Febr. 21 1991/*International Herald Tribune*, April 1991.
- *Asian Migrant Bulletin*, Vol.IV, No 2, 1996
- Asian Migrant Centre. *Unlad Kabayan, A Primer on Migrant Worker Re-entry programs (Migrant Savings for Alternative Investments.* Asian Migrant Centre Ltd, Hong Kong, 1995.
- ASI (Anti-Slavery International). *Forced Prostitution in Turkey: Women in the Genelevs.* ASI's Human Rights Series No. 6, 1993.
- ASI (Anti-Slavery International). "Early marriage". Representations to the Working group on Contemporary Forms of Slavery, 19th session, 1994.
- ASI. "Ritual Slavery: the Sexual Exploitation of the Devadasis". Representations to the Working group on Contemporary Forms of Slavery, 20th session, 1995a.
- ASI. "Fetish Slaves - the Trokosi system". Representations to the Working group on Contemporary Forms of Slavery, 20th session, 1995b.
- ASI. "Women and Property". Representations to the Working group on Contemporary Forms of Slavery, 20th session, 1995c.
- ASI. "Overseas Domestic Workers in the UK". Representations to the Working group on Contemporary Forms of Slavery, 20th session, 1995d.
- ASS (Anti-Slavery Society). "Domestic Workers, Report to the Working Group on Contemporary Forms on Slavery, 1990." In: Anderson, Bridget. *Britain's Secret Slaves. An Investigation into the Plight of Overseas Domestic Workers.* Anti-Slavery International & Kalayaan. ASI's Human Rights Series No 5, 1993.
- Australia. The Parliament of the Commonwealth of Australia, the joint Standing Committee on Foreign Affairs, Defence and Trade. *Human Rights and Progress towards democracy in Burma.* October 1995.
- Austria, Director General, Federal Ministry of the Interior, Vienna. "Recent international legal instruments and measures relating to the illicit trafficking in migrants: trends and efficiency". Discussion paper submitted by Manfred Matzka, 11th IOM seminar on Migration, Geneva, Switzerland, October 1994.
- Azize-Vargas, Yamila. "Prostitution in the Gambia". 1991.
- Azize-Vargas, Yamila, in collaboration with Kamala Kempadoo. "International Report Project on Trafficking in Women: Latin America and Caribbean Region". Draft report prepared for STV/GAATW. Puerto Rico, August 31 1996.
- Azize-Vargas, Yamila, con la colaboración de Kamala Kempadoo. *Tráfico de Mujeres para Prostitucion, Trabajo Domestico y Matrimonio: America Latina y el Caribe.* Informe Preliminar, Encuentro Regional Republica Dominicana 11 & 12 de diciembre de 1996. Report prepared for STV/GAATW.
- Azu, Masumi. In: *NGO's Report on the Situation of Foreign Migrant Women in Japan and Strategies for Improvement.* Edited by the Asian Migrant Worker's Research and Action Committee, for the 4th World Conference on Women, 1995.

B

- Bangladesh. *The Cruelty to Women (Deterrent Punishment), Ordinance 1983, Ordinance No. IX of 1984*, The Bangladesh Gazette Extraordinary, published by Authority, October 3 1983.
- Bangladesh. *Women and Child (Special Provision) Act 1995* (Act no XVIII of 1995)
- Bangladesh. *The Suppression of Immoral Traffic Act, 1933.* June 22 1993
- BATIS, Centre for Women. "Traffic in Women: Philippine country report". June 1996a.
- BATIS, Centre for Women. "Report on Philippine Laws regarding trafficking in Women". June 1996b.
- BATIS, Centre for Women. "Traffic in Women: Casestudies". International Human Rights Workshop, June 10-20, 1996, Bangkok, Thailand. June 1996c.
- BNWLA (Bangladesh National Women Lawyers Association). "Impact report December 1991 - June 1995." Dhaka, Bangladesh, 1995.

- Boer, Marga de. *Vrouwenhandel, Beleid in Beeld. Eindrapport 'Evaluatie van de PG-richtlijnen voor de opsporing and vervolging van vrouwenhandel'.* Willem Pompe Instituut voor Strafrechtswetenschappen, University Utrecht, May 1994.

- Boidi, Christina, Siegried Wistrcil et al. *Frauenmigration - Spiegel einer ungerechten Welt, Systematisierung der Erfahrungen von LEFÖ über Frauenmigration und Frauenhandel im internationale Zusammenhang.* LEFÖ, Vienna, Austria, 1996.

- Bond, Joanna. "Short summary of the marriage market in the US". Paper prepared for STV/GAATW.

- Brussa, Licia. "Migrant Prostitution". TAMPEP (Transnational AIDS/STD Prevention among Migrant Prostitutes in Europe Project). Mr de Graaf Stichting (The Netherlands), Comitato per i Diritti Civili delle Prostitute (Italy), Amnesty for Women (Germany), LEFÖ (Austria). Mr. de Graaf Stichting, Amsterdam, The Netherlands, 1996.

- Butegwa, Florence. "Preliminary report on Trafficking in Women in Africa". Uganda, August 24 1996. Paper prepared for STV/GAATW.

- Butegwa, Florence. *Trafficking in Women in Africa: a regional report.* Kampala, Uganda, January 1997. Report prepared for STV/GAATW.

C

- Cabezas, Amalia L. "Todas somos Putas: Some Theoretical Notes Towards the Study of Sex Work". Paper presented at the Regional Meeting on Trafficking in Women and Forced Labour in the Caribbean, Central and South America. Puerto Rico, May 24-26 1996.

- Cámara de Comercio de Bogotá. *La Prostitución en el centro de Bogotá.* Colombian Republic, 1991.

- Cámara de Comercio de Bogotá. *La Prostitución en el sector Chapinero de Santafé de Bogotá.* Colombian Republic, 1992.

- Cambodia: "Legal system and law enforcement on sex trafficking in Cambodia". No author, 1996.

- Canada: "Canada's paper for EU Conference on Trafficking in Women for Sexual Exploitation". Vienna, Austria, June 10-11 1996.

- Centrum voor Gelijkheid van Kansen en voor racismebestrijding (Centre for Equal Chances and for Fighting against Racism). *Trafficking in Human Beings, Towards a policy of common goodwill.* Evaluation Report on the process and results of the fight against the international trafficking in human beings. Brussels, Belgium, March 1996.

- Center for the Study of Human Rights. *Twenty-Five Human Rights Documents.* Center for the Study of Human Rights, Colombia University, New York, 1994.

- Chapkis, Wendy. "Prostitution, Prohibition and the Question of Sexual Slavery - Summary". In: *Conference book, Changing Faces of Prostitution,* Helsinki, 3-5 May, 1995. Published by Unioni - The League of Finnish feminists, 1996.

- COIN (Centro de Orientación e Investigación Integral). "Testimonios y Experiencias de Mujeres traficadas par Prostitución en Europa: Marisol, Carmen, Rosa, Laura, Altagracia, Sonia, Janet". Santo Domingo, Dominican Republic, 1995.

- COIN (Centro de Orientación e Investigación Integral). *Trabajadoras sexuales migrantes y no migrantes: Características Sociodemográficas, Condiciones de Vida, Expectativas y Experiencias.* Prepared by: Santo Rosariao, Luis Moreno, Dinnys Luciano, Francisca Ferreira, Mayra Tavares, Antonio de Moya. Santo Domingo, Dominican Republic, 1993

- Colen, Shellee. "Just a Little Respect: West Indian Domestic Workers in New York City". In: *Muchachas No More: Household Workers in Latin America and the Caribbean.* Eds. Chaney and Garcia Castro. Nueva Sociedad, Venezuela, 1993.

- Colimero Sarellano, Claudia. "Tráfico de Mujeres y Prostitución forzada en el Mexico". Paper presented at the regional meeting on Trafficking in Women and Forced Labour in the Caribbean, Central and South America, San Juan, Puerto Rico, May 24 - 26 1996.

- Colombian Republic. *Situación de la Ninez explotada sexualmente en Colombia.* Ministerio Público, Defensoría del Pueblo, Colombia. Serie Femina, no. 6. No date.

- Commonwealth Secretariate. "South Asia Regional Workshop on Protecting the Rights of Women and Children with special reference to International Trafficking and Migration". Dhaka, Bangladesh, 2 - 4 June 1992.

- Coomaraswamy, Radhika. *Preliminary Report submitted by the Special Rapporteur on Violence against Women, its causes and consequences in acoordance with Commission on Human Rights resolution 1994/45,* (E/CN.4/1995/42), November 1994.

- Coomaraswamy, Radhika. *Report of the Special Rapporteur on Violence Against Women, its causes and consequences, submitted in accordance with Commission of Human Rights resolution 1995/85* (E/CN.4/1996/53), February 1996.

- *Convention on the Elimination of All Forms of Discrimination Against Women* (CEDAW). December 18, 1979, 19 I.L.M. 33 (1980).

- *Convention for the Suppression of the Traffic in Persons and the Exploitation of the Prostitution of Others.* Approved by U.N. General Assembly resolution 317 (IV) of 2 December 1949.

- *Convention on the Protection of the rights of All Migrant Workers and their Families.* Adopted on 18 December 1990.

- Cordero, Tatiana. "Situación de la Prostitución forzada y el Tráfico de Mujeres en el Ecuador". Paper presented at the Regional Meeting on Trafficking in Women and Forced Labour in the Caribbean, Central and South America. San Juan, Puerto Rico. May 24 - 26 1996.

- Council of Europe. *Amended Summary of national replies to the questionnaire of forced prostitution and traffic in women*, CDEG (94)32. Steering Committee for Equality between men and women. Strasbourg, France, May 1994a.

- Council of Europe. *Synthesis of answers by the individual countries to the questionnaire on forced prostitution and traffic in women; Amended Tables.* CDEG (94)33. Steering Committee for Equality between men and women (CDEG), 8th meeting, Strasbourg, France, 21-23 June 1994b.

- Council of Europe. *Proposals for action to be taken in member states and in the framework of the Council of Europe.* Steering Committee for Equality between Women and Men, 11th Meeting, 27-29 March, 1996 and Meeting of the Presidents of Steering and other Committees of the Council of Europe on the follow-up to the work of the Group of Specialists on action against traffic in women and forced prostitution (EG-S-TP). CDEG (96) 6 rev., Strasbourg, France, 10 May, 1996.

- CWDA (Cambodian Women's Development Association). "The Prostitution Trafficking of Women". 1996.

- CWHR (Cambodian Women's Human Rights, Working Group on). "Notes on the Situation of Women working in Cambodia" (taken from a comprehensive report on *The Human Rights of Women in Cambodia* prepared by the Working group on Cambodian Women's Rights), January 1996.

D

- *Daily Nation*, Kenya. April 21, 1995.

- *Daily Star, The.* Dhaka, Bangladesh, April 26, 1995a.

- *Daily Star, The.* Dhaka, Bangladesh, August 24, 1995b.

- David, Natacha. Worlds Apart, Women and the Global Economy. International Confederation of Free Trade Unions, March 1996.

- Deutsche Hurenbewegung. *Prostitution - Job - Beruf - Arbeit, Broschüre zum Gesetzentwurf zur rechtlichen und sozialen Gleichstellung von Prostituierten mit anderen Erwerbstätigen.* Deutche Hurenbewegung, c/o Kassandra e.V. Nürnberg, January 1996.

- Doezema, Jo. "Choice in Prostitution". In: *Conference book, Changing Faces of Prostitution.* Helsinki 3 - 5, May, 1995. Published by Unioni - The League of Finnish feminists, 1996.

- Domingo Traspasso, Rosa. "Tráfico de Mujeres y Prostitución forzada en El Perú". Paper presented at the Regional Meeting on Trafficking in Women and Forced Labour in the Caribbean, Central and South America. San Juan, Puerto Rico. May 24 - 26, 1996. Puerto Rico, May, 1996.

E

- *East African Standard*, Kenya. April 22 & 24, 1996.

- *Europap 1994, Final Report.* Europap (European Intervention projects Aids Prevention for Prostitutes). Ghent, Belgium, 28 Febr. 1995.

- European Commission. *Report of the Conference on Trafficking in Women*, 10 - 11 June, 1996, Vienna, Austria (CAB./183/96-en), 1996a.

- European Commission. *Communication from the European Commission to the Council and the European Parliament on Trafficking in Women for Sexual Exploitation.* COM (96)567 final. Brussels, November 11 1996b.

- European Parliament. *Resolution on the Exploitation of Prostitution and the Traffic in Human Beings* (OJC 120), May 16 1989.
- European Parliament. *Resolution on Trade in Women* (OJC 268), October 4 1993.
- European Parliament. *Resolution on Trafficking in Human Beings* (A4-0326/95), adopted January 18 1996.
- *Express*. "St. Martin a staging post in prostitution racket", May 21, 1985, Trinidad and Tobago.

F

- Fehér, Lenke. "Forced Prostitution and Traffic in Persons". In: M. Klap et al.(ed), *Combatting Traffic in Persons.* Proceedings of the Conference on Traffic in Persons, held from 15-19 November 1994 in Utrecht and Maastricht. SIM Special No. 17, Institute of Human Rights, Utrecht, The Netherlands, 1995.
- Fernand-Laurent, Jean. *Report of Mr. Jean Fernand-Laurent, Special Rapporteur on the suppression of the traffic in persons and the exploitation of prostitution.* (E/1983/7) 17 March 1983.
- Ferreira, Francisca. "Prostitución y Tráfico de Mujeres en el República Dominicana". Paper presented at the regional meeting on Trafficking in Women and Forced Labour in the Caribbean, Central and South America. Puerto Rico, May 24-26, 1996.
- *Forward Looking Strategies.* Third World Conference on Women, Nairobi, Kenya 1985.
- Foundation for Women Thailand. *State Policies on Prostitution and their Impact on victims of trafficking in Women.* Thailand, 1994a.
- Foundation for Women Thailand. *International Workshop on International Migration and Traffic in Women, Chiangmai, 17-21 October 1994, Thailand.* Organized by Foundation for Women Thailand, Women's Study Center, Chiangmai, Women and Autonomy Centre, Leiden University, 1994.
- Foundation for Women, White Ink. *Our Lives, our Stories.* Research and Action Project on Traffic in Women, Foundation for Women, Bangkok, August 1995.

G

- GAATW. *Principles on which an effective Instrument to Combat Trafficking in Women should be based.* Bangkok, Thailand, August 1995.
- GAATW. *Draft Standard Minimum Rules for the Treatment of Victims of Trafficking in Persons and Forced Labour & Slavery-like Practices.* Bangkok, Thailand, June 1996.
- GAATW (Global Alliance Against Trafficking in Women). "Report of fact finding tour on trafficking in Nepal, India, Bangladesh, Hong Kong, Taiwan and Japan". Bangkok, June, 1996.
- Germany. *Beware! Traffic in Women, Information on Traffic in Women in West Germany.* Ministry of Youth, Family, Women and Health, Bonn, 1993.
- Germany. German Criminal Code.
- Guy, Donna J. *Sex and Danger in Buenos Aires: Prostitution, Family and Nation in Argentina.* University of Nebraska Press, United States, 1995.

H

- Hamilton, Cecily. *Marriage as a Trade.* 1909.
- Handayani, Sih. "Human Rights workshop for Women Activists Asian and Eastern European countries, Working on Traffic in Women, Indonesia case study". 1996.
- Harvard University, USA. "Violence Against Women in China", May, 1992. Unpublished report.
- Haveman, R., J.C. Hes. "Vrouwenhandel en Exploitatie van Prostitutie". In: *Het vrouwenverdrag: een beeld van een verdrag.* A.W. Heringa et al.,ed. MAKLU uitg., Antwerpen, Belgium/Amersfoort, The Netherlands, 1994.
- Haveman, Roelof. "Traffic in persons as a problem", in: M. Klap et al (ed), *Combatting traffic in persons.* Proceedings of the Conference on Traffic in Persons, held from 15-19 November 1994 in Utrecht and Maastricht. SIM Special No. 17, Institute of Human Rights, Utrecht, The Netherlands, 1995.
- Haveman, Roelof. *Strafbaarstelling van Vrouwenhandel.* 1996, dissertation. To be published in 1997.
- Heinrich Böll Foundation. *Conference: Sexwork, Sextourism and Trafficking in Women: a new Reality in Eastern Europe?* Prague, Czech Republic, 1996
- Heyzer, Noeleen, Geertje Luyklama-Nijeholt and Nedra Weerakoon, eds. *The Trade in Domestic Workers.* APDC Kuala Lumpur/Zed Books ltd., London and New Jersey, 1994.
- Hirsch, Michèle. Council of Europe, *Plan of Action*

Against Traffic in Women and Forced Prostitution, EG (96) 2. Strasbourg, France, 9 April 1996. ("The study represents the personal view of the author").
- HRIC (Human Rights in China). *Caught between tradition and the state - Violations of the human rights of Chinese Women.* New York, August 1995.
- Human Rights Watch. *A modern form of slavery, Trafficking of Burmese Women and Girls into Brothels in Thailand.* USA, 1993
- Human Rights Watch. "Bangladesh Women and Girls trafficked into Pakistan". In: *The Human Rights Watch Global Report on Women's Human Rights.* USA, 1995.
- Human Rights Watch/ Asia. *Rape for Profit, Trafficking of Nepali Girls and Women to India's Brothels.* Human Rights Watch, June 1995.
- Hummel, Diana. "Si piensas viajar a Europa". In: *ILA, Informationsstelle Latein Amerika, No.146*, June 1991, Germany.

I

- IGC (Intergovernmental Consultations). *Illegal Aliens: a preliminary Study.* Secretariat of the Intergovernmental Consultations on Asylum, Refugee and Migrations Policies in Europa, North America and Australia, June, 1995.
- IGC. *Summary description of legislation on aliens trafficking in states in Europe, North America and Australia.* Document: IGC/Traf/10/95(II). Secretariat of the Intergovernmental Consultations on Asylum, Refugee and Migration Policies in Europa, North America and Australia. December, 1995.
- *ILO (International labour Organization) Convention concerning Forced Labour (No.29).* 1930
- *ILO Convention on Freedom of Association (No. 87).*
- *ILO Convention concerning the Protection of Wages (No. 95).*
- *ILO Migration for Employment Convention (Revisited) (No.97).* 1949.
- *ILO Convention on Freedom of Collective Bargaining (no.98).*
- *ILO Equality of Treatment (Social Security) Convention (NO.118).* 1962
- *ILO Migrant Workers (Supplementary Provisions) Convention (No.143).* 1975
- *ILO Maintenance of Social Security Rights Convention (No.157).* 1982.
- ILO. *World Labour Report.* 1993.
- ILO. *ILO activities concerned with International Labour Migration and Migrant Workers.* International Labour Office. Geneva, April, 1995
- ILO. "Female Asian migrants: A growing but vulnerable workforce". In: *World of Work*, the magazine of the ILO, no. 15, March/April, 1996.
- Images Asia. "Burmese women sex workers in Thailand". Paper prepared for the NGO Forum on Women, Beijing, 1995. Thailand, 1995
- Images Asia. "Trafficking in women: some brief case study of Burmese women". Thailand, 1996.
- India: Immoral Traffic (Prevention) Act, 1956.
- *International Agreement for the Suppression of the White Slave Trade.* Signed in Paris, May 18 1904.
- *International Convention for the Suppression of the White Slave Trade.* Signed in Paris on, May 4 1910.
- *International Convention for the Suppression of the Traffic in Women and Children.* Geneva, Switzerland, September 30 1921
- *International Convention for the Suppression of the Traffic in Women of full* Age. Geneva, Switzerland, October 11 1933.
- *International Covenant on Civil and Political Rights.* December 16, 1966, 999 U.N.T.S. 171
- *International Covenant on Economic, Social and Cultural Rights.* December 16, 1966, 993 U.N.T.S. 3
- *International Convention on the Protection of the Rights of Migrant Workers and Members of their Family.* G.A. res. 45/158, annex, 45 U.N. GAOR Supp. (no.49A) at 262, U.N. Doc. A/45/49 (1990).
- IOM (International Organization for Migration). "Trafficking in Migrants", No. 5, *IOM Quarterly Bulletin*, 1994.
- IOM. Migration Information Programme, 1995. *Trafficking and Prostitution: the growing Exploitation of Migrant Women from Central and Eastern Europe*, Budapest, Hungary, May, 1995a.
- IOM. "Trafficking in Migrant Women: IOM Responses". Paper for Beijing, September 1995b.
- IOM. "Statement by Mr. Marco Gramegna, Preparatory meeting on Trafficking in Women", Brussels, 1 - 2 Dec. 1995c.
- IOM. Migration Information programme, 1996. *Trafficking in Women from the Dominican Republic for sexual Exploitation.* Budapest, Hungary, June, 1996a.
- IOM. Migration Information Programme, 1996.

Trafficking in Women to Austria for sexual Exploitation, Budapest, Hungary, June, 1996b.

- IOM. Migration Information Programme, 1996. *Trafficking in Women to Italy*, Budapest, Hungary, June, 1996c.

- IOM. *Trafficking of Women to countries of the European Union: Characteristics, Trends & Policy Issues*. Vienna, Austria, June, 1996d.

- IOM. Programme Information Sheet. *IOM Programmes for Trafficked Women and Children* (68/96). 1996e

- ISIS-WICCE. "Women living under muslim Laws". *Women's World, no 21-22*, December, 1989.

- IWRAW (International Women's Rights Action Watch). *1993. International Women's Rights Action Watch to CEDAW country reports*. Humphrey Institute, University of Minnesota, USA, December 1992.

J

- Japan. *Japanese Constitution*, Chapter II, Marriage, Art. 4 & 747.

- Japan. *Labour Standards Law*, Chapter 1, General Provisions, Art. 4 & 5. 1990.

- Japan. *Criminal Laws*, Articles 220-221 & 224-229, 1988.

- Japan. *Prostitution Prevention Law* (Law No. 118, May 24, 1956 Amended by Law No. 16 March 255, 1958).

- Japan. *Nationality Law* (Law No. 147, May 4, 1950)

K

- Kabeberi-Macharia, Janet (ed.). *Women, Laws, Customs and Practices in East Africa, Laying the Foundation*. WLEA Publications No.2, Nairobi, Kenya, 1995

- KALAYAAN-Justice for Overseas Domestic Workers. "1995: Slavery still alive", Conference Papers. London, 1995.

- Kawamura, Akio. "Traffic in women: from legal perspective. Japanese laws applicable to situations of the traffic in women". Japan, April, 1996.

- Kempadoo, Kamala. *Exotic Colonies: Caribbean Women in the Dutch Sex Trade*. University of Colorado at Boulder, USA. Ph.D. dissertation, 1994.

- Kempadoo, Kamala. "State Pimpage: Regulating Prostitution in the Dutch Caribbean". University of Colorado, USA, 1995.

- Kenya. "Comments upon City Court verdicts". 1996 (no author).

- Kenya. "Inside the brothels of Nakuru", *Weekend Mail*, June 10, 1993

- Kenya. "The sailors had docked so the girls expected heavy business", *Kenya Times*, May 22, 1994.

- Kenya. "Bid to give prostitutes a positive self image". *Kenya Times*, September 25, 1994.

- Kenya. "A light in the dark, commercial sex workers form AIDS self-help group. *Standard on Sunday Magazine*, November 13, 1994.

Kenya. "Corrupt owners giving us a bad name". *East African Standard*, December 18, 1995.

- Kenya. "Ban this illegal sextrade". *East African Standard*, April 15, 1996.

- Kenya. "AG's office reacts to sex trade scandal". *East African Standard*, April 16, 1996.

- Kenya. "Crackdown, police round-up 500 sex traders". *Sunday Standard*, April 21, 1996

- Kenya. "Twilight 'ladies' fail STD tests". *East African Standard*, April 22, 1996.

- Kenya. "War on sex traders, scores held in swoops", *East African Standard*, April 24, 1996.

- Kenya. "Police arrest 3.000 sex girls", by Alphonce Mung'ahu, *Sunday Standard*, April 28, 1996.

- Kenya. "Women fight for laws that are relevant to their needs". *The Sunday Nation*, May 19, 1996.

- Khan, Zarina Rahman, and Helaluddin Khan Arefeen. "Prostitution in Bangladesh", draft report. Dhaka, Bangladesh, 1992.

- Kootstra, Trijntje, ed. *One year La Strada, results of the First Central and East European Programme on Prevention of Traffic in Women*. Polish YWCA, PSF, STV, ProFem, Dutch Foundation Against Traffic in Women/La Strada Programme, September 1996.

L

- Lap-Chew, Lin. "Between Protection and Empowerment". Paper presented at the workshop on International Trafficking in Women, Conference on Human Rights, Vienna, Austria, June 1993.

- LAO, People's Democratic Republic of. Ministry of Labour & Social Welfare, "Report on the survey and the situation regarding the trafficking of children in the LAO PDR". 1995.

- LEFÖ (Lateinamerikanische exilierte Frauen in Österreich). "Strafrechtliche Aspekte des Frauenhandels". Vienna, Austria, 1996.
- LHRLA (Lawyers for Human Rights and Legal Aid). "The Flesh Trade: Report on Women's and children's Trafficking in Pakistan". Karachi, Pakistan, 1991.
- *Lianhe Zaobao*, newspaper, Singapore, 23 April 1996.
- Lim, Lin Lean, and Nana Oishi. *International Labour Migration of Asian Women. Distinctive Characteristics and Policy Concerns*. ILO, Geneva, February 1996.
- Limanowski, Barbara. "Trafficking in Women". Report from Poland. In: M. Klap et al (ed), *Combatting Traffic in Persons*. Proceedings of the Conference on Traffic in Persons, held from 15-19 November 1994 in Utrecht and Maastricht. SIM Special No. 17, Institute of Human Rights, Utrecht, The Netherlands, 1995.
- Lin, Yim Yuct. "China's workers: A Brief Description of Garment Workers in Pearl River Delta", key-note speech Studiedag: China: Rode Draak of Vijfde Tijger. Utrecht, The Netherlands, 1996.
- Luxemburg. *Prostitution in the EEC Member states. A Comparative Study of the existing Legal Position*. Directorate General for Research and Documentation, Luxemburg, 1985.

M

- Marie, Claude-Valentin. "The European Union confronted with population movements: reasons of state and rights of individuals, Paper no. 3", presented at the 11th IOM Seminar on Migration: International Response to Trafficking in Migrants and the Safeguarding of Migrant Rights, 26-28 October 1994.
- Matsui, Yayori. "Trafficking in Women and Prostitution in Japan". Tokyo, Japan, 1993 (?).
- Mens, Lucie van. *Prostitutie in Bedrijf*. Dissertation, Erasmus University, Rotterdam, The Netherlands, 1992.
- Migrant Women Worker's Research & Action Committee, The (ed.). *NGOs Report on the Situation of Foreign Migrant Women in Japan and Strategies for Improvement*, for the Fourth World Conference on Women, September 4-15, 1995, Bejing.
- Mill, John Stuart. *On Liberty*. 1859.
- Miller, Alice. Women in the Law Project of the International Human Rights Law Group. "Outline Presentation and Brief Analysis of United Nations and related International Action in the area of Migration and Traffic in Women". In: *International Workshop on International Migration and traffic in Women, Chiangmai 17 - 21 October 1994, Thailand*. Organized by Foundation for Women Thailand, Women's Studies Centre, Chiangmai, Women and Autonomy Centre and Leiden University, The Netherlands, 1994.
- *Monde Diplomatique, Le*. "Le Japon s'entrouve a l'immigration", Paris, France, August, 1990.

N

- *Nacional, El*. "Se asfixian 28 criollas en furgón". April 20, 1995, Dominican Republic.
- Netherlands, The. *Penal Code*, art. 250ter & 250bis.
- Netherlands, The. Ministry of Justice. *Vreemdelingencirculaire Slachtoffers Vrouwenhandel Hoofdstuk B 17* (Aliens Circular, Chapter B17 concerning victims of trafficking.) Den Haag, 1991
- Netherlands, The. Ministry of Justice. *Aanpak van Mensenhandel, Handleiding van de collegevergadering van Procureurs-Generaal*, May 1995
- Netherlands, The. *Basic Principles for a Code of Conduct within the Member States of the European Union to prevent and combat Trafficking in Women and Forced Labour & Slavery-like Practices*. Draft, presented by the Dutch Minister of Social Affairs and Employment in cooperation with the Minister of Justice at the "European expertmeeting on Recommendations for a code of conduct to prevent International Trafficking in Women", 10 December 1997, The Hague, The Netherlands, in preparation of the Ministerial Conference organized by the Netherlands Presidency of the European Union in conjunction with the EU Commission to be hold in April 1997.
- *News Report*, French Press Agency, February, 6 1996.
- *Newsweek*, August, 28 1996.
- NGO Forum on Women, Beijing '95, *Look at the World Through Women's Eyes, plenary speeches from the NGO Forum on Women, Beijing '95*. Ed.: Friedlander, Eva, NGO Forum on Women, Beijing '95 Inc., 1996.
- Niesner, Elvira, Estrella Anonuevo, Petchara

Songsiengchai-Fenzl. *A Women's Dignity is inviolable: a Trial on Trafficking in Women, Observations.* Research project commissioned by the Federal Ministry for Women and Youth. Frankfurter Institut für Frauenforschung, Frankfurt, Germany, 1991.

- Niewielski, A. Public Prosecutor, Ministry of Justice Public Prosecutors Office, Organized Crime Unit, Poland. "Paper on the problem of prosecuting crimes connected with the trade of women for their sexual exploitation in Poland". Presented at the La Strada Conference on Trafficking in Women, Warsaw, Poland, May 1996.

O

- O'Connor, Ann Marie. *The health needs of women working in prostitution in the Republic of Ireland.* Women's Education, Research and Resource Centre, University College Dublin, November 1994.
- Ohshimo, Shizuko & Carolyn Francis, HELP Asian Women's Shelter. *JAPAN Through the Eyes of Women Migrant Workers.* Japan Woman's Christian Temperance Union, Tokyo, 1989.
- Okumu Wengi, Jennifer (ed.). *Women and Law in East Africa. The Law of Succession in Uganda: Women, inheritance laws and practice - essays and cases.* WLEA Publications No. 1, Kampala, Uganda, 1994.
- Onitsuka, Tadanori, and Ayako Mizuno. *Summary Report on the Physical Abuses and Assaults by Immigration Enforcement Officers against Foreign Nationals in Japan at various stages of Compulsory Deportation Procedures, with Legal Commentary.* Report from Japan, Immigration Review Taskforce, Tokyo, March 1995.
- Oosterom, Ilona van. "De wetgeving op het gebied van vrouwenhandel en prostitutie in Rusland". Groningen, The Netherlands, 1994.
- *Outwrite, no. 39*, September 1995. "Dominican Government - protecting sex traders?" Dominican Republic, 1995.

P

- Pareja, Reynaldo and Santo Rosario. *Viage al exterior, Ilusiónes y Mentiras.* COIN, Santo Domingo, June 1992.
- Pheterson, Gail (ed). *Vindication of the Rights of Whores.* The Seal Press, USA, 1992.
- Pheterson, Gail. *The Prostitution Prism.* Amsterdam University Press, The Netherlands, 1996.
- Philippines, National Commission on the role of Filipino Women. "Philippine Plan for Gender-Responsie Development, 1996-2025, Violence against Women and Prostitution." Manila, Philippines, 1996
- *Platform for Action.* Fourth World Conference on Women, September 4-15, 1995, Bejing.
- Polania Molina, Fanny. "Prostitution and Trafficking in Women in Colombia", paper prepared for STV/GAATW. Utrecht, The Netherlands, 1996.
- Poudel, Meena. WATCH (Women Acting Together for Change, Nepal). "Trafficking in Women in Nepal: an overview". Paper prepared for the First Planning Meeting of Regional Project Against the Trafficking in Women in East, South East and South Asia, organized by International Movement Against All Forms of Discrimination and Racism (IMADR), March 15-16, 1994, Tokyo, Japan.
- Priscilla, Alexander. "Some Ideas regarding Prostitution and Migration. In: Klap, M. et al (eds), *Combatting Traffic in Persons, SIM Special No. 17*, Proceedings of the Conference on Traffic in Persons, held from 15-19 November 1994 in Utrecht and Maastricht. Netherlands Institute for Human Rights, Utrecht, The Netherlands, 1995.
- ProFem & Rozkos Bez Rizika. *Strassen und Grenzwege: Streetwork, Frauenhandel, HIV/AIDS Prävention, Prostituiertenorganisationen*, Prague, Czech Republic, 1996.

Q

- *Quehaceres, Ano 11, No. 7*, 24 de Julio, 1991, "Prostitución y Tráfico de Mujeres Dominicanas hacia Europa". CIPAF (Centro de Investigaciónes para la Acción Femenina), Santo Domingo, Dominican Republic, 1991.
- Quy, Dr. Le Thi. Center for Family and Women studies. "The Struggle against the Traffic in Women and Children in Vietnam", 1994.

R

- Rahman, Saira. "Across the Borders of Despair - Trafficking in Women and Children in Bangladesh". Bangladesh, 1995.
- Rayanakorn, Kobdul. *Special Study on Laws relating to Prostitution and Trafficking.* Foundation For

Women, Bangkok, Thailand, 1995.
- Rosario, Virginia O. del. "Mail-Order Brides: A case study of International Migration and Traffic in Women". In: *International Workshop on International Migration and traffic in Women, Chiangmai 17 - 21 October 1994, Thailand.* Organized by Foundation for Women Thailand, Women's Studies Centre, Chiangmai, Women and Autonomy Centre and Leiden University, The Netherlands, 1994.
- Roth, Claudia. *Report on immigration from Central and Eastern Europe.* (A3-0000/93). European Parliament, Committee on Civil Liberties and Internal Affairs of the European Parliament, 1993

S

- Safa, Helen. "Women and Industrialization in the Caribbean". *Anales de Caribe, vol.7-8*, La Habana, Cuba, 1987.
- Sanghera, Jyoti. "Preliminary Report on Forced Labour, Slavery-like Practices and Traffic in Women". Prepared for GAATW/STV. Canada, August 1996.
- Sanghera, Jyoti, Tracy Havlin & Amal Rana. *International Report Project, Regional Report on Traffic in Women: Canada.* Prepared for GAATW/STV. Canada, January 1997.
- Sangroula, Geeta. Institute for Legal Research and Resources, Nepal. "Paper on International and National Legal Instruments". Nepal, 1995.
- SANLAAP. "Women are for sale, trafficked women from Nepal and Bangladesh and other parts of India into Calcutta and Bombay presently called Mumbai". India, No date.
- Schuler, Margaret (ed.). *Freedom from Violence; Women's Strategies from around the World*, (1992). Women, Law and Development, UNIFEM publishers, USA, 1992.
- Shahid, Zulqarnain and Jabbar Khan. "Slave trade", in: *MAG*, Aug. 16-22, 1990, Karachi, Pakistan.
- Shamin, Prof. Ishrat. *Trafficking and sale of women and children: Bangladesh perspective.* Centre for Women and Children Studies, Dhaka, Bangladesh, June 1995.
- Silva, Dulin de. "Trafficking in Women: Sri Lanka". Sri Lanka, 1996.
- SIM (Netherlands Institute for Human Rights). Klap M. et al (ed.) *Combatting Traffic in Persons.* Proceedings of the Conference on Traffic in Persons, held from 15-19 November 1994 in Utrecht and Maastricht, The Netherlands. SIM Special No 17, Institute of Human Rights, Utrecht, The Netherlands, 1995.
- Simm, Gabrielle. "Sex, Guns and Money; a Feminist Critique of the Domestic and International Regulation of Prostitution in War". Australia, 1996.
- Sinha, Indrani. SANLAAP. "Glow Worms are dancing". In: *Report on the International Workshop on International Migration and Traffic in Women, Chiangmai, 17-21 October 1994, Thailand.* Organized by Foundation for Women Thailand, Women's Study Center, Chiangmai, Women and Autonomy Centre, Leiden University, The Netherlands, 1994.
- SINTRASEDOM (National Union of Household Workers, Colombia). "The History of our Struggle". In: *Muchachas No More, Household Workers in Latin America and the Caribbean.* Eds. Chaney and Garcia Castro. Nueva Sociedad, Venezuela, 1993.
- Skrobanek, Siriporn. "Exotic, subservient and trapped: Confronting prostitution and traffic in women in Southeast Asia". In: *Freedom from Violence, Women's strategies from around the World.* Women, Law and Development/ UNIFEM, publishers, Margaret Schuler (ed.), USA, 1992.
- Skrobanek, Siriporn. "The Globalization of Trafficking in Women". In: *International Workshop on International Migration and Traffic in Women, Chiangmai, 17-21 October 1994, Thailand.* Organized by Foundation for Women Thailand, Women's Study Center, Chiangmai, Women and Autonomy Centre, Leiden University, The Netherlands, 1994.
- Skrobanek, Siriporn. *The Diary of Prang.* Women Press/ Foundation for Women, Bangkok, Thailand, 1994.
- *Slavery Convention*, 1926.
- *Supplementary Convention on the Abolition of Slavery, the Sex Trade and Practices simular to Slavery*, 1956.
- Sobhan, Salmah. "Women labour Migration: the case of Bangladesh". 1992.
- Spring, Kathrin. *Gekauftes Unglück, Frauenhandel in der Schweiz.* Dokumentation 3/92, Caritas Schweiz/ FIZ Informationszentrum Dritte Welt/ SKF Schweizerische Katholishers Frauenbund, 1992.
- Studzinsky, Silke. "Die rechtliche Position von Opfern des Frauenhandels in Deutschland". Paper

presented at the La Strada Conference on Trafficking in Women, Warsaw, Poland, May 1996.
- STV (Foundation Against Trafficking in Women). *From the other side of the Sea; Lisa's Story.* STV, Utrecht, The Netherlands, 1991a.
- STV. *Report of the European Working Conference Against Trafficking in Women*, 4 - 5 July 1991, Amsterdam, The Netherlands, 1991b.
- STV/ Margreet Franssen. *Zicht op Vrouwenhandel, een methodiek van geïntegreerde begeleiding van slachtoffers van vrouwenhandel.* SWP Utrecht, 1994.
- STV. *International Newsbulletin*, Nrs. 1-4, 1994-1996
- STV/ Kerk & Wereld. *Report on the Polish-Dutch Seminar on Trafficking in Women*, 10-17 June 1994, Driebergen, The Netherlands. STV, Utrecht, The Netherlands, February 1995
- STV. *Background Study on Basic Principles for a Code of Conduct within the Member States of the European Union to Prevent and Combat Trafficking in Women.* STV, Utrecht, The Netheralnds, November 22, 1996.
- STV. *Barriers and Throughways, 1992-1994.* STV, Utrecht, The Netherlands, January 1995.
- *Sunday Nation, The.* May 19, 1996, Kenya.
- *Sunday Standard.* April 21 & 28, 1996, Kenya.
- Sutton, Alison. *Slavery in Brazil.* Anti-Slavery International Human Rights Series, no. 7, 1994.

T

- Taylor, Debbie. "Servile Marriage: a definition, a survey, and the start of a campaign for change". Oxford, United Kingdom, 1993.
- Tharan, Caridad. "Philippina Maids in Malaysia". In: *The Trade in Domestic Helpers: Causes, Mechanismes and Consequences.* Selected papers from the Planning Meeting on International Migration and Women, Quezon City, Philippines, 30 November -5 December, 1987. APDC (Asian and Pacific Development Centre), Kuala Lumpur, Malaysia, 1989.
- *Times of India*, New Delhi, India. July 25, 1995.
- Tkacz-Sztylkowska, Wieslawa. Criminal Division of the Polish Police Headquarters, Warsaw. "Prostitution and Traffic in Poland". In: *Report on the Polish-Dutch Seminar on Trafficking in Women*, June 1994, Driebergen, The Netherlands. Foundation Against Trafficking in Women (STV)/ Church & World (K&W), The Netherlands, February 1995.
- Truong, Than Dam. "Gender, International Migration and Social Reproduction: Implications for Theory, Policy and Networking". Paper presented at the conference on International Migration and Japan: Gender, Networking and Settlement, December 12-14, 1995, at PRIME, International Peace Research Institute, Meiji-Gakuin Universtity, Tokyo, Japan, 1995.

U

- Uganda. *Penal Code Act 1950*, amended 1990.
- UN, Wg. CFS. Report of the Working Group on Contemporary Forms of Slavery (CFS). *Draft Programme of Action for the Prevention of Traffic in persons and of the exploitation of the Prostitution of Others.* E/CN.4/Sub.2/1991/41, annex I, 1991.
- UN, CEDAW. *Recommandation no. 19 of the Committee on the Eliminiation of Discrimination and Violence against Women*, 1992.
- UN GA. *Declaration on Elimination of Violence Against Women.* Resolution adopted by the General Assembly (A/Res/48/104, 1994 GA Resolution), 1994a.
- UN GA. *Report of the Secretary General on Violence against Women Migrant Workers.* UN General Assembly, (A/49/354), September 1 1994b.
- UN GA. *Traffic in Women and Girls.* Resolution 49/166 of the General Assembly of the United Nations (A/Res/49/166), adopted 23 December 1994c.
- UN, CHR. *The question of integrating the rights of women into the human rights mechanisms of the United Nations and the Elimination of Violence against Women.* Commission on Human Rights Resolution 1994/45. 1994d.
- UN GA. *Traffic in Women and Girls.* Report of the Secretary General to the 50th session of the General Assembly (A/50/369), 24 August 1995a.
- UN. *The World's Women 1995: Trends and Statistics*, New York, 1995b.
- UN, CHR. *Resolution CHR/ECOSOC*, 10 April 1996, 52th session, adopted 19 April 1996 (E/CN.4/1-996/L.29), 1996a.
- UN, Wg. CFS. Report of the Working Group on Contemporary Forms of Slavery (CFS). *Programme of Action on the Traffic in Persons and the Exploitation of Prostitution of Others* (E/CN.4/sub. 2/ 1995/ 28/

Add.1), adopted by the Commission on Human Rights (CHR) in resolution 1996/61, entitled "Contemporary Forms of Slavery", 58th meeting, April 23 1996b.

- UN. *Report Expert Group Meeting on Violence Against Women Migrant Workers*. Manila Philippines, 27 May-31 May 1996. UN Division for the Advancement of Women, VAWMW/1996/1, June 1996c.

- USA. *Federal Mann Act*, Chapter 117 - Transportation for illegal sexual activities and related crimes.

V

- Veijalainen, Risto. "Migration, Discussion paper for the Migration Workshop". Conference on Trafficking in Women, EU/IOM, Vienna, Austria, June 1996.

- *Vienna Declaration and Programme of Action*, adopted by the UN World Conference on Human Rights on June 25 1993, Vienna, Austria, 1993.

- Vietnam: "Situation of Prostitution in Vietnam". (no author, 1996).

- Vleuten, Nelleke van der. *Survey on Traffic in Women, Policies and Policy-research in an International Context.* Research and Documentation Centre Women an Autonomy, Leiden University, The Netherlands, 1991.

W

- *Weekend Mail*, Kenya. June 10, 1993.

- Weinert, Patricia. *Foreign Female Domestic Workers: help wanted!* Working Paper, World Employment Programm. ILO, Geneva, March, 1991.

- Whitaker, Benjamin, Special Rapporteur. "Updating of the Report on Slavery, submitted to the Sub-commission in 1966". UN E/CN.4/Sub.2/1982/20

- White, Luise. *The Comforts of Home, Prostitution in Colonial Nairobi*. The University of Chicago Press, Chicago and London, 1990.

- Wijers, Marjan. "Supporting Victims of Trafficking". In: Klap, M. et al (ed.), *Combatting Traffic in Persons. SIM Special no. 17*. Proceedings of the Conference on Traffic in Persons, held from 15-19 November 1994 in Utrecht and Maastricht. Institute of Human Rights, Utrecht, The Netherlands, 1995.

- WODC. "Mensenhandel en -smokkel". *Justitiele Verkenningen 1 96*, WODC Ministry of Justice/ Gouda Quint, Den Haag, The Netherlands, January 1996.

Y

- Yirkinen, Marju (ed.). *Changing Faces of Prostitution*, Conference Book Helsinki 3 - 5 May, 1995. Unioni-The League of Finnish Feminists, 1996.

- Yudkin, Ruth. "Servile Forms of Marriage: the Issue of Women's Property Rights". ASI, April, 1996.

- Yunomae, T. "Commodified Sex: Japan's Pornographic Culture". *AMPO, Vol.24-4-Vol.26-1:55-9*, 1995.

Z

- Zambia. *Laws and Regulations protecting the Trafficking in Women, Prostitution and Slave-like Practices in Zambia*, no date or author.

- Zambia. *Penal Code*, Chapter XVI, Offences related to Marriage and Domestic Obligations.

- Zegveld, Liesbeth. "The Combat of Traffic in Persons within the Framework of the United Nations. In: Klap, M. et al (ed.), *Combatting Traffic in Persons. SIM Special no. 17*. Proceedings of the Conference on Traffic in Persons, held from 15-19 November 1994 in Utrecht and Maastricht. Institute of Human Rights, Utrecht, The Netherlands, 1995.

- Zlotnik, Hania. "Women as Migrants and Workers in Developing Countries". Paper Population Division United Nations, 1995.

ANNEXES

ANNEX 1 Questionnaire for NGOs

Utrecht, 15 April 1996

Re: Questionnaire/Report on Trafficking in Women and contemporary manifestations of Forced Labour & Slavery-like Practices in prostitution, domestic labour and marriage

L.s.,

Hereby we are sending you a questionnaire on trafficking in women and contemporary manifestations of forced labour & slavery-like practices with the request to complete it and return it to us.

Background to the Report

This questionnaire forms part of an investigation we are carrying out in the framework of a Report which the Foundation Against Trafficking in Women (STV), based in the Netherlands, and the Global Alliance Against Trafficking in Women (GAATW), based in Thailand, are compiling for the UN Special Rapporteur on Violence against Women, Mrs. Radhika Coomaraswamy, who was appointed by the United Nations Commission on Human Rights, at its fiftieth session in February 1994.
One of the forms of violence against women on which she will report in her third report to the Commission, in 1997, is "trafficking in women and forced prostitution".
After the publication of her preliminary report in February 1995, representatives of STV and GAATW had opportunity to discuss the issue with the Special Rapporteur. Following these discussions, the Special Rapporteur requested these two organizations to assist her by compiling a substantial report on this issue (annex 1). The Report will be global in character and will include a description and analysis of the current trends in trafficking in women, national and international legislative and administrative instruments, government and non-government efforts to address the issue at community level, as well as in-depth case studies.

Dubble objective of the Report

We believe that such a global report will also be extremely useful for furthering the work of NGOs and contribute to the search for more effective measures to combat and prevent trafficking. Next to providing the Special Rapporteur with the relevant information for her report to the Commission on Human Rights, we aim to bring together persons, organizations and networks and to identify and analyze strategies and shortcomings in current regulatory prac-tices. We hope that this will contribute to the development of a conceptual framework as well as stimulate new strategies which are based on the recognition of the human rights of women in all spheres of life and work.

Organization of the Research

STV is coordinating the research for information and the production of the final report.
We are collaborating with regional consultants in Asia/Pacific (Sarah Johnston), Africa (Florence Butegwa), S&C America & the Caribbean (Yamila Azize Vargas) and North America (Lisa Kois) who will coordinate the research and networking in these regions.
We are acutely aware that the most valuable information must come from persons and organizations who are actively addressing the issue in their own local situations, whether through providing services, advocacy on behalf of victims, or research to raise public and political awareness of the particular violations of women's human rights involved. Therefore we are sending this questionnaire to organizations who are working in various ways on this issue and whom we expect to have actual and/or specific information on their own local/ national/ regional situation. Many of those we have approached to ask their cooperation

have responded enthousiastically to the whole project, but for some of you this letter will be the first contact. We hope that you will agree with us on the importance of this activity and share with us your invaluable information and experience.

The questionnaire

The questionnaire concentrates on forced labour & slavery-like practices and trafficking in women for prostitution, domestic labour and marriage, since these are the most commonly known and researched situations. However, through the questionnaire, other areas may be identified where these practices occur and where further research is needed. The introduction to the questionnaire (annex 2) presents the framework for the whole report and explains how we developed working definitions of trafficking in women and of forced labour & slavery-like practices, based on our own work in the field and on present developments in the international discourse on the issue.

We hope our efforts to come to coherent definitions that connect to the reality of women will prove to be helpful to the work of NGOs, as well in help to focus the international debate by clarifying terms and concepts.

The questionnaire has 4 sections, which are explained in the Instructions for answering the Questionnaire (annex 3).

Deliberate ommissions

Although we are aware that trafficking in children occurs extensively and with devastating effects on those affected, the questionnaire will not address trafficking and forced labour & slavery-like practices with regard to children, since these practices take place in a different legal context and need a different approach and strategies.

There is also no specific section in the questionnaire on slavery-like practices and trafficking with regard to marriage. In our opinion this area needs in-depth research in order to understand all the complexities involved. We therefore will appreciate any specific information and case descriptions on trafficking for marriage which you could send us, so that we will be able to include the relevant aspects in the report.

The Special Rapporteur needs the basic information by the end of September 1996. In order to be able to process the responses to the questionnaire in time, we need to receive them by 31 MAY 1996. We plan to publish the Report by the end of 1996, and all those who have parti-cipated in this effort will receive a copy.

We are aware that we are asking a considerable effort from you to answer quite a substantial questionnaire, so we would like to thank you in advance for making the effort. We look forward to receiving your responses.

With kind regards,

Lin Lap-Chew, Marjan Wijers, Marjolein Sol
International Report Project, the Netherlands

Annexes 1 Recommendation letter from Mrs. R. Coomaraswamy
2 Introduction to the Questionnaire
3 Instructions for answering the Questionnaire

Radhika Coomaraswamy

United Nations Special Rapporteur on
Violence Against Women, including its
causes & consequences

ICES - 8, Kynsey Terrace, Colombo 8, Sri Lanka.
Telex: 23014 ICES CE Fax: 696618 Tel: 698048/685085
E - mail address: radhika@cmb.ices.ac.lk

8th November 1995

The Global Alliance Against Trafficking of Women is preparing a report for the Special Rapporteur on Violence Against Women, including its causes and consequences. I will be grateful if you would co-operate with the Alliance in the compilation and analysis of data regarding the problem of trafficking and forced prostitution for the 1997 Report to the Human Rights Commission.

Thank you for your co-operation.

Yours sincerely,

Radhika Coomaraswamy

Radhika Coomaraswamy

Objective of the survey

The objective of the survey is to obtain an overview of:

- the nature and extent of trafficking in women and contemporary manifestations of forced labour & slavery-like practices in prostitution, domestic labour and marriage;
- the national legislative and political instruments to combat trafficking and forced labour & slavery-like practices;
- the strategies of governmental and non-governmental organizations addressing the issue in their countries.

Necessity of a clear definition

A fundamental problem in responding to the issue of trafficking in women is the lack of a precise and unambiguous definition. The traditional concept of trafficking focusses only on prostitution and addresses mainly the `procurement' aspect, based on concern for 'innocent' girls who should be protected against being lured into brothels, but largely ignoring the abuses and the slavery-like conditions inside the brothels. Moreover, the traditional concept does not address the contemporary forms of trafficking, such as the traffic in women through commercial marriage bureaus and the trade in domestic workers.

Recent international documents also fail to offer a clear definition of trafficking in women. Some are even quite confusing, e.g. mixing up trafficking and illegal migration or smuggling of aliens, or simply equating trafficking with prostitution. Even the 1949 U.N. Convention on Trafficking In Women[1] fails to define the two most central terms of 'trafficking in women' and 'forced prostitution'.

However, a clear definition is necessary to develop measures which are effective and which do not give rise to unintended, undesirable side-effects for the women concerned. Without a good definition, attempts to deal with the problem will remain "wishful thinking" at best.

At worst they can cause repercussions which have repressive instead of emancipatory effects on the already precarious situation of the women likely to be affected.

Working definitions

We have developed the following working definitions in order to cover abusive working and living conditions and abusive brokerage practices occurring in both public and domestic spheres:

TRAFFICKING IN WOMEN.

All acts involved in the recruitment and/or transportation of a woman within and across national borders for work or services by means of violence or threat of violence, abuse of authority or dominant position, debt-bondage, deception or other forms of coercion.

FORCED LABOUR & SLAVERY-LIKE PRACTICES

The extraction of work or services from any woman or the appropriation of the legal identity and/or physical person of any woman by means of violence or threat of violence, abuse of authority or dominant position, debt-bondage, deception or other forms of coercion.

[1] Convention for the Suppression of the Traffic in Persons and the Exploitation of the Prostitution of Others, 1949.

Explanation of the working definitions

In formulating these definitions we went back to two international agreements: the League of Nations Slavery Convention of 1926 and the Supplementary Convention of 1956[2], which condemn all slavery-like practices, including debt-bondage[3] and forced marriage[4] and the ILO Forced Labour Convention no. 29[5]. These conventions have broad international acceptance and clearly describe the situations at hand. In the Slavery Convention the concept of 'ownership' is fundamental to slavery, which in art. 1.1 is defined as: "the status or condition of a person over whom any or all of the powers attaching to the right of ownership are exercised".

In art. 2 of the ILO Forced Labour Convention, forced or compulsory labour is defined as:

"all work or service which is extracted from any person under the menace of any penalty and for which the said person has not offered himself voluntarily".

Whereas the concept of "forced labour" in art. 1 of the ILO Convention is predominantly used for the relation between the state and the individual, art. 4.1 of the same Convention rules on state accountability regarding forced labour situations between individuals:

"the competent authority shall not impose or permit the imposition of forced or compulsory labour for the benefit of private individuals, companies or associations".

The crucial element in both definitions is coercion, which can take various forms, including but not limited to:

- violence or threat of violence, including deprivation of freedom (of movement, of personal choice);
- deception: a.o. with regard to working conditions or the nature of the work to be done;
- abuse of authority c.q. dominant position: this can range from confiscation of personal documents to place another person in a dependent position, abusing one's dominant social position, abusing one's natural parental authority or abusing the vulnerable position of persons without legal status;
- debt-bondage: pledging the personal services or labour of a person indefinitely as security for a debt, when the length and nature of the service is not clearly defined.

"Work or services": includes all domestic, sexual, reproductive or other services rendered under the above-mentioned conditions of coercion, regardless of whether these services are recognized as work, whether they take place under a work contract or whether they take place under a marriage contract.

"The appropriation of the legal identity and/or physical person" refers to the concept of partial or total ownership as used in the Slavery Conventions, but the word "appropriation" is used to denote the act of claiming ownership of a person, acting as if one owns the person.

[2] Slavery Convention, 1926; Supplementary Convention on the Abolition of Slavery, the Slave Trade, and Institutions and Practices simular to Slavery, 1956

[3] Art. 1a of the Supplementary Slavery Convention prohibits "Debt bondage, that is to say, the status or condition arising from a pledge by a debtor of his personal services or those of a person under his control as security for a debt, if the value of those services as reasonably assessed is not applied towards the liquidation of the debt or the length and nature of those services are not respectively limited and defined".

[4] Art. 1c of the Supplementary Slavery Convention prohibits "Any institution or practice whereby a woman without the right to refuse, is promised or given in marriage on payment of a consideration in money or kind to her parents, guardian, family or any other person or group", or whereby "the husband of a woman, his family, or his clan, has the right to transfer her to another person for value received or otherwise"

[5] ILO Convention no. 29 concerning Forced Labour, 1930

"Appropriation of the legal identity" can range from confiscating one's identity papers or supplying a woman with a false identity to the loss of one's legal personality under the marriage contract.

Principles underlying the definitions

The basic principle underlying both definitions is the (human) right of all women to have control over her own life and body. This includes the right of adult women working in prostitution to make personal choices regarding their lives and bodies.

The working definitions make a distinction between "trafficking", which comprises all the processes involved in recruitment and transportation of women under coercive conditions, and the situations of "forced labour & slavery-like practices" women are subjected to.

Trafficking can be the means to bring women into such situations, but not all such situations are the result of trafficking. On the one hand, women can be recruited and transported under conditions of coercion but not end up in a forced labour/slavery-like situation. On the other hand, women can find themselves in forced labour/slavery-like situations without having been trafficked. For instance, state regulations with regard to prostitution which entail withholding identity papers of prostitutes and closed state-controlled brothels make leaving prostitution or maintaining any control of working and living conditions virtually impossible, resulting in forced labour & slavery-like situations, without the occurrence of trafficking.

Through this distinction it is possible to make visible a broader range of forced labour & slavery-like practices to which women are subjected, and which may or may not be the result of trafficking. With coercion as the critical element, all working and living situations in which the personal freedom of women are curtailed, as well as the trafficking practices which are used to bring women into these situations can be addressed.

The knowledge and experience of those presently engaged in addressing the issues related to trafficking in women indicate that slavery-like practices, including forced labour, invariably occur in the sectors in which women basically lack legal protection through labour regulations or other legal provisions. These sectors are prostitution, domestic work and marriage, hence this questionnaire pertains to these three areas.

The questionnaire has 4 sections

A Organizational Information

B General questions on forced labour & slavery-like practices and trafficking in women with regard to prostitution, domestic labour and marriage

C Forced labour & slavery-like practices in prostitution / trafficking in women for prostitution

D Forced labour & slavery-like practices in domestic labour / trafficking in women for domestic labour.

All respondents have received sections A and B and are requested to complete these sections, which contain general questions. Sections C and D have been sent to selected respondents, because these sections contain questions requiring more specialised knowledge of the respective situations.

For each section that you have received

1 Please write as clearly as possible, preferably in block letters.

2 Many questions require you to fill in a number between 1 and 5, choosing one alternative from the following scale: **1 very frequently | 2 frequently | 3 occasionally | 4 rarely | 5 not**
If you don't know the answer to the question: **fill in 0**
If the question is not applicable: **fill in X** Please make sure that you fill in all the boxes, because it is important to know whether a question is not answered because the respondent does not know the answer or because she/he forgot to fill in one of the boxes.

3 Please do not be discouraged if you cannot answer a question fully. Answer as much as you can and go on to the next question. Every bit of information helps!

4 If you CAN have access to relevant information for a particular question, but do NOT have time to look it up, in order to fill in the response, please let us know by writing this in the margin. You can also send the unprocessed information to us.

5 The survey does not address children, i.e. persons under 18 (the UN regular standard).
If however, a different legal age is used in your country, you can use this standard in your answers, but please indicate that you are using a different age standard.

6 Section B: If you have knowledge of other areas where FL&SLP and/or TIW occur, please use the blank box "other..." in the appropriate questions to describe these. This is important to identify other areas where further research is needed.

7 You will probably need an average of 1½ hours to answer each section.

Please send the completed questionnaire by **31 MAY 1996**

to: **STV - International Report Project**
Post Box 1455
3500 BL UTRECHT
The Netherlands

Thank you!

WORKING DEFINITIONS

Forced Labour & Slavery-like Practices (FL&SLP)

The extraction of work or services from any woman or the appropriation of the legal identity and/or physical person of any woman by means of violence or threat of violence, abuse of authority or dominant position, debt-bondage, deception or other forms of coercion.

Trafficking in Women (TIW)

All acts involved in the recruitment and/or transportation of a woman
within and across national borders for work or services
by means of violence or threat of violence, abuse of authority or dominant position, debt-bondage, deception or other forms of coercion.

Explanations of some terms

- "your country" : the country in which you live and work and about which you will fill in the questionnaire.
- "third party" : all intermediaries - agents, procurers, pimps, brothel-keepers
- "GO" : governmental
- "NGO" : non-governmental

For section c: "categories" of women working in prostitution

- National prostitutes:women with the nationality of your country, who are working in prostitution in your country;
- Migrant prostitutes:migrant women from other countries, who are working in prostitution in your country. Migrant prostitutes can be either "LEGAL" (i.e. in possession of a valid staying permit) or "ILLEGAL" (i.e. without a staying permit);
- Out-national prostitutes:women with the nationality of your country, who are working in prostitution in other countries.

For section d: "categories" of women domestic workers (DWs)

- National DWs: women with the nationality of your country, who are working as domestic workers in your country;
- Migrant DWs: migrant women from other countries, who are working as domestic workers in your country. Migrant DWs can be either "DOCUMENTED" (with a contract and/or working permit) or "UNDOCUMENTED" (without a contract and/or working permit);
- OUT-national DWs: women with the nationality of your country, who are working as domestic workers in other countries.

NR.:

A ORGANIZATIONAL INFORMATION

1 Name of the organization (in your own language and in English) completing the questionnaire:

2 Contact person

Name: ______ Function: ______

Office hours / best time to reach you: ______

Languages spoken within your organization: ______

3 Full address of the organization ______

tel: ______ fax: ______ email: ______

4 Organizational information: How long has the organization been in existence, is it linked with government or political institutions? Number of staff and volunteers?

5 What is the main focus of your organization? (in 3 or 4 sentences)

6 Geographical area covered: (local/regional/national/international)

7 What kind of financial support does your organization have?

NR. COUNTRY:

B GENERAL QUESTIONS ON FORCED LABOUR & SLAVERY-LIKE PRACTICES AND TRAFFICKING IN WOMEN

I MANIFESTATIONS, TRENDS & DEVELOPMENTS

1] Do **forced labour & slavery-like practices (FL&SLP)** (according to the working definition) take place in your country in the following situations?
Please fill in:
1 very frequently 2 frequently 3 occasionally 4 rarely 5 not (0=don't know) (X=not applicable)
If possible, please give an estimate of the number of women involved at the time of this survey.

	occurrence (1-5)	Estimated number of women involved
FL&SLP take place in prostitution		
FL&SLP take place in domestic labour		
FL&SLP take place in marriage		
FL&SLP take place in other situations:		

The above estimations are based on:
[ ] government reports [ ] reports of NGOs [ ] own working experience
[ ] other, namely ______
(please cross all that apply)

2] Does **Trafficking in Women (TIW)** (according to the working definition) take place to, from, within or through your country for the following purposes?
Please fill in:
1 very frequently 2 frequently 3 occasionally 4 rarely 5 not (0=don't know) (X=not applicable)
If possible, please give an estimate of the number of women involved at the time of this questionnaire.

		occurrence (1-5)	Estimated number of women involved
TIW for prostitution takes place	**to** my country		
	from my country		
	within my country		
	through my country		
TIW for domestic labour takes place	**to** my country		
	from my country		
	within my country		
	through my country		
TIW for marriage takes place	**to** my country		
	from my country		
	within my country		
	through my country		
TIW takes place for other purposes			

The estimations are based on:
[ ] government reports [ ] reports of NGOs [ ] own working experience
[ ] other, namely ___________________________
(please cross all that apply)

3] With regard to TIW across borders: is your country: (please cross all that apply)
a] a sending country (country **from** which women are trafficked [ ] yes [ ] no [ ] don't know
b] a receiving country (country **to** which women are trafficked) [ ] yes [ ] no [ ] don't know
c] a transit country (country **through** which women are trafficked) [ ] yes [ ] no [ ] don't know

4a] If your country is **a sending country** (country of origin):
please write to which COUNTRIES OF DESTINATION women are trafficked from your country.

TIW **from** my country for	takes place FREQUENTLY to the following countries	takes place OCCASIONALLY to the following countries	don't know
prostitution			
domestic labour			
marriage			
other			

4b] If your country is **a receiving country** (country of destination):
please write from which COUNTRIES OF ORIGIN women are trafficked to your country.

TIW **to** my country for	takes place FREQUENTLY from the following countries	takes place OCCASIONALLY from thefollowing countries	don't know
prostitution			
domestic labour			
marriage			
other			

4c] If your country is **a transit country**: please write for which countries of origin and destination your country acts as a transit country.

TIW through my country for	FROM the following countries	TO the following countries	don't know
prostitution			
domestic labour			
marriage			
other			

5] Which of the following recruiting methods are used by traffickers?
Please fill in:
1 very frequently 2 frequently 3 occasionally 4 rarely 5 not (0=don't know) (X=not applicable)

Recruiting methods	TIW for prostitution	TIW for domestic labour	TIW for marriage
promise of work as waitress/cleaner			
promise of work as domestic worker			
promise of work as dancer/entertainer			
promise of marriage/marriage			
false job-contracts			
false marriage contracts			
kidnapping			
buying a woman from parents/legal guardian			
buying a woman from husband			
other			

6] Who are the recruiting agents?
Please fill in:
1 very frequently 2 frequently 3 occasionally 4 rarely 5 not (0=don't know) (X=not applicable)

Recruiting agents	TIW for prostitution	TIW for domestic labour	TIW for marriage
expected husband			
impresario/artist agencies			
marriage agencies			
individual marriage brokers			
job agencies			
family members			
friends			
acquaintances of family or friends			
strangers/accidental meetings			
government officials/law enforcers			
employers			
other			

7] How do you rate, for your country:
- public awareness of FL&SLP and/or TIW?
- media coverage of FL&SLP and/or TIW?
- political awareness/debate on FL&SLP and/or TIW?
Please fill in: 1 high 2 medium 3 low 4 not at all (0=don't know) (X=not applicable)

FL&SLP/TIW situations	public awareness	media coverage	political awareness/debate
FL&SLP in prostitution			
TIW for prostitution			
FL&SLP in domestic labour			
TIW for domestic labour			
FL&SLP in marriage			
TIW for marriage			

8] Have you observed any changes in manifestations and/or trends with regard to FL&SLP and/or TIW in your country during the last 5 years? [ ] yes [ ] no [ ] don't know

If yes, please describe the two most important changes you observed.

1	
2	

9] Has any research been done in your country during the last 10 years on FL&SLP and/or TIW with regard to:

a prostitution [ ] yes [ ] no [ ] don't know
b domestic labour [ ] yes [ ] no [ ] don't know
c marriage [ ] yes [ ] no [ ] don't know

If yes, please give references to this research. Send copies if possible. (If the research is not written in English, please give English translation of the title.)

2 LEGAL CONTEXT

10] How would you qualify the legal system governing prostitution in your country? Please cross ONE of the alternatives.

[ ] prohibitionist system: all prostitution is legally prohibited, anybody involved in prostitution (prostitutes, procurers, pimps, clients) is criminalized.

[ ] abolitionist system: prostitution per se is not an offence, but any involvement by third parties/all exploitation of the prostitution of others is prohibited.

[ ] regulatory system: prostitution is officially recognized and regulated through different forms of registration and other forms of control in the interest of public order and public health.

[ ] decriminalization/laborist system: prostitution is recognized as work and protected by the same laws as other types of work.

11] Does your country have any specific legislation with regard to:

a FL&SLP in prostitution [ ] yes [ ] no [ ] don't know
b TIW for prostitution [ ] yes [ ] no [ ] don't know
c FL&SLP in domestic labour [ ] yes [ ] no [ ] don't know
d TIW for domestic labour [ ] yes [ ] no [ ] don't know
e FL&SLP in marriage [ ] yes [ ] no [ ] don't know
f TIW for marriage [ ] yes [ ] no [ ] don't know

12] Have there been any major changes in the legislation of your country over the last 10 years with regard to:

a FL&SLP in prostitution	[ ] yes	[ ] no	[ ] don't know
b TIW for prostitution	[ ] yes	[ ] no	[ ] don't know
c FL&SLP in domestic labour	[ ] yes	[ ] no	[ ] don't know
d TIW for domestic labour	[ ] yes	[ ] no	[ ] don't know
e FL&SLP in marriage	[ ] yes	[ ] no	[ ] don't know
f TIW for marriage	[ ] yes	[ ] no	[ ] don't know

If yes, please describe the two most important changes.

1	
2	

3 CONTRIBUTING FACTORS

13] Which of the following factors in the countries of origin and/or of destination contribute to FL&SLP and/or TIW?
Please fill in:
1 very frequently 2 frequently 3 occasionally 4 rarely 5 not (0=don't know) (X=not applicable)

Contributing factors	In countries of origin	n countries of destination
poverty/unemployment		
national/local conflict/military presence		
cultural/religious practices		
development strategies (e.g. tourism)		
emigration/immigration laws & policies		
labour regulations		
laws & policies on migrant labour		
laws & policies on prostitution		
globalisation of the economy		
corruption of the authorities		
other		

4 CURRENT STRATEGIES TO STOP FORCED LABOUR & SLAVERY-LIKE PRACTICES AND TRAFFICKING IN WOMEN

14] Does your government have any specific policies on prevention, prosecution or victim support with regard to FL&SLP and/or TIW?
Please write in each box Y (yes) or N (no) or 0 (don't know) or X (not applicable)

Policies on	prostitution		domestic labour		marriage	
	FL&SLP	TIW	FL&SLP	TIW	FL&SLP	TIW
prevention						
prosecution of the offenders						
victim support						
other						

15] Is there any cooperation between your government and governments of other countries with regard to TIW?
Please fill in:
1 very frequently 2 frequently 3 occasionally 4 rarely 5 not (0=don't know) (X=not applicable)

Cooperation on	TIW for prostitution	TIW for domestic labour	TIW for marriage
prevention			
prosecution of traffickers			
victim support			
return programmes			
other			

16] Are there any NGOs in your country addressing FL&SLP and/or TIW with regard to:

a prostitution [ ] yes [ ] no [ ] don't know
b domestic labour [ ] yes [ ] no [ ] don't know
c marriage [ ] yes [ ] no [ ] don't know

If yes, what strategies do they employ to combat FL&SLP and/or TIW?
Please write in each box Y (yes) or N (no) or 0 (don't know) or X (not applicable)

Strategies employed by NGOs	FL&SLP/TIW in prostitution	FL&SLP/TIW in domestic labour	FL&SLP/TIW in marriage
informing women at risk			
advocacy			
victim support			
information/publications			
research			
raising public awareness			
lobbying for change in laws & policies			
other			

Please give names and addresses of organizations active in any of these fields.

17] What services are available to victims of FL&SLP and/or TIW in the various situations?
Please indicate whether the service is provided by governmental (GO) and/or non-governmental organization (NGO) by writing:
Y (yes) or N (no) or 0 (don't know) or X (not applicable) in each box.

Services	FL&SLP/TIW in prostitution		FL&SLP/TIW in domestic labour		FL&SLP/TIW in marriage	
	provided by GO	provided by NGO	provided by GO	provided by NGO	provided by GO	provided by NGO
counselling						
legal assistance						
medical assistance						
financial assistance						
safe shelters						
return programmes						
witness protection						
other						

Please give names and addresses of organizations who provide victim support.

5 RECOMMENDATIONS

18] What are the two most important things that should change in your country to combat FL&SLP in the various situations?

1	
2	

19] What are the two most important things that should change in your country to combat TIW for the various purposes?

1	
2	

6 STATISTICS

20] If possible, please give an estimation of:
a] the total number of national and migrant women working in prostitution respectively domestic labour at the time of this questionnaire.
b] the percentage of a. (total number), working under conditions of forced labour & slavery-like practices as defined in the working definition.
c] the percentage of women working under FL&SLP-conditions, who have been trafficked into this situation.
d] the percentage of the total number of cases of FL&SLP/TIW that is reported to the authorities.

	a total number	**b** % of **a** working under conditions of FL&SLP	**c** % of b. trafficked into this situation authorities	**d** % of cases reported to the
national women working in prostitution				
migrant (non-national) women working in prostitution				
national women working as domestics				
migrant (non-national) women working as domestics				

The above estimations are based on:
[ ] government reports [ ] reports of NGOs [ ] own working experience
[ ] other, namely ________________________________
(please cross all that apply)

If it is not possible to give the requested estimations, please indicate why.

21] What is your opinion on the working definitions? Do you think they are helpful to clarify concepts and focus the international debate?

End of Section B
Thank you.

NR. COUNTRY:

C FORCED LABOUR & SLAVERY-LIKE PRACTICES IN PROSTITUTION / TRAFFICKING IN WOMEN FOR PROSTITUTION

In order to get a more precise understanding of the prevalence of forced labour & slavery-like practices and trafficking in prostitution we will use the following "categories" of women working in prostitution:

- NATIONAL PROSTITUTES: women with the nationality of your country, who are working in prostitution in your country;
- MIGRANT PROSTITUTES: migrant women from other countries, who are working in prostitution in your country. Migrant prostitutes can be either "LEGAL" (i.e. in possession of a valid staying permit) or "ILLEGAL" (i.e. without a staying permit);
- OUT-NATIONAL PROSTITUTES: women with the nationality of your country, who are working in prostitution in other countries.

Please do not be discouraged if you cannot answer for all the categories. Answer as much as you can and go on to the next question. Every bit of information helps!

I MANIFESTATIONS, TRENDS & DEVELOPMENTS

1] With regard to your country: do situations of forced labour & slavery-like practices as described in the working definition occur among the different categories of women working in prostitution? Please fill in:
1 very frequently 2 frequently 3 occasionally 4 rarely 5 not (0=don't know) (X=not applicable)

	occurrence of FL&SLP
National prostitutes	
Migrant prostitutes/legal	
Migrant prostitutes/illegal	
Out-national prostitutes	

2] With regard to your country: does trafficking in women for prostitution as described in the working definition occur among the different categories of women working in prostitution?
Please fill in:
1 very frequently 2 frequently 3 occasionally 4 rarely 5 not (0=don't know) (X=not applicable)

	occurrence of TIW
National prostitutes	
Migrant prostitutes/legal	
Migrant prostitutes/illegal	
Out-national prostitutes	

3] Which of the following forms of coercion are used by traffickers?
Please fill in:
1 very frequently 2 frequently 3 occasionally 4 rarely 5 not (0=don't know) (X=not applicable)

Forms of coercion	national prostitutes	migrant prostitutes/legal	migrant prostitutes/illegal	out-national prostitutes
violence or threat with violence				
abuse of authority or dominant positition				
deception regarding conditions of work, wages, etc.				
deception regarding the nature of work				
debt-bondage				
using false papers				
other				

2 LEGAL CONTEXT

4] Is it possible to work in prostitution on a legal basis
a for nationals [ ] yes [ ] no [ ] don't know
b for migrant women [ ] yes [ ] no [ ] don't know

If yes, under which conditions?

For nationals
For non-nationals

5] Do your laws on prostitution make a difference between:
a prostitution by consent and prostitution under coercion [ ] yes [ ] no [ ] don't know
b 'third party involvement' by consent and 'third party involvement' under coercion [ ] yes [ ] no [ ] don't know
c legal and illegal prostitution [ ] yes [ ] no [ ] don't know
d legal and illegal 'third party involvement' [ ] yes [ ] no [ ] don't know

6] Are prostitutes subjected to special registration? [ ] yes [ ] no [ ] don't know

If yes, can women de-register and leave prostitution when they want? (please cross ONE of the alternatives)
[ ] yes, without any problem
[ ] yes, but records will be kept and can be used against her
[ ] no, records will be kept which will make it very difficult to find another job
[ ] no, once you are registered as a prostitute, it is virtually impossible to leave prostitution
[ ] other, namely ______________________________

7] Are prostitutes allowed to have their own associations/organizations?
[ ] yes [ ] no [ ] don't know

If not, please explain.

8] Do the laws of your country specifically exclude prostitutes from legal emigration/immigration?
[ ] yes [ ] no [ ] don't know

9] Do women working in prostitution in your country have any form of legal protection against coercion, abuse or violence under the following laws?
Please fill in Y (yes) or N (no) or 0 (don't know) or X (not applicable)

	national prostitutes	migrant prostitutes/legal	migrant prostitutes/illegal
criminal laws			
labour laws/regulations			
civil laws			
other			

If you answered one or more of these questions with Y (yes), please explain.

10] - Which of the following acts related to prostitution does the law of your country prohibit?
Column 1: please fill in Y (yes), N (no) or (don't know) or X (not applicable)
- Are these laws enforced?
Column 2: please fill in:
1 very frequently 2 frequently 3 occasionally 4 rarely 5 not (0=don't know) (X=not applicable)

The law prohibits	Y/N/0	Is the law enforced?
prostitution per se		
prostitution without license/registration		
prostitution outside permitted areas		
solliciting/loitering		
procurement/pimping per se		
procurement/pimping of minors		
procurement/pimping with the use of coercion		

- more next page -

procurement across borders		
procurement across borders with the use of coercion		
brothel keeping per se		
brothel keeping without license		
brothel keeping when minors are involved		
brothel keeping with the use of coercion		
buying of sexual services (clients)		
other		

11] With regard to prostitution involving minors: what is the age of consent under your law?
[ ] 16 years [ ] 18 years [ ] 21 years [ ] other, nl ________ years
(please cross ONE of the alternatives)

12] Does the criminal law of your country contain specific provisions prohibiting trafficking in women for prostitution? [ ] yes [ ] no [ ] don't know

If yes,
a what is prohibited? (please give the definition of trafficking in your country's criminal law.)

b what is the maximum penalty? _____ years/months/days (circle) and/or (circle)______ US$ fine
c what is the average penalty? _______ years/months/days (circle) and/or (circle)______ US$ fine

13] Do these provisions also apply:
a when TIW takes place within national boundaries [ ] yes [ ] no [ ] don't know
b when the woman has worked in prostitution before [ ] yes [ ] no [ ] don't know
c when the woman knew she was expected to work in prostitution [ ] yes [ ] no [ ] don't know
d when the woman wants to continue to work in prostitution [ ] yes [ ] no [ ] don't know

14] Is coercion a necessary condition in your country's LEGAL definition of TIW?
(Please cross ONE alternative)
[ ] no, any procurement/recruitment for prostitution within and across borders is considered to be trafficking, regardless of the woman's will and regardless of any coercion is used.
[ ] no, any procurement/recruitment for prostitution of women across borders is considered to be trafficking, regardless of the woman's will and regardless of any coercion is used.
[ ] yes, only procurement/recruitment with the use of coercion is considered to be trafficking.
[ ] other ____

15] What constitutes 'coercion' under your law? *(Please cross ALL that apply)*
[ ] violence [ ] threat of violence
[ ] abuse of authority/dominant position [ ] deception
[ ] other ____

16] Does the criminal law of your country contain specific provisions prohibiting forced labour & slavery-like practices in prostitution as defined in the working definition?
[ ] yes [ ] no [ ] don't know

If yes,
a what is prohibited? (please give the definition of forced labour & slavery-like practices in prostitution in your country's criminal law.)

b what is the maximum penalty? _____ years/months/days (circle) and/or (circle) _____ US$ fine
c what is the average penalty? _______ years/months/days (circle) and/or (circle) _____ US$ fine

17] Are there any provisions for victims of trafficking and/or forced labour & slavery-like practices in prostitution to obtain compensation for damages? [ ] yes [ ] no [ ] don't know

If yes, please explain.

3 VICTIMS SITUATION AND NEEDS

18] Which of the following characteristics of forced labour & slavery-like practices apply to the living and working conditions of the different categories of women working in prostitution?
Please fill in:
1 very frequently 2 frequently 3 occasionally 4 rarely 5 not (0=don't know) (X=not applicable)

Living and working conditions	national prostitutes	migrant prostitutes/legal	migrant prostitutes/illegal	out-national prostitutes
psychological abuse (threats, name calling, insults, humiliation, etc.)				
physical abuse (hitting, kicking, beating, threatening with violence, etc.)				
sexual assault or rape (incl. attemped or threathened)				
illegal confinement (movements controlled/ restricted, no permission to leave working place, or allowed out only with chaperone)				
isolation (prohibited from normal social contacts, interception of letters/phone calls)				

- more next page -

threat of reprisals against family/relatives				
debt-bondage				
identity papers/passport confiscated (and not obtainable on departure)				
false identity papers				
personal belongings are taken away				
not paid regularly and/or paid less than agreed				
not paid at all				
no right to refuse certain customers/forced to have a certain number of customers per day				
no right to refuse certain sexual acts				
no right/opportunity to use condoms				
no access to medical and health care				
dangerous abortion practices/forced abortion				
compulsory HIV/AIDS testing				
not having a bedroom (forced to sleep in working space)				
not having a bed or nothing to sleep on				
more than 12-hour workdays normally				
denial of time off / denial of holidays				
no regular food (given left-overs, regularly denied food, insufficient food)				
forced to recruit sisters/girl friends into prostitution				
constant fear of police arrest				
other				

19] What factors inhibit women to escaping when they have become a victim of FL&SLP and/or TIW? Please fill in:
1 very frequently 2 frequently 3 occasionally 4 rarely 5 not (0=don't know) (X=not applicable)

Barriers to escape	national prostitutes	migrant prostitutes/legal	migrant prostitutes/ illegal	out-national prostitutes
movements are controlled by the criminal network				
violence by the criminal network				
fear of reprisals by the criminal network against herself, children, family or friends				
debt-bondage / fear of retribution against her parents/relatives for defaulting her debt				

- more next page -

no money				
no or false identity papers				
fear of reprisals or arrest by the authorities				
fear of reprisals by the authorities against family/friends				
fear of deportation				
fear of rejection by her family				
fear of rejection or moral condemnation by society				
family is dependant on her income				
not wanting to return home empty-handed				
lack of alternative employment				
involvement of own government/embassy				
other				

In your opinion, what are the two most important measures that should be taken to help women escape/change their situation?

1	
2	

20] What problems do victims of FL&SLP and/or TIW face when they return home?
Please fill in:
1 very frequently 2 frequently 3 occasionally 4 rarely 5 not (0=don't know) (X=not applicable)

Problems women face on returning home	migrant prostitutes/legal	migrant prostitutes/illegal	out-national prostitutes
rejection by her family			
stigmatization/rejection by society			
harassment by the authorities of her own country			
arrest/detention by the authorities of her own country			

- more next page -

reprisals by the criminal network against herself or family/relatives			
caught again by traffickers			
debts that cannot be paid off			
no earning/employment possibilities			
no housing			
psychological problems			
medical/health problems			
HIV/AIDS positive			
no medical care			
left to prostitution because of no other possibilities			
other			

What are the two most important measures that should be taken to support migrant women who became victim of FL&SLP and/or TIW when they return home?

1	
2	

4 CURRENT STRATEGIES TO STOP FORCED LABOUR & SLAVERY-LIKE PRACTICES AND TRAFFICKING IN WOMEN

21] Which of the following provisions does your government provide to encourage/facilitate victims of FL&SLP to report to the authorities?
Please fill in Y (yes) or N (no) or 0 (don't know) or X (not applicable)

Provisions to facilitate reporting	national prostitutes	migrant prostitutes/legal	migrant prostitutes/illegal	out-national prostitutes
confidential counselling/ victim support				
specially trained police officers				
safe shelters				

- *more next page* -

witness protection				
free legal aid				
provision against immediate deportation				
legal residence during investigations				
legalization of residence status if the victim cannot/does not want to return home				
assistance in returning home				
special support programmes for returnees				
other				

22] What support services are provided by NGOs?
Please fill in Y (yes) or N (no) or 0 (don't know) or X (not applicable)

Support services provided by NGOs	national prostitutes	migrant prostitutes/legal	migrant prostitutes/illegal	out-national prostitutes
counselling/social assistance				
medical/health services				
safe shelters				
legal assistance				
assistance to leave prostitution				
other				

23] Is there any special government policy to detect and prosecute those charged with FL&SLP and/or TIW? [ ] yes [ ] no [ ] don't know

24] Which of the following factors act as a barrier for women to report FL&SLP and/or TIW to the authorities?
Please fill in:
1 very frequently 2 frequently 3 occasionally 4 rarely 5 not (0=don't know) (X=not applicable)

Barriers to report to the authorities	national prostitutes	migrant prostitutes/legal	migrant prostitutes/illegal	out-national prostitutes
fear of deportation				
fear of reprisals by the traffickers				
fear that she herself will be punished/arrested				
fear that her situation will become known to her family/community				
outstanding debts				
need to financially support her family				

- more next page -

lack of confidence in the legal system				
lack of knowledge of her rights/the legal system of the country				
officials themselves are involved in FL&SLP/TIW				
corruption of authorities				
language barrier				
attitudes of law-enforcers				
shame				
no access to legal assistance				
other				

25] If women file a complaint: how are complaints handled by officials in your country?
Please fill in:
1 very frequently 2 frequently 3 occasionally 4 rarely 5 not (0=don't know) (X=not applicable)

Handling of complaints	occurrence
women are believed	
complaints are taken seriously	
complaints are investigated	
complaints result in prosecution	
prosecution results in a conviction	
offenders are sentenced to imprisonment	
offenders are fined	
other	

26] Do victims of FL&SP and/or TIW suffer ill-treatment by the authorities?
[ ] yes [ ] no [ ] don't know

If yes, which kind of ill-treatment are they subjected to?
Please fill in:
1 very frequently 2 frequently 3 occasionally 4 rarely 5 not (0=don't know) (X=not applicable)

Nature of ill-treatment by the authorities	national prostitutes	migrant prostitutes/legal	migrant prostitutes/illegal	out-national prostitutes
harassment by the police				
harassment by immigration officers				
arrest/detention as prostitute				
arrest/detention as illegal alien				

- more next page -

arrest/detention for illegal exit from the country				
arrest/detention for false/no identity papers				
arrest/detention for violation of laws on infectuous deseases				
compulsory admission in a rehabilitation centre/penal reform centre				
expulsion				
woman is sent back to brothel keeper/ procurer				
refusal to give back identity papers/issue new identity papers				
compulsory blood testing on HIV/AIDS				
other				

5 RECOMMENDATIONS

27] Do you have any recommendations to prevent and combat FL&SLP and/or TIW in prostitution:

a for the UN

b for governments

c for NGOs

6 STATISTICS

28] Please give your estimation of the number of women that become victim of **TIW** (according to the working definition) in your country per year. ______________

29] What percentage of victims of TIW files a legal complaint? (circle the best estimate)

< 2%	2-10%	11-30%	31-50%	51-70%	71-90%	>90%

30] What percentage of the complaints results in prosecution? (circle the best estimate)

< 2%	2-10%	11-30%	31-50%	51-70%	71-90%	>90%

31] What percentage of cases prosecuted results in a conviction? (circle the best estimate)

< 2%	2-10%	11-30%	31-50%	51-70%	71-90%	>90%

32] Please give your estimation of the number of women that become victim of **FL&SLP** (according to the working definition) in your country per year. ______________

33] What percentage of victims of FL&SP files a legal complaint? (circle the best estimate)

< 2%	2-10%	11-30%	31-50%	51-70%	71-90%	>90%

34] What percentage of the complaints results in prosecution? (circle the best estimate)

< 2%	2-10%	11-30%	31-50%	51-70%	71-90%	>90%

35] What percentage of cases prosecuted results in a conviction? (circle the best estimate)

< 2%	2-10%	11-30%	31-50%	51-70%	71-90%	>90%

36] If data are available, please fill in the following table with your estimations.

	1990	1991	1992	1993	1994	1995
number of complaints filed by victims of FL&SLP/TIW						
number of complaints that resulted in prosecution						
number of cases prosecuted that resulted in a conviction						

The above estimations are based on
[ ] government reports [ ] reports of NGOs [ ] own working experience
[ ] other, namely ______________________________
(please cross all that apply)

If it is not possible to give the requested estimations, please indicate why.

End of Section C
Thank you

NR. COUNTRY: ....

D FORCED LABOUR AND SLAVERY-LIKE PRACTICES IN DOMESTIC LABOUR / TRAFFICKING IN WOMEN FOR DOMESTIC WORK

In order to get a more precise understanding of the prevalence of forced labour and slavery-like practices (FL&SLP) and trafficking in women (TIW), we will use the following categories of women domestic workers (DWs):

- National DWs=women with the nationality of your country, who are working as domestic workers in your country;
- Migrant DWs=migrant women from other countries, who are working as domestic workers in your country. Migrant DWs can be either DOCUMENTED (with a contract and/or working permit) or UNDOCUMENTED (without a contract and/or working permit).
- OUT-national DWs=women with the nationality of your country, who are working as domestic workers in other countries;

Please do not be discouraged if you cannot answer for all the categories. Answer as much as you can and go on to the next question. Every bit of information helps!

I MANIFESTATIONS, TRENDS & DEVELOPMENTS

1] Do situations of FL&SLP (Forced Labour & Slavery-Like Practices) as described in the working definition occur among the different categories of DWs working in your country?
Please fill in:
1 very frequently 2 frequently 3 occasionally 4 rarely 5 not (0=don't know) (X=not applicable)

	occurrence of FL&SLP
national DWs	
migrant DWs/documented	
migrant DWs/undocumented	
out-national DWs	

2] Does TIW (Trafficking in Women) for domestic labour as described in the working definition occur among the different categories of DWs working in your country?
Please fill in:
1 very frequently 2 frequently 3 occasionally 4 rarely 5 not (0=don't know) (X=not applicable)

	occurrence of FL&SLP
national DWs	
migrant DWs/documented	
migrant DWs/undocumented	
out-national DWs	

3] Which of the following forms of coercion are used by traffickers?
Please fill in:
1 very frequently 2 frequently 3 occasionally 4 rarely 5 not (0=don't know) (X=not applicable)

Forms of coercion	national DWs	migrant DWs/ documented	migrant DWs/ undocumented	out-national DWs
violence/threat of violence				
abuse of authority/dominant position				
deception regarding conditions of work or service				
deception regarding nature of work or service				
debt-bondage				
using false papers				
other				

2 LEGAL CONTEXT

4] Are domestic workers protected by labour legislation or regulations in your country?
a national DWs [ ] yes [ ] no [ ] don't know
b migrant DWs/documented [ ] yes [ ] no [ ] don't know
c migrant DWs/undocumented [ ] yes [ ] no [ ] don't know
d out-national DWs [ ] yes [ ] no [ ] don't know

5a] Are there any special measures undertaken by your government to regulate recruitment and placement of migrant domestic workers?
Column 1: please fill in Y (yes), N (no) or 0 (don't know) or X (not applicable)
5b] Are they enforced?
Column 2: Please fill in:
1 very frequently 2 frequently 3 occasionally 4 rarely 5 not (0=don't know)(X=not applicable)

recruitment and placement	Y/N/D	Measure enforced? (1-5)
emigration clearance to leave country		
ban/restriction on direct hiring		
minimum standards for work contracts		
licensing/regulation of private recruiters		
operation of recr. agency by state		
security bond requirement		
ban/limit recruitment fee charged to worker		
contribution to Welfare Fund		
restriction on passport issue		
regulation of job advertising		
trade test requirement		

- ***more next page*** -

compulsory use national employment service		
restriction on selected occupations		
no objection certificate requirement		
compulsory service in country before departure		
ban on female domestic workers		
specification of transport carrier		
periodic inspection recruitment establishment		
pre-departure briefing		
restriction on country of employment		
renewal of contract clearance		

Source: M. Abella (1985) " Overseas Employment Administration: A Review of Policies and Procedures" in R. Owen, *Migration Workers in the Gulf*, Report No. 68, London, The Minority Rights Group.

6] Are domestic workers allowed to have their own associations/organizations?
[ ] yes [ ] no [ ] don't know

If not, please explain

7] Do domestic workers in your country have any form of legal protection against coercion, abuse or violence under the following laws:
Please fill in Y (yes) or N (no) or 0 (don't know) or X (not applicable).

	national DWs	migrant DWs/documented	migrant DWs/undocumented
criminal laws			
labour laws/regulations			
civil laws			
other			

If you answered one or more of these questions with Y (yes), please explain.

8a] Does the criminal law of your country contain specific provisions prohibiting trafficking in women for domestic labour? [ ] yes [ ] no [ ] don't know

If yes,
a what is prohibited?

b what is the maximum penalty? __________ years/months/days (circle) and/or ________ US$ fine
c what is the average penalty? __________ years/months/days (circle) and/or ________ US$ fine

8b] Does the criminal law of your country contain specific provisions prohibiting forced labour & slavery-like practices in domestic labour? [ ] yes [ ] no [ ] don't know

If yes,
a what is prohibited?

b what is the maximum penalty? __________ years/months/days (circle) and/or _______ US$ fine
c what is the average penalty? __________ years/months/days (circle) and/or _______ US$ fine

9] Are there any provisions for victims of FL&SLP in and/or TIW for domestic labour to obtain compensation for damages? [ ] yes [ ] no [ ] don't know

If yes, please explain.

10] Which of the following characteristics of FL&SLP apply to the living and working conditions of the different categories of domestic workers in your country?
Please fill in:
1 very frequently 2 frequently 3 occasionally 4 rarely 5 not (0=don't know) (X=not applicable)

Living and working conditions*	national DWs	migrant DWs/ documented	migrant DWs/ undocumented	out-national DWs
psychological abuse (threats, namecalling, shouting insults, threats)				
physical abuse (hitting, shoving, spitting, kicking, beating, etc)				
sexual assault or rape (including attempted and threatened harassment)				
illegal confinement (movements controlled and restricted, no permission to leave household, or allowed out only with chaperone)				
isolation (prohibited from normal social contacts, interception of letters, phone calls)				
threat of reprisal against family/relatives				
debt-bondage				
identity papers/passport confiscated by employer (and not obtainable on departure from employment)				
alse identity papers				
personal belongings taken away and not returned				
not paid regularly and/or paid less than agreed in contract				
not paid at all				
no access to medical and health services				
not having a bed-room (forced to sleep in hall-way, kitchen, bathroom, storeroom)				
not having a bed or nothing to sleep on				
more than 12-hour workdays normally				
denial of time off / denial of holidays				
no regular food (given left-overs, regularly denied food, insufficient food)				
lack of respect for cultural/religious customs & beliefs				
constant fear of police arrest				
compulsory HIV/Aids testing				
other				

* This list is adapted from a report of Kalayaan (Justice for Overseas Domestic Workers, London)

11] Which factors inhibit women from escaping when they become victims of FL&SLP and/or TIW?
Please fill in:
1 very frequently 2 frequently 3 occasionally 4 rarely 5 not (0=don't know) (X=not applicable)

Barriers to escape	national DWs	migrant DWs/ documented	migrant DWs/ undocumented	out-national DWs
movements are controlled by traffickers/ employers				
violence by traffickers/employers				
fear of reprisals by traffickers/				
employers against family/friends/herself				
debt-bondage/fear of retribution against family for not paying debt				
having no money				
having no identity papers or false papers				
fear of arrest by authorities				
fear of deportation				
dependence of family on her income				
not wanting to return home empty-handed				
ack of alternative employment				
involvement of own government/embassy				
lack of knowledge of laws and her rights				
other				

In your opinion, what are the two most important things that would help women to escape/change their situation?

1	
2	

12] What problems do victims of FL&SLP and/or TIW face when they return home?
Please fill in:
1 very frequently 2 frequently 3 occasionally 4 rarely 5 not (0=don't know) (X=not applicable)

- more next page -

problems women face when they return home	migrant DWs/ documented	migrant DWs/ undocumented	out-national DWs
no alternative employment/ financial coercion			
psychological problems			
no housing			
medical problems			
lack of skills			
shame for coming home empty-handed			
break down of family relationships			
other			

In your opinion, what are the two most important measures that should be taken to support migrant domestic workers who became victims of FL&SLP and/or TIW on returning home?

!	
2	

4 CURRENT STRATEGIES TO STOP FORCED LABOUR & SLAVERY-LIKE PRACTICES AND TRAFFICKING IN WOMEN

13] Which of the following provisions does your government provide to encourage victims of FL&SLP and/or TIW to report to the authorities?
Please fill in Y (yes) or N (no) or D(don't know) or X (not applicable).

Provisions to facilitate reporting	national DWs	migrant DWs/ documented	migrant DWs/ undocumented	out-national DWs
confidential counselling /victim support				
specially trained police officers				
safe shelters				
witness protection				
free legal aid				

- more next page -

provision against immediate deportation				
legal residence during investigations				
legal residence if the victim cannot return home				
assistance in returning home				
support programmes for returnees				
other				

14] What support services are provided by NGOs?
Please fill in Y (yes) or N (no) or D(don't know) or X (not applicable).

Support services available	national DWs	migrant DWs/ documented	migrant DWs/ undocumented	out-national DWs
counselling/social assistance				
health/medical services				
safe shelters				
legal assistance				
unemployment assistance				
assistance to return home				
assistance on return				
up-grading/training				
other				

15] Is there any government policy to detect and prosecute those charged with FL&SLP in and/or TIW for domestic work? [ ] yes [ ] no [ ] don't know

16] Which of the following factors act as a barrier for domestic workers to report FL&SLP and/or TIW to the authorities?
Please fill in:
1 very frequently 2 frequently 3 occasionally 4 rarely 5 not (0=don't know) (X=not applicable)

Barriers to report to the authorities	national DWs	migrant DWs/ documented	migrant DWs/ undocumented	out-national DWs
fear of losing visa sponsorship				
fear of deportation				
fear of reprisals by the traffickers/agents				
fear that she herself will be punished/arrested				
outstanding debts				
financial dependence of family				

- more next page -

lack of confidence in the legal system				
lack of knowledge of her rights/the legal system of the country				
language barrier				
corruption of authorities				
attitudes of law-enforcers				
officials themselves are involved in FL&SLP/TIW?				
lack of knowledge of/access to support mechanisms, e.g. legal assistance				
other				

17] If women file a complaint: how are complaints handled by officials in your country?
Please fill in:
1 very frequently 2 frequently 3 occasionally 4 rarely 5 not (0=don't know) (X=not applicable)

Handling of complaints	occurrence
women are believed	
complaints are taken seriously	
complaints are investigated	
complaints result in prosecution	
prosecution results in a conviction	
offenders are sentenced to imprisonment	
offenders are fined	
other	

18] Do victims of FL&SLP and/or TIW risk ill-treatment by the authorities and law-enforcers?
[ ] yes [ ] no [ ] don't know

If yes, indicate which kind of ill-treatment are they subjected to?
Please fill in:
1 very frequently 2 frequently 3 occasionally 4 rarely 5 not (0=don't know) (X=not applicable)

nature of ill-treatment by the authorities	national DWs	migrant DWs/ documented	migrant DWs/ undocumented	out-national DWs
harassment by the police				
arrest/detention as prostitute				
compulsory admission in a rehabilitation centre/ penal reform centre				
arrest/detention as illegal alien				

- more next page -

arrest/detention for illegal exit from the country				
expulsion				
woman is sent back to brothel keeper/procurer				
harassment by immigration officers				
arrest/detention for false/no identity papers				
refusal to give back identity papers/issue new identity papers				
compulsory blood testing on HIV/AIDS				
arrest/detention for violation of laws on infectuous deseases				
other				

5 RECOMMENDATIONS

19] Do you have any recommendations to prevent and combat FL&SLP in and/or TIW for domestic labour,

a for the UN

b for governments

c for NGOs

20] If data are available, please fill in the following table with your estimations:

	national DWs	migrant DWs/ documented	migrant DWs/ ndocumented	out-national DWs
a total numbers of DWs				
b percentage of a. working under conditions of FL&SLP				
c percentage of b. trafficked into this situation				
d percentage of cases of FL&SLP and/or TIW reported to the authorities				
e percentage of d. investigated				

The above estimations are based on
[ ] government reports [ ] reports of NGOs [ ] own working experience
[ ] other, namely ______________________________
(please cross all that apply)

If statistics are not available, please explain why.

End of section D
Thank You

ANNEX 2 Questionnaire for International Organizations

NR.:

B QUESTIONS ON TRAFFICKING IN WOMEN AND FORCED LABOUR & SLAVERY-LIKE PRACTICES

Please use extra sheets if you need more space to answer the questions.

1a] Has your organization carried out any studies or research concerning TIW/FL&SLP with regard to:

prostitution	[ ] yes	[ ] no
domestic labour	[ ] yes	[ ] no
marriage	[ ] yes	[ ] no

1b] What were the most significant findings of these studies/research?

____

____

____

1c1] Are there reports of these studies/researches available?

[ ] yes [ ] no

1c2] If yes, could you please give the references to these reports/researches? If possible, could you please send them to us? (If necessary we will reimburse costs.)

____

____

____

2a] Has your organization initiated programme(s) in any of these fields?

[ ] yes [ ] no

2b] If yes, please fill in the attached "Programme Information Form" - one for each of the programmes; please make as many copies as you need.
If no, please go on to question 3.

3a] Has your organization formulated any policies with regard to TIW and FL/SLP in the fields of

prostitution	[ ] yes	[ ] no
domestic work	[ ] yes	[ ] no
marriage	[ ] yes	[ ] no

3b] If yes, please describe briefly the main points of these policies. If available, please send us a copy of such policy statements.

____

____

____

4a] Is your organization involved in any networks on these issues:

NATIONAL [ ] yes [ ] no
Name, address, tel/fax/email of network(s)

REGIONAL [ ] yes [ ] no
Name, address, tel/fax/email of network(s):

INTERNATIONAL [ ] yes [ ] no
Name, address, tel/fax/email of network(s):

5a] Does your organization have any plans for future initiatives in this area?
[ ] yes [ ] no

5b] If yes, please describe these briefly. If available, please send us a copy of these proposals.

6] Does your organization have any recommendations for action against Trafficking in Women and/or Forced Labour & Slavery-like Practices in prostitution, domestic labour and marriage?

PROGRAMME INFORMATION FORM - Part of Question 2

Questions on Trafficking in Women and Forced Labour & Slavery-like Practices

1] Name of programme

____

____

____

2] Time-span of implementation

____

____

____

3] Names of cooperating organizations

____

____

____

4] Objectives

____

____

____

5] What are the principles underlying the specific approach of the programme; has there been any change in this approach over time?

____

____

____

6] How did this initiative come about?

____

____

____

7] How is the programme funded?

____

____

____

8a] Has the programme ended? [ ] yes [ ] no

8b] If yes, what were the most concrete results of the programme?

____

____

____

9a] If the programme has ended, has there been an evaluation? [ ] yes [ ] no

9b] If yes, what, briefly, are the conclusions of the evaluation?

____

____

____

10] If available, please send us any printed materials concerning the programme.

____

____

____

ANNEX 3 Questionnaire for Embassies

NR. .... COUNTRY: ....

QUESTIONS ON TRAFFICKING IN WOMEN AND FORCED LABOUR & SLAVERY-LIKE PRACTICES IN PROSTITUTION, DOMESTIC LABOUR AND MARRIAGE

1a] Have there been any official reports or surveys concerning trafficking in women and/or forced labour & slavery-like practices with regard to prostitution, domestic labour or marriage?
[ ] yes [ ] no [ ] not known

1b] If yes, could you please give the references to these reports/surveys?
If possible, could you please send us a copy.

____

____

____

2a] Does your country have any specific legislation or official government policies concerning trafficking in women and/or forced labour & slavery-like practices with regard to prostitution, domestic labour and/or marriage? [ ] yes [ ] no [ ] not known

2b] If yes, could you please describe such legislation/policies prescribed?
(Please send us a copy of the texts of any laws or regulations related to trafficking and/or forced labour & slavery-like practices.)

____

____

____

3a] Is it possible to work as a prostitute legally:

a	for nationals	[ ] yes	[ ] no	[ ] not known
b	for migrant women	[ ] yes	[ ] no	[ ] not known

3b] If yes, under which conditions?

For nationals

____

____

____

For migrant women

____

____

____

4a] For migrant women, is it possible to work as a domestic worker legally?
[ ] yes [ ] no [ ] not known

4b] If yes, under which conditions?

____

____

5] - Which of the following acts related to prostitution does the law of your country prohibit?
Column 1: please fill in Y (yes), N (no) or 0 (not known)
- What is the maximum penalty?
Column 2: please fill in the number of years/months/days and/or the fine in US$)
- What is the number of convictions during the last 5 years (1991-1995)?
Column 3: please fill in the number of convictions, if available.

The law prohibits	Column 1 Y/N/0	Column 2 Maximum penalty years/months/days and/or US$ fine	Column 3 Number of convictions during the last 5 years (1991-1995)
prostitution per se			
prostitution without license/registration			
prostitution outside permitted areas			
solliciting/loitering			
procurement/pimping per se			
procurement/pimping of minors			
procurement/pimping with the use of coercion			
procurement across borders			
procurement across borders with the use of coercion			
brothel keeping per se			
brothel keeping without license			
brothel keeping when minors are involved			
brothel keeping with the use of coercion			
buying of sexual services (clients)			
other			

6a] Does your country have any specific (migration, labour, criminal) legislation or policies concerning migrant women working in prostitution or domestic labour and/or migrant women married to nationals of your country? [ ] yes [ ] no [ ] not known

6b] If yes, could you please describe these laws/policies?

____

____

____

7a] Have there been any major changes in your country's legislation or government policies concerning trafficking and/or forced labour & slavery-like practices during the last 5 years (1991-1995)?
[ ] yes [ ] no [ ] not known

7b] If yes, could you please describe these changes.

____

____

____

8a] Is there any police cooperation on the national or international level to prevent and combat trafficking and/or forced labour & slavery-like practices? [ ] yes [ ] no [ ] not known

8b] If yes, could you please describe this cooperation.

____

____

____

9] Does your country have any specific government policies concerning: (Please tick where appropriate)

	yes	no	not known
the prevention of trafficking in women and/or forced labour & slavery-like practices?			
the tracing and prosecution of offenders?			
encouraging of victims to press charges?			
the provision of medical, legal, social, financial, psychological or other assistence to victims?			
legal possibilities for victims to claim compensation for economic, physical and psychological damages?			
granting a temporary residence permit to victims in order to enable them to take legal action against the offenders and to regain control over their life?			
assistence to victims in returning home?			
granting a permanent residence permit to victims if they cannot return home?			

10a] Do (migrant) women who are working in prostitution or in domestic labour or married to nationals of your country have any form of legal protection against violence, abuse or coercion?
[ ] yes [ ] no [ ] not known

10b] If yes, please describe the relevant laws and whether they are enforced.

____

____

____

11] If statistics are available, could you please fill in the following table

	in 1995
national women working in prostitution	
migrant women working in prostitution	
national women working as domestics	
migrant women working as domestics	
migrant women married to nationals of your country	

12a] If statistics are available, could you please fill in the following table

	Total of the last 5 years (1991 - 1995)
number of migrant women working in prostitution who were expelled	
number of migrant women working as domestics who were expelled	
number of migrant women married to a national of your country who were expelled	

12b] On which grounds were they expelled?

re. migrant women working in prostitution:
re. migrant women working as domestics:
re. migrant women married to a national of your country:

13] If statistics are available, could you please fill in the following table

	Total of the last 5 years (1991 - 1995)
number of women who filed a complaint under the laws you mentioned in question 2	
number of court cases that took place	
number of persons convicted	

We would appreciate very much to receive any relevant information and/or documents.

End of questionnaire
Thank you

ANNEX 4 List of Respondents to the questionnaires (NGOs, International Organizations and Embassies)

Organizations who returned a completed questionnaire

Australia

Australia, *End Child Prostitution in Asian Tourism (ECPAT)*
Australia, *Prostitutes Collective of Victoria*

Asia

Bangladesh, *Association for Community Development (ACD)*
Bangladesh, *Center for Women & Children Studies*
China, *Yunnan/Australian Red Cross*
Hong Kong, *Action for Reach Out*
Hong Kong, *Helpers for Domestic Helpers*
India, *SANLAAP*
India, *Rural Resource Women's Organization (SANGRAM)*
Japan, *HELP, Asian Women's Shelter*
Japan, *Kanagawa Women's Space*
Nepal, *Maiti*
Nepal, *Women acting together for change (Watch)*
Philippines, *National Commission on the Role of Filipino Women*
Taiwan, *Grassroots Women Workers' Centre (GWWC)*
Thailand, *Office of the National Commission on Women's Affairs (ONCWA)*
Thailand, *Office of the Attorney General*
Thailand, *Centre for the Protection of Children's Rights (CPCR)*
Thailand, *Images-Asia*
Thailand, *Good Shepherd Sisters-Fountain of Life Center*
Vietnam, *IOM mission*

Europe

Belgium, *Pag-asa*
Bulgaria, *Association Animus*
Czech Republic, *Bliss without Risk*
Czech Republic, *ProFem*
Denmark, *KULU-Aarhus*
England, *Kalayaan*
Finland, *Stakes*
Germany, *Amnesty for Women*
Germany, *Ban Ying*
Ireland, *Filipino-Irish Group*
Italy, *Associazione Donne Semza Confini*
Italy, *Casa delle Donne per non subire violenza*
Italy, *Khantara Group*
Netherlands, *Foundation against Trafficking in Women (STV)*
Poland, *La Strada*
Romania, *National Assocation of University Women*
Slovenia, *Slovenian Ecology Movement*
Spain, *IEPALA/AMDE*
Switzerland, *Caritas*
Switzerland, *FIZ*
Turkey, *Women for Women's Human Rights*
Ukraine, *Ukrainian Center for Women's Studies*

Africa

Cameroon, *Association de lutte contre les violences faits aux femmes (ALVF)*
Cameroon, *Fesade*
Mali, *AJM*
Mali, *APDF*
Namibia, *Legal Assistance Centre*
Nigeria, *Ms. Grace Osakue*
Tanzania, *Ms. Helen Kijo-Bisimba*
Zambia, *Young Women's Christian Association (YWCA)*

North America

Canada, *Prostitutes Empowerment Education Recovery Society (PEERS)*
Canada, *Philippine Women Centre of B.C.*
Canada, *Status of Women Canada*
USA, *Farmworker Legal Services of New York*
USA, *Women's Justice Center*

South-, Central America, Carribean

Curaçao, *Kamala Kempadoo*
Dominican Republic, *Centro Orientacion e Investigacion Integral (COIN)*
Dominican Republic, *Coordinadora Organizaciones no Gubernamentales del Aera de la Mujer*
Ecuador, *Pan American Health Organization-World Health Organiation (OPS/OMS)*
Mexico, *Comunicacion e Informacion de la Mujer Asociasion Civil (CIMAC)*
Mexico, *Mujeres por la salud en acción contra el Sida AC*
Peru, *Movimiento El Pozo*

INTERNATIONAL ORGANIZATIONS WHICH RETURNED A QUESTIONNAIRE

1 **African Centre for Democracy and Human Rights Studies (ACDHRS),**
(Promotion of democracy and human rights in accordance with African Charter; research on inheritance and marriage laws in Senegal and Kenya)

2 **Anti-Slavery International**
(Elimination of slavery in all its forms; advocacy, lobbying, public campaigning. Specific FL/SLP/TIW programmes, wrt domestic workers and prostitution; not yet marriage)

3 **Bilance**
(Financing programmes in developing countries: COIN, EcPat, Ecumenical Coalition on Third World Tourism)

4 **CAFOD/Medical Missionaries of Mary**
(no TIW programmes; work on HIV/Aids)

5 **CARITAS Switzerland**
(funding; research on prostitution and marriage)

6 **CLADEM-Peru**

7 **European Human Rights Foundation (EHRF)**

8 **European Women's Lobby**
(no TIW programmes)

9 **Euro Step**
(no TIW programmes)

10 **HIVOS (Humanist Institute for Cooperation with Developing Countries)**

11 **International Organization for Migration**
(research, inter-governmental cooperation, return projects)

12 **Quaker Council for European Affairs**
(Research '92: The Trafficking of Women to Europe)

13 **Women's International Network**
(Female genital mutilation; WIN NEWS)

The following (national) organizations completed a questionnaire for international organizations

Reden The Nest, Denmark
Ain o Salish Kendra (ASK), Bangladesh

Embassies which returned a completed questionnaire

Europe

Austria, *Ministry of Women Affairs*
Czech Republic, *Ministry for Foreign Affairs*
Germany, *Ministry for Family Affairs, Senior Citizens, Women and Youth*
Hungary, *Ministry of Labour, Office of the Status of Women*
Luxembourg, *Ministère de la Promotion Féminine*
Slowak Republic, *Presidium Slowak Police*
The Netherlands, *South-African Embassy*
Spain, *Ministerio de Trabajo y Asuntos Sociales, Instituto de la Mujer*

ANNEX 5

Tables of countries of origin and destination

- *Trafficking in Women for Marriage*
- *Trafficking in Women for Domestic Work*
- *Trafficking in Women for Prostitution*

TRAFFIC IN WOMEN FOR MARRIAGE

Read as country of destination

FROM ↓ / TO →	**EUROPE**	Ireland	Germany	Switzerland	Netherlands	Italy	Spain	Belgium	United Kingdom	France	Turkey	Bosnia	Slovenia	Czech Rep	Bulgaria	Romania	Poland	Ukraine	Russia	Bela-russia
EUROPE																				
Ireland																				
Germany																				
Switzerland																				
Netherlands																				
Italy																				
Spain																				
Belgium																				
United Kingdom																				
France																				
Turkey																				
Bosnia						▼														
Slovenia			▲																	
Czech Rep																				
Bulgaria																				
Romania																				
Poland			◆	◆		◆		◆												
Ukraine			▲	▲					▲	▲					▼					
Russia						▼			▼						▼					
Bela-russia																				
NORTH AMERICA																				
USA																				
Canada																				
SOUTH AMERICA																				
Curaçao																				
Dominican Rep			▲	◆		▲														
Peru			▲																	
Mexico																				
Ecuador																				
Guatamala																				
El Salvador																				
Brasil					▼	▼														
Colombia																				
Argentina																				
Mauritius					▼															
Cuba																				
AFRICA																				
Zambia																				
Tanzania																				
Nigeria																				
Mali										▲										
Cameroon			▲		◆					▲										
Kenya					▼															
Somalia																				
Malawi																				
Chad																				
Benin																				
Central Africa																				
Ivory Coast					▼															
Seychelles																				
Cape Verde																				
Gabon																				
Ghana					▼															
ASIA & PACIFIC																				
Bangladesh																				
Nepal																				
Thailand			◆	▼	▼				▼											
Japan																				
Hong Kong																				
India																				
China																				
Philippines			◆	▼				◆	▲											
Vietnam																				
Taiwan																				
Indonesia																				
Burma																				
Sri Lanka									▼											
Pakistan																				
Singapore																				
Korea																				
Malaysia					▼															
AUSTRALIA																				
Australia																				
MIDDLE EAST																				
Lebanon																				
UAE																				
Saoudi Arabia																				
Israel																				
Dubai																				

FROM ↓ / TO →	**NORTH AMERICA**	USA	Canada	**SOUTH AMERICA**	Curaçao	Dominican Rep	Peru	Mexico	Ecuador	Guatamala	El Salvador	Brasil	Colombia	Argentina	Mauritius	Cuba
EUROPE																
Ireland																
Germany																
Switzerland																
Netherlands																
Italy																
Spain																
Belgium																
United Kingdom																
France																
Turkey																
Bosnia																
Slovenia																
Czech Rep																
Bulgaria																
Romania																
Poland																
Ukraine																
Russia																
Bela-russia																
NORTH AMERICA																
USA																
Canada																
SOUTH AMERICA																
Curaçao																
Dominican Rep																
Peru		▲														
Mexico		▲														
Ecuador																
Guatamala																
El Salvador																
Brasil																
Colombia																
Argentina																
Mauritius																
Cuba								▼								
AFRICA																
Zambia																
Tanzania																
Nigeria																
Mali																
Cameroon																
Kenya																
Somalia																
Malawi																
Chad																
Benin																
Central Africa																
Ivory Coast																
Seychelles																
Cape Verde																
Gabon																
Ghana																
ASIA & PACIFIC																
Bangladesh																
Nepal																
Thailand																
Japan																
Hong Kong																
India																
China																
Philippines																
Vietnam																
Taiwan																
Indonesia																
Burma																
Sri Lanka																
Pakistan																
Singapore																
Korea																
Malaysia																
AUSTRALIA																
Australia																
MIDDLE EAST																
Lebanon																
UAE																
Saoudi Arabia																
Israel																
Dubai																

FROM ↓ / TO →	**AFRICA**	Zambia	Tanzania	Nigeria	Mali	Cameroon	Kenya	Somalia	Malawi	Chad	Benin	Central Africa	Ivory Coast	Seychelles	Cape Verde	Gabon	Ghana
EUROPE																	
Ireland																	
Germany																	
Switzerland																	
Netherlands																	
Italy																	
Spain																	
Belgium																	
United Kingdom																	
France																	
Turkey																	
Bosnia																	
Slovenia																	
Czech Rep																	
Bulgaria																	
Romania																	
Poland																	
Ukraine																	
Russia																	
Bela-russia																	
NORTH AMERICA																	
USA																	
Canada																	
SOUTH AMERICA																	
Curaçao																	
Dominican Rep																	
Peru																	
Mexico																	
Ecuador																	
Guatamala																	
El Salvador																	
Brasil																	
Colombia																	
Argentina																	
Mauritius																	
Cuba																	
AFRICA																	
Zambia																	
Tanzania																	
Nigeria																	
Mali																▲	
Cameroon																	
Kenya																	
Somalia																	
Malawi																	
Chad																	
Benin																	
Central Africa																	
Ivory Coast																	
Seychelles																	
Cape Verde																	
Gabon																	
Ghana																	
ASIA & PACIFIC																	
Bangladesh																	
Nepal																	
Thailand																	
Japan																	
Hong Kong																	
India																	
China																	
Philippines																	
Vietnam																	
Taiwan																	
Indonesia																	
Burma																	
Sri Lanka																	
Pakistan																	
Singapore																	
Korea																	
Malaysia																	
AUSTRALIA																	
Australia																	
MIDDLE EAST																	
Lebanon																	
UAE																	
Saoudi Arabia																	
Israel																	
Dubai																	

FROM ↓ / TO →	**ASIA & PACIFIC**	Bangladesh	Nepal	Thailand	Japan	Hong Kong	India	China	Philippines	Vietnam	Taiwan	Indonesia	Burma	Sri Lanka	Pakistan	Singapore	Korea	Malaysia	**AUSTRALIA**	Australia	**MIDDLE EAST**	Lebanon	UAE	Saoudi Arabia	Israel	Dubai
EUROPE																										
Ireland																										
Germany																										
Switzerland																										
Netherlands																										
Italy																										
Spain																										
Belgium																										
United Kingdom																										
France																										
Turkey																										
Bosnia																										
Slovenia																										
Czech Rep																										
Bulgaria																										
Romania																										
Poland																										
Ukraine																									▲	
Russia																										
Bela-russia																										
NORTH AMERICA																										
USA																				▲						
Canada																										
SOUTH AMERICA																										
Curaçao																										
Dominican Rep																										
Peru																										
Mexico																										
Ecuador																										
Guatamala																										
El Salvador																										
Brasil																										
Colombia																										
Argentina																										
Mauritius																										
Cuba																										
AFRICA																										
Zambia																										
Tanzania																										
Nigeria																										
Mali																										
Cameroon																										
Kenya																										
Somalia																										
Malawi																										
Chad																										
Benin																										
Central Africa																										
Ivory Coast																										
Seychelles																										
Cape Verde																										
Gabon																										
Ghana																										
ASIA & PACIFIC																										
Bangladesh							◆								▲											
Nepal						▲	◆																			
Thailand																										
Japan																										
Hong Kong																										
India																								▲		
China				▲	▼											▲										
Philippines																	▲			▲						
Vietnam								▲			▲															
Taiwan					▲																					
Indonesia											▲															
Burma							▼																			
Sri Lanka																										
Pakistan																										
Singapore																										
Korea																										
Malaysia																										
AUSTRALIA																										
Australia								▲	▲																	
MIDDLE EAST																										
Lebanon																										
UAE																										
Saoudi Arabia																										
Israel																										
Dubai																										

Responses to survey-questions 4a + 4b (Section B): If your country is a **SENDING COUNTRY** (country of origin): please write to which **COUNTRIES OF DESTINATION** women are trafficked from your country / If your country is a **RECEIVING COUNTRY** (country of destination): please write from which **COUNTRIES OF ORIGIN** women are trafficked to your country.
Indicated are the countries which respondents mention under the category "frequently".

4a Vertical bar ▲ traffic in women for marriage takes place **FROM** these countries to ... (horizontal bar)

4b Horizontal bar ▼ traffic in women for marriage takes place **TO** these countries from ... (vertical bar)

Traffic in women for domestic work

Read as country of destination

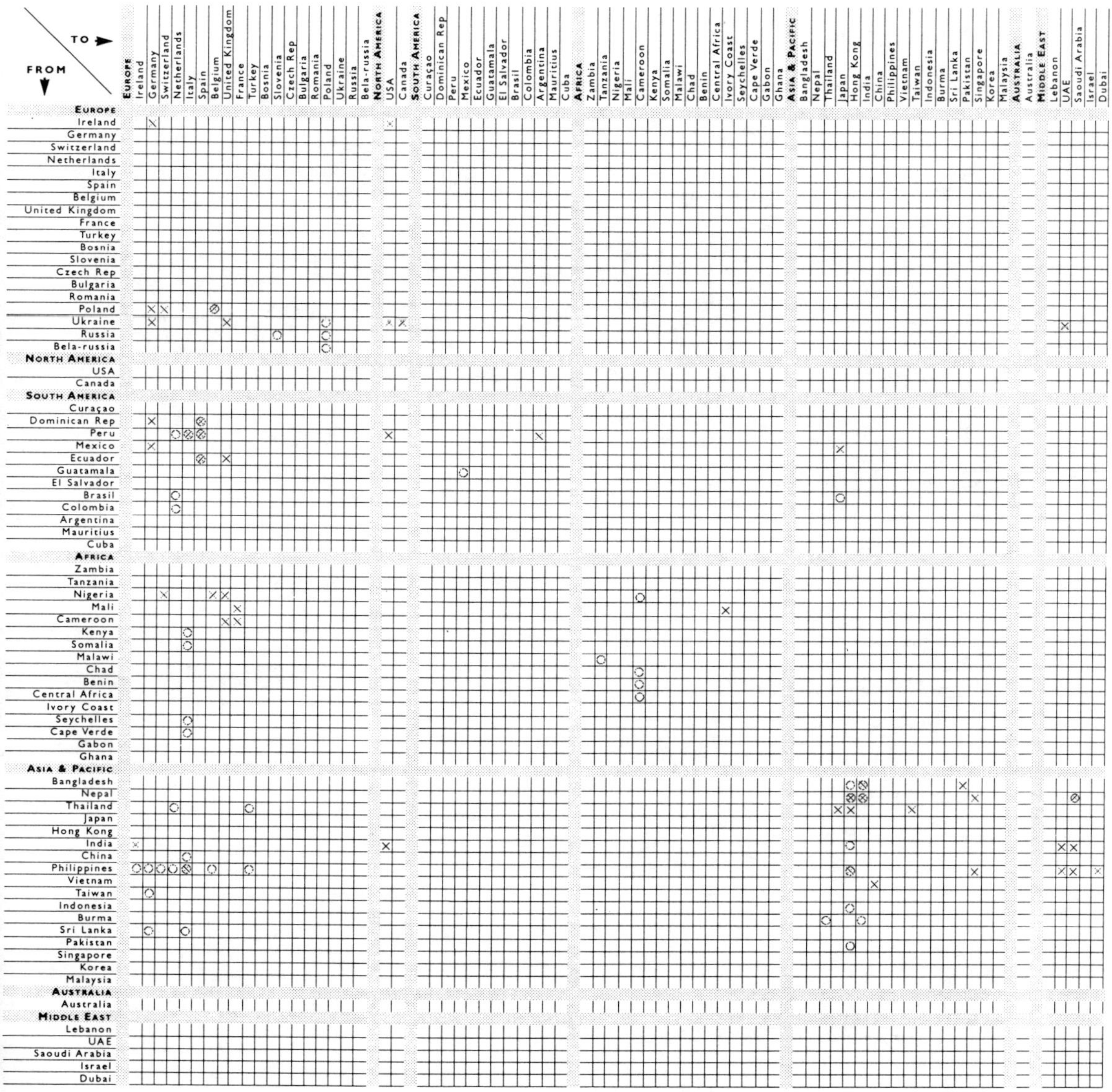

Responses to survey-questions 4a + 4b (Section B): If your country is a **SENDING COUNTRY** (country of origin): please write to which **COUNTRIES OF DESTINATION** women are trafficked from your country / If your country is a **RECEIVING COUNTRY** (country of destination): please write from which **COUNTRIES OF ORIGIN** women are trafficked to your country.
Indicated are the countries which respondents mention under the category "frequently".

4a Vertical bar	×	traffic in women for domestic work takes place **FROM** these countries to ... (horizontal bar)
4b Horizontal bar	○	traffic in women for domestic work takes place **TO** these countries from ... (vertical bar)

Traffic in women for prostitution

Read as country of destination

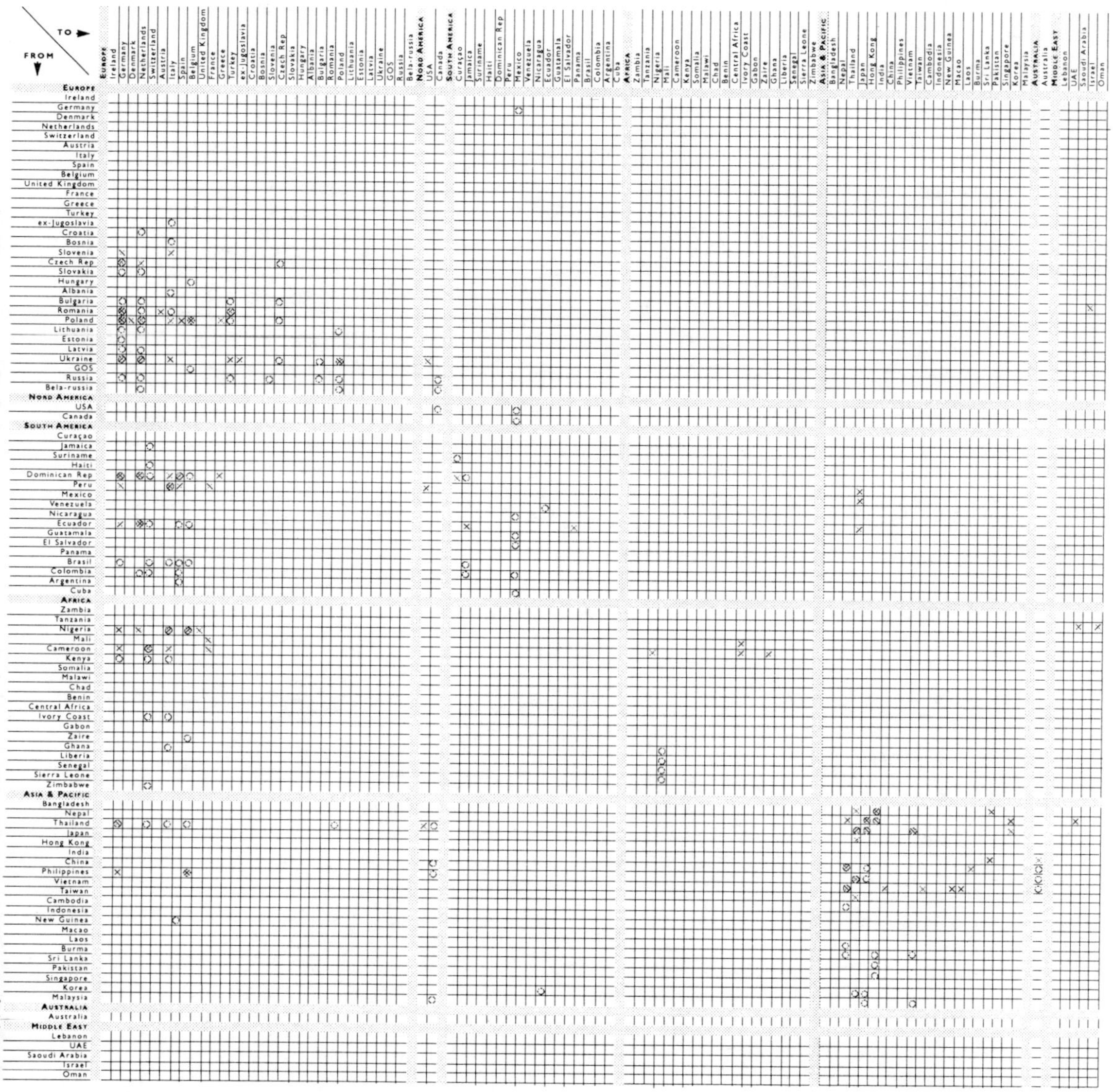

Responses to survey-questions 4a + 4b (Section B): If your country is a **sending country** (country of origin): please write to which **countries of destination** women are trafficked from your country / If your country is a **receiving country** (country of destination): please write from which **countries of origin** women are trafficked to your country.
Indicated are the countries which respondents mention under the category "frequently".

4a Vertical bar	×	traffic in women for prostitution takes place **FROM** these countries to ... (horizontal bar)
4b Horizontal bar	○	traffic in women for prostitution takes place **TO** these countries from ... (vertical bar)

ANNEX 6 Draft Standard Minimum Rules for the Treatment of Victims of Trafficking in Women and Forced Labour & Slavery-like Practices

DRAFT PROPOSAL OF STANDARD MINIMUM RULES FOR THE TREATMENT OF VICTIMS OF TRAFFICKING AND FORCED LABOUR AND SLAVERY LIKE PRACTICES (SMR)

The idea for the NGO draft of standard minimum rules for the treatment of victims of Trafficking and Forced Labour and Slavery Like Practices (SMR) arose out of discussions during the October 1994 International workshop on International Migration and Traffic in Women, organised by the Foundation for Women in Thailand. It became clear that existing treaties and covenants directly addressing trafficking in women were ineffective, owing in part to:

- Their failure to provide a comprehensive definition of trafficking
- Their failure to address basic rights of women as the basis of action
- Their lack of enforcement mechanisms
- Their limited scope, as they addressed only trafficking for prostitution and not other purposes.

At the same time it seemed likely that NGOs and governments could agree on focusing on basic human rights protection for persons who are trafficked, which are basic principles in UN and international standards.

There are many documents and agreements which can be used for the protection of the human rights of trafficked persons but do not make concrete enough recommendations to be of any practical use. We would like to develop a document which draws together these principles, and makes solid, practical recommendations.

Our recommendations could be used as a guide for governmental actions, given they are based on agreements the governments have already entered into. As such, the recommendations would have a strong potential, both politically and practically to be adopted.

The Foundation for Women initiated the first draft of the recommendations, based on research on the concrete reality of trafficked women. The International Human Rights Law Group (Women in Law Project) placed the recommendations into a human rights framework. Various NGOs involved in the discussion through GAATW agreed that the minimum rules should extend to protect victims of forced labour and slavery-like practices. The term 'standard minimum rules for the humanitarian treatment of trafficked persons' was mentioned at the 50th session of the UN General Assembly, and at the 52nd session of the UN Commission on Human Rights, and governments were invited to consider the development of standard minimum rules.

DRAFT

Standard minimum rules for the treatment of victims of trafficking in persons and forced labour & slavery-like practices

Drafted by the Global Alliance Against Traffic in Women and The Foundation For Women, in cooperation with The International Human Rights Law Group Women In Law Project, and the Foundation Against Trafficking in Women.

The following Standards aim to protect the human rights of those individuals who have been victim of trafficking in persons and the related forced labour & slavery-like practices, in particular the right to control over one's mind, body and life.[1]

Keeping in mind that victims of trafficking and the related forced labour and slavery-like practices are not criminals but victims of crime, governments should take all necessary steps to reform any law or policy that punishes, criminalizes or marginalizes the victims of these practices and to ensure them the humane treatment stated below.

Recognizing that traffickers exploit poverty, gender violence, armed conflicts, and other conditions which subordinate persons and which they may seek to escape, protection must be given to individuals in situations which render them vulnerable to deception as well as physical, psychological and economic coercion and violence.

Governments should take all necessary steps to ensure victims of trafficking and forced labour & slavery-like practices the equal protection of the law and to guarantee them the rights and fundamental freedoms of all individuals, including the freedom of movement and residence in each State, the freedom to choose one's place of residence, the right to safely return to one's own country, and the right to seek asylum or otherwise legalize one's status in the country of destination.

[1] See also International Covenant on Civil and Political Rights (ICCPR), art. 1 & 8; Protection of the Rights of All Migrant Workers, 1990, art. 16 para 1 & 2; Slavery Convention, 1926; Supplementary Convention on the Abolition of Slavery, the Slave Trade, and Institutions and Practices Similar to Slavery 1956, Preamble ("Considering that freedom is the birthright of every human being..") and art. 1.

DEFINITIONS

Trafficking In Persons

All acts involved in the recruitment and/or transportation of a person within and across national borders for work or services by means of violence or threat of violence, abuse of authority or dominant position, debt-bondage, deception or other forms of coercion.

Forced Labour & Slavery-like Practices

The extraction of work or services from any person or the appropriation of the legal identity and/or physical person of any person by means of violence or threat of violence, abuse of authority or dominant position, debt-bondage, deception or other forms of coercion.

Background of the definitions

The above formulated definitions go back to two international agreements: the League of Nations Slavery Convention of 1926 and the Supplementary Convention of 1956[2], which condemn all slavery-like practices, including debt-bondage[3] and forced marriage[4] and the ILO Forced Labour Convention no. 29[5].These conventions have broad international acceptance and clearly describe the situations at hand. In the Slavery Convention the concept of 'ownership' is fundamental to slavery, which in art. 1.1 is defined as:
"the status or condition of a person over whom any or all of the power attaching to the right of ownership are exercised".
In art. 2 of the ILO Forced Labour Convention, forced or compulsory labour is defined as:
"all work or service which is extracted from any person under the menace of any penalty and for which the said person has not offered himself voluntarily".
Whereas the concept of "forced labour" in art. 1 of the ILO Convention is predominantly used for the relation between the state and the individual, art. 4.1 of the same Convention rules on state accountability regarding forced labour situations between individuals:
"the competent authority shall not impose or permit the imposition of forced or compulsory labour for the benefit of private individuals, companies or associations".

The crucial element in both definitions is coercion, which can take various forms, including but not limited to:

2 Slavery Convention, 1926; Supplementary Convention on the Abolition of Slavery, the Slave Trade, and Institutions and Practices simular to Slavery, 1956.

3 Art. 1a of the Supplementary Slavery Convention prohibits "Debt bondage, that is to say, the status or condition arising from a pledge by a debtor of his personal services or those of a person under his control as security for a debt, if the value of those services as reasonably assessed is not applied towards the liquidation of the debt or the length and nature of those services are not respectively limited and defined".

4 Art. 1c of the Supplementary Slavery Convention prohibits "Any institution or practice whereby a woman without the right to refuse, is promised or given in marriage on payment of a consideration in money or kind to her parents, guardian, family or any other person or group", or whereby "the husband of a woman, his family, or his clan, has the right to transfer her to another person for value received or otherwise"

5 ILO Convention no. 29 concerning Forced Labour, 1930

- violence or threat of violence, including deprivation of freedom (of movement, of personal choice)
- deception: with regard to working conditions or the nature of the work to be done
- abuse of authority, dominant position: this can range from confiscation of personal documents to place another person in a dependent position, abusing one's dominant social position, abusing one's natural parental authority or abusing the vulnerable position of persons without legal status
- debt-bondage: pledging the personal services or labour of a person indefinitely as security for a debt, when the length and nature of the service is not clearly defined.

"WORK OR SERVICES" include all domestic, sexual, reproductive or other services rendered under the above-mentioned conditions of coercion, regardless of whether these services are recognized as work, whether they take place under a work contract or whether they take place under a marriage contract.

"THE APPROPRIATION OF THE LEGAL IDENTITY AND/OR PHYSICAL PERSON" refers to the concept of partial or total ownership as used in the Slavery Conventions, but the word "appropriation" is used to denote the act of claiming ownership of a person, acting as if one owns the person.

"APPROPRIATION OF THE LEGAL IDENTITY" can range from confiscating one's identity papers, supplying a person with a false identity to the loss of one's legal personality under the marriage contract.

"COUNTRY OF ORIGIN": the country of origin of the trafficked person.

"COUNTRY OF DESTINATION": the country of destination of the trafficked person.

"TRANSIT COUNTRY": the country en route from the country of origin to the country of destination, often for the purpose of preparing false passports, marriage documents, visas.

Obligations of all countries: destinations,transit and origins

1 The following shall be guaranteed to all victims of trafficking and forced labour & slavery-like practices:
  - Freedom from persecution or harassment by those in positions of authority.
  - Adequate, confidential and affordable medical and psychological care by the State or, if no adequate State agency exists, by a private agency funded by the State.
  - Strictly confidential HIV testing service shall be provided **ONLY IF** requested by the person concerned. Additionally, any and all HIV testing must be accompanied with appropriate pre- and post-test counselling. The Standard provided in the UN Centre for Human Rights and World Health Organization Report of an International Consultation on AIDS and Human Rights, Geneva, July 1989 shall be adopted.
  - Access to a competent, qualified translator during all proceedings, and provision of all documents and records pursuant to having been victim of trafficking and/or forced labour & slavery-like practices.[6]

[6] See also, Protection of the Rights of all Migrant Workers. Art. 16. par 5.

- Free legal assistance.
- Legal possibilities of compensation and redress for economic, physical and psychological damage caused to them.
- The personal history, the alleged 'character' or the current or previous occupation of the victim shall not be used against the victim, nor serve as a reason to disqualify the victims complaint or to decide not to prosecute the offenders. The offenders cannot use as a defence the fact that the person is or was at any time, for example, a prostitute or a domestic worker.
- The victim's history of being trafficked and/or being subjected to forced labour & slavery-like practices shall not be a matter of public or private record and shall not be used against her, her family or friends in any way whatsoever, particularly with regard to the right to freedom of travel, marriage, search for gainful employment.

2 The State in the territory under whose jurisdiction the trafficking and/or forced labour & slavery-like practices took place shall take all necessary steps to ensure that the victim, if he or she wishes so, may press criminal charges and/or take civil action for compensation against the perpetrator(s)[7].

3 If the victim is not recognized as citizen by the country of origin for any reason, the country of origin must consider on the balance of probabilities whether that person was born in and/or has spent most of her/his life in the country of origin and if so, accord that person nationality of the country of origin. If the country of origin will not accept the victim, the country of destination must treat her as a national of that country under the Convention on the Status of Stateless Persons (1960).

4 The State must ensure the right of all people within its jurisdiction to be free from being sold by any other person[8] and/or from being subjected to forced labour and slavery-like practices in accordance with the ILO Convention no. 29 concerning Forced Labour, art. 1.4.1.

Obligations of destination and transit countries

5 In addition to the above, and in order to ensure the victim's ability to remain in the country during all proceedings pursuant to having been victim of trafficking and/or forced labour & slavery-like practices, the victim shall, for the duration of her stay, be guaranteed:
- Resident status, in order to take legal action against the offenders and to regain control over her life
- Adequate and safe housing
- Access to all State provided health and social services
- Adequate financial support
- Opportunities for employment, education and training

6 Victims of trafficking and/or forced labour & slavery-like practices shall not be held in a detention centre at any time, including during proceedings against the offenders.

[7] See International Covenant on Civil and Political Rights, art. 2.3

[8] See Supplementary Convention on the Abolition of Slavery, the Slave Trade, and Institutions and Practices Similar to Slavery 1956, Art. 1 Par C Sub Par i-iii.

7 Victims of trafficking and/or forced labour & slavery-like practices shall have access to the embassy/consulate of their home country or, if trafficked into a country without an embassy/consulate representation, they shall have access to a diplomatic representative of the State that takes charge of the home country's interests or any national or international authority whose task it is to protect such persons.[9]

8 Victims of trafficking and/or forced labour & slavery-like practices shall not be prosecuted for the use of false travel or other documents and/or visas pursuant to their predicament

9 Victims who wish to do so, shall be enabled to apply for permanent residence under internationally agreed upon covenants. Guidelines recognizing gender-based persecution as grounds for asylum should be followed.

10 Victims of trafficking and/or forced labour & slavery-like practices shall be guarenteed the right to legal representation during criminal or other proceedings against her or him that may result in detention, deportation or loss of legal status. If she cannot afford to pay, legal representation shall be provided without cost.[10]

11 The burden of proof prior to and during any prosecution of a person alleged to be quilty of trafficking and/or forced labour & slavery-like practices lies with the prosecution, not with the victim. The victim shall not be placed in detention prior to the trial of the offender.

12 If a person is convicted of trafficking and/or subjecting another person to forced labour & slavery-like practices, any or all funds in his/her possession shall be used to pay any debts the victim incurred as a consequence of being trafficked and/or subjected to forced labour & slavery-like practices. Additionally, adequate compensation shall be granted to the victim.

13 The State shall provide the necessary funds for the victim to return to her/his home country.

14 If a victim of trafficking and/or forced labour & slavery-like practices person is arrested under the criminal law of the country for committing a crime :
- As a result of physical, psychological or economic duress or coercion by the person(s) who trafficked her and/or subjected her to forced labour & slavery-like practices: these circumstances shall be considered in any defence of duress or coercion raised by the victim during the pre-trial and trial proceedings and as mitigation in sentencing if convicted.
- Against the person who trafficked her and/or subjected her to forced labour & slavery-like practices, including homicide.
- The history of trafficking and/or being subjected to forced labour & slavery-like practices shall be permitted in support of a plea of self-defence and as a mitigation during sentencing if convicted.

[9] See 38 (2) of the Standard Minimum Rules For the Treatment of Prisoners 1955.

[10] See ICCPR, art.14.3 ; Protection of all Persons under any Form of Detention, Prin.17, para 1 & 2, Prin.18, para 1-5

Obligations of countries of origin

15 Victims of trafficking and/or forced labour & slavery-like practices who return to their home country shall not be imprisoned or detained for facts pursuant to their predicament, nor for the use of false travel and other documents.

16 The State shall protect victims of trafficking and/or forced labour & slavery-like practices and their family members from reprisals of the perpetrators, including people in positions of authority.

17 The State shall not do anything to prevent or obstruct the voluntary movement of citizens, including victims of trafficking and/or forced labour & slavery-like practices, out or into the country at all times.[11]

18 The State shall use diplomatic channels and resources in destination and transit countries to protect their nationals abroad.

The Global Alliance Against Traffic in Women
PO BOX 1281, BANGRAK POST OFFICE, BANGKOK 10500, THAILAND
Tel (662) 864-1428
Fax (662) 864-1637

[11] See Universal Declaration of Human Rights, Art. 13; ICCPR, art.12 family, or his clan, has the right to transfer her to another person for value received or otherwise"

ANNEX 7 Members of the Advisory Committee and Regional Consultants

Members of the Advisory Committee

Siriporn Skrobanek	Coordinator Global Alliance Against Trafficking in Women (GAATW), Bangkok NGO/ community activities and networks
Lesley Roberts	Ex-director Anti-Slavery International, London UN/ International Human Rights instruments and agencies and their processes
Gail Pheterson	Psychologist, publicist, lecturer, Paris/Amsterdam Migration (labour) processes and consequences, including migratory prostitution processes
Roelof Haveman	Criminal Law Lecturer, University of Leiden Legislations and juridical processes
Welmoed Koekebakker	Head of Asia Department, Humanist Institute for Cooperation with Developing Countries (HIVOS), member of the Board of STV International cooperation

Regional Consultants

Yamila Azize-Vargas	Latin America and Caribbean
Florence Butegwa	Africa
Lisa Kois / Joanna Bond / Jyoti Sanghera	North America and Canada
Siriporn Skrobanek / Sarah Johnston	Asia and Pacific

ANNEX 8 Information on the [illegible] Alliance Against Trafficking in Women (GAATW)

THE GLOBAL ALLIANCE AGAINST TRAFFICKING IN WOMEN (GAATW)

International Coordination Office:
191 Sivalai Condominium, Isaraphab Road 33,
Bangkok 10600, Thailand.
Tel: (662) 864 - 1427/ (662) 864 - 1428
Fax: (662) 864 - 1637
E-mail: GAATW @ mozart.inet.co.th

The **Global Alliance Against Trafficking in Women (GAATW)** was formed at the International Workshop on International Migration and Traffic in Women in Thailand in October 1994.

We are a feminist alliance who wish to coordinate the action on trafficking in women. Our definition of trafficking is the transportation of women from one place to another in order to subject them to actual and unlawful power by means of violence or the threat of violence, or by abusing a position of authority arising from a relationship or by misleading another person. Trafficking is not only for the purposed of forced prostitution, but for a range of activities which include any form of forced labour in the formal and informal sphere, for example, domestic services and services related to the sex industry.

Our aim is not to stop the migration of women but to ensure the protection of the human rights of those involved. Our strategy is to promote the involvement of grassroots women in all work against trafficking in women to ensure that any work done addresses the real problems. We work to empower women rather than treat them as victims.

Objectives

1 To improve practical support and advocacy work at all levels
2 To make alliances with international organisations
3 To enforced and utilise the existing international instruments to address existing and future problems
4 To examine the need for new international instruments
5 To promote and facilitate research on the issue

Activities

To achieve the above mentioned objectives **GAATW** is currently running the following rojects.

* *International Report on Trafficking in Women*

GAATW is completing a research project to provide the United Nations Special Rapporteur on Violence against Women with up-to-date and accurate information about current trafficking patterns and conditions and strategies to combat trafficking.

* ***International Human Rights Training***

Trafficking is a violation of human rights and treating it as such allows the use of UN mechanisms and instuments. A human rights training is organizing for **GAATW** members in Asia, Eastern Europe, Africa and South America.

* ***Development of handbook for Assisting Trafficked Women***

A handbook aimed at agences who assist trafficked women. It will provide guidance regarding care and counseling, legal and health issues as well as suggestions on influencing regional and national authorities and media.

* ***Development of a manual on Rights and Practicalities for Migrant Workers***

The manual would include information for women who wish to migrate on their rights as migrant workers, dangers and difficulties. They may encounter and organisations that they can turn to in countries of origin and destination.

* ***Launching and Supporting the adoption of The Minimum Standard Rules for the Treatment of Trafficked Persons***

* ***Research on Trafficking of women in Cambodia and Vietnam***

ANNEX 9 Information on the Foundation Against Trafficking in Women (STV)

STV

FOUNDATION AGAINST TRAFFICKING IN WOMEN (STV)

P.O. Box 1455, 3500 BL UTRECHT, The Netherlands
Tel: (31) 30 - 2716044 Fax: (31) 30 - 2716084
E-mail: S.T.V@inter.NL.net

member of the Global Alliance Against Traffic in Women (GAATW)
GAATW Coordination: 191 Sivalai Condominium, Isaraphab Road 33,
Bangkok 10600, Thailand.
Tel: (662) 864 - 1427 / (662) 864 - 1428
Fax: (662) 864 - 1637 E-mail: GAATW@mozart.inet.co.th

The Foundation Against Trafficking in Women (STV) was initiated in the early 80's in response to the then highly publicised issue of prostitution tourism. Women's organizations, development NGOs and various action groups, especially in the regions where mass tourism was becoming the alternative paradigm for development, were awakening to the fact that not only the natural resources but also the human resources, namely the young women, of their countries were being traded for foreign exchange.
Officially set up in 1987, STV's first campaigns were aimed at developing and refining national legislation and litigation for addressing trafficking in women. This was necessary in order to increase visibility of the problem in the Netherlands, to be able to offer support to the victims of trafficking and to build up legal jurisprudence through prosecution of traffickers.

* In 1988, a ruling was obtained under the Aliens Laws to prevent migrant women who may have become victims of trafficking from being evicted before investigations have been done. *"Paragraph B17"* of the Dutch Aliens Law now states that at the least suspicion of trafficking, a woman will be allowed time to consider pressing charges. When she has done so she will be allowed to stay in the Netherlands until the whole juridical process has been completed. In 1993 this provision was extended to witnesses who were willing to testify for the prosecution in trafficking cases.

* In 1989 the Attorney-General's office issued instructions for dealing with cases of trafficking and formulated a new legal definition. This states that a person is guilty of traffic in persons "who induces another into prostitution by violence or an act of violence or by threatening violence or an act of violence, or by using his or her authority ensuing from an actual relationship, circumstance or by misrepresentation, or who undertakes any action which he or she knows or could reasonably suspect, may bring the other into prostitution". In 1994 the relevant article in the Dutch Penal Code (Art.250ter) was changed to include this basic definition, among other specifications. The maximum sentence for trafficking was raised from 5 to 6 years. In cases involving minors, severe physical violence and organized trafficking the maximum sentence is 10 years.

STV combines elements of anti-violence programmes and pro-rights campaigns while working in the following areas:

Support and Assistance: organizing social support and practical assistance for the victim-survivors, (safe shelter, legal aid, finances for basic needs, medical services, counselling). This forms an essential element of the programme. Through direct contact, and in the process of assistance work, first hand insight is gained into the motivations and the dilemmas of women who have been deceived or coerced into prostitution, or who find themselves working under unfree and exploitative conditions. To date, STV has assisted more than 800 women from Asia, Africa, the Caribbean, South America and Central and Eastern European countries. STV has published a book describing the methodology developed for victim support work and is currently integrating the support work into the programmes of main-stream social work institutions, shelters, etc.

Advocacy and Campaigning: in the fields of legislation and litigation, social policies, migrant womens' rights, (migrant) prostitutes' rights, assistance programmes and to strengthen political commitment to combatting trafficking in women. The interest and welfare of the women concerned is the basis of all advocacy work and political campaigning. Work in this area takes place at national, European and international levels.

Information and Training: documentation and information services, tailored to inform specific relevant groups in the society are aimed at increasing public awareness of the issue. Training and consultancy services are designed to enable interested and qualified persons to participate in the various tasks of the Foundation or to initiate their own activities to address the issue.

Publications: STV publishes a quarterly magazine "Keerzijde" which carries current news and national and international developments in legislation and policies concerning trafficking in women, as well as thematic articles. Occasional publications are produced when appropriate or necessary.

Prevention: through collaboration with divers organizations in specific countries on concrete issues, projects and cases:
- cooperating in research projects, conferences and seminars
- supporting/participating in prevention initiatives in sending and receiving countries (currently, one such project is in progress. "LA STRADA" is a joint prevention project with organisations in Poland, the Czech Republic and Ukraine.
- participating in training seminars in sending and receiving countries

International Networks, in order to influence international policies and actions:
- in 1991 STV initiated a European Network against Trafficking in Women
- in 1993 STV launched an International Campaign to build up an international lobby for review of existing international instruments to prevent and combat trafficking
- in 1994 STV participated in launching the Global Alliance Against Traffic in Women
- in 1995 STV participated in the Fourth World Conference on Women and extended its network among human rights', migrant workers' and development organizations.
- in 1996/1997 STV is implementing the International Report Project a joint initiative with the Global Alliance Against Traffic in Women. This project will produce a global report on trafficking in women which will be presented to the UN Special Rapporteur on Violence against Women while at the same time stimulating and developing initiatives among NGOs to address the issue at local and national levels.